Arkansas Women

Arkansas Women

THEIR LIVES AND TIMES

EDITED BY

Cherisse Jones-Branch and

Gary T. Edwards

The University of Georgia Press   *Athens*

© 2018 by the University of Georgia Press
Athens, Georgia 30602
www.ugapress.org
All rights reserved
Set in Minion Pro by Graphic Composition, Inc.

Most University of Georgia Press titles are
available from popular e-book vendors.

Printed digitally

Library of Congress Cataloging-in-Publication Data

Names: Jones-Branch, Cherisse, editor. |
Edwards, Gary T., editor.
Title: Arkansas women : their lives and times /
edited by Cherisse Jones-Branch and
Gary T. Edwards.
Description: Athens, Georgia : University of Georgia
Press, [2018] | Series: Southern women: their lives
and times | Includes bibliographical references
and index.
Identifiers: LCCN 2017058463 | ISBN 9780820353319
(hardcover : alk. paper) | ISBN 9780820353333 (pbk. :
alk. paper) | ISBN 9780820353326 (ebook)
Subjects: LCSH: Women—Arkansas—History. |
Women—Arkansas—Social conditions. |
Arkansas—History.
Classification: LCC HQ1438.A8 A75 2018 |
DDC 305.409767—dc23
LC record available at https://lccn.loc.gov
/2017058463

Contents

Acknowledgments ix

Introduction
CHERISSE JONES-BRANCH AND GARY T. EDWARDS 1

Women in Early Frontier Arkansas
"They Did All the Work except Hunting"
SONIA TOUDJI 5

Bondwomen on Arkansas's Cotton Frontier
*Migration, Labor, Family, and Resistance
among an Exploited Class*
KELLY HOUSTON JONES 27

Amanda Trulock (1811–1891)
Yankee Mistress of the Old South
GARY T. EDWARDS 46

Women of the Ozarks in the Civil War
"I Fear We Will See Hard Times"
REBECCA A. HOWARD 72

Freda Hogan (1892–1988)
A Socialist Woman in Huntington, Arkansas
MICHAEL PIERCE 93

Senator Hattie Caraway (1878–1950)
A Southern Stealth Feminist and Enigmatic Liberal
SARAH WILKERSON FREEMAN 109

Hilda Kahlert Cornish (1878–1965)
A Community Volunteer and Civic Leader:
The Birth Control Movement in Arkansas
MARIANNE LEUNG   133

Adolphine Fletcher Terry (1882–1976)
Seventy-Five Years of Social Activism in Arkansas
DIANNA OWENS FRALEY   156

Sue Cowan Morris (1910–1994)
An Educator and the Little Rock, Arkansas, Classroom
Teachers' Salary Equalization Suit
JOHN A. KIRK   179

Daisy Lee Gatson Bates (1913?–1999)
The Quest for Justice
ELIZABETH JACOWAY   197

Edith Mae Irby Jones (1927–)
"Brilliant . . . Black Pilgrim, Proud Pioneer" and the Integration
of the University of Arkansas School of Medicine
YULONDA EADIE SANO   223

Mary L. Ray (1880?–1934)
Arkansas's Negro Extension Worker
DEBRA A. REID   237

Dr. Mamie Katherine Phipps Clark (1917–1983)
American Psychologist and Arkansas Native
LORETTA N. MCGREGOR   262

Mary Sybil Kidd Maynard Lewis (1897–1941)
"I'm from the South and I've Got Plenty of Rhythm"
MICHAEL B. DOUGAN   275

Mary Celestia Parler (1904–1981)
Folklorist and Teacher
RACHEL REYNOLDS   287

Contributors   305

Index   309

Acknowledgments

As coeditors, we extend a special thank-you to the fourteen contributors to this volume. Everyone was extraordinarily busy, but each generously provided their expertise and, far more important, their patience over the years necessary to complete this project. We are further grateful for the support from Arkansas State University's Department of History. We could not wish for better colleagues. We have been most fortunate to work with, first, Nancy Grayson, former editor in chief, and later, Lisa Bayer, director, at the University of Georgia Press; they believed in this project and assured us time and time again that our experiences as coeditors were perfectly normal. We also thank Katherine Grace La Mantia for sending emails to keep us on task. A heartfelt thank-you is due to Elizabeth Payne, coeditor of *Mississippi Women: Their Histories, Their Lives*, and Sarah Wilkerson Freeman and Beverly Bond, coeditors of *Tennessee Women: Their Lives and Times*, for their guidance and support as we completed our volume on Arkansas women. And, finally, we thank our families: Ezell Branch III, and Michelle and Cacie Edwards for their love and encouragement. You have made this journey worthwhile.

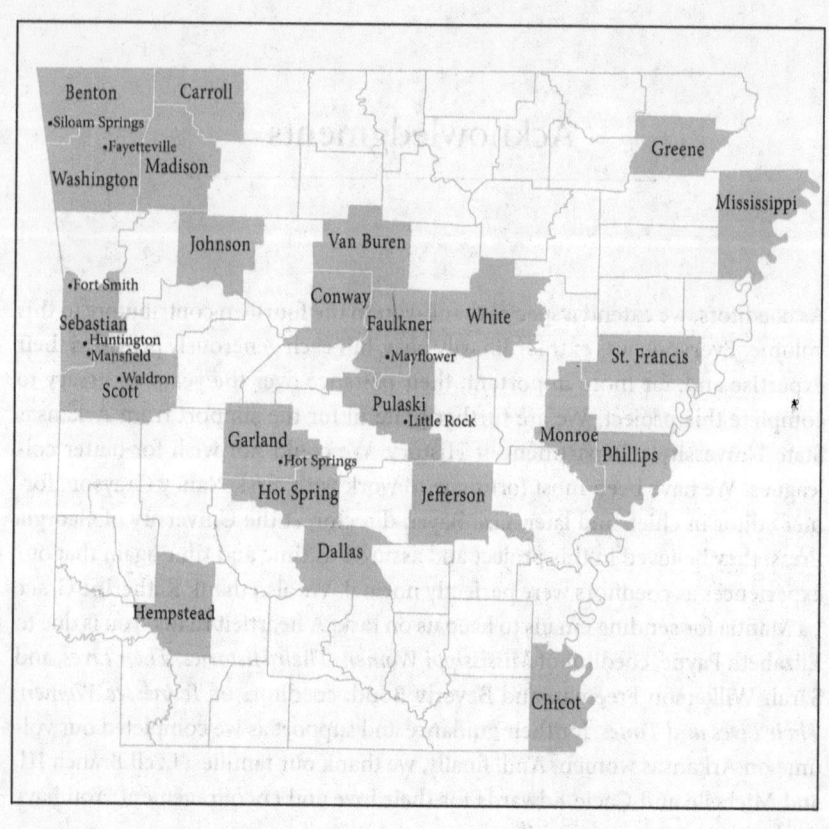

Arkansas Women

Introduction

CHERISSE JONES-BRANCH AND GARY T. EDWARDS

❀ ❀ ❀

Arkansas Women: Their Lives and Times explores women's experiences across time and space from the state's earliest frontier years until the late twentieth century. This collection of fifteen biographical essays productively complicates Arkansas history by providing a multidimensional focus on women, many of whose stories have not been told, with a particular appreciation of how gender and race informed and nuanced the times in which they lived.

Arkansas, a mid-South state, is both racially and geographically diverse. Carved out of the 1803 Louisiana Purchase, Arkansas was granted statehood in 1836. Its history encompasses the stories of people from prehistoric times until the twenty-first century. Native American cultures like the Quapaw, Caddo, and Tunica had long been present in Arkansas, and their interactions with Europeans resulted in an intercultural exchange that enhanced colonial sojourns around the state and buttressed the economies of both groups until Native Americans were removed from Arkansas in the 1820s and 1830s. The story of intercultural exchange in Arkansas was also informed by the presence of black and white women. Women assumed key roles in building both communities and institutions in the state. With the support of progressive governors and legislators, women were granted the right to vote in Arkansas primary elections in 1917 before women obtained suffrage nationwide. Additionally, through the efforts of such organizations as the Arkansas Woman Suffrage Association, Arkansas became the twelfth U.S. state and the second southern one to ratify the Nineteenth Amendment in 1919.

Like other southern states, Arkansas was invested in the institution of slavery, yet it was only in its second generation by the time the state seceded from the Union in 1861. The bulk of political power, however, resided in the Arkansas Delta where most enslaved African Americans in the state labored. This temporal lag impacted race relations in Arkansas in such a way that led to its becoming an enigma among southern states. Indeed, after the Civil War, as the state legislature actively suppressed Ku Klux Klan activities, approximately two hundred thousand southern black people flocked to Arkansas to access economic and political opportunities.[1]

The state's history is further influenced by its various geographic regions (the Ozark Mountains, the Arkansas River valley, the Ouachita Mountains, the Coastal Plain, and the Delta, which runs along the Mississippi River) and its long-standing reliance on agricultural production, factors that continue to define Arkansas's character as a state in the twenty-first century. Many of the chapters in this book reflect this rural geographic diversity while some reflect Arkansas's modest urban landscape, found primarily in Little Rock. Many of these Arkansas women oriented themselves to place by spending significant time out of the state. For some, their travels muted any desire to question the state's entrenched status quo. Others, however, were inspired to prod their fellow Arkansans to change and expand their worldview beyond the state's stereotypical parochialism.

Like the rest of the nation, Arkansas has witnessed and has been impacted by historical change. Arkansans have suffered losses during every war in which the United States has engaged. They have further been affected by the changes wrought by Jim Crow laws, migration, and the civil rights movement. Yet through all of this, the voices and experiences of Arkansas's women, with a few exceptions, have largely remained silent and invisible. Furthermore, the exceptions have failed to speak significantly to the depth and breadth of women's lives in Arkansas in ways that illuminate their complexity, nuance, and interconnectedness across time, state, and region.

The literature about women in Arkansas has grown very slowly since the 1980s. Although archives and repositories around the state are teeming with women's history collections, few of them have resulted in publications about Arkansas women. One of the first volumes to comprehensively explore Arkansas women's stories was Elizabeth Jacoway's *Behold, Our Works Were Good: A Handbook of Arkansas Women's History* (1988). More recently, new monographs have emerged. Among them are Grif Stockley's *Daisy Bates: Civil Rights Crusader from Arkansas* (2005), Stephanie Bayless's *Obliged to Help: Adolphine Fletcher Terry and the Progressive South* (2011), David Margolick's *Elizabeth and Hazel: Two Women of Little Rock* (2011), Charlotte Tillar Schexnayder's *Salty Old Editor: An Adventure in Ink: A Memoir* (2012), Elizabeth Griffin Hill's *A Splendid Piece of Work, 1912–2012: One Hundred Years of Arkansas's Home Demonstration and Extension Homemakers Clubs* (2012) and *Faithful to Our Tasks: Arkansas's Women and the Great War* (2017), Nancy Hendricks's *Senator Hattie Caraway: An Arkansas Legacy* (2013) and *Notable Women of Arkansas from Hattie to Hillary: One Hundred Names To*

Know (2016), Beth Brickell's *The Disappearance of Maud Crawford* (2014), and Bernadette Cahill's *Arkansas Women and the Right to Vote: The Little Rock Campaigns, 1868–1920* (2015). While this new scholarship is significant, it still largely fails to examine the many differences that exist among Arkansas women.[2]

The essays included in *Arkansas Women* intentionally reflect this diversity by showcasing stories about women from the Arkansas frontier, those who were political, social, and health activists, and women who contributed to the state's music, folklore, and agriculture. Not all of the women portrayed in these pages were native Arkansans. However, their long-term presence in Arkansas has informed the contours of gender history and women's history in the state. This collection, by its very design, intentionally recasts Arkansas history by placing women at the center of the narrative. These biographies show women who lived complicated lives in Arkansas from the time before statehood through the twentieth century.

The first four chapters of this book consider the stories of women on Arkansas's frontier. Sonia Toudji's "Women in Early Frontier Arkansas: 'They Did All the Work except Hunting'" examines the often overlooked importance of gender before Arkansas became a state. In doing so, she unearths the narratives of indigenous women and their interactions with European men. Kelly Houston Jones continues this story with "Bondwomen on Arkansas's Cotton Frontier: Migration, Labor, Family, and Resistance among an Exploited Class." She broadens the history of the southern slave experience by focusing on bondwomen of African descent who were forcibly moved to Arkansas from the seaboard to labor on cotton plantations. Jones further explores bondwomen's agency and autonomy as they navigated motherhood and their roles as members of the larger enslaved community.

Gary Edwards's contribution, "Amanda Trulock: Yankee Mistress of the Old South," expands the historiography by speaking to the nuances and complexities of Connecticut-born Amanda Beardsley Trulock, who for twenty-one years was the mistress of a plantation near Pine Bluff, Arkansas, in Jefferson County. His chapter demystifies the southern belle stereotype and grapples with how a woman born in New England interpreted and accepted the system of slavery into which she married. Finally, Rebecca Howard's "Women of the Ozarks in the Civil War: 'I Fear We Will See Hard Times'" provides a new and unique interpretation of women who lived in the northwestern portion of the state, which was less impacted by concerns about slavery yet was still influenced on both the homefront and the battlefield by a violent national conflict.

The next portion of the book examines individual Arkansas women's political, social, and cultural activism in the twentieth century. Michael Pierce's "Freda

Hogan: A Socialist Woman in Huntington, Arkansas" and Sarah Wilkerson Freeman's "Senator Hattie Caraway: A Southern Stealth Feminist and Enigmatic Liberal" provide clear examples of this activism, and both of these chapters underscore the diversity of women's political experiences and influence in the state in the first few decades of the twentieth century.

Included in this section are stories about women who were change agents in their communities. Marianne Leung's "Hilda Kahlert Cornish: A Community Volunteer and Civic Leader and the Arkansas Birth Control Movement," Dianna Fraley's "Adolphine Fletcher Terry: Seventy-Five Years of Social Activism in Arkansas," John Kirk's "Sue Cowan Morris: An Educator and the Little Rock, Arkansas, Classroom Teachers' Salary Equalization Suit," and Elizabeth Jacoway's "Daisy Lee Gatson Bates: The Quest for Justice" all chronicle their subjects' social activism in ways that unearth women's concerns about and responses to health and educational access for marginalized populations in Arkansas communities.

The next chapters analyze women who were Arkansas "firsts": Yulonda Sano's "Edith Mae Irby Jones: 'Brilliant . . . Black Pilgrim, Proud Pioneer' and the Integration of the University of Arkansas School of Medicine," Debra Reid's "Mary L. Ray: Arkansas's Negro Extension Worker," and Loretta McGregor's "Dr. Mamie Katherine Phipps Clark: American Psychologist and Arkansas Native." The volume ends with Michael Dougan's "Mary Sybil Kidd Maynard Lewis: 'I'm from the South and I've Got Plenty of Rhythm'" and Rachel Reynolds's "Mary Celestia Parler: Folklorist and Teacher," both of which further discussion about women's contributions to Arkansas's rich cultural heritage.

This single volume should not be considered a comprehensive treatment of women's history in Arkansas. *Arkansas Women: Their Lives and Times* is, rather, a tentative beginning designed to inspire the mining of the voluminous and as yet largely untapped resources on Arkansas women located around the state and beyond. The chapters herein merely serve as a guide to unearthing Arkansas women's diverse lives, experiences, and perspectives.

NOTES

1. Story Matkin-Rawn, "'The Great Negro State of the Country': Arkansas's Reconstruction and the Other Great Migration," *Arkansas Historical Quarterly* 73, no. 1 (Spring 2013): 1–41.

2. The website of the Arkansas Women's History Institute has an extensive list of older articles and books on Arkansas women. See http://www.arkansaswomen.org/bibliography.html (accessed August 24, 2017).

Women in Early Frontier Arkansas

"They Did All the Work except Hunting"

SONIA TOUDJI

❈ ❈ ❈

In May 1749, Marie Genevieve Baury, a French settler and resident at the Arkansas Post, was taken captive when Chickasaws, Choctaws, and Abekas joined forces, attacked the post, and killed several Frenchmen. Initially, she remained among the Chickasaws, who must have debated her fate. Rather than adopting her into the tribe, the Chickasaws, already involved in trading captives as slaves, sold her to their neighbors.[1] In 1751, Marie Genevieve found herself among the English colonists and lived at Charleston for six months. By May 16, 1754, now referred to as the widow Baury, Marie Genevieve was living in New Orleans. It is not clear, however, whether her husband was killed in the earlier raid or under other circumstances.[2] The end of her story remains a mystery. Women's voices in the early American frontier are mostly lost to history, since they left almost no direct records of their thoughts. According to a prominent scholar, Daniel K. Richter, in order to overcome these hard realities, "we can only try to look over [women's] shoulders ... to try to hear [their] voices when they emerge from the surviving documents" to reconstruct the conditions in which they lived.[3] This has been the situation with colonial Arkansas women, particularly those of European origin or descent, "partly because women married early, and during the time of their 'coverture,' as their marital condition was called, they suffered from certain civil disabilities."[4]

Since the 1990s, scholars have produced a number of acclaimed studies of colonial Arkansas. These histories of the early frontier usually focus on the process of exploring, civilizing, and settling the "savage" scenery and its Native inhabitants.[5] Dominated by male presence, the stories of women remain in the background. Rethinking early Arkansas history to incorporate women as equal players is necessary in order to have a fully painted picture of these frontiers and to offer a complete story of Arkansas women as a whole. This chapter is an attempt to uncover the past lives of some Arkansas women, recovering their contributions to frontier life from the early encounters of the late seventeenth century to the Louisiana Purchase in 1803. Historical records have described women of early Arkansas as industrious and hard workers, especially due to their crucial roles as food producers and in reproduction, which were essential in establishing and strengthening the population in the colony. Significantly, the women of the Caddo, Osage, and Quapaw nations that inhabited Arkansas were at the heart of the diplomatic process as mediators and peace builders during the encounters on the frontier. In this chapter I shed more light on the hidden stories of early Arkansas women within their socioeconomic and political settings and reexamine their contributions to the market economy in the Mississippi valley frontier.

The Caddos, who occupied the contemporary territory of eastern Texas, also stretched their settlements along the Red and Ouachita rivers in Arkansas. This Caddoan-speaking group is known as the Kadohadachos.[6] Archaeological and anthropological studies of Natives in contemporary Arkansas help us understand the role and place of these indigenous women.[7] Matrilineal, the Caddo society operated under a different socioeconomic and political organization. For instance, during house construction, a task performed by men among other Native nations, it was the women's task to gather bundles of long grass to thatch the roof and walls. Additionally, the first recorded Spaniards who visited them described the Caddos as sedentary farmers because each family chose a site to build a house and plant crops. Women planted fields of corn, beans, watermelons, sunflowers, and tobacco. A planting ritual honored the women as they began their work in the fields, while the harvest ceremony in the fall was the largest celebration of the year. In addition to their physical labor outside, Caddo women performed the household tasks. Most food was cooked in the form of a stew. Green corn was roasted and ground into flour, which was mixed with water, formed into loaves, and baked on hot stone slabs. Caddo women, however, were better known for their crafts, including baskets and mats woven from cane splints, which served both domestic and ritual needs. Their pottery, decorated with intricate designs, served as platters, bowls, and jars, which became commodities for trade.[8]

Subsequent to the Spanish expedition and prior to the French exploration in late seventeenth-century Arkansas, the Dhegihan-speaking indigenous nations migrated from the east as a result of wars with the Iroquois Confederacy, claimed the lower Mississippi valley, and made it their home. Passed down for generations, the Native story explains how, during the long journey from the lower Ohio River valley, a big storm separated some brothers during their crossing of the river. The Wa-Sha-She (the Osage), meaning the "children of the middle water," went up the river and established themselves in the upper Arkansas River valley, around the Missouri River, and controlled vast territories of northern Arkansas to the White River. The O-Gah-Pah, meaning the "people who went downstream," set up their villages around the confluence of the Mississippi and Arkansas rivers and came to be known as the Quapaw.[9]

Both the Osage and the Quapaw based their socioeconomic and political organization on kinship, placing women and their labor at the center of their societies. In their tradition, the labor was divided between the men and women. While child-rearing was the responsibility of the whole family, women cultivated and cooked corn, beans, and squash, and from the forest, they gathered nuts, fruits, seeds, and roots, contributing to a productive agricultural economy. As in most indigenous societies, farming came to be women's work, and they controlled the food they produced. The ceremonial planting of corn was at the heart of the Osage traditional teachings for the women. When the Buffalo and Corn songs were sung, the elders invited the women to be present in order to receive instructions in the rites they had to follow when planting corn. During the ceremony, the instructor explained to the women that the planting of the field was their responsibility and that it had to do with "the feeding of your children." The planting ritual required the women to rise with the sun. For this task, the women were to paint the parting of their hair in red to "represent the path of the force of the day and [it] will make the paths of all the animals converge toward you, for upon them you and your children must depend for food."[10] This responsibility also placed the Osage woman in the position of a provider.

At the political and spiritual levels, Quapaw and Osage women worked to maintain peace within their nations and to support them during war. Both nations were split into two divisions, the Sky and the Earth, each of which was subdivided into clans. To bind the members and create kinship bonds within the tribe, exogamy regulated marriage among both the Osage and Quapaw. The young men and women had to look outside their clan and moiety for marriage partners.[11] Through these marriages, the Native women became diplomatic tools within as well as outside the tribe. Spiritually, during wartime, as the Osage warrior raided, killed, and captured the enemy, the Osage woman sent him courage through prayers for his success. The woman's duty began with the pre-battle ceremony and carried to the battlefield through the song *Rite of Vigil and the Sending of Courage*. As the warrior began his journey, usually at night, the woman was required to remember him. The ceremony continued: "Before the sun rises on the fifth morning, [the Osage woman] must arise and go out of your house and take from the earth a bit of soil and put it on your head. You must give all your thoughts to the warrior who has gone against the enemy.... in this way you will aid him. When the shadow of evening comes ... remove from your head the soil of earth repeating these words: 'I remove from my head the soil of the earth and wipe my hands upon the body of the chief of our enemies that he may come to his death at the hands of our warriors.'"[12] According to Athanase de Mézières, lieutenant governor of the Natchitoches district of the Caddos, the Osages had made of the region a "pitiful theatre of outrageous robberies and bloody encounters."[13] These rituals became part of the Osage woman's routine since the Osage people were engaged in constant warfare against neighboring enemy nations with which they competed for political power and control over the region's resources.

Similarly, the Osage emphasized women's reproductive abilities, which allowed the growth of the population within the nation and the increase of its political and economic power. Osage women performed the most basic requirement for the survival of a people by giving birth and raising children to adulthood. In the second part of the *Rite of Vigil and the Sending of Courage*, the Osage woman was instructed on her duties as a mother: "you have a child. There is in you the same desire that there is in all good mothers to bring your children successfully to maturity. In this, you need the aid of a power that is greater than that of the human being."[14] It was also the instructor's task to teach the Osage woman about the rite by which an appeal could be made to the power that was to bless her child. As additional Europeans arrived in the valley, settlers and explorers recorded their observations on the early encounters with these Native groups, which allows us to sketch women's lifeways and understand and assess their role in their seventeenth- and eighteenth-century societies.

As part of Europeans' colonial aspirations and conquest of North America, Arkansas Natives witnessed "explorers" encroaching on their lands one after the other. The French were the first Europeans to establish a permanent settlement among Arkansas's Natives. Father Jacques Marquette, a priest, and Louis Joliet, a merchant, launched an expedition from New France into the interior of the North American continent. They reached Arkansas in June 1673 and were welcomed by the Quapaws, who informed the French visitors that the Mississippi River empties into the Gulf of Mexico. The French explorers headed back to Quebec, the heart of New France, with the news of their discovery.[15] As a result, the French Crown ordered René-Robert Cavelier, sieur de La Salle, to launch more expeditions to expand the colony southward. In 1682, Robert La Salle, who claimed the territory of La Louisiane in the name of the king of France at the Quapaw village of Kappa, reached the mouth of the Mississippi River. Soon, Frenchmen left France and New France to pursue fortune and adventure in the new territories, including Arkansas. Henri de Tonti, who accompanied La Salle, in 1686 set up the Arkansas Post, the first permanent settlement in French colonial Louisiana, for trade among the Quapaws.[16]

Despite the first French exploration and the beginning of settlements, the number of European and African women present in the French colony of Louisiana was almost insignificant. Similar to the stories of Native women, the stories of Arkansas women of European and African descents, as well as their roles in the early frontier, are yet to be uncovered. The first Frenchwomen came to Louisiana as part of La Salle's expedition of twenty-one; by 1687, there were seven women. The initial French government in Louisiana began at Ocean Springs, Mississippi, and then transferred to the environs of Mobile, Alabama, in 1701.[17]

In 1717, the French Crown gave Louisiana to John Law, a Scottish financier, for settlement through his Compagnie d'Occident. The company granted land to settlers and to entrepreneurs who wished to establish plantations in the colony.[18] Between 1717 and 1721, a population of 5,303 men, 1,215 women, and 502 children, mostly natives of France and some from Germany, were transported to Louisiana.[19] Most of the female immigrants were the wives and daughters of concessionaires, farmers, workers, and soldiers; however, at least 150 of them came from poorhouses and prisons in France. Records also reveal single women workers, such as Marie Delure, a dressmaker, and Françoise Chatrency, a laborer.[20] As part of the colonial project, the first two slave ships, *Le Duc du Maine* and *L'Aurore*, brought rice seeds as well as enslaved Africans to French colonial Louisiana under the auspices of John Law's Company of the Indies, arriving in 1719. There were more than 600 Africans brought to Louisiana for agricultural labor by Law.[21] In 1721, Law's ships disembarked 2,000 enslaved people from West Africa to produce crops for the colony's subsistence and exports.[22] Among them was *Le Fortuné*, which brought 303 enslaved people, including 64 women and 11 girls. Between 1726 and 1731, thirteen slave ships landed in Louisiana, and by 1746, the African population numbered 4,738 individuals, outnumbering the 3,400 Europeans.[23]

During the first decades of settlement, a civil government was set up to rule the French colony, and the Coutume de Paris (the French customary law) and the edicts of the king regulated the colony and dictated the legal status of women in Louisiana. According to article 25 of the Coutume, "le mari est seigneur," the husband is the lord. This legal system restricted women's rights severely, and they could not perform any legal act without their husband's consent. However, the law offered a certain level of economic protection, at least in theory. For instance, a married woman could act independently in business as a *marchande publique* (public merchant) and be active in her husband's mercantile affairs. The husband could not contract or obligate her separate property, possibly acquired through inheritance or by marital gift, without her consent. In the case of a second marriage, the new husband had marital powers over the woman but not over her property. In becoming a widow, a woman gained both legal and financial independence.[24] This law both restricted and protected the lives of colonial Arkansas women.

In 1724, a code of laws to govern the Africans, the Code Noir, was enacted in Louisiana. The code had already defined the system of slave labor and regulated race relations in the Caribbean colonies.[25] The Code Noir severely governed some aspects of the lives of enslaved people, with an emphasis on cross-racial intimate intercourse. Enslaved people in French Louisiana were unable to petition to be sold away from a cruel owner and could not claim the right of self-purchase. The law prohibited manumission without the permission of the government or the Superior Council and also prohibited freeing slaves in wills.[26] The code also forbade the sale of young children separately from their mothers. It is, however, unclear how real this protection was in actual practice. The code restricted whites' behavior as well: they could not marry or live in concubinage with "mulattoes" or blacks, whether enslaved or free. In 1726, Father Raphael, the Capuchin vicar general of Louisiana, reported violations of the code by the colonists, who "maintained young Indian women or negresses to satisfy their intemperance.... [It was] enough to scandalize the church and to require an effective remedy."[27]

Colonial women's inferior legal status did not prevent their contribution to the early frontier; their labor and their reproductive ability were at the heart of the agricultural export economy in the French colony. Similarly, Louisiana grew as it depended on the deployment of enslaved Africans to boost its economy and secure its frontiers. African women performed many tasks in the settlers' households, including cleaning, cooking, and working in the agricultural fields. Others worked on plantations where they did all the exhausting work of growing indigo, tobacco, and sugar.[28] While women's physical labor was important, historiography has brought to light the essential role of reproduction in making the natural increase of population possible in the frontier life of the North American colonies. "Slaveowners contemplated women's reproductive potential with greed and opportunism," Jennifer Morgan writes.[29] The reassessment of colonial women's contribution to the early frontier must keep in perspective their role as bearers of children, making life sustainable. European women's roles in the French colony included their reproductive potential, since populated settlements became key to maintaining sovereignty over the claimed territories.

Early censuses reveal a small presence of both European and African women at the Arkansas Post. During the first decades of settlement in Louisiana, nearly 90 percent of the colonial population was concentrated in and around New Orleans and on the Gulf Coast. Established by colonial officials, the interior posts, including Arkansas, worked to secure access and preserve trade networks with the Native people. In 1721, the Company of the Indies granted a large concession in Arkansas to John Law himself. Soon after, a hundred French indentured servants, a few German farmers, a number of African slaves, and about twenty soldiers arrived at the Arkansas Post. A year later, the company moved most of the enslaved Africans nearer to New Orleans and freed a number of the indentured French servants. Unable to farm virgin land, which was difficult to cultivate, only twenty Frenchmen, six slaves, and an additional thirty settlers who lived among the Quapaws, remained. Quickly, more settlers abandoned the area, leaving a total of thirty men, women, and children. Those who stayed immediately gave up farming and became full-time hunters, depending on the Quapaws for agricultural produce. In 1726, records of the colonial population in Louisiana showed only fourteen settlers in Arkansas, including three women of European descent and one "Indian slave" (gender undisclosed).[30]

Throughout the eighteenth century, the Arkansas Post did not provide much stability and security for its settlers, especially women, thus discouraging newcomers. As a labor force at the post, especially during the hunting season when the men left the settlement—for roughly six months—the few European women and the enslaved African women engaged in a wide variety of activities. While conducting trade was restricted to the European men, Arkansas women, white and black, took care of the daily domestic tasks in the frontier households, such as child-rearing, cooking, serving, and cultivating small gardens of vegetables and tobacco. Throughout the first half of the eighteenth century, it appears that the villagers at the post were not equipped with an outdoor oven for baking bread, a common feature in other colonial towns of the era, an indication that there was no reliable production of grains. The successful cultivation of swampy and flooded lands was no easy task, if not impossible, but the biggest challenge for the women at the post was security. Even with the French military presence and Quapaw protection, the settlement was subject to raids from neighboring Native nations. In May 1749, a Chickasaw-British raid resulted in the killing of six Frenchmen and the taking captive of eight women and children, including Marie Genevieve Baury, whose story opened this chapter.[31] While most of the captives were later ransomed, Marie Genevieve was sold to the British.

While the records are scarce, it is clear that the colonial government and the French Crown understood the importance of women's ability to procreate in order to sustain settlements in the colony. Although they claimed the large territories of New France and Louisiana, the French remained relatively weak by contrast to the Spaniards and the British. Thus, populated settlements became key for French survival during the race for land. As early as 1714, Louisiana governor Antoine Laumet de Lamothe Cadillac characterized the French colonists of Louisiana as "a mass of rapscallions from Canada, without subordination, with no respect for religion, and abandoned in vice with Indian women, whom they prefer to French girls."[32] The same year, Father Henri Roulleaux de La Vente argued that "in order to populate the colony [we need] to permit marriages between Frenchmen and Catholic Indian women."[33] However, as long as the Frenchmen remained among the Natives and their wives and children remained "uncivilized," these unions neither populated nor benefited the colony. In 1715, writing from Dauphin Island in what was then lower Louisiana, French administrator Jean-Baptiste du Bois Duclos expressed his opposition to intermarriage between Native women and Frenchmen. He reported that Frenchmen legally married to Native women in the Illinois Country were "Indianized," while "their wives had changed nothing or at least very little in their manner of living." As a result, the governor-general of New France, Pierre Rigaud de Vaudreuil, reversed the policy and banned intermarriages in 1715.[34] In fact, post commandants and governors in French Louisiana frequently asked for Frenchwomen from the homeland to strengthen the settlement.

In response to these requests, French authorities sent women from France in an attempt to solidify the settlements in Louisiana. The king agreed to send one hundred women annually to increase the colonial population; twelve women taken from a house of correction in Paris arrived at the colony by 1713. After their arrival, the king's "daughters," as they came to be known, were supposed to live with Sister Gertrude, a Catholic nun, until they might marry. As the Frenchwomen remained unmarried, Duclos, Louisiana's commissary-general, suggested that the "girls were too ugly and badly formed to secure the affections of the men," and added that in the future, "if they were only to be offered girls as ugly as these they would rather attach themselves to Indian females."[35] More young women were sent from France in response to the officials' complaints concerning the need for wives. In 1720, twenty-five women arrived from a house of correction, the Saltpetriere, in Paris. In 1727, a vessel arrived with a few women who, unlike many others who had been sent to Louisiana, had not been taken from a house of correction.[36] By 1749, Governor Jean-Baptiste Le Moyne de Bienville could describe Louisiana as a "healthy place [where] women are very fertile."[37] Regardless, the arrival of a larger number of Frenchwomen in Louisiana did not mark an end to the sexual relations between Frenchmen and Native women; however, marrying Native women often was a matter of practicality rather than preference.

During this early period, Native American women's labor in the household and in the field remained crucial to life and the market economy on the frontier. Native American women were a labor force for their communities that sustained economic exchange with the Europeans. The contribution of Osage women, for example, was evident in the articles they produced, mainly for cooking, and exchanged in long-distance trade networks. Osage women used the peelings stripped from canes to make fine strainers, while other strainers with larger openings were used to sift grains. They made baskets to carry corn and other produce they grew in their yards. With feathers from the tails of turkeys, "which they [knew] how to arrange," the women made fans for themselves and for European women.[38] They sold or exchanged these small articles to the French for European goods, such as cooking pots and knives. Jean-Baptiste Le Moyne de Bienville, the cofounder and governor of Louisiana, complained in an undated memoir that the Quapaws were "very lackadaisical and lazy and depended entirely on the work of their women for the necessities of life."[39] Quapaw men hunted turkey, deer, and buffalo, as reported by Father Paul Du Ru, who traveled up the river from New Orleans. Du Ru described the Quapaw women as harder working than the men.[40] In addition to household chores, cooking, and rearing children, the women tilled the soil, sowed, and reaped. Frenchman Henri Joutel admired a field of four or five square miles from which the Quapaw harvested "corn, pumpkins, melons, sunflowers, beans, as well as lots of peaches and plums." Joutel explained the different sorts of corn bread prepared by the Arkansas women, which they served with smoked meat. They cooked all kinds of dishes and "did all the work except hunting."[41]

For the fur trappers, to whom European women were useless, the Native women's work was essential to maintaining the frontier economy. Cleaning furs and dressing skins were deemed women's work, and without a good skin dresser, a trapper, hunter, or skin buyer was severely handicapped. According to Dumont de Montigny, the indigenous women were "very hardworking.... When her husband kills a deer or a buffalo, he never brings it home.... he tells her where to find the animal and she walks in her husband's track[s] to find it and carries it to the hut." The woman cooked what she needed and traded the rest of it to the French, or she smoked the meat and dried it in order to preserve it.[42] In Arkansas, both the Quapaw and the Osage supplied fur to the colony of Louisiana. The French took advantage of their expertise in working skins and pelts, as the Arkansas Post produced deerskins.[43]

Osage women's work on hides was central to tribal life and, now, to their economic and diplomatic relations with the Europeans. The Osage used both raw and tanned hides in their daily lives. Some of the hides were used with the hair still on them, but often the hair was removed. Women removed the hair from buffalo hides using the ash-lye method. They boiled the hide in a water and wood ash solution, which loosened the hair, making it easier to scrape off. However, for hides to be used in making bags, the Osage women hammered off the hair with a rounded stream stone. Then the hide was covered with buffalo dung on both sides and kept moist for three to five days before tanning. The hide was cleaned with buffalo brain. Once the oil of the brain loosened the fibers, they laid the hide over a log and beat it with a stick until it was pliable. The hide was then smoked and stored.[44] The Osage woman's skills with hides and in the fields were critical for the Osage man, whose status depended on his wife's reproductive and productive abilities as well as his ability to provide for and protect his family. These same skills also proved to be critical for the French trappers and traders on the early frontier.

Historian Juliana Barr has suggested that women represented peace and played a crucial role in early frontier diplomacy. In fact, the presence of women or their absence was an indication of peace or threat. For instance, during the encounter between Spanish explorers and Caddos in the late seventeenth century, although Spanish women were absent, the portrait of the Virgin Mary carried by the Spaniards prevented the Caddos from identifying them as potential enemies. Additionally, the Spaniards explained how the Virgin was their mother and the mother of all the Caddos as well. As a result, the Caddos drew parallels between the Virgin Mary and the Mother from their creation story, which made the Caddos identify with the Spaniards, who now became brothers and allies.[45]

Similarly, women lay at the heart of Native nations' diplomacy, and they were at the center of the tribes' hospitality. Because women grew, gathered, prepared, and served the food, they came into intimate contact with the guests and potential allies. As they arrived among the Natives, the Europeans were delighted by the hospitality of the "savages" and the treatment offered by their women. In fact, when Hernando de Soto ventured into contemporary Arkansas in 1542, the Spanish conquistador reported an attempt by the Natives to establish a kinship with him. The chief of the Casqui nation welcomed the Spaniards and then expressed his desire to offer "de Soto one of his daughters to unite his blood with that of so great a lord."[46] Instead, de Soto, who failed to understand Native diplomacy, attempted to pass for a god. Unsuccessful, he died with no glory and no legacy. Similarly, Spaniard Jacinto de Barrios was scandalized by the Frenchmen among the Caddo who regarded "the Indians so highly that civilized persons marry the Indian women without incurring blame."[47] Along with

Native women being "Europeanized" among the Spaniards, Frenchmen might be "Indianized" and serve, along with their métis offspring, as a bridge between the two peoples.⁴⁸

Native women and Frenchmen engaged in intimate and socioeconomic interactions that sustained diplomatic and economic relations that benefited the two peoples throughout the eighteenth century. Among the Quapaw, hospitality was at the center of kinship while women were at the heart of hospitality. On March 12, 1682, when the Quapaw welcomed Robert La Salle, Father Membre recalled "the courtesy and fine treatment we received from these barbarians. They let us lodge where we wanted, swept the place clean for us, and gave us firewood for the three days we spent with them." Membre was pleased by the treatment that the Quapaw women, with "pretty white complexions," gave the Frenchmen. They were "so well formed that we were in admiration of their beauty and their modesty," wrote Membre. According to him, the Frenchmen were convinced that the Quapaws' hospitality and friendship "gives idea of the good-hearted qualities of these savages."⁴⁹ The French seemed to understand the importance of the kinship established by La Salle to preserving the Quapaws' friendship and loyalty.

Intermarriage enabled the Quapaws to create stronger bonds with French Creoles.⁵⁰ During La Salle's expedition among the Caddos in 1684, Henri Joutel, commander of a company, asserted that when Barbier, a Frenchman whose full name is unknown, went out hunting, Joutel usually "sent with him some women and maids, to help the hunters to dress and dry the flesh. Barbier used to slip aside from the company, with a young maid he had kindness for." After Barbier expressed his desire to leave to marry that young woman, Joutel asked the priest to marry them. Joutel added that following this example, other Frenchmen asked for the same privilege, and he indicated that he had blessed many of these unions himself.⁵¹

During the first decades of the eighteenth century, the French royalty relied on a *coureur de bois* (woodsman), Etienne de Veniard, sieur de Bourgmont, who lived among the Osage and Missouri nations, to establish Fort d'Orleans in 1723.⁵² He influenced five tribal chiefs to travel across the Atlantic to seal diplomatic ties with the king of France two years later.⁵³ As part of the delegation that traveled to Paris, a Missouri woman, identified as a chief's daughter, took an active diplomatic role. In Paris, the Duchess of Orleans arranged for the baptism of the "sauvagesse" in Notre Dame de Paris, and stood as her godmother. She also arranged the Native woman's marriage to a French officer, a sergeant identified only as DuBois, who had served Bourgmont during his explorations on the American Plains and then on the trip to France.⁵⁴ The couple and the rest of the delegation came back to the Mississippi valley with gifts that symbolized the kinship between the king and his "children" and the reciprocal obligations between their nations. These unions, friendships, and alliances illustrate the ties between the French settlers and the Arkansas Natives that persisted even after the diplomatic treaties ended with the transfer of Louisiana to Spain in 1763. As the balance of power changed at the end of the French and Indian War, the French attempted in vain to convince the Arkansas Natives that they were maintaining their previous diplomatic relations through the Spaniards, but Arkansans, Natives, and French settlers all resisted Spanish authority.

Because the French and the Natives lost the French and Indian War, the British and the Spaniards advanced into the French territory of Louisiana in accordance with the 1763 Treaty of Paris. On paper, the great war for empire was ended, and the Louisiana territory west of the Mississippi River became Spanish. In reality, the territory, in many aspects, remained French and Indian. Since the Spanish Crown was slow to send officials to begin their rule in Louisiana, the residents continued life as if they were still in a French colony. The laws and the Coutume de Paris, which had governed the colony during the French regime, remained essentially unchanged under the initial Spanish colonial governance. As the Spaniards enacted laws to govern the newly acquired colony, settlers and Natives resisted the change. In March 1766, the first Spanish governor of Louisiana, Antonio de Ulloa, in an attempt to control the economics of the colony, issued new commercial decrees that changed trade practices. Merchants who had been accustomed to trading with French ports in the Caribbean, in addition to conducting illegal commerce with the nearby British colonies, resisted the governor's new trade decrees. The leaders of New Orleans's business community led an insurrection in 1769 that forced Ulloa to leave.[55] In theory, Spanish was the official language, and French authorities were replaced by Spanish ones; in actuality, many Frenchmen still held offices, and French remained the most important language in the colony. Because few Spaniards lived in the region, St. Louis, Louisiana, maintained its French character and French language.[56]

However, when the Crown appointed Alejandro O'Reilly as governor in 1769, the laws that regulated the lives of enslaved Africans, including enslaved women in Arkansas, changed under the Spanish colonial government. O'Reilly instituted reforms to encourage economic exchange between Louisiana and other Spanish colonies. Economic prosperity during the Spanish era brought more African slaves into the colony; the enslaved population reached 5,000 individuals and grew even larger with the expansion of plantation agriculture in the 1770s. The rapid growth of the slave population prompted tighter restrictions on their social and economic actions. Unlike the Code Noir, Spanish law did not protect the African slave family: children could be sold separately from their parents. Slaves were, however, able to purchase their freedom, buy their family members, and go to court to seek a remedy if they were badly treated by their owners. A large number of enslaved Africans petitioned and sued for their freedom while many slaveowners voluntarily emancipated their slaves. As a result, communities of free people of color developed throughout the colony, including the Arkansas Post. The Spanish Census of 1769 had counted 9 male slaves, 7 female slaves, and no free blacks or mulattoes at the Arkansas Post. In 1785, more than a decade after the Spanish law was in place, the Arkansas Post's total population of 196 individuals included 31 free people of color and 17 slaves.[57] Although the record does not disclose gender, it is possible that the freed slaves included women, since the Spanish law was not gender specific and allowed African women in Arkansas to buy their freedom.

Like the French, the Spanish colonial government understood that families, implying the presence of women, were important for the stability and therefore prosperity of the Arkansas Post. In 1769, the Arkansas Post housed thirty white women in addition to the seven enslaved women. In 1768, Captain Alexandre Chevalier DeClouet, commandant of the post during the Spanish era, succeeded in getting four outdoor ovens built for baking bread; however, the inhabitants were still unable to produce grains and were reduced to trading liquor to the Quapaw for corn. As the French and African women continued their work in the fields, flooding undermined their labor. The 1779 flood, for instance, submerged the post as the inhabitants saw their crops destroyed, their livestock drowned, and their houses collapse. Soon, Captain Balthazar de Villiers relocated the post permanently to higher ground. De Villiers hoped, like other officials before him, to attract farmers and create "a respectable settlement." A year later, nine American families, refugees of the American Revolution, arrived, followed by a petition from other families from South Carolina asking for permission to settle.[58] Although most of the residents continued to hunt as their main source of income, about a dozen families eventually began to produce a significant wheat crop after the post relocated. In the spring of 1780, de Villiers reported, "an American family composed of nine persons has arrived to stay. They came from Illinois and ought to be followed by several others, all farmers. This is going to give this post a stability, which it has never had. I am doing my best to encourage them."[59] By the 1791 Census, there were twenty-seven households, and sixteen of them were headed by farmers (*cultivateurs*). The largest slaveowner (thirty-seven slaves) living at the post was the widow Ménard, a merchant and farmer, who became one of the most productive farmers growing wheat, corn, and tobacco. The Census of 1798 counted approximately four hundred habitants, the highest number throughout colonial times, including thirty families that produced a crop, mostly corn, some wheat, and tobacco. The number of mulatto and black slaves reached fifty-six.[60] While migration partially explains the population growth at the post, women's reproductive capabilities continued to serve the frontier.

Women of European descent contributed to the natural increase of the population. On December 5, 1743, Catherine Landrony, daughter of Joseph and Marie Landrony, was the first white child recorded as born at the post. A year later, Catherine's sister, Marie Antoine, was born. Between 1780 and 1793, baptismal records, which are incomplete, reveal that a total of thirty-three children of European descent were born at the post.[61] Perhaps the case of the widow of Joseph Francoeur, Marie Jeanne, an Indian or métis, opens a window into these women's role in populating and also connecting the early frontiers. In the 1768 Census of Inhabitants of Arkansas Post by Alexandre DeClouet, Marie Jeanne Francoeur is reported to have had three sons and six daughters—Agnes, Angelique, Susanne, Catherine, Marie Jeanne (known as Maria Juana in the Spanish records), and Marianne. Agnes married Jean Jollin, a native of La Rochelle, France, and they lived in St. Genevieve, Illinois. Their daughter Agnes Jaulin was baptized on December 10, 1770. Angelique, who married Joseph Turgeon in 1770, lived in Kaskaskia, Illinois. On June 5, 1770, at Pointe Coupée, Susanne married Pierre Julien Chevalier de Montcherveaux. Catherine married Jean Baptiste Chenier, a native of Illinois and resident of St. Charles Parish, in 1771. She gave birth to two sons: Jean Baptiste Chenier Jr. and Joseph Chenier. The records from St. Louis Cathedral, New Orleans, show the marriage on July 5, 1783, of Maria Juana (Marie Jeanne) and Antonio Pino, who later had two sons.[62] One colonial Arkansas woman, Marie Jeanne Francoeur, by giving birth to six daughters, thus managed to create a web of connections between the post and different frontier settlements throughout the colony of Louisiana.

The Catholic Church records for the Arkansas Post show that Frenchmen continued to rely on Native women (either wives or captives) for their necessities. During his visit among the Quapaw in 1772, Jean Bernard Bossu declared that it was "a pleasure seeing these women who were showing a great affection toward the French, they prefer them to the Spanish."[63] In 1784, Jacob (Jacobo) Dubreuil, commandant of the post, reported in his Census of the three villages of the Arkansas Quapaws a total of 308 females of all ages out of a total population of 708. Few officials or travelers clearly documented French-Native liaisons, and of the European-Native marriages actually recorded in official and sacramental records in eighteenth-century Arkansas, only one clearly involved a Quapaw woman—that between Michael Bone and Marie Louise. However, recent scholarship has pointed at the hidden unions between Frenchmen and Arkansas Native women throughout the eighteenth century. Further, Native women were often victims of a highly organized slave trade in the region. The Catholic Church records of the 1790s reveal several instances of Frenchmen who fathered children with women of indigenous origin (including Osage, Cances—now known as Kansas—and Paducah), presumably captives. A larger list of Native women who gave birth to children of unknown fathers can be drawn from these records. By 1791, two women identified as métis served the post's residents as seamstresses.[64]

As wives, concubines, or captives, Native women were so necessary that Frenchmen disregarded the Spanish law about Indian slavery to maintain their lifestyle in frontier Arkansas. The Spanish law was beneficial to the enslaved Natives, who won their freedom under the new regime. In 1763, there were about one hundred Indian slaves in lower Louisiana. In 1769, as the Spanish government officially took over the administration of Louisiana, the law prohibited the further enslavement of Natives and the selling of Natives already in slavery, proclaiming future descendants of Indian women to be free by law. The Spanish Crown published a decree on December 7, 1769: "the wise and just laws of His Majesty very expressly forbid subjects of any quality or condition whatsoever to make any Indian a slave or to possess any such, under any pretext whatever, even though there be an open war against that Indian's nation. In Consequence whereof, all subjects of His Majesty, and even all transients, are expressly forbidden to acquire, purchase, or take over any Indian slaves."[65] In 1770, a year after the Spanish law took effect, Lieutenant Governor Athanase de Mézières complained about French hunters in Arkansas's St. Francis River area and described them as "the most wicked persons, [who] live so forgetful of the laws"; many "have not returned to Christian lands" for several years and lived "their scandalous lives in public concubinage with the captive Indian women whom for this purpose they purchase among the heathen, loaning those of whom they tire to others of less power, that they may labor in their service, giving them no other wage than the promise of quieting their lascivious passions."[66] The same year, however, in a letter addressed to François Demazellières, commandant of the Arkansas Post, the Francoeur brothers declared that the hunters along the Arkansas River who "requested permission to marry the savage women with whom they are living and by whom they have had children, in the Roman Apostolic church, did not have the money or the food to go to New Orleans."[67] Because Native women were so necessary to the Europeans' survival, Frenchmen who kept captive Indian women found ways around the Spanish law: they used terms such as "captive," "slave," "domestic," "concubine," and "wife" interchangeably, making the women's status difficult to define, in case of law enforcement.

The Osages, via their women, expanded control over the Arkansas River valley and provided New Orleans with the largest quantity and the best quality of fur. They occupied a very strategic site that connected to the Great Plains. The revenues from the fur and skin trade at the Arkansas Post with the Osages alone averaged $18,750 annually by the end of the colonial era. Osage women continued to carry out their regular tasks of child-rearing, tending the gardens, and preparing the meals, and they built their houses and most of the interior furniture and utensils as well. Most critical to the Frenchmen were the Osage women's role in preparing buffalo and deer hides for the European market. It was the tradition among the Osage on the hunts that the men cooked the ribs while the women were busy preparing the meat and the hides. Osage women cleaned and dressed thousands of furs and shaved and tanned most of them to make leather. Their skills were so necessary for the hunt that during the winter, the Frenchmen took some women with them to prepare the hides with fleshers and metal scrapers. Historian John Mathews concluded that the interest the coureurs de bois, the French woodsmen, had in the Osage had to do with their women because "they all took the widows or married the girls."[68] Hundreds of individual *voyageurs* worked along the rivers and streams of Louisiana, exchanging guns, ammunition, and other goods for furs and skins. As a result, the French coureurs de bois and voyageurs fraternized with the Natives, learned their languages, ate their food, and married the women.[69] In fact, during the second half of the eighteenth century, the Chouteau family built St. Louis using indigenous labor and collecting the most "precious fur from throughout the region."[70] The Chouteau brothers, Auguste and Pierre, had been students of the Osages since their adolescent years and married into the tribe. Through the Osage wives, the Chouteaus and the Osages gradually became intimate and business partners, forging a kinship that maintained their monopoly on the fur business during the second half of the eighteenth century. Because of his connections with the Osage and his economic power in the region, Pierre Chouteau was appointed to become the U.S. Indian agent for the district of Louisiana, and was selected to escort the Osage delegation to visit the president in Washington, D.C., in 1804.[71]

The aristocratic women of Arkansas throughout the eighteenth century contributed to frontier life similarly, although they experienced it differently. Perhaps what is most unusual about this group of women is their presence in the historical records. Although these women are still identified as the wives or daughters of colonial officials, they are more than numbers in a census about female population or being part of a household. Uniquely, the upper-class colonial Arkansas women became part of the recorded stories about the Arkansas Post, and their names and even their portraits have survived. For instance, when Ensign Pierre Louis Petit de Coulange was assigned to the Arkansas Post, his wife accompanied him to the frontier. Shortly after, on September 23, 1732, their daughter, Marie Françoise, was born in Arkansas, as her tombstone in a New Orleans cemetery reveals. By the time she was seven years old, Marie Françoise lost her father to a Chickasaw warrior, and she moved to New Orleans with her mother. She grew up to give birth to a son, Charles Melchior de Vilemont, who served as one of the last colonial commandants of the Arkansas Post between 1794 and 1802.[72]

Another colonial Arkansas elite woman, Marie Madeleine Broutin Delinó de Chalmette, also accompanied her husband, who was appointed commandant at the Arkansas Post, and she witnessed the infamous Chickasaw raid of May 1749. Like the rest of the women at the post, Marie Madeleine experienced the insecurity and the violence of frontier Arkansas. And like Marie Françoise, Marie Madeleine's contribution to Arkansas was giving birth to Jean Ignace Delinó de Chalmette, who served as commandant of the post from 1790 to 1794. Marie Madeleine's daughter, Victoire Delinó de Chalmette (1777–1868), and Marie Félicité Vallière de Vaugine (1770–1806), the daughter of Commandant Don Joseph Vallière, spent a few years at the post during their childhood, but eventually enjoyed a privileged life in the city of New Orleans and received a proper education that included music and dancing lessons. Marie Félicité attended the school at the Ursuline convent—built in 1753 and still standing in the French Quarter in today's New Orleans—since there were no educational opportunities at the post at all. Last, Captain Alexandre Chevalier DeClouet, commandant of the post, saw his wife, Louise Favrot, serving the frontier as she attended the sick brought to the post during an epidemic. Before 1769, when the DeClouet family left Arkansas, Louise offered the post's chapel some luxury items as gifts.[73] These examples show the lives of Arkansas's ruling class in the colonial era: they faced the isolation, violence, and diseases of the typical frontier experience regardless of age, class, and gender.

By the turn of the nineteenth century, the lifestyle in the colony looked similar to what it had been at the beginning of settlement. Reporting on his 1802 travels, Perrin du Lac revealed: "The inhabitants, almost all originally French emigrants from Canada, are hunters by profession. . . . More than half the year one finds in this village only women, children, and old people. . . . On their return home [the men] pass their time in playing games, dancing, drinking, or doing nothing, similar in this as in other things to the savage peoples . . . whose habits and customs they acquire."[74] On August 17, 1803, George Gillespie from St. Louis exclaimed at "the news of the day" that "the French have ceded Louisiana to the Americans for six million *piastres*."[75] The purchase of the French colony by President Thomas Jefferson signaled the end of a colonial frontier and the beginning of a new era, as Arkansas became part of the American unorganized territory. During the colonial era, through their presence, and their sexuality, Arkansas women contributed to survival on the frontier, while their wombs provided the population necessary to settle the land and their labor carved out wealth. What the purchase meant for Americans, and its consequences for colonial Arkansas women, is covered in the following chapters.

NOTES

I am grateful to Judge Morris Arnold, an expert in colonial Arkansas history, who has read my work and provided important feedback.

1. Because of the demand for female slaves/captives, the Chickasaw-English raids against the Arkansas Post continued until the end of the American Revolution. On August 3, 1783, Captain of Infantry Jacob Dubreuil, commander of the Arkansas Post, requested the return of the captives and some property, taken in April of the same year, from James Colbert, a British trader, who allied with the Chickasaws and resided in the Chickasaw Nation (see 545 in the following source). Fort Charles III, "Arkansas Reports for the Year 1783, by Anna Lewis," *Mississippi Valley Historical Review* 20, no. 4 (1934): 537–49.

2. Petition of Marie Genevieve [Baury], Colonial Records of South Carolina, Documents Relating to Indian Affairs, 1754–1765, 37–38, Core Family Papers, box 22, file 15, MC1380, Special Collections, University of Arkansas, Fayetteville.

3. Daniel Richter, *Facing East from Indian Country: A Native History of Early America* (Cambridge, Mass.: Harvard University Press, 2001), 9.

4. Jeannie Whayne, Thomas A. DeBlack, George Sabo III, and Morris S. Arnold, *Arkansas: A Narrative History* (Fayetteville: University of Arkansas Press, 2013), 81.

5. A leading scholar in the field, Morris Arnold, looked at the early Arkansas societies and the laws that governed Natives, Europeans, and Africans. Arnold's work includes *Unequal Laws unto a Savage Race: European Legal Traditions in Arkansas, 1686–1836* (Fayetteville: University of Arkansas Press, 1985); *Colonial Arkansas, 1686–1804: A Social and Cultural History* (Fayetteville: University of Arkansas Press, 1991); and *The Rumble of a Distant Drum: The Quapaws and the Old World Newcomers, 1673–1804* (Fayetteville: University of Arkansas Press, 2000). Kathleen DuVal developed the concept of "Native ground" and applied this encounter pattern to the lower Mississippi valley, home to a few large and relatively cohesive tribes, in her *The Native Ground: Indians and Colonists in the Heart of the Continent* (Philadelphia: University of Pennsylvania Press, 2006). George Sabo III traced the history of Arkansas Natives from precontact to their removal to the Indian Territory in the early nineteenth century in his *Paths of Our Children: Historic Indians of Arkansas* (Fayetteville: Arkansas Archeological Survey, 2001). See also Joseph Key's "The Calumet and the Cross: Religious Encounters in the Lower Mississippi Valley," *Arkansas Historical Quarterly* 61 (Summer 2002): 165.

6. Todd Smith, *Louisiana and the Gulf South Frontier, 1500–1821* (Baton Rouge: Louisiana State University Press, 2014), 38.

7. George Sabo's work offers an overview of the cultural beliefs and practices as well as the sociopolitical structures of three different tribes of French Louisiana, including what is today Arkansas.

He explores the lives of the Quapaws, Osages, and Caddos and developments from the ancient prehistoric era to the twentieth century. The period before the encounter with the French explorers and settlers is pertinent to my work. Sabo, *Paths of Our Children*.

8. Following Hernando de Soto's death in 1542, the remaining members of his expedition, about three hundred individuals, headed westward hoping to join the Spanish settlements in Mexico. Traveling along the Ouachita River, the journey took them to southwest Arkansas (between Malvern and Arkadelphia), where they encountered the Caddo people. Sabo, *Paths of Our Children*, 19–20, 50–52.

9. Velma Seamster Nieberding, *The Quapaws: Those Who Went Downstream* (Miami, Fla.: Dixons, 1976); David Baird, *The Quapaw Indians: A History of the Downstream People* (Norman: University of Oklahoma Press, 1980); and Baird, *The Quapaw People* (Phoenix, Ariz.: Indian Tribal Series, 1975).

10. The women were then instructed on how to gather ceremonially the roots of the water lily for food for their little ones. "The water lily with which you feed your children is also a sacred food and should be gathered with proper ceremony. It is a symbol of life." For the complete story of the ceremony, see Garrick A. Bailey, ed., *The Osage and the Invisible World: From the Works of Francis La Flesche* (Norman: University of Oklahoma Press, 1999), 176–79.

11. Baird, *Quapaw People*, 7.

12. Bailey, *The Osage*, 79.

13. Smith, *Louisiana*, 157.

14. Bailey, *The Osage*, 79.

15. Roger Coleman, *The Arkansas Post Story: Arkansas Post National Monument* (Santa Fe, N.M.: National Park Service, 1987), 6.

16. Arnold, *Unequal Laws*, 1; Arnold, *Rumble of a Distant Drum*, 15.

17. Vaughan Baker, "*Cherchez les Femmes*: Some Glimpses of Women in Early Eighteenth-Century Louisiana," *Louisiana History* 31 (1990): 21–37, 23; Lawrence Powell, *The Accidental City: Improvising New Orleans* (Cambridge, Mass.: Harvard University Press, 2012), 3.

18. Arnold, *Colonial Arkansas*, 9.

19. Daniel Usner, *Indians, Settlers, and Slaves in a Frontier Exchange Economy: The Lower Mississippi Valley before 1783* (Chapel Hill: University of North Carolina Press, 1992), 33.

20. These women were on board the *Loire*, which left the port of Lorient in 1720, bound for the Sainte Catherine concession at Natchez. Usner, *Indians, Settlers, and Slaves*, 47.

21. John Mathews, *The Osages: Children of the Middle Waters* (Norman: University of Oklahoma Press, 1982), 188.

22. Usner, *Indians, Settlers, and Slaves*, 32.

23. Gwendolyn Midlo Hall, *Africans in Colonial Louisiana: The Development of Afro-Creole Culture in the Eighteenth Century* (Baton Rouge: Louisiana State University Press, 1992), 9, 64.

24. Edward Haas, *Louisiana's Legal Heritage* (Pensacola, Fla.: Perdido Bay Press, 1983), 7.

25. Judith Kelleher Schafer, *Slavery, the Civil Law, and the Supreme Court of Louisiana* (Baton Rouge: Louisiana State University Press, 1994), 1.

26. «Code Noir; ou, Loi Municipale, Servant de Reglement pour le Governement et Administration de la Justice, Police, Discipline et le Commerce des Esclaves Négres, dans la Province de la Louisianne, entreprit par Délibération du Cabildo en Vertu des Ordres du Roi,» article 16, Xavier University Archives, New Orleans, Louisiana; Schafer, *Slavery*, 2. Spain transferred Louisiana back to France in 1801 in a secret treaty, but France did not take possession of the colony until November 30, 1803. Twenty days later, the Americans took possession of the territory, but during those

twenty days the French reenacted the Code Noir and ordered its strict enforcement. After the Louisiana Purchase, the newly created Superior Court of the Territory of Orleans declared Spanish law, rather than French law, to govern the territory unless it conflicted with American law.

27. Code Noir, articles 6 and 19; Usner, *Indians, Settlers, and Slaves*, 50.

28. Kimberly Hanger, *Bounded Lives, Bounded Places: Free Black Society in Colonial New Orleans, 1769–1803* (Durham, N.C.: Duke University Press, 1997), 7.

29. Jennifer Morgan, *Laboring Women: Reproduction and Gender in New World Slavery* (Philadelphia: University of Pennsylvania Press, 2004), 7.

30. Usner, *Indians, Settlers, and Slaves*, 48.

31. Smith, *Louisiana*, 118.

32. Albert James Pickett and McAdory Owen Thomas, *History of Alabama and Incidentally of Georgia and Mississippi from the Earliest Period* (Birmingham, Ala.: Webb Book, 1900), 188.

33. Jennifer Spear, "Colonial Intimacies: Legislating Sex in French Louisiana," *William and Mary Quarterly* 60, no. 1 (2003): 75–98, quote on 75.

34. Sophie White, *Wild Frenchmen and Frenchified Indians: Material Culture and Race in Colonial Louisiana* (Philadelphia: University of Pennsylvania Press, 2012), 34; Saliha Belmessous, "Assimilation and Racialism in Seventeenth- and Eighteenth-Century French Colonial Policy," *American Historical Review* 110, no. 2 (2005): 322–49.

35. Duclos was hoping that "beautiful" single young women from Paris would counteract the tendency toward intermarriage and have an effect on "the whiteness and the purity of blood in [their] children." Carl J. Ekberg, *Stealing Indian Women: Native Slavery in the Illinois Country* (Urbana-Champaign: University of Illinois Press, 2007), 25.

36. Pickett and Thomas, *History of Alabama*, 154. In his research, Vaughan Baker showed that the king's ships sailing out of the ports of La Rochelle and Lorient transported ninety-six single women, known as the "king's daughters," to Louisiana between 1717 and 1721. Baker, "*Cherchez les Femmes*."

37. The original quote from Bienville's letter reads: "on dois remarquer que l'air est tres sain et les femmes tres fecondes!" Archives Nationales, Paris, Archives Colonial, subser. C13A, 30:257.

38. Dumont de Montigny, "The History of Louisiana," 153–54, National Archives, Washington, D.C.

39. Morris Arnold suggested that the memoir most likely dates to the 1730s. Arnold, *Rumble of a Distant Drum*, 41.

40. Journal of Paul Du Ru, 1700, National Archives, Washington, D.C.

41. Henri Joutel, "An Historical Journal of the Last Voyage Performed by Monsr. de La Salle," 134, National Archives, Washington, D.C..

42. Montigny, "History of Louisiana." Although the account is not describing a particular tribe, but rather Indians in Louisiana in general, the Quapaw women probably had similar duties.

43. Jean-Baptiste Le Moyne de Bienville, "The Indians of Louisiana, Their Populations and the Trading That Can Be Done with Them," National Archives, Washington, D.C.

44. Louis F. Burns, *Osage Indians: Customs and Myths* (Tuscaloosa: University of Alabama Press, 1984), 106.

45. Juliana Barr, *Peace Came in the Form of a Woman: Indians and Spaniards in the Texas Borderlands* (Chapel Hill: University of North Carolina Press, 2007), 35.

46. In 1539, de Soto reached the west coast of Florida, accompanied by seven hundred individuals, including soldiers, craftsmen, priests, and at least two women, to establish a settlement in the New World. De Soto crossed the Mississippi River in 1541 and explored the Mississippi River valley in search of gold, which he never found. De Soto followed the White and Arkansas rivers and explored the region for two years, during which he encountered several Native tribes, including the

Casqui, Pacaha, Tula, Anilco, and Guachoya. Sabo, *Paths of Our Children*, 8, 13, 16; Buckingham Smith, *Narratives of the Career of Hernando de Soto in the Conquest of Florida as Told by a Knight of Elvas* (New York: Bradford Club Series, 1991), 115.

47. Barr, *Peace Came*, 87–88.

48. Sonia Toudji, "'The Happiest Consequences': Sexual Unions and Frontier Survival of French and Quapaws at the Arkansas Post," *Arkansas Historical Quarterly* 70 (Spring 2011): 45–56.

49. Philip Marchand, *Ghost Empire: How the French Almost Conquered North America* (Toronto: McClelland and Stewart, 2007), 352.

50. Baird, *Quapaw People*, 30; Key, "Calumet and the Cross," 165.

51. Joutel, "Historical Journal," 72, 128, 155.

52. Bourgmont wrote two accounts of what he saw during his expeditions to the west: *The Exact Description of Louisiana* (1713) and *The Route to Be Taken to Ascend the Missouri River* (1714). See Kristie Wolferman, *The Osage in Missouri* (Columbia: University of Missouri Press, 1997), 26.

53. Mathews, *The Osages*, 204.

54. Elliott West, "The West before Lewis and Clark: Three Lives," in his *The Essential West* (Norman: University of Oklahoma Press, 2012), 143.

55. Bennett Wall et al., *Louisiana: A History* (Wheeling, W.Va.: Harlan Davidson, 1997), 57.

56. Wolferman, *The Osage in Missouri*, 34.

57. Usner, *Indians, Settlers, and Slaves*, 107, 114; Hall, *Africans in Colonial Louisiana*, 304; Schafer, *Slavery*, 2.

58. Morris Arnold, *The Arkansas Post of Louisiana* (Le Petit Rocher, France: Editions aux Arks, 2013), 4, 17–19.

59. De Villiers to Galvez, May 15, 1780, Papeles de Cuba, file 192, Archivo General de Indias, Seville, Spain.

60. Smith, *Louisiana*, 190; Arnold, *Arkansas Post of Louisiana*, 24.

61. Dorothy Core, *Abstract of Catholic Register of Arkansas, 1764–1858* (Almyra, Ark.: Grand Prairie Historical Society, 1976), 74, 10–17.

62. Core Family Papers, box 24, file 4, from Cathedral Records, Funeral Register, 1772–1790, 8.

63. Jean Bernard Bossu was a French naval officer who traveled up the Mississippi valley and left an extensive account of his observations on the French colony and its inhabitants. He claimed to have visited the Quapaws in 1751, 1756, and 1770–1771. During his first trip, the Quapaws adopted Bossu, who acted as a military advisor during their war against the Chickasaws. See Bossu, *Nouveaux Voyages dans l'Amérique Septentrionale: Contenant une Collection de Lettres Écrites sur les Lieux, par l'Auteur, à Son Ami, M. Douin ... ci-devant Son Camarade dans le Nouveau Monde* (Amsterdam: Changuion, 1777), 106.

64. Papeles de Cuba, file 107, folio 6, Archivo General de Indias, Seville, Spain; Toudji, "Happiest Consequences," 49; Arnold, *Arkansas Post of Louisiana*, 24.

65. Usner, *Indians, Settlers, and Slaves*, 7, 108; Patricia Cleary, *The World, the Flesh, and the Devil: A History of Colonial St. Louis* (Columbia: University of Missouri Press, 2011), 112.

66. Herbert Eugene Bolton, ed. and trans., *Athanase de Mézières and the Louisiana-Texas Frontier, 1768–1780* (Cleveland, Ohio: Arthur H. Clark, 1914), 1:166–69.

67. Letter from Francoeur brothers to Commandant Demazellières, June 17, 1770, Translations of French and Spanish Documents, 1712–1785, Archivo General de Indias, Seville, Spain; Arkansas Post Investigation, Arkansas Colonial Papers, Special Collections, University of Arkansas Libraries, Fayetteville.

68. Arnold, *Colonial Arkansas*, 62; DuVal, *Native Ground*, 109; Mathews, *The Osages*, 17, 84, 98.

69. Mathews, *The Osages*, 116. In the French trading system the licensed trader, the voyageur, represented a vital link between French government officials and the Native tribes. The license stated the amount of goods he had to trade, the Indians with whom he would trade, the route to be taken to his destination, the number of his employees, and even what he would pay for the furs he purchased. The coureurs de bois, however, were unlicensed traders and trappers who lived beyond the control of French officials. Gilbert C. Din and A. P. Nasatir, *The Imperial Osages: Spanish-Indian Diplomacy in the Mississippi Valley* (Norman: University of Oklahoma Press, 1983), 27–28.

70. William E. Foley and C. David Rice, *The First Chouteaus: River Barons of Early St. Louis* (Urbana-Champaign: University of Illinois Press, 1983), 9.

71. Stephen Aron, *American Confluence: The Missouri Frontier from Borderland to Border State* (Bloomington: Indiana University Press, 2009), 121.

72. Arnold, *Arkansas Post of Louisiana*, 53.

73. Ibid., 50–57.

74. François Marie Perrin du Lac, *Voyage dans les Deux Louisianes* (Paris: N.p., 1805), 360.

75. Chouteau Family Papers, Missouri History Museum, St. Louis.

Bondwomen on Arkansas's Cotton Frontier

Migration, Labor, Family, and Resistance among an Exploited Class

KELLY HOUSTON JONES

Enslaved women in Arkansas navigated the horrors and hardships of bondage while burdened with the added strain of carving cotton acreage from the southern wilderness. This chapter discusses the migration, labor, family, and resistance that shaped the lives of bondwomen on the cotton frontier. Whites forced enslaved women from their homes and families in the east to the western margins of the Old South both in the slave trade and with the migration of white families. These women labored in the homes and fields of whites seeking to profit on the fertile frontier and from the rising cotton prices of the 1850s. Slave women struggled to nurture children and relationships despite their precarious circumstances. These Arkansas women resisted slavery in a variety of ways, ranging from passive and indirect to fiercely violent. All the while, they labored under a system that blurred the boundaries of their womanhood.

Scholars have paid too little attention to the topic of bondwomen in Arkansas. This gap is largely due to the bias toward the older eastern South and away from the trans-Mississippi region. But general studies of enslaved women, and those focusing on points east, do not necessarily represent the experience in Arkansas, on the southern periphery. Orville Taylor's *Negro Slavery in Arkansas*—still, after more than fifty years, the only published history of slavery in Arkansas—gives little attention to the slaves' point of view, and even less to enslaved women. General works focused on antebellum Arkansas provide glimpses of slave life, but do not wade very deeply into the lives of slave women.[1] There is a compelling need to expand the story of black women and slavery in Arkansas's historiography.

A few enslaved women probably entered French colonial Arkansas in the 1720s, but it was the antebellum era that witnessed an exponential increase in the institution. Women forcibly migrated to Arkansas were part of the more than 875,000 bondpeople who were removed from the seaboard South to the cotton kingdom between 1820 and 1860. Slave importation (along with some natural increase) boosted Arkansas's slave population by 136 percent between 1850 and 1860. By 1860, more than 111,000 enslaved people resided in Arkansas, owned by more than 11,000 masters. Of Arkansas slaves in 1860, 54,941, or 49 percent, were women, a proportion similar to other southern states. Reflecting the importation of enslaved men, the state's most intensive plantation districts in southwestern Arkansas and along the Arkansas River exhibited lower proportions of slave women to men, dipping as low as 47 percent. The highest proportions of slave women to slave men occurred in northern Arkansas, reaching more than 62 percent on the Missouri border.[2]

These women came into Arkansas from all over the South. In interviews conducted by the Works Progress Administration (WPA) in the 1930s, many former slaves told of their families' origins in Virginia, Tennessee, and North Carolina. Historians estimate that around 60–70 percent of this forced migration was due to the domestic slave trade. New Orleans and Memphis were the two main large-scale slave trading points for Arkansas, though slave sales took place all over the state. The waves of incoming slaves continued, bringing generations of women and their children to the southern periphery.[3]

Women often entered Arkansas's slave trade via the mismanagement of debts by eastern white men. This was the case for a woman known only as Peggy. In 1802, Peggy was gifted to Fanny Stovall of Granville County, North Carolina, when she married Obadiah Liggin. The couple moved twelve miles away into Virginia. Five or six years later, Obadiah sold Peggy to satisfy a debt. Unhappy with his son-in-law's sale, Fanny's father bought Peggy back. But in order to allow Fanny to receive Peggy's labor without risking her sale by Obadiah, Mr. Stovall (his full name is unknown) "verbally loaned" the enslaved woman to Fanny for her lifetime. Peggy stayed with the Liggin family, but Fanny's father had Peggy brought over to his home every Christmas, around the time he settled his accounts for the year, in order to claim ownership of her and keep her from being sold to pay Liggin's debts. The yearly visit circumvented the law, which equated five consecutive years of possession with ownership, and may have eased Peggy's fears of being sold again at the whim of Obadiah. This continued until Stovall died in 1820, leaving a will that explicitly gave Peggy to Fanny and provided that she could not be sold to pay Liggin's debts. Nevertheless, when Obadiah died four years later, Peggy was sold at auction to satisfy the debts of the estate, sold two more times, and then taken to Arkansas by William B. Easely in 1835 or 1836, remarkably with her four children.[4] Although

Peggy left no record of her ordeal, such treatment reveals a capricious fate, at best, for enslaved women who found themselves in Arkansas.

But while the majority of the forced migration of slave women occurred in connection with the slave trade, many came to the cotton frontier with westward-traveling white families, although exactly how many is unknown. Slave women likely would have preferred to move with familiar white family groups than via individual sale or as part of a trader's wares. These family moves were initiated by men like James Hines Trulock, of a wealthy South Carolina family, who took his new Connecticut bride to southwestern Georgia in 1837, then moved on to finally settle in Jefferson County, Arkansas. All of Trulock's forty slaves made the trip except one elderly man. Bondwomen could also be moved when absentee planters expanded their holdings westward, as was the case for the thirty women of seventy-eight slaves who were moved into Chicot County, Arkansas, from Mississippi when elite slaveholder Rice C. Ballard added Wagram Plantation to his extensive westward-growing cotton acreage sometime in the mid-1850s. And although slaveowners might not have agreed on a transfer of ownership, slave women could be sent to the marginal South by whites for the use of migrated family members. This was the case for Amelia (or Parmelia), who was sent by a white family in Kentucky to nurse a relative in Conway County, Arkansas, in 1840.[5]

Several factors could combine to force women to the cotton frontier. The practice of gifting slaves to newly married daughters, the prevalence of slaveholders' debts, and westward migration could coalesce to create a perfect storm of uncertainty for enslaved women and their families. South Carolina slaves owned by William Pond fell victim to such a series of events. In 1833, Pond deeded (in trust) to a family friend a slave woman named Maria and her children Stephen, Emily, and Harriet, for the exclusive use of his wife, Mary Pond, and their children "to prevent them from being sold in one of his drinking sprees." Mary Pond died six years later, and the troubled widower, seeking a fresh start and a better income, moved hundreds of miles west to Hot Spring County, Arkansas, with his children and slaves. All of Maria's children were able to come along except Stephen, who was left in South Carolina to secure Pond's debt. But in 1844, Pond sold Maria's children Emily, Harriet, Tom, and Peter for $900 total, while keeping all of his other slaves.[6]

As indebted slaveholders like Pond struggled to keep their operations afloat, seeking fresh beginnings on the South's periphery, slave families like Maria's were separated and displaced. Cynthia and her children suffered this upheaval during Arkansas's territorial years. In Kentucky in 1826, Thomas Humphreys willed Cynthia (and any future children) to his daughter, Susan Mills, "to be enjoyed by her during her lifetime, and then to descend to her lawful heirs." After four years, Susan and her husband, Ambrose Mills, moved to southeastern Arkansas. Three years later, Ambrose died and Susan sold Cynthia and her eleven-year-old child for $500.[7] Arkansas was not only a destination but also a crossroads for slave women pushed to the southern periphery. Mary Overton was born in Tennessee but was moved when she was very young to Carroll County, Arkansas, by the Kennards. When she was four years old, she was gifted to the master's daughter, who married James Cox. She traveled with them to Fort Graham in Hill County, Texas.[8] As whites sought to provide for the economic well-being of their growing and moving families, slaves paid the price.

Whatever the immediate causes for the move west, overland journeys from the seaboard South to the trans-Mississippi cotton frontier were considered inconvenient by whites, but must have been nearly unbearable for bondpeople. Jenny and Celia were among the women and men moved by John Mebane Allen and his family from Alamance County, North Carolina, to Ozan Township in Hempstead County, Arkansas, in the fall of 1852. With each bridge and river and with each passing night spent in camp, Jenny and Celia would have been conscious of the greater distance being put between themselves and the families and friends they were forced to leave behind. The trek was physically uncomfortable as well. The group usually traveled upward of fifteen miles per day and could cover as many as twenty-five miles in a day. In two weeks, the party had crossed into Tennessee.[9]

While they doubtless understood that the cotton frontier would mean great changes for them, some indication of the differences of their bondage in Arkansas would have been noticeable to the Allen slaves as soon as they crossed the Mississippi River; even counties just opposite each other could differ markedly in some respects. In those years, counties on the east side of the Mississippi boasted almost five times more acreage in improved farmland than Arkansas's counties along the west bank. Jenny and Celia may have felt uneasy with the much less developed landscape. The enslaved population also dropped by more than 75 percent across the river, further indicating to the women that they had crossed into a more isolated part of the slave South.[10]

The problems of rough roads and overturned wagons impeded the party's progress. The group camped by the roadside or stayed at churches or with strangers. There was usually a good bit of resting on the weekends, however. The chores of preparing food and hauling water to the night's camp would have especially burdened the weary slave women. Sometimes, due to bad weather or other inconveniences, the party settled in for the night without dinner, and often water was scarce. It is reasonable to assume that the effects of such shortages would have been felt more severely by the enslaved members of the party. While Allen recorded discomfort and "low spirits" among the whites during the trip, the enslaved people must have felt absolute desolation. Finally, the cheerless caravan reached the Arkansas River on November 12, but they were unable to immediately cross. The next day, they waited "all day in consequence of so many wagons being before us."[11]

After passing through southern Arkansas, Jenny, Celia, and the rest of the Allen slaves finally arrived at their new neighborhood and could begin to take stock of the latest site of their bondage on November 20, when the party camped twelve miles east of Washington in Hempstead County.[12] With the journey from the seaboard South to their destination on the cotton frontier complete, these women, along with the rest of the slaves in their company, would have been painfully aware of their final separation from home.

But not all slaves completely lost their connection to their former home. "Aunt Jenny" (as whites called her) kept up a correspondence with people in North Carolina, at least between 1852 and 1864. Celia and other black people are also mentioned in letters from North Carolina, but none of them seem to have sent or received their own.[13] Jenny was able to "hear all the news" of births, deaths, injuries, illnesses, slave sales, and even enslaved newcomers on several different farms back east through letters that mostly came from her master's sisters. And while this channel seems to have been a major source of information, news was not only disseminated by women. For example, letters to John Allen from his uncle included notes like "Tell Jenny that Betsy had a fine boy this morning." News could be accompanied by messages from other slaves back in North Carolina, such as when "Uncle Bob" sent greetings to "Aunt Jenny" and Celia; he wanted them to know that he had experienced a religious conversion and was very happy. All of this information allowed Jenny to maintain and update her construction of the black neighborhood back home from hundreds of miles away.[14]

In addition to receiving news from North Carolina, Jenny served as a conduit for information about herself and other slaves in Hempstead County with roots in North Carolina, though this messaging passed through whites' hands. Perhaps dictating her missives to John Allen's wife, "Aunt Jenny" consistently sent letters to white people in North Carolina. This gave her the opportunity to maintain the sources of information about her loved ones back home and send her own messages of affection and news to them from distant Hempstead County, Arkansas.[15]

Thus, the move to the cotton frontier created a great disruption in the life of the Allen slaves, but their ties with those back east were not completely severed, due largely to the favored position of Jenny. Jenny's community continued to include connections with those from whom she had been separated, albeit by delicate threads. The Allen letters indicate that "Aunt Jenny" probably made a visit back to North Carolina with John Allen and his wife in late 1860 or early 1861. Clues, such as a note to Jenny informing her of an upcoming slave marriage with an urging for Jenny to attend, suggest that a visit was planned near the end of 1860.[16] Continued news and a visit back to her old home in North Carolina would have gone far to widen the scope of Jenny's constructed networks of family and friends, which stretched beyond her new home in southwest Arkansas and carried on for years after her forced migration west.

Jenny's circumstances were extremely unusual, as most enslaved Arkansans would have known little if anything about the fates of their loved ones from whom they had been separated. Migration that took place with white families, outside the slave trade per se, could mean a greater degree of family cohesion, but did not guarantee stability. Jenny and Celia were not the only ones to make such journeys with slaves who were already part of their communities. Westward movement in groups helped women to keep the important bonds of family and friendship. This would have been treasured by Emma Moore's parents, who came from Tennessee to Arkansas together, and by Molly Finley's grandmother, who was lucky enough to have been purchased along with her sons, all making the journey from Kentucky to Tennessee to Arkansas together.[17]

The life of a female slave in Arkansas consisted of unending toil exacerbated by white expectations that blurred the boundaries of gender. Sallie Crane said, "They would call on you to work like men and you better work too."[18] But while general accounts of slave women's labor in the American South are abundant, the work experiences of enslaved women in Arkansas have received almost no attention. *Negro Slavery in Arkansas* does not interrogate the significance of women's labor nor its effect on slave family life. Slave women exhibited remarkable grit under the heavy workload. With clear admiration of her ancestors' strength of mind and body, Adrianna Kerns recalled that her aunts "could handle a plow and roll logs as well as any man." Lou Fergusson recalled having to work in the fields even in the sleet.[19]

Bondwomen were essential members of the agricultural labor force, taking up the main work of the crop when men were assigned to other tasks, as they often were on new and large farming operations. This allowed for the crop routine to continue even when men were needed for heavier work. This was so often the case on the Wagram Plantation of Chicot County that absentee owner Rice C. Ballard's overseer wrote him for new hoes, explaining, "The women will be the main workers of the crop and these hoes are heavier than I am in the habit of giving to men."[20] Slave women's attention to the crop allowed for the other work to progress. Women performed the yearly task of gathering corn while men raised a new stable at Wagram Plantation in 1857. And in 1854, when John Brown sent the men to build his new home in a nearby town, enslaved women cleaned up the fields in preparation for the new cotton crop. Women were critical at picking time as well. "Hands at new ground until diner [sic]. In evening women picking," John Brown noted in November 1852. He moved the men from picking to clearing new land by December, but kept the women picking well into January 1853. In fact, at Brown's plantation, women were the last to stop picking the 1852 crop in early 1853, and the first to begin picking the next crop in August 1853.[21]

Women's role in cotton picking was not supplementary, but central to the effort of making cotton farms pay. This was especially true when the rhythm of the crop cycle was interrupted by bad weather, other work, or unexpected delays. The records of Shugart's plantation list several women's daily picking totals in 1859. Men and women both averaged nearly 100 pounds of cotton harvested per day. A woman named Lucy averaged 131 pounds per day, picking more than 800 pounds in a given week.[22] Records of slaves' daily cotton-picking totals over the course of thirty workdays in Chicot County further reveal the importance of women in that effort. Lithia worked twenty-nine of those thirty days, picking 6,752 pounds, averaging nearly 233 pounds each day. Her haul was a higher total and average than Bill, who picked the most out of the men on the farm. He picked twenty-eight of the thirty days, bringing in 6,204 pounds—around 500 pounds less than Lithia. Bill also averaged fewer pounds per day—221.5. Because Bill probably was capable of picking more than he did, these figures indicate that Bill was often at other work besides picking, leaving more of that task to Lithia and others.[23]

Women worked the cotton year after year, while family milestones punctuated the crop routine. In 1859, the beginning of the crop cycle coincided with an addition to the Ballard slave community when Lucille's baby was born on January 1. In 1857, also on the Ballard place, the demanding planting season had been a time for celebration when Martha Ann, eighteen years old, and George Turner, nineteen, were married on a Saturday. After a long week of clearing land and planting, the overseer noted, "They are all now enjoying themselves" in celebration of the union. Martha Ann and George cultivated a new beginning in their relationship as well as the cash crop. But the burden of crop work could be intensified by grief. On the same day that the first cotton boll opened on Shugart's plantation in 1839, Fanny's child died. The slaves were forced to pull fodder the next day, burying Fanny's child that rainy evening before the picking season began in earnest.[24]

Women also toiled outdoors at tasks associated with rural infrastructure. They might be sent to work on roads by area slaveholders, often for a couple of days at a time. John Brown's slaves spent several days building a bridge in 1853. Lucindy Allison told a WPA interviewer that her mother was required to help "grade a hill" and build a road when she was enslaved. Here again, distinctions between men's work and women's work fell away. Black women's bodies were pooled like taxes and forced into public labor to literally build the southern frontier. Of course, their labor was crucial to the maintenance of private land as well. The Ballard slaves had to manage the yearly flooding of that farm on the unruly Mississippi River. The work of women was central to the effort of juggling that task with the regular crop work. In the spring of 1857, while men continued to plow and clear land, overseer John Pelham required eight "of the stoutest women" to carry dirt to the low places for two days.[25]

Laboring in the fields worked against slave women's family lives. In the South as a whole, the cotton boom of the 1850s coincided with a decline in fertility and an increase in miscarriages among slave women, along with an infant mortality rate twice that of whites, although it is not clear to what extent this trend affected Arkansas women. Pregnancy and childbirth could be dangerous for slave women, whose bodies were commodified by whites. In a WPA interview conducted in the 1930s, 107-year-old former slave Hannah Allen recounted the story of a slave woman delivering her baby in the field. The woman had apparently been worked too hard in the heat, gave birth out in the open, and had to be attended to by a doctor.[26]

But apart from the physical ramifications, their labor encroached on the time that mothers were able to devote to the care of their children. Whites clearly placed the care of their own youngsters above the needs of the children of their slaves. Molly Finley tended to her siblings while her mother worked at the wide spectrum of tasks expected of her. More rarely, the work routine of bondwomen could mean that white women would step in to care for their children. Apparently, the enslaved children on the Horton farm stayed in a house together with "Miss Mary," the mistress, during the day while their parents worked. Becky, a bondwoman on Bullock's plantation would come to the mistress's house at about 10 a.m. every morning to feed her baby, presumably stopping in for more feedings throughout the day.[27] Thus, mothers worked as best they could to fit childcare into their time in ways allowed by their masters and farm managers. John Pelham at Wagram revealed some annoyance at this necessity in a letter to his employer during the very wet spring in March 1857: "I will make the two women with young children clear [the field] of cotton stalks and level it. . . . I have had them filling up about the gates, cleaning yard[,] repairing quarter fence etc. since they quit work on the Levee as it was rather troublesome to ferry them over the chute as often as they would have to come over."[28] Mandy Tucker explained to a WPA interviewer, "I didn't know nothin' bout my mother and father cause it was night when they went to work and night when they come in." Dinah Perry recalled that her mother was gone to the fields every day by the time she woke in the morning. Harriet Payne experienced a similar scenario on the Chaney place: "We wouldn't see our mammy and daddy from early in the morning till night when their work was done." After their long workdays, slaves would return to their quarters and prepare an evening meal from their weekly rations. But, on some places, after finishing their work in the field, in the evenings women set to additional tasks assigned to them, such as washing or spinning cloth.[29]

But slave women did their best to prevent whites' labor demands from destroying their family and social life. As recorded marriages and births show, family life did go on despite the difficulties. Although two-parent family units were less common on the plantations of Arkansas than in other southern states, enslaved parents were able to keep meaningful family connections alive. Slaves in Arkansas took an active role in choosing their partners and caring for the children who resulted from their pairings. The socialization of enslaved children leaned on the institutions created by the slaves themselves. Affection existed between family members despite uncertain circumstances.[30]

Older women were often assigned to lighter physical tasks, like milking and churning, but also served as mentors and caregivers among the enslaved people. A common—and important—duty for older women was to watch slave children during the day. These women might be expected to feed the children so that their parents would not have to prepare a meal for them when they returned from work in the fields.[31] Older women learned many skills that made them valuable contributors to the productivity and health of the farms on which they lived. For example, bondwomen in their later years could be an important source of medical knowledge. O. W. Green's grandmother worked under a doctor for several years, receiving training in his methods of healing. But the master would whip her to scare her from sharing these medical secrets. This woman lived in the tension between white male dominance over "scientific" medical knowledge and the power of black folk medicine and midwifery. Medical knowledge conferred power on slave women among whites and blacks, and allowed them to alleviate the suffering of others in the slave community. Figures such as the "old doctor woman," whom Mandy Tucker remembered from Cockrill's plantation, reinforced gendered divisions of labor while simultaneously providing a challenge to white male authority.[32]

Slavery offered a painfully brief childhood. Like older women, girls were assigned numerous jobs that were less physically demanding. Emma Moore remembered sitting at the cotton gin as a small girl, periodically tapping the mule that powered the mechanism by walking laps in the gin house. Children would keep needed fires burning; run errands; sweep; gather brush, trash, and rocks from the yard; pick up chips left behind by adults chopping wood; and carry water. When they got older, enslaved youngsters took on jobs like feeding chickens, driving cows, nursing children, washing, milking, churning, and carrying wood. Older children also worked in the cotton fields by helping adults in picking or helping to move the sacks or baskets down the rows while adults picked. When old enough, they were assigned a row to pick for themselves. While still a young girl, Adeline was given to her master's newlywed daughter as a domestic servant. But, being only five years old, Adeline lacked the knowledge, skill, and physical strength to work to the satisfaction of her new mistress, and she was sent back to her master to mature for a couple of more years. Although young children and the elderly were unable to perform the most physically demanding work, their tasks were important and were expected to be completed in a timely manner.[33]

On large plantations, certain slave women were designated for house work only. Although these women were kept out of the fields, they worked hard and much was demanded of them. Laboring in the house meant closer proximity to whites, and frequently it meant closer scrutiny. House work encompassed cooking, sewing, weaving, cleaning, washing clothes, and caring for the white children. In homes with fewer slaves, all of this fell to the one or two women who worked in the home. In North Carolina, Molly Hudgens's mother was sold to Judge Allen, a widower who brought her to Monroe County, Arkansas. Her household responsibilities would have been even greater than in a home with a mistress, though perhaps with less oversight. Her duties included sewing and caring for two other slave children, who had been brought to the Allen workforce without parents. Laura Shelton's mother and grandmother both worked in the house. Her mother performed chores like churning and watching children, while her grandmother prepared the food for everyone on the plantation. Harriet Daniel, a planter's daughter in Dallas County, Arkansas, recalled, "We children had never been required to wash our own faces," since enslaved women and girls in domestic work were responsible for the upkeep of white bodies.[34]

Domestic work did not necessarily mean strictly indoor work, nor Sundays off. The advantages of house work over field work have been historically exaggerated. Harriet McFarlin Payne recalled, "Some of the slaves were house negroes. They didn't go to work in the fields, they each had their own job around the house, barn, orchard, milk house, and things like that." She remembered "washday," when a few women would spend the entire day scrubbing clothes, possibly drawing the water from a nearby spring. On Cockrill's plantation in Jefferson County, this chore was completed every Sunday evening. Hannah Jameson described the task as taking place well into Sunday nights, by the light of a pine torch, if need be.[35]

The WPA narratives reveal a rich tradition of spinning, weaving, and sewing among Arkansas's slave women. Many slaveholders used the skills of enslaved women to clothe all of their slaves. This practice saved money and was convenient for whites. Charles Dortch's mother worked both the loom and the spinning wheel in Dallas County. Joe Bean described the weaving operation on Bean's plantation, close to Fayetteville in Washington County: "Not far from the big house was a rock building used for the looms[.] In there they made cloth and thread, and they [made] it for anybody what come there with cotton or wool." Much of the spinning for the Pattillo family was done by Solomon Pattillo's mother, Fannie. Slave women at this task might produce nine or ten yards of cloth per day.[36]

But as much as their labor encroached on time they would have rather spent caring for their children, slave women in some circumstances actually worked under a routine that kept them close to their little ones. On Jack Hall's plantation along the Arkansas River in Jefferson County, Senia Rassberry and her sister both worked in the house where their mother was a cook. At least this arrangement meant close proximity to their mother, even if she was busy. In these situations, the special bonding between mother and child could be possible despite the workload. For example, as a child Eva Strayhorn ran errands and completed odd jobs around the house on the Newton farm in Clarksville, Johnson County; she remembered fondly the moments when she was able to help her mother cook. Although Ellen Briggs Thompson's mother had to work in the fields owned by the Mitchell family of Hempstead County, she was at least able to spend time with her grandmother, who worked in "the big house" cooking, making clothes, and caring for children. But enslaved domestics were expected to put the needs of the white family first. "Just like a cow would leave a calf," Mary Jane Hardridge bluntly described the requirement that her mother, a domestic worker, accompany the Scull family on trips away from the plantation. Although "she'd hate to do it," Hardridge's mother had to travel with the white family on their frequent vacations.[37]

For many slave women in Arkansas (and all over the South) there existed no clear distinction between house work and field work. Women in bondage were expected to do what was asked of them, no matter the type of work. Only the largest plantations could afford to assign certain women strictly to domestic work. Molly Finley's mother "was a nurse and house woman and field woman if she was needed," as was Minnie Stewart's mother, who sewed for the mistress in the house, but could also be found in the field. Their work ranged from hoeing and plowing to milking, cooking, weaving, and more. Mollie Barber said of her mother, "seem lak she done 'bout ever'thing." Betty Brown explained that there was only one slave family on the Nutt farm in Greene County, Arkansas. Thus, her mother cooked, weaved, tanned leather, made moccasins, and trapped and hunted game. Some women experienced a seasonal shift from field work to house work. Sarah was moved from picking cotton to spinning for some time on Ballard's Chicot County plantation in December 1857. Similarly, the women working on John W. Brown's plantation probably welcomed being assigned to spinning in the cold months after the cotton was in and before new crops were to be planted. When the time was right, they were moved back into the fields to complete tasks like pulling cotton stalks to make room for the new plants.[38]

In addition to their family time and sense of womanhood, slavery also threatened women's health. House work might result in burns and blisters, while field work could prove more dangerous, resulting in injuries from tools or draft animals or from sheer exhaustion. Bondwomen suffered from common illnesses like dropsy and colds, as well as those unique to females. An overseer on R. Ç. Ballard's place vaguely noted "some of the women complaining of the womb" in early 1858. It may be that women could capitalize some on the ignorance of male overseers about women's health, allowing them to fake particularly female ailments, as Paulina and Jane might have been doing to cause Ballard's overseer to frustratedly report that they were "complaining about as usual." But a woman on that plantation, whose name was never mentioned in the sources, lingered with breast cancer for months before passing away in May 1859. Whites had little patience for slave women with what they perceived as unfitness, whether physical or dispositional. In one lawsuit, a slave woman named Fanny was described as "worth less than nothing" because she was "sickly and drunken." There were other dangers on the cotton frontier. In April 1858, three enslaved girls were killed on George Brodie's farm when a fire broke out in the slave quarters.[39]

Slave women relieved the burdens of their bondage in various ways according to their personalities, priorities, and circumstances. Their resistance was often passive or subtle, effective without involving an outright challenge to white authority. Like enslaved men, women commonly resisted work demands. Martha Jones, who probably cooked for Ballard's plantation and also worked in the field, may have been exaggerating an illness to get out of work until a new overseer arrived and called her bluff. He wrote to Ballard, "Sent her out and she tried to stop the same day but failed and has done very well since." Some women refused to accept limitations on their religious lives, such as O. W. Green's grandmother, who repeatedly received punishment for taking part in "shouting." Women like Green's grandmother and Ellen Briggs Thompson's grandmother insisted on providing religious leadership for their children and grandchildren, risking brutal punishment.[40]

In addition to work slowdowns and covert religious practices, enslaved women practiced more direct physical resistance. Although men were more likely to run away, women could and did flee their masters. In 1833, a woman named Tenns ran away with Pleasant and Pete from Chicot County. A slave woman, presumably a captured runaway, escaped from the Pulaski County jail in 1823. In January 1839, Henry Shugart noted that "Old Polly" had run away on the sixteenth but was back on the eighteenth. The punishment for flight could be severe. Sallie Crane was forced to wear a "buck and gag" for three days as punishment for running away. This restraint position immobilized the body and kept the mouth full of a cloth or piece of wood, preventing eating, drinking, and speaking. Crane described the horror of being unable to simply clean the saliva that dripped down her body during the punishment, showing her interviewer the scars remaining where flies and maggots had settled into her chest. Slave women risked these tortures for the chance to reunite with loved ones. This was a strong motivation for Sophia, who ran after her sale and removal from her children in northwest Arkansas in the 1830s. Although she was brutally whipped for it, Sophia ran to see her children, whom "she seemed much devoted to," time and again. While Sophia disappears from the record, it is probable that she never saw her children again, illustrating the hard reality that women's direct resistance was risky and unlikely to secure long-term benefits.[41]

Slave women could also become violent toward masters and overseers. In Cross County, Mandy Buford's sister was fiercely defended by their mother, who threatened to chop the riding boss "in pieces" if he tried to execute his plan to lay the pregnant woman in the hole he had prepared for her face-down whipping. While this particular story might be larger than life, bondwomen's physical protectiveness of female relatives, especially those carrying children, is not hard to believe. Neither are the violent thoughts of resistance and meditations on revenge that would have swirled in many of their minds. Some women carried out these musings, like the unnamed St. Francis County woman who crept up behind her master, James Calvert, in 1849. Turning a tool of daily domestic work into a deadly weapon, she struck Calvert with a mallet intended for "beating hominy." Women resisted an inherently violent system both in the heat of the moment and in plotted attacks.[42]

In addition to outright retaliation, women were also moved by complex motives that called for a combination of strategies. The story of Martha, a middle-aged domestic servant on R. C. Ballard's plantation, although hard to follow in the sources, demonstrates an ability to play whites against each other. Martha was reportedly "stolen" from Chicot County and turned up in Memphis with a couple of white men. After being apprehended in circumstances that are not altogether clear in Ballard's cryptic correspondence on the matter, she was taken to New Orleans to be sold. Martha had alerted whites when another slave in New Orleans, Anthony, ran away (perhaps to Natchez) when he was about to be sold to Helena, only to suspiciously disappear herself soon after. Martha had reported to whites that her previous "captors" were in the area before her last disappearance, and she was presumed to be somewhere in Texas with the same white man who had "kidnapped" her before. Although she was willing to inform on another slave in order to gain the trust of the whites who held her in New Orleans, there was clearly a level of cooperation between Martha and whoever kept spiriting her off.[43]

Enslaved women played whites off each other within households as well. Discord in the Rose household of Chicot County was directly related to Mary, William Rose's domestic servant, taking advantage of his northern-born wife, Nancy. Nancy eventually filed for divorce, claiming, in addition to other insults, that William encouraged the slaves to disobey her, making life at the plantation unbearable. It seems that Mary had been in charge of the Rose household, a small plantation keeping around twenty slaves, since William had moved there in 1839. By the time Nancy arrived in 1841, Mary had been running the Rose home how she pleased for long enough to resent intrusion. Mary easily benefited from Nancy's inexperience in slaveholding and had noticed William's scorn for his new wife. Mary routinely ignored Nancy's orders, knowing that William would not enforce them. A witness claimed that Nancy showed bruises on her arm inflicted not by her husband (which surely would have gone further to strengthen Nancy's case) but by Mary. Mary had instilled such fear in Nancy that the mistress sometimes refused to eat Mary's cooking, in case the food was poisoned. Supposedly referring to his wife as a "lazy trifling white woman" (as opposed to a hardworking black woman like Mary), William would have encouraged any already existing disdain for Nancy in Mary. Mary was able to successfully place herself in charge of the Rose household and defend her position by establishing supremacy over the new mistress of the house.[44]

Women who were enslaved worked to secure their freedom using whites' own systems, though not always successfully. Mourning, a Hempstead County bondwoman, risked much in the hope of freeing her child, who had been fathered by a white man she worked for. Before his death, store owner James H. Dunn of Hempstead County acknowledged his paternity of Mourning's daughter Eliza (presumably conceived while she was hired out to him). Before he died, Dunn made it clear that he wanted to purchase their daughter and manumit her. After Dunn's death, Mourning gave her owner, James Moss, $300 that Dunn had entrusted to her to go toward the purchase of Eliza. The money was Mourning's only hope for Eliza's freedom since Dunn's passing, but it was stripped from her because Dunn's heirs claimed the money as part of Dunn's estate. Although it is unclear whether Mourning was able to regain the money and use it to ensure her daughter's freedom, she saw how attempts to follow the rules set by whites did not guarantee success.[45]

A rather well-known and successful freedom suit is the case of *Daniel v. Guy*. Probably in the late 1830s, Abby Guy, born to a mulatto woman named Polly who died before the journey, came to Arkansas from Alabama with William Daniel and his brother. Sometime after they arrived in southern Arkansas, Abby, who might have had a white father and was described as having a very light complexion and straight hair, began to live separately from the Daniels. Abby and her children, Elizabeth Daniel, Mary Daniel, John Guy, and Malissa Arnold, lived as free whites beginning in 1844, farming in Bayou Bartholomew in Ashley County, Arkansas. Abby made her own contracts, paid her own debts, and hired men to do work on her farm, such as hauling cotton and moving fences. She was able to board her oldest daughter and pay for her schooling. For some period of time, she lived as the wife of a white man with the last name of Guy, though they were not married, and he passed some land to her when he died. Abby and her children also socialized and attended church as whites with whites. But William Daniel began claiming Abby as a slave after about 1856, causing her to sue for the freedom of herself and her children.[46]

Abby struggled to prove her whiteness to a group of people who adhered to the "one-drop rule"—the notion that any bit of black "blood" defined an individual as nonwhite. This was crucial because blackness assumed enslavement. After lengthy discussions in the courtroom about hair, skin color, and nose shape, at one point Abby and her children were asked to remove their shoes and socks and show their feet to the jury, in order that a doctor's theories of blackness and foot shape could be tested. In addition to revealing notions of race, this case demonstrates the importance of migration. Abby Guy was able to establish her own household, relationship, and social life as a free person, and raise her children as free people, because her community had never known her as a slave. Her looks made this possible, to be sure, but both Abby's slave mother—the main indicator of enslaved status—and William's father, James

Daniel, who had owned Abby and her mother, had died years before the move to Arkansas. In order to prove Abby's slave origins, the attorneys for Daniel called witnesses who had known Abby and Daniel in Alabama. This testimony turned out to be much more important than that describing her whiteness. Abby won her case, but she and her children were forced to work as slaves for some time during the legal proceedings. Here, the cotton frontier provided just enough chaos for a woman to slip unnoticed from slavery to freedom for a while. Her light skin and persistence eventually secured that freedom legally for herself and her children.[47]

Bondwomen of Arkansas negotiated the hardships of slavery on the South's periphery the best they could. Uprooted from points east, countless enslaved women were marched to the trans-Mississippi cotton frontier as traders' wares or with migrating whites. There, bondwomen toiled under the lashes of whites, who commodified and masculinized them in their quest to profit from fresh cotton land. Slave women cleared the forests of the Old South, carving out wide patches of earth in which they seeded King Cotton and harvested the cash crop year after year in a routine that intertwined with their family and social lives. Women worked hard to navigate their enslavement in ways that allowed them to cultivate relationships and mother their children, sometimes risking all in attempts to protect or reunite with those they loved. Slave women were each born with unique personalities and goals, and they pushed against their oppression in myriad ways, ranging from quiet and cautious to downright violent in their resistance to the burdens of their bondage. Their misfortunes and successes are a crucial part of the story of early Arkansas women.

NOTES

1. Orville Taylor, *Negro Slavery in Arkansas* (1958; repr., Fayetteville: University of Arkansas Press, 2000); Donald P. McNeilly, *The Old South Frontier: Cotton Plantations and the Formation of Arkansas Society, 1819–1861* (Fayetteville: University of Arkansas Press, 2000); S. Charles Bolton, *Arkansas, 1800–1860: Remote and Restless* (Fayetteville: University of Arkansas Press, 1998).

2. See Ira Berlin, "Migration Generations," in his *Generations of Captivity: A History of African-American Slaves* (Cambridge, Mass.: Belknap, 2003), 161–244; Steven Deyle, *Carry Me Back: The Domestic Slave Trade in American Life* (New York: Oxford University Press, 2005), 43; Joseph C. G. Kennedy, *Population of the United States in 1860, Compiled from the Original Returns of the Eighth Census* (Washington, D.C.: U.S. Government Printing Office, 1864), 12–13, 503–4.

3. Deyle, *Carry Me Back*, 44; George E. Lankford, ed., *Bearing Witness: Memories of Arkansas Slavery* (Fayetteville: University of Arkansas Press, 2003), 23–24; Edward E. Baptist, "'Stol' and Fetched Here': Enslaved Migration, Ex-Slave Narratives, and Vernacular History," in *New Studies in the History of American Slavery*, ed. Edward E. Baptist and Stephanie M. H. Camp (Athens: University of Georgia Press, 2006), 243–44, 252–54; Brief in the Case of Elijah Brown, box 60, Disallowed

Claims of U.S. Colored Troops, 1864–1893, 54th USCT, Records of the Pay and Bounty Division, Records of the Accounting Officers of the Department of the Treasury, RG 217, National Archives and Records Administration (hereafter NARA). For additional examples of places of origin, see Lankford, *Bearing Witness*, 36, 66, 104, 126, 134, 45, 53, 104. See also Michael Tadman, *Speculators and Slaves: Masters, Traders, and Slaves in the Old South* (Madison: University of Wisconsin Press, 1989); Walter Johnson, *Soul by Soul: Life inside the Antebellum Slave Market* (Cambridge, Mass.: Harvard University Press, 1999).

4. Whitfield v. Browder, 13 Ark. 143–150 (1852).

5. Sarah Brooke Malloy, "The Health of Our Family: The Correspondence of Amanda Beardsley Trulock, 1837–1868," MA thesis, University of Arkansas, 2005, 1–2, 22; Bounty Claim for Lewis Pettis, Disallowed Claims of U.S. Colored Troops, 1864–1893, 54th USCT, Records of the Pay and Bounty Division, Records of the Accounting Officers of the Department of the Treasury, RG 217, NARA; Wagram Plantation journal, ser. 5, box 30, folder 457, Rice C. Ballard Papers, Southern Historical Collection, University of North Carolina, Chapel Hill (hereafter Ballard Papers); James M [illegible] to Col. R. C. Ballard, subser. 1.3, box 7, folder 108, ibid.; Menifee's Administrators v. Menifee et al., 8 Ark. 9 (1847).

6. Pond v. Obaugh, 16 Ark. 95 (1855).

7. Maulding et al. v. Scott et al., 13 Ark. 88–95 (1852).

8. Lankford, *Bearing Witness*, 53.

9. John Allen journal, 9–11, John Mebane Allen Papers, Southern Historical Collection, University of North Carolina, Chapel Hill (hereafter Allen Papers).

10. Together, Chicot, Crittenden, Desha, Phillips, and Mississippi counties, Arkansas, had 82,706 acres in improved farmland and 9,410 slaves in 1850. That same year, Tipton, Shelby, and Lauderdale counties, Tennessee, and De Soto, Tunica, Coahoma, Bolivar, and Washington counties, Mississippi, together had 397,672 acres in improved farmland and 42,195 slaves. Alamance County, North Carolina, had 98,260 improved farm acres and was home to 3,196 slaves in 1850. U.S. Census, 1850, Productions of Agriculture, Slave Population. In 1860, Chicot, Crittenden, Desha, Phillips, and Mississippi counties, Arkansas, together had 229,905 acres in improved farmland and 24,018 slaves. Shelby and Lauderdale counties, Tennessee, and De Soto, Tunica, Coahoma, and Bolivar counties, Mississippi, had a total of 501,589 acres in improved farmland and 51,440 slaves in 1860. Data for Washington County, Mississippi, are missing from the 1860 Census enumeration. Alamance County, North Carolina, had 110,655 acres of improved farmland and was home to 3,445 slaves in 1860. U.S. Census, 1860, Productions of Agriculture, Slave Population.

11. Allen journal, 9–11, 14–16.

12. Ibid., 17.

13. See transcripts of letters to John Mebane Allen, 1852–1864, Allen Papers. About one-third of the letters to Allen from North Carolina in that period include some greeting or note to "Aunt Jenny," mostly those from Fannie Thompson and Mary Jane Allen. John Allen did own slaves in 1850; see U.S. Census, 1850, Slave Population, Alamance County, N.C.

14. Mary Jane Allen to brother and sister, January 18, 1853; John Scott to nephew, September 24, 1852; Lizzie K. Allen to brother and sister, August 1, 1858; M. J. Allen to brother, December 14, 1859; Mary Jane Allen to Aunt Jenney [sic], June 21, 1856, all in Allen Papers.

15. Mary Jane Allen to brother and sister, August 13, 1857; M. J. Allen to brother, June 8, 1858, both in Allen Papers.

16. M. J. Allen to brother, November 28, 1860, Allen Papers.

17. Lankford, *Bearing Witness*, 15, 24.

18. Ibid., 269, 86, 71, 72, 102, 136; Jacqueline Jones, *Labor of Love, Labor of Sorrow: Black Women, Work, and the Family, from Slavery to the Present* (1985; repr., New York: Vintage, 1986) 17.

19. Lankford, *Bearing Witness*, 140.

20. H. L. Berry to Col. Ballard, April 4, 1857, subser. 1.3, folder 256, Ballard Papers.

21. Jno. B. Pelham to Col. Ballard, October 16, 1857, subser. 1.3, folder 260, Ballard Papers; John Brown diary, January 4, 9, 11–14, 16, 21, and 23, 1854; October 13 and November 6, 1852 (quotation); January 14 and 25, August 30, 1853, microfilm, University of Arkansas Libraries, Fayetteville.

22. Shugart plantation journal, microfilm, n.p., University of Arkansas Libraries, Fayetteville.

23. Maggie Walker Benton diary, 1861, Arkansas State Archives, Little Rock.

24. H. L. Berry to Col. Ballard, January 8, 1859, subser. 1.3, folder 322, Ballard Papers; Jno. B. Pelham to Col. Ballard, February 28, 1857, ibid., folder 253; Brown diary, February 12, 1853; Shugart plantation journal, August 2 and 3, 1839.

25. Brown diary, July 31, 1852, August 4 and 10, 1853; Lankford, *Bearing Witness*, 71; Jno. B. Pelham to Col. Ballard, February 22, 1857, subser. 1.3, folder 253, Ballard Papers; Jno. B. Pelham to Col. Ballard, March 4, 1857, ibid., folder 254.

26. Jones, *Labor of Love, Labor of Sorrow*, 19, 35; Lankford, *Bearing Witness*, 353.

27. Lankford, *Bearing Witness*, 107, 23, 245, 368, 15, 210, 214, 30, 124, 376, 50; Margaret Jones Bolsterli, *A Remembrance of Eden: Harriet Bailey Bullock Daniel's Memories of a Frontier Plantation in Arkansas* (Fayetteville: University of Arkansas Press, 1993), 61–62.

28. Jno. B. Pelham to Col. Ballard, March 4, 1857, subser. 1.3, folder 254, Ballard Papers.

29. Lankford, *Bearing Witness*, 210, 214, 30, 185, 376, 24, 317–18, 164, 165.

30. Carl H. Moneyhon, "The Slave Family in Arkansas," *Arkansas Historical Quarterly* 58 (Spring 1999): 35–44; Jones, *Labor of Love, Labor of Sorrow*, 13.

31. Brown diary, February 7 and 22, 1854; Lankford, *Bearing Witness*, 371, 4, 102, 305, 244, 124, 216, 376, 50.

32. Lankford, *Bearing Witness*, 48, 214; Sharla M. Fett, *Working Cures: Healing, Health, and Power on Southern Slave Plantations* (Chapel Hill: University of North Carolina Press, 2002), 4–5, 111–15.

33. Wilma King, *Stolen Childhood: Slave Youth in Nineteenth-Century America*, 2nd ed. (Bloomington: Indiana University Press, 2011), xxi–xxii, 71–106; Lankford, *Bearing Witness*, 122, 164, 197, 370–71, 4, 102, 305, 244, 124, 216, 13, 15, 23, 104, 136, 379.

34. Lankford, *Bearing Witness*, 22, 86, 95, 108, 185, 359, 362, 259, 289, 246–47, 124; Bolsterli, *Remembrance of Eden*, 49.

35. Jones, *Labor of Love, Labor of Sorrow*, 27; Lankford, *Bearing Witness*, 366, 30, 215, 165.

36. Lankford, *Bearing Witness*, 185, 95, 104, 107, 381; Madelyn Shaw, "Slave Cloth and Clothing Slaves: Craftsmanship, Commerce, and Industry," *Journal of Early Southern Decorative Arts* 34 (2013), www.mesdajournal.org/2012/slave-cloth-clothing-slaves-craftsmanship-commerce-industry.

37. Lankford, *Bearing Witness*, 211, 223, 170, 196.

38. Jones, *Labor of Love, Labor of Sorrow*, 22; Lankford, *Bearing Witness*, 23, 166–67, 20, 260, 128–29; Jno. B. Pelham to Col. Ballard, December 5, 1857, subser. 1.3, folder 264, Ballard Papers; Brown diary, February 5–7 and 26, March 1, 1853.

39. H. L. Berry to Col. Ballard, December 17, 1857, subser. 1.3, folder 265, Ballard Papers; H. L. Berry to Col. Ballard, January 18, 1858, ibid., folder 268; H. L. Berry to Col. Ballard, June 1, 1859, ibid., folder 308; Porter v. Clements, 3 Ark. 367 (1841); H. C. Buckner to Col. R. C. Ballard February 4, 1860, subser. 1.3, folder 324, Ballard Papers; *Arkansas Gazette*, April 10, 1858.

40. Jones, *Labor of Love, Labor of Sorrow*, 21; Jno. B. Pelham to Col. Ballard, February 28, 1857, subser. 1.3, folder 253, Ballard Papers; Kelly Houston Jones, "'A Rough, Saucy Set of Hands to Manage': Slave Resistance in Arkansas," *Arkansas Historical Quarterly* 71 (Spring 2012): 12.

41. *Arkansas Gazette*, September 18, 1833, October 14, 1823; Shugart plantation journal, January 16–18, 1839; Lankford, *Bearing Witness*, 136; Jones, "Rough, Saucy Set of Hands," 6–7.

42. Jones, "Rough, Saucy Set of Hands," 15–16, 19.

43. Peete and Raglan to Mr. Ballard, [April 1858], subser. 1.3, box 18, folder 277; W. Cox and Co. to Col. R. C. Ballard, May 6, 1858, ibid., folder 278; C. M. Rutherford to Coln. Ballard, May 16, July 5 and 6, 1858, ibid., folder 283, all Ballard Papers.

44. Rose v. Rose, 9 Ark. 508, 3, 11, 16, 43–45, 48, 56, 63, 69 (1849), Arkansas Supreme Court Briefs and Records, ser. 1, box 48, folder 3148, University of Arkansas, Little Rock, Bowen School of Law and Pulaski County Law Library; U.S. Census, 1850, Slave Population, Chicot County, Ark.

45. Moss v. Sandefur, 15 Ark. 381–88 (1854).

46. Daniel v. Guy, 19 Ark. 121–38 (1857) and 23 Ark. 50 (1861). Abby Guy's case is explored in more detail in Robert S. Shafer, "White Persons Held to Racial Slavery in Antebellum Arkansas," *Arkansas Historical Quarterly* 44 (Summer 1985): 134–43.

47. Daniel v. Guy (1857, 1861).

Amanda Trulock
(1811–1891)

Yankee Mistress of the Old South

GARY T. EDWARDS

❈ ❈ ❈

The plantation known as Prairie Place had become a shell of itself by the summer of 1865. "There is nothing on the place," the resident mistress complained, "nor money to get anything with." The following spring she was still uncertain how to proceed. In a letter to her sister, she expressed the full measure of her apathy: "Somehow it seems as though I have nearly lost all interest in almost everything, that I hardly know what is going on around me." Physically and emotionally exhausted from self-described "trials and troubles," she contemplated taking a trip to "have a little rest." Amanda Trulock was fifty-five when she wrote these words, and after twenty-one years in Arkansas she had accumulated her share of struggle and losses: a difficult migration from Georgia and a deceased child, a deceased husband, a destructive war, and the emancipation of her human property. Trulock was justifiably weary. Later that year she followed her own advice and left her grown children behind to "have a little rest" in her native New England. Just a few years earlier she had been certain she would finish out her days on a southern plantation. But she never returned to live in Arkansas and passed the last twenty-five years of her life in the region of her birth.[1]

Amanda Beardsley Trulock (1811–1891) is a rare example of a northern woman, born and raised in Bridgeport, Connecticut, who married a Georgia cotton planter; she later migrated to Arkansas and eventually became a plantation proprietor and the sole mistress of sixty-two slaves near Pine Bluff. Like many slaveowning widows of the Old South, Trulock was a very competent financial manager. But she delegated many other responsibilities, a surprising amount, to an enslaved man, Reuben. Their relationship reveals a distinctive example of antebellum enslavement, which combined an unusual mixture of white leniency and black autonomy. Trulock also shares some things in common with the tiny handful of New England women who married into slaveholding families at the time. Most informative of these commonalities (or perhaps the most surprising, depending on one's preconceptions) was her immediate acceptance and selective advocacy of slavery during her twenty-nine years of residency in the South. In at least three other areas her personal narrative is unusual compared to either New England expatriates or native white southerners. First, she actually chose to leave the urban North specifically for a married life in the rural South, unlike most of her female contemporaries who first came as tutors and later married planters.[2] Second, she spent every summer of the 1850s in Bridgeport, gradually leaving all her children there to attend school while she returned to Arkansas in the autumn with different members of her extended family. Third, Trulock permanently abandoned the South after the Civil War, again unlike other New England transplants. Arguably, Amanda was in and out of Connecticut so frequently she may have stunted the development of any long-term affinity for the rural South. This was exacerbated during the Civil War, which she viewed more as a trial of personal endurance rather than as a situation in which she should support either side. However, it was suffering the entire war on her plantation that seemed to effectively extinguish her desire to rebuild in a postslavery Arkansas.

Trulock's story is a revealing chronicle about an oscillating identity of place at a time when sectional identity rose to its polarizing apogee. Ultimately her identity took shallow root in the South and returned to its cosmopolitan beginnings. Ironically, Amanda Trulock had little in common with most of the women who lived in Arkansas during her twenty-one years of intermittent residency, but her uniqueness provides a contrast that casts the lives of others in a brighter light. She was an "Arkansas woman" of sorts, but only of the rarest kind and ultimately only on her terms.

In contrast to the voluminous correspondence she wrote while in Georgia and Arkansas, there is comparatively little primary evidence about Amanda Beardsley Trulock before she married and moved to the South. Early genealogical data point back to a Puritan ancestor, William Beardsley, an artisan who arrived in Connecticut in 1635. During the American Revolution Amanda's great-great-grandfather briefly served as a captain in the Continental Army. By the nineteenth century the Beardsleys of Bridgeport were a respectable family of sufficient means and members of the Congregational Church. Thus Amanda's authentic "Yankee heritage" could not have been better established. The eldest of three children, Amanda remained close to her siblings, Bronson and Marcia, throughout her life. Amanda presumably received a competent education, based on her many descriptive letters and the interest she showed in the education of her children.³

Amanda Beardsley was already twenty-six years old when she married James Trulock. The circumstances of the young planter's business in Bridgeport are unclear, although the two families shared a common acquaintance in Bainbridge, Georgia.⁴ Amanda's relatively advanced age invites speculation about her motive, since matrimony was the catalyst for her dramatically altered life. Even though New England women delayed marriage, Amanda seemed cognizant of the implications of her age. Indeed she retrospectively described herself as an "old maid" but appeared resigned, if not content, with that social status. Additionally, the example of her younger sister, Marcia, who never married, suggests that the Beardsleys did not pressure their daughters to take a husband in order to avoid "spinsterhood." Furthermore, Amanda was apparently happy during her twelve years of marriage to "one of the kindest, and most affectionate of husbands." Her assertive personality in the future strongly suggests that she would not have remained in an unhappy marriage—even in the face of the prevailing social expectations of her time. Last, there was frequent speculation about James and Amanda returning to live in Bridgeport throughout their marriage. This is highly suggestive that similar discussions took place during their courtship and that Amanda may have moved to the South thinking she might be away no more than a few years. Taking all this into consideration, it seems plausible that she married James Trulock on terms of her choosing rather than to avoid any negative consequences of remaining unmarried.⁵

Amanda almost certainly possessed little personal knowledge of black people (free or enslaved) prior to her marriage, but her ready acceptance of slavery when she experienced it in person is an informative reflection of the white mentality in the antebellum North. It is certainly a rebuke to any easy conclusions of a broad-based antipathy to the "peculiar institution" by white northerners in general. In the first place, Amanda received the courtship of James Trulock with the full knowledge of his economic standing. She understood that he owned slaves. She also knew that if she accepted his proposal, she would become a southern plantation mistress of slaves. However, it is also clear from her letters that she could not have comprehended what that really entailed; she seemed largely unfazed by the thought of it at the time. Her courtship and marriage are also important reminders that America was very much a nation that was half-slave and half-free in 1837. The Beardsleys were not ardent abolitionists, although Bronson apparently questioned slaveownership's compatibility with Christianity. And while Connecticut was no longer a slave state, it was no bastion of racial equality; indeed, William Lloyd Garrison derided it as the

"Georgia of New England" in 1835. Thus there was no compelling reason that Americans from free states and slave states should not come together in various social exchanges, including matrimony. A young lady from Connecticut would not automatically be repulsed by a Georgia bachelor simply because he owned slaves.[6]

The day after they were married, Mr. and Mrs. James Trulock began a thirteen-day trip to Georgia, where Amanda met her husband's extended family and observed human slavery up close for the first time. Overall, Amanda's description of her initial journey to the South reveals a strong inclination toward approval of all she surveyed. A new bride with a new life set before her, she had every motivation to cultivate an optimistic outlook. Perhaps as anticipated, she found her husband's siblings and mother all perfectly agreeable. And they, in turn, embraced her with sincerity; Amanda noted, "they have a very exalted opinion of the yankees." When the couple finally arrived at James's plantation, Magnolia Place, the effect was truly dramatic. Amanda described a boisterous reunion where all the slaves rushed out to "welcome home their Master and to be introduced to their new Mistress, each one separately. I can assure you that was a very interesting scene and one that is entirely out of my power to describe but which will long be remembered by me, as an area of my life worthy of note." Amanda was pulled in by the gravity of this transitional moment. "And then to think of the responsibility and charge that I am about to participate in," she explained, "for life together with thirty Negroes that are consined [sic] to our care, which have souls as well as ourselves, is no trifling thing." However, she simultaneously espoused a benign attitude and confessed that upon arriving in Georgia her opinion was now quite different "with regard to the Negroes . . . for certainly they are the happiest people in the world for they have no cares." Building on this halcyon premise, and fully cognizant that this was now her life too, Amanda summarily validated every aspect of the "peculiar institution." She concluded that slaves did not work half as hard as white farmers in the North; a cook prepared their food especially for them; they sang and danced in the evenings; and they were untroubled by aspirations toward wealth. Within a few days she felt comfortable enough to order them about the house.[7]

It is plausible to conclude that Amanda fervently hoped to see slavery in a positive light in justification of her matrimonial choice, and her earliest experiences all reinforced this. No doubt this was partly facilitated by the enslaved people themselves, who perceived in the arrival of their "Yankee mistress" a rare opportunity to make a good first impression. One may imagine the negative effect of an alternative scenario where Amanda witnessed a violent punishment on the day of her arrival. Instead she saw jubilant slaves who received her almost like the new queen of their principality. Indeed, this analogy to a feudal state was implied by Amanda when she portrayed Magnolia Place as "a little City of our own in the Pine woods." James further encouraged Amanda, somewhat in the fashion of a medieval monarch. "My dear don't do that," he often chided, "let the Negroes do it." But the strongest adhesive that cemented her early affinity for slavery was the slave children. No doubt prompted by the adults, the children were precociously attentive to Amanda as they politely greeted her and regularly inquired after her health. She, in turn, found them charming and much less quarrelsome than white children. Through them she grew toward a personal acceptance of the institution of slavery in an ever-broadening way. Within five months Amanda's opinions had solidified. She declared the Trulock slaves "much better off than the Negroes and well might I say, many of the poor white people of the North." Thus Amanda was now like many other slaveholders who viewed the loss of personal freedom as an inconsequential effect of an otherwise productive and benevolent social institution.[8]

Amanda spent the next seven years in Georgia, where she grew fully into her new setting and all that married life entailed. By all accounts she was essentially contented and declared so to her family: "You all thought that I should not like the country . . . [but] I should think that a country life particularly at the south, would be much more desirable. . . . I say give me the country where I can enjoy the free and open air and seek my own amusement, independent of any." She had generally good relationships with her husband's extended family and was particularly close to her sister-in-law Elizabeth Trulock, who joined the household in 1841. Amanda was continually learning about her adopted region and frequently compared it to New England. Her letters also reveal an increasing understanding of production costs and the tenuous profit margins on a cotton plantation in the wake of the Panic of 1837. The two greatest changes during this time were motherhood and James's moderate quest for better cotton lands in southwestern Georgia. In prolific succession Amanda gave birth to Victoria (1839), Bronson Van Buren (1840), Felecia (1841), Burton (1842), and Eugenia (1844). Tragically, Felecia died within a few months, yet Amanda accepted it with a resigned fortitude frequently displayed in her correspondence. And when two separate moves within a few miles of their original home proved unsatisfactory, James gave full expression to his wanderlust. The Trulocks moved more than five hundred miles away to the southwestern cotton frontier in Arkansas.[9]

Both the journey and the transition to Arkansas were eventful and difficult. In early 1845 the Trulocks and their slaves traveled by ship from Florida to Pine Bluff. Nearly everyone suffered bouts of violent sea sickness. Many were taken with fever and chills, while all endured excessive rain aboard a poorly heated ship. Baby Eugenia was overpowered by these issues. She lingered for seven days and died onboard as they traveled up the Mississippi River. Forced to improvise, James and Amanda preserved her remains in whiskey and buried her once they docked. Yet even in her grief Amanda was heartened by some generous passengers who offered their sympathy and shared their medicine with her family. Coincidentally they were also to be some of her new Arkansas neighbors, and she praised them as "the kindest people I ever met with in my life." Fortified by this prospect the Trulocks began their new life, but all, black and white, struggled with illness in their new setting for an extended period. And while the neighbors were an asset, Amanda still found the neighborhood to be a remote frontier society. In particular Arkansas's roads were too rough for travel except by horseback, and there was no suitable school that Amanda could discern. But James had procured a rental house, and the slaves were clearing new fields for cotton. Within a year they were in their own home, which they eventually called Prairie Place, situated about eight miles from Pine Bluff.[10]

Thus the Trulocks were part of a great influx of cotton planters into the Delta, but Amanda was slow in building affection for her new state. Many of her neighbors believed that Arkansas gave settlers more than their fair share of sickness, especially during the first two years, but afterward, they declared, it was the same as elsewhere. "They would not give Arkansas for any other state they have lived in," Amanda observed, "but I do not think that I can say that." Amanda also discerned that her husband was not as "well pleased" with their new home as he hoped, but he would not say so. One reason he did not speak on the topic was because Amanda and her sister-in-law Elizabeth regularly seized the opportunity: "[We] tell him that we cannot see what his object was in selling out and sacrificing so much to come to this sickly place that Elizabeth and myself keep him strait [sic]." Obviously there was palpable tension among the three white adults in the household, yet some of this appears to be no more than a necessary ventilation of emotions so that life could proceed. Improvements and expansion helped the process along. They hired a tutor, Anne Kirkwood from Massachusetts, and she mitigated their concerns about schooling, but James and Amanda both thought a northern education was in their children's future. Area planters also sent their daughters to study under Kirkwood, which meant that several young girls often resided at the Trulocks, essentially forming a tiny boarding school. Anne also served as a replacement for Elizabeth's role in the household when Elizabeth married William Cantrell and moved a few miles away in 1848. Amanda began to enjoy social calls to other plantations and received ample company in return—even boasting that she had "twenty five to dine at my table several times." And in the midst of it all, Arkansas became the place of birth of two more sons, Marshall (1848) and James Hines (1849). The Trulocks' enslaved laborers also increased both naturally and through purchase. This opened the possibility of greater financial gain as Amanda and James looked toward their future together. But when it finally arrived, the future proved dramatically different.[11]

Amanda's life was transformed when her husband became ill and died just before Christmas in 1849. She struggled to find words to explain the heartrending news to her family, "for my feelings can be better imagined than described." Nevertheless, she painted a vivid portrait of James's deathbed and the trauma of her young children, who could not fully comprehend the effects of the death of their father. Widowhood would have been disruptive in any circumstance, but it easily could have instigated the end of her life in Arkansas. And few would have blamed her if it had. The Beardsleys were all in Connecticut and the Trulocks in Georgia, Amanda's children were years away from adulthood, and some fifty slaves wondered what the mistress would do. Amanda's father and brother immediately encouraged her to get her finances in order and move back to Connecticut with the children. However, for the near term at least, Amanda was resolute. She invoked James's wish that the plantation be kept up, and on the surface that seemed a plausible justification, albeit somewhat reactionary in her state of grief. However, Amanda also noted that James had purchased "a great deal of land within the last year which has been a source of anxiety to me" because it had increased their debt. Citing the counsel of her closest acquaintances, Amanda announced that she hoped to get out of debt in two years. This course of action seemed to be firmly in her mind even as she informed her family of her widowhood. When her father pressured her to leave Arkansas, she composed her most pointed rebuttal. "You know nothing about a plantation, and slaves," she declared. "And even if you were to come here and stay for years, it would be impossible for you to have the same feelings I have. . . . it may seem strange to you, but this is my home and it is in my interest to remain here for the present at least." Thus she moved decisively and filed for guardianship over her children, procured supplies to see them all through the next year, and turned her attention to the management of the plantation.[12]

Amanda accepted the burden of responsibility alone, but she was also well served by three men, two white and one black, during the important transitional year of 1850–1851. First, William Cantrell, Elizabeth Trulock's husband, acted as a kind of proxy for his deceased brother-in-law. This was facilitated to an even greater degree by Elizabeth's untimely death just a few months before James's. As a widower himself Cantrell nobly offered his assistance to Amanda, whom he apparently still considered his kin. Amanda was exceptionally grateful and stated, "I shall expect to have him [to] advise with and have the farm carried on as usual." Cantrell was counted as a member of the household and appears to have been the primary manager of the plantation that year, according to the Census. Next, her brother, Bronson, arrived in the fall and stayed through the winter. It seems likely that he arrived with the intent of persuading his sister to sell everything and leave Arkansas. While working on that goal he provided trustworthy counsel and assistance with her debt management. Although he failed to convince her to move, he at least left with a better understanding of Amanda's affairs, which meant Bronson could offer competent advice in the future. But more surprisingly Bronson seems to be the one who changed his mind. Before he returned to Connecticut he insisted that his sister remain a mistress of slaves. Six years later Amanda reminded him of his powerful words at the time: "You yourself advised me . . . after seeing my peculiar situation, always to keep [these] people with me . . . [that] it would be wrong for me to part with them, and that you would never give your consent to it." Last, and most important in the long term, an enslaved man named Reuben did the most to facilitate Amanda's "peculiar situation." Amanda endowed Reuben with remarkable authority and, although a slave, Reuben acted in a capacity that was comparable to a white overseer or even something akin to a comanager of the plantation.[13]

Amanda's handling of Prairie Place through Reuben is so unusual that it compels a reexamination of her overall relationship with slavery. It is plausible to conclude that she followed the precedent established by her husband, who was arguably a lenient master based on the evidence. For instance, James was quite comfortable leaving his plantation for months at a time; he allowed slaves to sell their own surplus produce for fifty or sixty dollars in annual income; and he himself had already authorized Reuben to do important managerial tasks, like select and buy mules. Additionally, there is evidence that James must have worked side by side with his slaves on some occasions, such as when they were clearing new land. For her part Amanda had always entrusted the slaves to serve her needs with increasing levels of autonomy in ways that enhanced her own personal freedom. Motherhood stimulated remarkable trust in this regard. Amanda apparently had difficulty breastfeeding, and she sometimes relied on enslaved women for that and otherwise resorted to bottle feeding. This initiated a situation where all of her young children developed such an attachment to their enslaved caregivers that the children often preferred them to Amanda. In fact the first time she left any of them alone, it was for two full nights with only the slaves to watch over her two-year-old and five-month-old. Amanda was also entirely unfazed by the open display of slaves' literacy. Reuben and Orren sent occasional letters to her and other family members when they visited Connecticut. Orren even received some religious tracts in return from Amanda's sister, Marcia, which he read and saved with great appreciation. And, while this conclusion is subjective, there is no clear evidence that corporal punishment was regularly dispensed by the Trulocks. Of course it would be very unlikely for Amanda to write her family that she either struck a slave or ordered someone to do so. But the overall texts and tone of her letters leave no strong suggestion of the employment of physical coercion. The only time she wrote of any personal discipline was earlier in Georgia when she "was displeased with one of my house girls and sent her in the fields." On the other hand, Bronson's observations of Arkansas slavery revealed his revulsion for the violence and abuse that was endemic to enslavement. He chastised whites who "beat their servants in a very savage manner with ropes, whips, [and] sticks of wood." And he deplored "the almost universal licentiousness of the [white] men with the black women [which] is looked upon by most of the white women as a matter of course." But Bronson apparently excluded his sister's household from this condemnation as evidenced by his conclusion that her situation with plantation slavery was "peculiar." In the final analysis Amanda's distinctive relationship with Reuben bears out her unusual personal history with the broader institution of slavery. Thus she generally grew in her advocacy of slavery on terms that may not have been widely practiced by most of her slaveowning peers.[14]

All things considered, widowhood eventually proved to be a time of greater financial stability for Amanda—made possible in no small part by her decision to allow Reuben greater managerial authority. It's plausible to conclude that the transition to Reuben's oversight was without incident as evidenced by the example where he selected and purchased mules. In that instance Amanda facilitated Reuben's purchase by setting up the details of the payment herself even though James was still alive at the time. This suggests that such cooperation between Amanda and Reuben had already become routine. Additionally, Amanda had previously described Reuben's indispensability before her husband's death. "It sometimes appears to me," she observed, "that we could not be able to carry on a farm without him and in fine I think that he does better than any white man that Mr. T. could hire which would cost him not less than 400 [dollars] board and all considered." Amanda's conclusion that Reuben was better than a white man must partly be understood as a reflection of the generally low reputation of white overseers across the Old South. However, this also reveals that she understood Reuben's service provided measurable financial savings. His record of dependability only reinforced her decision to rely on him more after she became a widow. For Reuben's part, he later reported to a

Freedmen's Bureau officer that at that tragic moment in her life, Amanda fully comprehended her vulnerable financial state and pointedly asked for Reuben's help. She "told him [Reuben] that she had no one to rely upon but him, and placed her all in his hands." And Reuben, in turn, was moved "by this touching confidence." Thus Amanda apparently made a conscious decision. She allowed Reuben's oversight to expand to an unprecedented level.[15]

Amanda's plantation was largely self-sufficient in food and grew more profitable as evidenced by her frequent descriptions of Reuben's activities. And Amanda almost exclusively referred to them as if they were essentially in Reuben's domain while she remained focused on the financial, domestic, and social activities that had always most concerned her. But Reuben frequently conveyed a fretful disposition to his mistress in which every contingency was a potential threat to their prosperity. This anxiety informed Amanda's observations, but it cannot diminish Reuben's demonstrable success over the next decade. For instance, in some years there was not quite enough pork for the plantation's annual sustenance, but most of the time there was. In 1853, after Reuben supervised the butchering of seventy hogs (including forty-eight in a day), Amanda observed that he was in high spirits over the prospect that "we shall not have meat to buy [this year]." Likewise, Prairie Place raised such a prodigious crop of corn, increasing from 2,500 bushels in 1850 to 6,000 bushels in 1860, that there was often a marketable surplus. More important, the cotton crop was robust as Reuben increased it from 140 bales in 1850 to an incredible 450 bales before the Civil War. A primary reason for this was the accompanying increase in improved acreage (cleared and fenced land) overseen by Reuben. Prairie Place went from 300 to 550 improved acres during this period. Reuben was persistent in expanding the plantation's tillable acreage, as Amanda noted: "no matter what he has to do he will clear some land every year." To maximize efficiency more outbuildings were constructed. While Reuben consulted Amanda on their placement, there is a sense in her descriptions that she did not have any preference, other than that they be completed, so Reuben decided independently in many cases. For instance, a bigger warehouse was needed to store the baled cotton until it could be shipped. According to Amanda, Reuben selected a location and then changed his mind and built it "not far from the gin house as he did not like to risque [sic] the cotton so far from home." A new gin house turned into a concern when they agreed to upgrade to steam power. Amanda perceived that the complexity of the new technology vexed Reuben: "this gin house troubles him very much because he does not understand it to his satisfaction [and he] is afraid that we shall be affected some way." Eventually, Reuben was satisfied, and Amanda no longer wrote of it after skilled workmen installed it and cotton production increased.[16]

Amanda surely had disagreements with Reuben, but the only ones she mentioned were related to his seemingly unbridled ambition to expand agricultural operations. In this regard there is further evidence of Reuben's unconventional position in Amanda's household as she described his success at an annual competition against local white planters to see who could produce the most per hand. "The most trying time with him is the Spring of the year," she explained, "particularly if he is not ahead of his neighbors." A surprising comment reveals the full scope of his autonomy; Amanda once lamented that he was actually planting too much cotton. "I thought the hands would have to work to [sic] hard," she reasoned, "but when he has his mind made up on any one thing, it is almost impossible to change it." If Amanda had really wanted less cotton planted, it seems that it would have been so. Her concession is indicative of her easy acceptance of Reuben's greater agricultural knowledge and that time generally validated most of his decisions.[17]

Ironically, Amanda's greatest conflict with Reuben was in response to his unusual proposition that she should buy additional slaves. The issue arose when Reuben concluded that the neighbors were purchasing more slaves and he felt as if Prairie Place was losing ground by comparison. He approached Amanda with a specific request to be allowed to "have all he made over sixteen thousand dollars next year—that he might invest it in *blacks* . . . as Mistress was so unwilling to buy any." Amanda could not casually dismiss Reuben's idea because he apparently knew exactly how much money she needed each year, so he requested accordingly. Furthermore, he pressed her constantly on the topic for several months. She took his proposal seriously, but it presented a genuine conundrum in her eyes. "If I continually try to keep him back and oppose all of his plans for advancing the interest of the place," she explained, "I shall be the means of killing his ambition and deadening his energies—in which case what will become of the place[?]" Amanda's family—her father, Bronson, and Marcia—were all consulted on the idea since Reuben's proposal ultimately exposed one of Amanda's previously unstated convictions. She did not want to buy more enslaved people. In what must have been the final word in one of their periodic exchanges on the issue, Amanda attempted to extinguish the entire idea: "I told him [Reuben] a few days since that I did not expect to buy any more [slaves] and that I did not want them even if they were given to me." This was a remarkably candid confession. In every other respect regarding agricultural production, Amanda always followed Reuben's counsel. This, however, was apparently a line that Amanda did not wish to cross, and it would never have come to light but for Reuben's persistence.[18]

Upon closer examination this incident tells us something about how Amanda's slaves perceived slavery and how Amanda's family perceived their status as slaveowners through her. While Reuben's true reasons for his proposal cannot be entirely discerned, it is plausible that he was simply motivated by self-preservation. It eventually came to light that local planters often goaded Reuben that Amanda was only interested in the cash value of the plantation and that she would certainly sell out and return to the North. On this occasion Reuben was disturbed by a credible neighborhood rumor that Amanda might receive an offer of $100,000 for the whole place, including the slaves. On the verge of tears he pleaded with her to seek the advice of Bronson before she left for the summer since Reuben feared the family in Connecticut would persuade her to accept. Seen in this light Reuben's proposal makes more sense. It was his preemptive counteroffer to make Amanda just as rich, the only way he knew how, and without the sale of anyone close to him. With this hypothesis in mind, all of Reuben's success at plantation management can be reimagined in a different light. What Amanda saw as Reuben's ambition for its own sake, or simply to outdo the other plantations in the neighborhood, may have actually been his long-term strategy to continue the status quo under a lenient mistress. At the same time this episode demonstrates that all the Beardsleys had been pulled deeper into slavery by Amanda's widowhood. The Beardsleys were resigned to the fact that through Amanda they were a family of slaveowners, but none could apparently tolerate the thought of being slave traders too. Amanda referenced a letter from her father that seemed to finally put the issue to rest. Beardsley had apparently sent his daughter extensive calculations that supported his ideas about the plantation far into the future. "I read it to Reuben," she wrote, "[and] he was pleased with it." Although she appreciated her father's input, Amanda was uncertain if she could "apply it to a practical use as I am not in the habit of looking forward a hundred years." This sounds cryptically like he may have proposed some kind of gradual emancipation for the next generation. Whatever her father meant, Amanda did not purchase any more slaves while she observed that Reuben's disposition improved that spring.[19]

An incident involving an enslaved woman named Caroline reveals Amanda's experience as a slaveowner to have been more typical than does the evidence from her relationship with Reuben. The sudden pregnancy of Caroline, an important house worker who was regularly mentioned in Amanda's letters, inspired dialogue over the topic of paternity. Responding to her sister's inquiry Amanda answered, "you wished to know who was Caroline's favored one, it was one of the workmen, I do not know as anything will ever come to light." Presumably this referred to one of the men who briefly had stayed on the plantation during the construction of the new cotton-gin house. This incident raises some interesting ideas about her relationship with her slaves because Amanda had ascertained that the child's father was white before Caroline gave birth. Such knowledge would primarily have come from Caroline. It seems that it did, Amanda believed her—and indeed it turned out to be so. Amanda later observed that Caroline's daughter was "certainly quite a pretty baby and as white as any child for anything I can see at present—quite to[o] bad! Don't you think so?" In many respects Amanda's response to Caroline's child reinforced her brother's observation that white women tacitly accepted biracial children as an immutable fact of plantation life. However, as a widow without any sons living at home at that particular time, Amanda was relieved of the anxiety of wondering if the men in her family were sexually exploiting any enslaved women.[20]

Widowhood and the sustainability of Prairie Place allowed Amanda to reconnect with her New England roots to a degree that never existed when she was married. Up to now her physical connection with Connecticut had been intermittent, but she and James had still managed three visits to Bridgeport over the course of their marriage. However, the Trulocks had also expressed a desire for their children to be educated in the North, and eighteen months after James's death the time seemed right to Amanda. The older children had initially continued their studies under the tutelage of Anne Kirkwood, but when she took other employment Amanda carried Victoria (age twelve), (Bronson) Van Buren (age eleven), and Burton (age eight) to Bridgeport in the summer of 1851. Leaving three of her five living children under the care of her family virtually guaranteed that she would return to Connecticut every summer. In an ironic twist, the decade generally proved to be a period of familial stability even though Amanda was separated from those children most of that time.[21]

Amanda's annual migrations to Connecticut were highly uncommon in the nineteenth century. Such regular travel to New England would have distinguished her among most company in the antebellum South, but among Arkansans it was truly extraordinary. Even though members of the planter elite traveled regularly, her 2,800-mile round trip every summer and autumn was distinctive. The vast majority of the mileage was traveled by boat with the Arkansas River being the most capricious section due to low water levels. Consequently, the travel time varied widely, and the trip could take twenty to thirty days one way. However, railroad connections improved dramatically, and by the end of the decade she might travel by rail to Chicago and then Cairo, Illinois, where she resumed via water. And in a striking display of her independent spirit, there is no clear evidence that she regularly traveled with any adult males. Instead, she developed a pattern where a different female family member would return with her to Arkansas for the winter and then travel back with her to Connecticut the following summer. Amanda typically left Arkansas in the later part of June and returned in October. She was able to leave because Reuben and all the other slaves carried on so efficiently, apparently without any white adults regularly present.[22]

By 1851 Amanda regularly left Prairie Place to Reuben and the other enslaved people for months at a time. Amanda apparently considered this routine and left no hint of any special justification for this action. Besides, Reuben already managed the farming activities, so if all the white adults temporarily left, there were no pressing domestic activities to oversee until they came home. Whenever Amanda returned, the manner of Reuben's reception indicates that he had been given authority to watch over the place during her absence. Returning from her first annual journey to Connecticut after James's death, she described her pleasure at what she found. "Reuben had everything done that lay in his power," she exclaimed, "had the house all cleaned and scoured, and the carpet down and curtains all put up, and everything done that I requested." Indeed, Reuben typically did extra things, like build a new smokehouse or kitchen, while Amanda was away and often had pound cake and pumpkin pies ready in abundance upon her arrival. Whenever she returned via steamboat, the vessel cruised past the border of her property and stopped at the plantation's dock, which was still a considerable distance from the house. On one occasion the boat inauspiciously arrived at midnight, and she assumed the captain would have to ring the bell only to discover "before the boat had landed Reuben, Ephraim, and Orren [were already] there with two horses for us." Indeed, when the boats could not run up the Arkansas River she would send word from the Mississippi River town of Napoleon, Arkansas, for Reuben to come and fetch her. Overall, Reuben seemed to have such command of the place while she was in Connecticut that even her two youngest boys were apparently entrusted to his care. Hines, at two years old, was so young he no longer recognized her when she returned that first autumn. But Hines accompanied Amanda in 1856 and spent the rest of his childhood in Connecticut starting in 1857. Thus, by 1856, Prairie Place became devoid of white inhabitants entirely during Amanda's annual treks to the North.[23]

Because Amanda's travel between the two main sections of the country coincided with the burgeoning sectional tensions of the 1850s, it invites speculation as to whether she ever displayed any strong support for either place. For the most part she did not, since her situation compelled the exercise of personal diplomacy in the matter. Amanda chose to live part of each year in the two sections of the country that were growing increasingly suspicious of one another. With all of her family in one section and all of her finances in the other, she seemed to favor the stability of an equilibrium between the two. This was the only way to live peacefully among her neighbors in both places. However, the mere fact of her regularity in appearing in and disappearing from one section and then the other must have rendered her a conspicuous source of information to curious people in both regions. It can be instructive to compare her with the example of the contemporary figure Frederick Law Olmsted, a northerner who famously traveled south during the same decade. Olmsted wrote so that northern readers could understand a region few would ever visit, and, perhaps predictably, he was critical of the Old South.[24] Amanda had no need of such secondhand knowledge because she already possessed an intimate understanding of both areas. And she had good reason to refrain from open criticism of either region as long as she lived in both.

Still, there were some cultural differences that continued to bind Amanda to New England and others that bound her to the South. The clear preference for a New England education was one, even though James had also shared it, and it was especially fortuitous that Kirkwood had arrived from Massachusetts to be the family tutor. Additionally, Amanda was frequently sentimental (a rarity for her) about missing Thanksgiving in Connecticut. This was exclusively a New England holiday at the time, and the fact that it was largely unobserved in the South served to deepen her uncharacteristic melancholy over the occasion. We can never know other things, like whether Amanda had a strong accent that identified her as a native New Englander. It's possible that she borrowed speech from both regions just enough to sound like an outsider in each. Along that same line Reuben once joked that her continual trips might eventually "make a yankee" of her before she was done. On the other hand, Amanda's residence on a southern plantation made her seem culturally bound to the South by default. And in one important respect she was culturally very close to southern common folk: Amanda lived in a log cabin. Prairie Place was apparently a nice log home with a hall and a few modest rooms. Amanda made improvements to it, like adding an extra chimney and accessorizing with curtains and carpets, but it was not a Greek Revival mansion. While it was not uncommon for antebellum planters to live in a cabin on the frontier, many chose to build something more substantial within their first decade. Amanda certainly could have afforded a beautiful mansion, but financing her children's education and traveling to visit them were more important. This also must have suited her temperament since she once declared that she did not envy the "splendid mansions" of some of her neighbors. Confirming this view, she even began to refer to the house as "Prairie Cottage," which better reflected its unpretentious style. At six years old even young Hines understood the difference and amused Amanda when he complained that they lived in a "hut."[25]

By the end of the antebellum era, Amanda had achieved much for herself and her family in Arkansas and Connecticut. She had become a shrewd cotton planter through the vital service of Reuben and established an honorable but savvy reputation as a businesswoman. In recognition of this her neighbors periodically solicited her financial help. She loaned some of them money at 10 percent interest, and in some cases held mortgages as security. Land that she did not wish to cultivate was often rented to various tenants. Amanda was also opportunistic. Once she bought land and paid for it with baled cotton. She reckoned that the difference in the price of local cotton versus the price in New Orleans, after accounting for the expense of shipping, was a better tradeoff during that particular phase of the market cycle. She also received offers to buy her entire estate in recognition of her success but did not seriously entertain them. In one curious case Amanda was briefly pursued (via letter) by a shameless gold digger. The fact that he learned of her through passenger gossip on a steamboat to Little Rock only reinforces the breadth of Amanda's reputation as a woman of means. She summarily dismissed the flirtatious charlatan as deranged but entertaining. Ultimately, and most important, the prosperity of Prairie Place extended all the way to Bridgeport. Amanda had long been sending money for her father to invest on her behalf, especially after she became a widow. Evidence from the 1860 Census suggests that Amanda's children and the extended family were basing their livelihoods, some entirely and others partially, on the profits of the cotton plantation in Arkansas.[26]

Although the 1850s were a time of rising national anxiety over slavery, Amanda was arguably an apolitical person who was seldom impassioned by the polarizing sectional politics of her era. Her husband had been a staunch Democrat who wore his politics on his sleeve. Likewise, her sister, Marcia, seemed to be developing an affinity for the Republicans as early as the 1856 election. When the Democrats won the contest, Amanda playfully teased, "Hurra[h]! for Buchannan [sic]." But that was a rare outburst. Although she regularly read newspapers filled with political opinion, she usually limited her discussion of them to personal items. Even when Harriet Beecher Stowe's *Uncle Tom's Cabin* (1852) instigated a firestorm of rhetoric, her commentary was only that the book had caused "a great stir." But the most political and revelatory confession of Amanda's truest feelings about slavery as an institution is revealed in her enthusiasm for another novel: *The Cabin and Parlor*. Her cousin Nellie, visiting from Connecticut, read the entire book aloud while Amanda recovered from an illness one winter. Amanda was struck by what she considered the book's insightful portrayal of what slavery was like in reality. She was eager to recommend it to her family. "I wish you would get it and read it aloud," she exclaimed. "Also tell

Mr. L. Sterling I wish he would read it as I think that will give him a more correct idea of slavery or rather a more correct idea of it than I could give him." The recommendation that an acquaintance read it reveals that slavery was discussed and debated during Amanda's visits to Connecticut. In fact, it sounds rather like a particular argument had occurred, and Amanda was offering a rejoinder in the form of this novel.[27] Her strong endorsement of this text offers the best opportunity to comprehend what Amanda thought, for in understanding it we may better understand her.

The Cabin and Parlor was one of many proslavery novels written as a reactionary protest against *Uncle Tom's Cabin*. The briefest synopsis of the book reveals common themes and stock characters from the genre of anti-*Tom* literature but also striking similarities to Amanda's own life. The story begins with Uncle Peter, a kindly old slave who manages the family plantation to the great satisfaction of all. But upon the planter's death his adult son and daughter, Horace and Isabel, must sell everything and seek work to support their mother. Isabel becomes a teacher, and Horace migrates north, where he suffers and dies as a "white slave" of industrial capitalism. During his pitiful demise, Horace is befriended by a southern slaveowner named Walworth, who regularly travels to the North and carries his dying words back to Isabel. A romance ensues, and Walworth recoups the plantation, including the slaves, after he marries Isabel. All the while, Uncle Peter has been especially sympathetic toward Isabel and only wishes to repay her for her family's kindness. At the end he is content to once again be her slave. The novel's penultimate paragraph has Uncle Peter refusing emancipation: "No, God bless yer, I'd rather be a slave here, under a good masser, dan a free colored man North. By'm bye, p'raps, my chil'en may take yer offer, ef de Lord, by dat time, opens de way for de African." The conclusion admonishes elite whites to be benevolent in their authority: "Whether you live in the North or the South, *be the good master*; ... the laboring classes, be they called operatives or slaves, have no friend but God, if you, their employers or owners, are not that friend."[28]

Amanda's approval of this novel could tell us many things, but it suggests at least two important ideas. First, it is easy to conclude that Amanda saw in Uncle Peter her own slave Reuben. In reality Reuben was more complicated than Amanda may have ever realized, but on the surface he seemed much like Uncle Peter. This must have validated her idealized view of Reuben as a slave who simply wanted to serve for the sake of service itself. Second, the book was a pointed indictment against the "white enslavement" of the laboring poor in the North at the hands of heartless capitalists. This could have allowed Amanda to draw a comparison in which black enslavement was infinitely better. Ironically, what supposedly made slavery better was its permanence. Slaves should not be emancipated; if they were, the implication was that they would surely suffer an even worse fate than that currently endured by the "white slaves" of the North. This justification fit with Amanda's earliest experiences in Georgia and was probably reinforced by her brother when he admonished her to keep her human property. After all these years Amanda was at ease with slavery, and in her own way she was ready to defend it on terms that reflected her experience.

Amanda's world was transformed by the Civil War, which set events into motion that ultimately convinced her to return to Connecticut permanently. Initially, Amanda probably saw the war as nothing more than a great inconvenience to be briefly endured. She made her annual trip to Bridgeport during the summer of 1860, but it is not clear who, if anyone, returned with her in the autumn. She did not attempt to visit Connecticut in 1861, but her oldest son, Bronson Van Buren Nichols (now called Nichols), apparently managed to reunite with her that year. At twenty-one years old Nichols was now the first white adult male to reside at Prairie Place in a decade. Postal service was disrupted in 1861, and mother and son lost all communication with Connecticut for the next two years. But the war did not physically come to their doorstep until the Union army occupied Pine Bluff in September 1863. Up to that time, life at Prairie Place must have been close to normal except for the growing instability of the cotton market. Amanda reported that they still had sufficient food, with the exception of coffee, and apparently all the slaves continued the plantation's routine despite the uncertain future. A return to Connecticut was not viable, so Amanda and her son endured most of the war together.[29]

In many respects, Nichols and his younger brother Burton serve as the best evidence of Amanda's war experience and overall attitude toward the conflict. Through them we may perceive her resignation to endure the war as a personal burden rather than a societal one. Likewise, her sons reflect her ambiguous attitude toward the Confederate and Union causes alike. First and foremost Nichols was an apparently healthy young man who, despite his age and situation, never served in the Confederate military—and never wanted to serve either side, for that matter. This suited Amanda, who purchased him a draftee replacement for more than $3,000 in Confederate script and lavished praise on her son for his devotion to her comfort and security. In her first letter to Connecticut after the Union occupation of Pine Bluff, she declared that no child could have done more for their mother than Nichols had for her during the previous two years. "He has stayed by me night and day and done everything that he could . . . while other young men have left their mothers to get along the best they could," she explained. "I hope he will be remembered for it." This is a shockingly honest confession. Amanda was proud of her son for staying beside her, rather than joining the Confederate army like scores of other young men in the neighborhood. Amanda would never have vocalized this pride in Arkansas. However, considering the intended audience for her letter, it reveals that the Beardsleys would have agreed. Nichols's duty was to Amanda first. And the Confederate cause, in particular, was not worthy of the family's voluntary support. Second, it appears that Amanda and Nichols took oaths of loyalty to the Union fairly soon after the occupation. This is evidenced by their open participation in the cotton market in the spring of 1864. Producing cotton inside federal lines entailed numerous restrictions, not the least of which was the disavowal of rebellion. However, this probably should not be viewed as ardent Unionism on their part. More likely it conveys detachment from the politics of both causes and the desire to return to the antebellum status quo.[30]

Equally important, Burton was no more a willing combatant than his older brother. Amanda addressed a topic of family debate as to whether Burton should join his mother and brother in Arkansas in 1863. She worried that it was "to[o] great a risk . . . [as] they will soon be conscripting all in this vicinity." However, Amanda was obviously worried that either side might come for Burton when she speculated that she could no longer acquire the amount necessary to purchase a Union army substitute. "I do not suppose we have got three hundred dollars in greenbacks," she concluded. In the spring of 1864 the brothers traded places: Nichols went back to Connecticut, and Burton returned to Arkansas to help his mother. It was a short-lived reunion as Burton was conscripted by the Confederates within a few weeks. Amanda took comfort that both sons had not been caught in the draft, although it was disconcerting to wait out the year until Burton came home. For the rest of the war, she cautioned Nichols to stay in Connecticut since she believed he would "have to go immediately into one or the other armys [sic]" if he returned.[31]

The neighborhood around Prairie Place spiraled down into a state of societal chaos in late 1863 as Amanda stoically endured the final nineteen months of the war. Although the U.S. Army secured Pine Bluff, the outlying regions devolved into a no-man's land controlled by neither side but picked over by both as well as by bands of Confederate deserters. Amanda described the inexorable loss of nearly everything that could be carried off unless she hid it. She wryly noted in the summer of 1864 that she mostly spent her time in moving and hiding her "things from place to place and then in looking for them when I want them." After Burton was conscripted, Amanda was entirely alone except for one formerly enslaved woman, America, and her young children. Amanda exhibited genuine gratitude for America's presence and confessed, "the truth is I could not remain here on this place [without her]." When another former slave, Harry, returned in the autumn, Amanda felt some relief. She still had several bushels of corn well hidden, and they even sowed some winter wheat for the coming spring. Despite the loss of so much, Amanda remained modestly hopeful that they could now all "get along quite comfortably through the winter." But she doubted they could remain there another year without some change.[32]

There is no record as to the precise moment when Amanda knew that emancipation was inevitable, but there is some information about the moment of its final fulfillment at Prairie Place. The evidence suggests that all the Trulock slaves had left her and Nichols in the autumn of 1863. It is likely that some of them soon returned and apparently stayed on as contracted laborers. On December 7, 1863, she wrote that "the servants we have hired here are sick a good deal." This reference is the first clear indication that emancipation had actually occurred. Six enslaved men on the place used their new freedom to join the Union army. All the others seemed to be working on local abandoned plantations under federal oversight. Amanda received occasional news about them and noted, "Reuben and many others are still on the Roan [sic] place." By his own account, Reuben stayed with Amanda till the end. In an exchange that was summarized in a Freedmen's Bureau report, Reuben explained to the agent that all the other slaves left Prairie Place before he and his family did. Only after Union officers assured Reuben that the Emancipation Proclamation was true, and only then, "he also came quietly in." At that moment Reuben was finally a free man and Amanda was no longer a slaveowner.[33]

Amanda had the rest of the war and, in some ways, the rest of her life to ruminate over the outcomes of emancipation. Still, she expressed early cynicism that freedom could not meet the expectations of those who viewed it as a panacea. For instance, two months before the end of the war she noted that her former slaves still had not received their pay for last year's work on the Roane Plantation. She further calculated that "eighteen of our servants have died since they left this place.... that is more than have died in twenty years before." With biting sarcasm she concluded, "so, you see they are freeing them very fast." This comment overlaid a deep reservoir of emotion that only emancipation could have tapped. Obviously, she viewed the liberty of black people as a chaotic and even lethal policy. But she confused the effects of emancipation with the effects of war on all refugees, which was dire for black and white alike. We may also return to her worldview, exemplified in *The Cabin and Parlor*, that enslavement had enabled black people to flourish under the controlled protection of the plantation. Releasing them into a free labor market was cruel and unjust. Reuben himself demonstrated the vicissitudes of freedom. He apparently had been given the position of "boss-workman" at the Roane Plantation. But with payment delayed for all of the workers, Amanda learned that he too was forced to survive through the most common of labor. "Reuben was [now] cutting boat-wood," she declared, "just like an[y] other nigger." Amanda had never before referred to him in this way. Her usage of this epithet was uncharacteristic, and it laid bare the intensity of her bitterness at his abandonment. Ironically, Reuben's successful plantation management must have further reinforced Amanda's inverted view of human nature, at least for people of color. Although Amanda could not see it, Reuben had never flourished *because* of enslavement but in spite of it.[34]

Amanda stayed in Arkansas for a year after the war, but she already seemed ready to leave the plantation to her children and return to New England. Burton returned from Confederate service in the summer of 1865, and in the autumn Victoria joined them from Bridgeport. Finally Amanda returned in the summer of 1866 to Connecticut, where the rest of her family must have greeted her warmly. She rested in the knowledge that two of her grown children watched over the plantation. The others would inevitably follow to claim the legacy created by their father, protected by their mother, and expanded by a slave. It's not clear if Amanda planned to remain in Connecticut permanently in 1866 or if this was intended to be the renewal of her antebellum travel pattern. However, her adventurous zest for long-distance travel had clearly evaporated. In 1865 she had declared, "I feel as though I have lost all confidence in my traveling capacity." Thus Amanda may have thought that if she could ever see Bridgeport again, she would never leave it. The remaining children in Connecticut spent much of 1867 preparing to return to Arkansas to join their siblings in the fall. Amanda must have had plenty of time to think through whether she would go with them. It seems she made a conscious choice not to go back to Arkansas, even to be with her children. Furthermore, there was now palpable sibling rivalry over the future control of Prairie Place specifically and financial squabbles generally. Amanda lamented, "I cannot allow myself to think very strongly on the subject without almost making me sick." This may have given her extra incentive to remain in New England where she could play the peacemaker for her children from afar. However she came to her decision, by 1870 so many changes had transpired that Amanda must have long since resolved to leave well enough alone. All four of her sons lived at Prairie Place along with Nichols's wife and their two-year-old son. Amanda's youngest son, James Hines, turned twenty-one that year, and as adults everyone had to come to a mutual understanding on the long-term division of the estate. Victoria had married a Union officer in Arkansas, given birth to a daughter, Clara, and then suddenly died at the age of thirty. Victoria's husband sent Clara to Connecticut, where Amanda and Marcia raised her together. The two sisters shared a house on Park Avenue in Bridgeport, where Amanda died in 1891. She apparently never returned to Arkansas again.[35]

Amanda Beardsley Trulock is a curious anomaly in the history of Arkansas's women. She embodies so many counterintuitive impulses that she defies easy categorization: she was a native of urban Bridgeport, but she was perfectly at ease on a rural Delta cotton plantation; she was a slaveowner who defended slavery, but she would not participate in the slave market; she was a Yankee who lived in the Confederacy, but she attempted to keep her sons from fighting for either side; and she was a mother who longed to be with her children, but she was absent for most of their childhoods. In the final analysis she is too distinctive to be very representative of Arkansas women of her era. This seems to be punctuated by her deeper and more abiding affinity for New England. Of course if James had lived to an old age, the story would have gone differently. Thus, if we return to the narrative arc of her life, the decisive crossroads seems to have been when she became a widow. Why did she not return to Connecticut then? The answer is threefold. She did not return because of James's wish to continue the plantation for the ultimate benefit of their children; because of the couple's joint desire to educate the children in the North, which could be financed by the plantation; and because of her own revulsion at the consequences of releasing any of her slaves, which was apparently shared by her family. However, one way or another, these three issues were all resolved by 1866. With that being the case, nothing compelled Amanda's presence in Arkansas. Furthermore, the trauma of the war and the arduous chore of rebuilding was unappealing compared to the comforting familiarity of Connecticut with its extensive network of kin and nostalgic memories. And Amanda knew that her children could always make the trip to Bridgeport just as she did. In the end, Amanda's life is a surprising example of the exception to the rule. Her greatest value is that she helps us see the Arkansas women of her era by showing us the ways in which she was different from most of them.

NOTES

1. This chapter is primarily based on approximately 150 letters written by Amanda Beardsley Trulock from 1837 to 1867 and a few others written by her husband, James, and daughter Victoria. I cite both the Trulock Family Papers, University of Arkansas Libraries, Special Collections, Fayetteville (hereafter UAFSC), and the Trulock Family Letters, University of Central Arkansas Archives, Conway (hereafter UCAA). For the information in this paragraph, see Amanda Trulock to brother,

February 4, 1857, UCAA; Amanda Trulock to son and daughter, July 20, 1865, Amanda Trulock to sister, May 9, 1866, both UAFSC.

Trulock has been the subject of two theses: Sarah Brooke Malloy, "The Health of Our Family: The Correspondence of Amanda Beardsley Trulock, 1837–1868," master's thesis, University of Arkansas, 2005; Rebecca Norman Prestwood, "Amanda Trulock: A Connecticut Yankee in Antebellum Arkansas," master's thesis, University of Central Arkansas, 1996.

2. Tryphena Fox and Dolly Lunt Burge are two well-known examples, from Massachusetts and Maine, respectively, of tutors who married southern slaveholders. Northern migrants to the Old South tended to have more antislavery feelings than native southerners, but this was highly subject to their unique circumstances, and many became more proslavery over time. Wilma King-Hunter, ed., *A Northern Woman in the Plantation South: Letters of Tryphena Blanche Holder Fox, 1856–1876* (Columbia: University of South Carolina Press, 1993); Christine Carter, ed., *The Diary of Dolly Lunt Burge, 1848–1879* (Athens: University of Georgia Press, 2006); Dennis Rousey, "Friends and Foes of Slavery: Foreigners and Northerners in the Old South," *Journal of Social History* 35 (Winter 2001): 373–96.

3. Nichols Beardsley is listed among the pew holders at the Congregational Church in 1835. By 1850 he had accumulated $7,000 in real estate wealth. U.S. Census, 1850, Fairfield County, Conn., 2; Samuel Orcutt, *A History of the Old Town of Stratford and the City of Bridgeport, Connecticut* (Fairfield County Historical Society, 1886), 1:633, 2:1130, 1142; Application of Trulock Burton Hatheway, in *Sons of the American Revolution Membership Applications, 1889–1970* (Louisville, Ky.: National Society of the Sons of the American Revolution), 244:216–18; Malloy, "Health of Our Family," 3.

4. Trulock family lore suggests that James had an additional acquaintance who was the captain of a ship that frequented Bridgeport, and he supposedly provided mutual introductions. Walter N. Trulock, "A Family Memoir," *Jefferson County Historical Quarterly* 8, no. 1 (1979): 30–33.

5. In 1850 the median age of first marriage for women in New England has been estimated, by some, to be as high as 24.9 years. J. David Hacker, Libra Hilde, and James Holland Jones, "The Effect of the Civil War on Southern Marriage Patterns," *Journal of Southern History* 76, no. 1 (2010): 42, 52; Amanda Trulock to Bronson Beardsley, January 30, 1838; Amanda Trulock to father, August 27, 1841, both UCAA.

6. Three years after she left New England, the free black population of Fairfield County, Connecticut, was no more than 2.5 percent of the total population. Amanda referred to the condition of free blacks in the North from time to time and that would plausibly be based on some previous firsthand observations. Bronson Beardsley must have expressed reservations about slavery because an undated letter he received from James Trulock has Trulock defending Christian slaveownership to his brother-in-law. Finally, many scholars have supported Garrison's observation that free states like Connecticut still contained deep currents of "virulent racism." Matthew Warshauer, *Connecticut in the American Civil War: Slavery, Sacrifice, and Survival* (Middletown, Conn.: Wesleyan University Press, 2012), 2–3; Amanda Trulock to Nichols Beardsley, March 21, 1838, and James Trulock to Bronson Beardsley, n.d., both UCAA; U.S. Census, 1840, Population Schedule, Fairfield County, Conn.

7. Amanda Trulock to Beardsley family, October 24, 1837, UCAA.

8. Amanda Trulock to Beardsley family, Bronson Beardsley, and Marcia Beardsley, October 24, 1837, March 21 and June 5, 1838, all UCAA; King-Hunter, *Northern Woman*, 13.

9. Amanda Trulock to Bronson Beardsley, January 30, 1838; Amanda Trulock to mother, January 24, 1842, both UCAA.

10. Amanda Trulock to mother, December 29, 1844, February 22, 1845, both UCAA.

11. Nineteenth-century settlers linked topography and climate directly to health, and migrants to Arkansas generally believed an acclimation period was imperative. See Conevery Bolton Valencius, *The Health of the Country: How American Settlers Understood Themselves and Their Land* (New York: Basic, 2002), 23; Donald P. McNeilly, *The Old South Frontier: Cotton Plantations and the Formation of Arkansas Society, 1819–1861* (Fayetteville: University of Arkansas Press, 2000), 61–67; Amanda Trulock to father, March 1845; Amanda Trulock to mother, September 3, 1845; Amanda Trulock to brother, June 14, 1847, all UCAA.

12. As a slaveholding widow, Amanda was now a member of a group that was statistically more vulnerable to economic instability. Kirsten Wood, *Masterful Women: Slaveholding Widows from the American Revolution through the Civil War* (Chapel Hill: University of North Carolina Press, 2004), 37; Amanda Trulock to father and mother, December 23, 1849; Amanda Trulock to father, March 1850, both UCAA.

13. William Cantrell was thirty-seven years old and identified as a member of the Trulock household that year and as a "farmer" by occupation. This was Bronson Beardsley's second trip to his sister's plantation; he had visited her in Georgia nine years earlier. Reuben was not described as either an "overseer" or "driver" in Amanda's correspondence, and the notion of a "black overseer" is problematic within the nomenclature of slave historiography. Nevertheless, there is sufficient evidence that a few slaves in the Old South sometimes had broad managerial powers similar to Reuben's. William L. Van Deburg, "The Slave Drivers of Arkansas: A New View from the Narratives," *Arkansas Historical Quarterly* 35, no. 3 (Autumn 1976): 231–45; William Wiethoff, "Enslaved Africans' Rivalry with White Overseers in Plantation Culture: An Unconventional Interpretation," *Journal of Black Studies* 36, no. 3 (2006): 429–55; U.S. Census, 1850, Jefferson County, Ark.; Amanda Trulock to mother, March 5, 1841, and Amanda Trulock to brother, February 4, 1857, both UCAA; Bronson Beardsley to father, mother, and sister, November 21, 1850, February 12, 1851, Beardsley and Trulock Family Letters, private collection of Burton Hatheway, Fairfield, Conn., cited in Malloy, "Health of Our Family," 93–94.

14. James Trulock used a white overseer for at least one year in Georgia (1839). Based on that, it would be plausible to conclude that Amanda had some personal knowledge of the physical coercion that was the norm in slavery. James sometimes wrote of being physically sore after arduous labor clearing some of his new land. This has to be considered uncommon behavior and is highly suggestive of James's unconventional management style. Six letters written by Reuben and Orren have survived. Amanda sometimes even received short dictations from Reuben, which she put into her letters. James Trulock to Polly Beardsley, August 2, 1846; Amanda Trulock to mother, March 18, 1839, June 30, 1848; Amanda Trulock to father, March 21, 1838, April 16, 1839, February 17, 1840; Amanda Trulock to sister, February 15, 1848; Amanda Trulock to brother, December 25, 1852, all UCAA; Bronson Beardsley to father, mother, and sister, February 12, 1851, cited in Malloy, "Health of Our Family," 93–94.

15. *Report of the General Superintendent of Freedmen, Department of the Tennessee and State of Arkansas for 1864* (Memphis, Tenn., 1865), 74; James Leslie, "The Reuben and Orren Letters," *Jefferson County Historical Quarterly* 18, no. 4 (1990): 12–30; Amanda Trulock to sister, March 16, 1846, UCAA.

16. William K. Hutchinson and Samuel Williamson, "The Self-Sufficiency of the Antebellum South: Estimates of the Food Supply," *Journal of Economic History* 31, no. 3 (1971): 591–612; Amanda Trulock to sister, January 14, 1853, January 5 and March 11, 1854, all UCAA; U.S. Agricultural Census, 1850, Jefferson County, Ark., 52; U.S. Agricultural Census, 1860, Jefferson County, Ark., 4.

17. Reuben's exact management method over the field slaves is largely unknown. One unverifiable incident passed down in Trulock family lore suggests that Reuben used force and hit slaves on the head with the end of a hoe. More likely is a primary account of his habit of commencing daily labor earlier than most other planters. If so, then Reuben may have incentivized faster work by offering an earlier quitting time when the day's tasks were accomplished. James W. Leslie, "The Reuben and Orrin [sic] Letters: 1852–1855," *Jefferson County Historical Quarterly* 18, no. 4 (1990): 10–21; Trulock, "Family Memoir," 30; Amanda Trulock to sister, December 15, 1853, Amanda Trulock to father, March 7, 1853, both UCAA.

18. Revealing the depth of her conviction on this issue, Amanda was out of useful house workers at this time (primarily due to sickness) and was doing more of her own domestic work than usual. She could have justified the purchase of a house worker, but she refrained. Amanda Trulock to sister, November 18, 1856, January 3, 1857, Amanda Trulock to brother, February 4, 1857, all UCAA.

19. Amanda had prior experience with this issue because James had sold and purchased some enslaved people while they lived in Georgia and purchased others from Virginia after they moved to Arkansas. She portrayed this as a financial necessity but expressed no obvious empathy for the slaves' predicament. However, it is still plausible that she may have comprehended some of the human trauma inflicted by the slave trade and did not wish to revisit it. Amanda Trulock to brother, May 20, 1845, Amanda Trulock to sister, April 6, 1857, both UCAA.

20. Amanda once wrote of a Mr. Clements and his men, who were to construct the new gin house, but there was an extensive delay before construction. It seems likely that she was referring to them again when she later stated, "I must tell you that our gentlemen boarders have finished and left, and that I have paid them in full by draft." A few lines later she spoke of Reuben's pleasure over the new gin house. Amanda Trulock to sister, May 1, 1854, December 17, 1855, November 18, 1856, all UCAA.

21. James and Amanda traveled to and from Bridgeport at least twice from Georgia (1838 and 1842) and once from Arkansas (1847). None of Amanda's letters written after March 1858 until the start of the Civil War have survived. But it is plausible to assume that she continued to visit her children each summer.

22. Amanda Trulock to sister, May 1, 1854, UCAA.

23. Upon her return in 1851 Amanda found that her older son had been deathly ill while she was away. Caroline and Reuben conveyed a tale of personal frustration in getting the neighbors Dr. and Mrs. Wright to come in time to attend to young Marshall. This suggests that the slaves were taking care of the boys and were responsible for seeking outside white assistance, even though it proved painfully slow in this instance. The incident also reveals Amanda's predisposition to believe her slaves, even against the actions of whites, when she surmised that there was not "any doubt about the children being badly treated." Amanda Trulock to one and all, October 1851; Amanda Trulock to all at home, September 29, 1857, both UCAA.

24. John C. Inscoe, ed., *Selections from the Cotton Kingdom by Frederick Law Olmsted* (New York: Bedford/St. Martin's, 2014).

25. Amanda Trulock to one and all, November 12, 1845, October 1851; Amanda Trulock to sister, December 17, 1855, all UCAA.

26. The Census does not explicitly state sources of income but suggests that the Beardsleys had some financial benefit from Amanda's plantation and her slave property. In 1850 and 1870 Nichols Beardsley had only $7,000 in real estate wealth, most likely his house and land in the town of Bridgeport. But in 1860 he had $40,000 in personal income, most likely assets given by Amanda. In 1870 Nichols no longer had any personal income, but Amanda, now home from Arkansas, had

$40,000. Likewise, in 1860, Amanda's sons living in Connecticut had $20,000 in real estate and $10,000 in personal property each, even though none of them were yet twenty-one. U.S. Census, 1850, Fairfield County, Conn., 2; U.S. Census, 1860, Fairfield County, Conn., 48; U.S. Census, 1870, Fairfield County, Conn., 116; Amanda Trulock to sister, December 1, 1854, November 12, 1857, Amanda Trulock to father, November 29, 1857, all UCAA.

27. Amanda Trulock to sister, February 2, 1853, November 18, 1856, both UCAA.

28. J. Thornton Randolph, *The Cabin and Parlor; or, Slaves and Masters* (Philadelphia: T. B. Peterson, 1852), 325.

29. Amanda Trulock to family, September 1863?; Victoria Trulock to mother, October 18, 1863, both UAFSC.

30. The Trulocks' successful participation in the cotton market is suggested by the fact that Amanda sent $15,000 for her father to invest on behalf of her children in June 1864. Such income must have been "greenbacks" made from the recent legal trade of cotton in the occupied regions. Furthermore, it is plausible that the slaves had picked a large amount of cotton before emancipation was fully realized, and Nichols was left to gin whatever he could, with minimal assistance, throughout the following winter. Carl Moneyhon, "From Slave Labor to Free Labor: The Federal Plantation Experiment in Arkansas," *Arkansas Historical Quarterly* 53, no. 2 (Summer 1994): 137–60; Amanda Trulock to family, September 1863?, Amanda Trulock to son, March 7, 1864, Amanda Trulock to father, June 9, 1864, all UAFSC.

31. *Confederate Veteran* 6, no. 9 (1898): 433; Amanda Trulock to all, August 1, 1864, September 20, 1864, both UAFSC.

32. Amanda Trulock to son and daughter, July 10, 1864; Amanda Trulock to all, August 1 and September 20, 1864; Amanda Trulock to son, October 27, 1864, all UAFSC.

33. Freedmen's Bureau records confirm that Nichols had previously contracted the labor of fourteen freedmen by March 1864. Six men with the surname Trulock (Elbert, George, James, Moses, Phillip, and Thomas) were enlisted in the Fifty-Fourth U.S. Colored Infantry—a unit formed in Arkansas. Soldiers and Sailors Database, National Park Service, http://www.nps.gov/civilwar/soldiers-and-sailors-database.htm (accessed August 29, 2017); General Index to Pension Files, 1861–1934, National Archives and Records Administration (hereafter NARA), roll T288_479, Elbert Trulock; George E. Lankford, ed., *Bearing Witness: Memories of Arkansas Slavery, Narratives from the 1930s WPA Collections* (Fayetteville: University of Arkansas Press, 2003), 178; Freedmen's Bureau Field Office Records, Arkansas, 1864–1872, M1901, roll 20, Letters Sent, 1864–1866, 1868, 10, NARA; *Report of the General Superintendent of Freedmen*, 74; Amanda Trulock to daughter, December 7, 1863; Amanda Trulock to son and daughter, November 13, 1864, both UAFSC.

34. Report of July 1, 1864, Office of Superintendent of Freedmen, State of Arkansas, Department of Arkansas, RG 393, NARA, cited in Moneyhon, "From Slave Labor to Free Labor," 147; Amanda Trulock to children, February 3, 1865, UAFSC.

35. *Bridgeport City Directory, 1891*, 512; Amanda Trulock to children, June 18, 1865; Amanda Trulock to Major G. W. Davis, October 3, 1866; Amanda Trulock to daughter, September 13, 1867, all UAFSC.

Women of the Ozarks in the Civil War

"I Fear We Will See Hard Times"

REBECCA A. HOWARD

❦ ❦ ❦

All Arkansas women were impacted by the Civil War, but northwest Arkansas women navigated its perils the earliest and the longest. Whether Confederate or Union, white or black, women in the four most northern and western counties of Arkansas faced a complex situation during the Civil War.[1] For four years, they moved their families in response to battle lines or the changing military affiliations of their men, faced violence, dared to maintain homes in the midst of a guerrilla war, and, if enslaved, endured or celebrated changes in their status and location as the war reshaped freedom and race.[2] The Civil War in the Ozarks was fought around and among women, warping the structure of the society to the point that women took on roles, made decisions, and often controlled households far beyond the usual mores of nineteenth-century society.

When scholars and others consider the American Civil War, women are usually relegated to the homefront. Viewed as far from the physical battle lines, they are seen occasionally engaging in changed and expanded roles in their household, perhaps coping with societal disorder, or even struggling with hunger and physical hardship when their men go off to fight. If women had a role on the battlefront, it was often an auxiliary one as nurses or camp followers. Occasionally, women claimed more exotic roles, perhaps as dashing spies or dressed as men so as to engage in battle. Scholarship since the 1990s, however, has revealed that these divided designations rarely held true for southern women during the Civil War.[3] Across the Upper South especially, women took active roles in fighting occupation or destabilizing the Confederacy from within, even stepping into the political realm to push officials on policy.[4] Near northwest Arkansas in Missouri, women even supported male relatives in the guerrilla fight, if they were not actively participating themselves.[5] Women in northwest Arkansas were no different. They dealt with homefront and battlefront issues to the point where those lines were indelibly blurred. And this confusion began early: the 1862 Battles of Pea Ridge and Prairie Grove destabilized the area and led to three years of guerrilla fighting as the Union army struggled to impose order. This conflict shaped the wartime experiences of women in the area no matter their political affiliation. Further, the isolation of the Ozarks and the relative newness of its communities exacerbated the conditions experienced by northwest Arkansas women. Most communities in the region were less than two decades old and lacked the extensive political systems and multigenerational kinship networks that supported women in the established communities of the eastern part of the Confederacy.

The Arkansas counties of Benton, Carroll, Madison, and Washington were in many ways a frontier in 1860. Though part of the Ozark Mountains, the rolling prairies of the Springfield Plateau gave the four counties of northwest Arkansas some of the best farmland in the region. This drew settlers even though travel to the state capital was difficult and the area was isolated by geography. The population of northwest Arkansas nearly doubled between 1850 and 1860. The boom was centered in Washington County, with Fayetteville as its county seat, and made the county one of the most densely settled in the frontier state by 1860.[6] Bentonville, Huntsville, and Carrollton, the county seats of Benton, Madison, and Carroll counties, respectively, also saw growth during the 1850s and the establishment of rudimentary political and social systems.[7] However, with little more than two decades of settlement there were few ancestral homes or holdings, no dynasties in local politics, and only a handful of families with well-established fortunes. Outside of the small number of wealthy slaveholders in the region, the Census generally reflected an intergenerational tradition of westward movement for most of the population. The oldest members of most families were born in Virginia or North Carolina. In turn, their sons and daughters were born in Tennessee or Illinois, and only the grandchildren were born in Arkansas. Women made up slightly less than half of the total population. Enslaved women made up slightly more than half of the African American population, which was roughly 10 percent of the total. Women of this region were accustomed to movement and experienced in frontier survival. Every bit of that background would be put to use during the war.[8]

The women of northwest Arkansas experienced the Civil War as a contested yet inconclusive occupation, though "occupation" is a rather generous description of the level of control exerted by either Confederate or Union troops. LeeAnn Whites and Alecia Long define an occupied space as one where "the home front and the battlefield merged, creating a new kind of battlefield and an unanticipated second front, where some civilians—many of whom were women—continued resisting what they perceived as illegitimate domination."[9] This merging of the homefront and the battlefront is especially relevant for northwest Arkansas. No one was safe in the area as early as the Battle of Pea Ridge in March 1862. Afterward, law and order were gradually replaced by military rule and covert violence. By late 1864, military farm colonies established by the U.S. Army sheltered Unionist and Confederate women alike from guerrilla action.[10] Like many parts of the upland South, the Arkansas Ozarks experienced numerous regular and irregular interactions throughout the war. Northwest Arkansas women lived with a sense of occupation even if the main armies were far away.[11]

The combined presence of regular and irregular troops quickly strained the region's meager sources of food and shelter and burdened the lives of any women who remained. Despite the population surge of the 1850s, the region was still lightly settled compared to regions farther east, and the addition of thousands of troops in the area made the situation unsustainable. Many of the means for producing food, clothing, and basic farm implements were destroyed in the first year of the war. By 1863, after enduring two formal battles in the area and numerous shifts in regional control, the means for most residents of northwest Arkansas to subsist were severely depleted. First neglected by the Confederacy, then separated entirely, the only surplus food into the region came through federal supply lines. Local men were involved in the fighting, either formally with one of the armies or informally with irregular bands. Even men not in service were often separated from their homes and families, on the run, or hiding out in the hills and caves to avoid conscription. As a result, independent of men, northwest Arkansas women protected their homes and farms. Many became refugees as they sought safer and better-supplied locations for themselves and their families. By the winter of 1862–1863, the women of northwest Arkansas faced violence and starvation on a scale most other southerners, even in other border areas, would not see for another year. By late 1864, troops and guerrilla bands had relentlessly ground down the residents and resources until nothing was left; no people, no crops, no livestock. Only those too poor to leave, especially dogged, or under the explicit protection of the Union army remained.[12]

The challenge in understanding the occupation of northwest Arkansas during the Civil War is that loyalties were fluid, and affiliation shaped women's experiences. Women can generally be divided into three groups: enslaved women, Confederate-affiliated women, and Union-affiliated women. Depending on who was doing the occupying and when, "occupation" meant very different things to Confederate-identified women than it did to Union-identified women. Further, enslaved women saw the Union advance as anything but occupation; it was liberation delivered. Enslaved women had the least control of their circumstances. They were subject not only to the decisions of the men in their family unit but also, until emancipation, to the desires of their slaveholder. Confederate-affiliated women were known as such through the service of the men in their family or their expressed personal conviction. In northwest Arkansas, many of these women were among the earlier settlers in the area, wealthier, and closely tied to the slave system. Finally, Union-affiliated women, similar to their Confederate counterparts, were defined as such either through the association of their male relatives with the Union cause or, if free to do so, because they had made their personal convictions known. Unionist women were less likely to have been members of slaveholding families prior to the war, though there were a few. Many of these women came to the Union cause over the course of the war, as men who were originally conscripted into the Confederate army became disillusioned with the cause and joined the other side, or as conditions declined in the area and necessity required Union affiliation for survival.[13]

Gender politics of the nineteenth century generally viewed men as the exclusive head of the household, but it would be erroneous to assume that all Ozark women deferred to their husbands on issues as large as secession and rebellion. "My husband was loyal at the start," Elizabeth Martin of Washington County stated in her 1878 testimony to the Southern Claims Commission, "but then listened to [Confederate general Thomas C.] Hindman's big tales and turned Rebel and went South." Martin did not join her husband. Their two sons fought for the Union. In fact, the pair remained estranged until at least the 1880 Census, where Elizabeth Martin was listed as married, but the head of her household. Reconciliation only appears to have come in death. James Martin died in 1882, and Elizabeth was buried at his side two years later.[14] The persistence of their separation in life reveals the depth of wartime loyalties and the continued influence of the conflict. Elizabeth Martin received such admiring testimony from neighbors and authorities in the 1870s despite the fact that she disregarded nineteenth-century feminine mores. She defied her husband and perhaps even turned his sons against him. After the war was over, she lived separately from him for years. Women on a frontier like northwest Arkansas in 1860, experienced with hardship and travel, could exercise more of their own agency than modern observers might expect when it comes to analyzing the crisis that faced the nation.

Racial and political identity intersected with wartime conditions to create a vast range of experiences for northwest Arkansas women. Displacement, violence, loss, and interaction with military entities were all common. Yet each experience was shaped by the circumstances of the individual woman. For example, displacement was common for many women, no matter their prewar status or wartime affiliation, but race and political affiliation strongly affected where, when, and how a woman was displaced. Most northwest Arkansas women left their homes during the war years: some women moved to the safety of neighbors or the Union lines within the same area, and some traveled to different counties or states. Even fiercely independent Elizabeth Martin saw her house burned and was forced to move. For enslaved women, the alternatives were different: some northwest Arkansas slaveholders freed their slaves and embraced the Union, many took their slaves south, and some slaves self-emancipated and went north, especially to Kansas. In the early years of the war, many white women in slaveholding families evacuated with their families and slaves to friendlier and more secure environs, but some remained on the farm, often without men, to prevent an accusation of abandonment that could result in the confiscation of land. There were no easy choices. High levels of both guerrilla and military violence in the area and the scarcity of food in the later years of the war made departing the region an appealing option no matter the affiliation of the family. Vulnerability to violence, the loss of loved ones, and formal interactions with military entities were also affected by the racial and political identity of women, creating such a complex situation in northwest Arkansas that there is simply no single Civil War experience to which one can point to understand the experiences of all women in the area. The war was a challenging and often brutal experience for all women.

African American women were the most vulnerable people in society at the outbreak of the Civil War. Violence during the war forced these women to move, often with little regard to their wishes. Further, most African Americans had been brought to the Ozarks in the 1850s; emancipation freed many women to leave and at least attempt to find family and friends who had remained in the East. As a result, in northwest Arkansas, the African American population dropped from 2,502 individuals in 1860 to only 1,043 in 1870.[15] Combined with the fact that enslaved women were hardly encouraged to write down their experiences, there are few sources that capture the Civil War from their perspective. The best are the slave narratives collected by the Federal Writers' Project in the 1930s, and there are a few claims made by former slaves to the Southern Claims Commission, a federal program to reimburse loyal southerners for losses incurred during the war, which operated in the 1870s.[16] Yet the stories of these women elucidate the experience of a population often completely forgotten in most histories of the Civil War in the Ozarks.

Mary Myhand and Adeline Blakely were former slaves interviewed by volunteers with the Federal Writers' Project during the Great Depression. Myhand

and Blakely were young in 1860, and both had uncommonly close relationships with their owners during and after the war. Both Myhand and Blakely were in their early teens when the war broke out and were reliant on their mistresses even after emancipation. Myhand had no living parents, and Blakely at seven years old had been a gift to her mistress when she married. Their brief statements in the 1930s reveal youths' perspectives on the displacement and violence that were inherent to the war in the Ozarks. Mary Myhand lived on a farm south of Siloam Springs in Benton County, near the border with Indian Territory. She was owned by the Farley family and recalled, "I was a little tod of a girl when the war came up." No matter one's age or status in society, accurate information was a luxury for everyone, and rumors as much as facts often drove decision-making. Myhand remembered, "One day word come that the 'Feds' were coming through and [would] kill all of the old men and take all the boys with them." This prompted her master to take his grandson and Myhand's brother to Texas. "I was so scared," she said. "I followed them for about half a mile before they found me and I begged so hard they took me with them." Myhand was in Texas for about a year before "the Feds gave the women on our place orders to leave their home. Said they owned it now." The Farley women had arrived in Texas just as the South surrendered, and the family moved back to Benton County. Myhand lived with the Farleys for the next twenty years. For such a brief statement, Myhand revealed one of the essential ways in which gender divided the experience of war. Men were indeed in danger in northwest Arkansas, and it was not uncommon for male heads of households to take male slaves and young white boys south in an attempt to prevent loss of life and property. Women, however, were usually left behind in the Ozarks to spare them the hardships of the road and perhaps to protect the remaining physical property, with the hope that federal troops would not harass lone women. For the Farleys, this does not appear to have been effective, since Myhand noted that the house was burned and federal troops confiscated the land.[17]

In contrast, Adeline Blakely was enslaved by a Washington County family living in Fayetteville. Where Myhand experienced the war in a rural setting, Blakely lived in a town that changed hands multiple times during the war. Like Myhand, Blakely chose to remain with her mistress during the war and beyond, stating, "I wanted to stay in the only home I had ever known." Blakely's owner also remained in northwest Arkansas while other members of the mistress's family fled south. "The War separated lots of [white] families," Blakely observed, mentioning that Parks, the father of her owner, took "all his slaves and all his fine stock, horses and cattle and went South to Louisiana following the Southern army for protection." It appears from Blakely's stories about the Civil

War that she spent the entire time in Fayetteville, since she related her mistress saving the Masonic building from being burned and her own experience of bringing a meal to a "crazy Confederate soldier" who had attempted to burn down the courthouse and had been locked up for his own safety.[18]

Though Myhand and Blakely had different experiences during the war, as young black women largely raised by their white mistresses, they survived it in similar ways. It does not appear that Myhand had any direct contact with federal troops, whereas Blakely lived in a town that was regularly occupied by the Union army, yet both women acknowledged that federal troops separated slaves from their masters. However, it seems that neither woman viewed the federal army as a liberating force. Myhand begged to be taken to Texas with her master, and Blakely remained in her familiar home. Some of this sentiment can be explained by the limits of the slave narratives themselves; interviewers rarely dug into the psychological motivations of their subjects, and decades of time might have smoothed memories. Yet the fact that both women chose to remain with their mistresses for decades after the war is illuminating. Young enslaved women with neither blood nor even fictive adult kin experienced the war differently than other enslaved women. Where, exactly, could they have gone on their own after emancipation? Guerrilla warfare made the region unsafe for everyone. Leaving would have meant trading known circumstances for unknown—both women had likely been raised to respond to the quirks, rules, and foul moods of their mistresses—and venturing out into a region so devastated by war that adult white women were starving to death was simply not a reasonable decision for either girl. Far from taking an easy or cowardly path in response to emancipation, Myhand and Blakely made choices that ultimately ensured that they survived.

Enslaved women with families experienced displacement, interaction with federal troops, and freedom differently than Myhand and Blakely did. Some sixty years earlier than the Federal Writers' Project narratives, the 1875 testimony of Fannie Bean Maxey in a Southern Claims Commission deposition revealed how a girl in a black family responded to war and freedom. Mark Bean, a planter in Washington County, owned Maxey's family.[19] Caesar and Mary Bean were the parents of a number of children, including Fannie, who met and married Ran Maxey, a veteran of the Second Kansas Colored Regiment, in Fort Smith, Arkansas, after the war.[20] In 1875, Caesar Bean filed with the Southern Claims Commission for reimbursement of the loss of a mule. According to Bean's sworn testimony, sometime after the Battle of Pea Ridge in early 1862, Mark Bean decided to leave Washington County and took his slaves south to the plantation of his recently married daughter near the Arkansas River in Johnson

County, about one hundred miles away. However, federal troops soon occupied Johnson County too, and at some point in the fall of 1863, a portion of the Bean clan moved to Texas, leaving behind the Caesar Bean family and one mule. In his first stated interaction with federal troops, Bean left his family in Johnson County in the winter of 1863 for Clarksville in an attempt to enlist in the Union army. The inspecting surgeon rejected the nearly sixty-year-old Bean, and he went to work in a government sawmill instead. When federal troops confiscated the mule, only Bean's wife and children were present, leaving Fannie Bean Maxey to later testify in the claim.[21]

The Bean women experienced displacement and contact with federal troops, but had a far different experience than Myhand and Blakely. "The first federal troops came and occupied the county where we was living," Fannie Bean Maxey stated. "A party of 10 or 12 soldiers, as well as I remember, under a Captain Clare came to where we was living. It was in the afternoon, they passed by our house, [went] to a pasture where mule charged in the claim was running, they caught him and returned by the house where we lived. My mother told them to leave the mule that he belonged to my father, the claimant, but they refused to give him up, said they wanted him." Despite the protestations of the two women, the troops took the mule and left.[22] Fear of federal troops drove Mark Bean south just as it did Mary Myhand's owner, but testimony in the Bean claim draws a clear correlation between the actual arrival of federal troops and freedom. According to the men who testified in Caesar Bean's claim, when federal troops arrived in Johnson County, the Bean slaves started moving—not under the command of their now absentee owner, but by their own choice. Fannie Bean Maxey, however, was left on a farm with her mother and younger siblings. Freedom for her came in growing crops for the benefit of the family and in the image of her mother confronting white men about property owned, not by her master, but by her husband. Further, Maxey, ensconced in a black family unit, was not tethered to a white family for survival. The Bean family settled in Van Buren shortly after the war, where they lived in a community of former slaves, including some from the Bean Plantation.[23] Instead of remaining in a white household and never marrying, as Blakely did, or delaying marriage, as Myhand did, Maxey married and had children.[24] As the stories of Myhand, Blakely, and Maxey show, violence and displacement were experienced by enslaved women in the Ozarks. The conditions under which they were enslaved, however, and especially their access to kinship networks, shaped their response to that violence and displacement and, ultimately, their experience of freedom.

Though the Bean women survived the hardships of displacement, not all northwest Arkansas women were so lucky. Hermannsburg in far western Washington

County, on the border with Indian Territory in 1860, had been settled over the previous decade by immigrants from Germany. Brothers Johann (Jean) and Karl Hermann were the leaders of the settlement and were married to sisters Nani and Lina, respectively. The sisters were born in Germany and had migrated to the United States with their father in the early 1850s. Their husbands also migrated around the same time. Germany and much of Europe had faced its own unrest starting in the late 1840s, and many Germans left in search of opportunity and stability. The Hermanns found both of those in northwest Arkansas, at least briefly. By 1860, the two couples had nine children between them and substantial holdings in the area. Their most prosperous enterprise was a steam-powered mill, which processed corn and wheat, sawed lumber, and carded wool.[25]

When the war came, the location of Hermannsburg along a flatter and more accessible north-south route through Washington County, as well as its proximity to Indian Territory, made their situation vulnerable. After the Battles of Pea Ridge in March 1862 and Prairie Grove in December, the situation became dire. Lina recorded in her diary scavenging by "starving secessionists" at the mill and on the morning of November 15, 1862, woke to find her home surrounded by troops she eventually determined to be part of Hindman's Confederate army. Lina Hermann was decidedly resistant to this development. "I have been ordered to cook for the soldiers," she recounted. "I have tied a bandage over one eye and tell them I am not well and will cook only for the sick and wounded. I am tired of cooking for secessionists. Nani cooks for them and out of gratitude four soldiers stole everything they could lay hands on from her."[26] Lina resisted the occupation by feigning sickness and shared a number of incidents in her diary that asserted she was not cowed by the presence of hostile troops. The men of Hermannsburg soon left to find protection with the Union forces, and Lina and Nani both indicated this was the safest option, noting more than once their relief that the men were not around when Confederate troops arrived to scavenge. The women debated for nearly a month how long their hidden supplies would last, their chances for survival on the road, and the advisability of staying at Hermannsburg. They wrote in their diaries nearly every other day, always mentioning scavenging and confrontations with occupying troops. Political or military affiliation mattered little as they noted theft and violence from Confederates, Cherokees, and Unionists alike. On December 18, 1862, their brother Fritz Wilhelmi arrived with a military escort of a hundred men to take them to Union general Francis Herron's camp. "How glad I will be to leave here," Lina stated.[27]

Reflecting on the journey out of northwest Arkansas, Karl Hermann later noted of the Christmas Day they spent on the road in 1862, "The Christ-child had lost its magic that day. Satan was ruling the land."²⁸ It was a common practice by General Herron to grant protected passage out of northwest Arkansas to Unionist refugees, but the journey itself was fraught with hardship. The Hermann group, numbering nearly twenty, was granted permission to travel with a Union commissary train to Rolla, Missouri. Johann Hermann took ill before leaving Arkansas and spent most of the trip prone in a wagon. It took the family four months to get to Washington, Missouri, outside of St. Louis. There Nani died, leaving behind five children under the age of ten. Johann, her husband, wrote the final entry in her diary: "Here ends the diary of my beloved Nany [sic]. At her request I am adding the conclusion. On the 30th of April at 8:30 o'clock in the morning my poor wife died after six days' illness. She called me to her bed and said: 'Jean, tell me the end—I cannot find the words for the end—bring my diary and my pen and ink—you write the end.'"²⁹ Despite the loss of Nani, the Hermanns' journey did not end in St. Louis. Some members of the family went back to Germany to wait out the war. The Civil War had ended the hopes of their small German community of making a new life in the Arkansas Ozarks. Only a few would ever return to Arkansas, and none on a permanent basis.³⁰ Despite the fact that the Hermann women had achieved the highest level of security available to women in the nineteenth century—they were educated, married, and ran two of the most prosperous households in northwest Arkansas—even they were not safe from the hardships of war.

Displacement was a nearly universal experience for northwest Arkansas women, and in most cases it was precipitated by violence, either the presence of fighting nearby or specific violence against and the loss of loved ones. Because of the destruction and massive movement of people during the Civil War, it can be difficult to determine who was killed, where, and why. The Southern Claims Commission documented a surprising number of incidents of violence against Unionists as individuals sought to prove they had maintained their loyalty to the United States during the conflict. These claims were made in the 1870s, and a number were made by women. They tell stories of murder and movement, loss and hardship. Margaret Champlin and Elizabeth High of Carroll County, Jane Lewis of Washington County, and Eliza Buttram of Benton County all testified to the murders of their husbands in front of them, either on their property or actually in their home. Champlin's husband was killed by rebels in front of her in January 1864, leaving her widowed with four children under the age of twelve.³¹ High's husband was killed by "rebel bushwhackers" in 1863 in the family home in front of her and her sons, ages eight and ten. She remained on their farm, located near the Missouri line, even after her husband's death, until January 1865, when she sought refuge with federal troops at Cassville, Missouri, some forty miles away. "My reason for moving to Missouri," she stated, "was that the rebels had robbed me of about everything I had to live upon and I was compelled to leave to procure subsistence and I also went for the protection of the federal forces as I feared personal violence from the rebel bushwhackers."[32]

For women in these areas, gender offered only dubious protection. On the night of October 5, 1864, Jane Lewis's husband, who had been released from Union service due to an injury, was dragged from their home in Washington County and killed by rebels in front of her and their nine children. The Confederates then threatened to burn the house down with the children inside, but left with a warning for the family to leave. Lewis packed up her family and moved closer to the Union lines near Mt. Comfort, outside of Fayetteville.[33] Eliza Buttram's husband, William, was "murdered at home in July 1862 by the Rebel Bushwhackers because he was [a] Union man, and they told me they killed him for that reason, and him a laying a corpse in the yard where they shot him down." Buttram quickly left for Missouri with her two small children and father-in-law.[34] The contested, occupied space of northwest Arkansas was not just a place of resistance to an illegitimate military, but truly a place where the homefront and the battlefield merged. What that meant for many northwest Arkansas women, no matter their status before the war, was violence, death, and loss. These men did not die on a faraway battlefield. These women abruptly lost the heads of their households in their very presence. They had to adjust immediately and decide if, when, and where to move their families. Many had the support of extended family networks, but even that could not make up for the sudden loss of their husbands on the homefront.

While violence led many women to leave northwest Arkansas, another portion of the population experienced displacement through their connection with the Union army. Women with husbands, fathers, or brothers in Union service in the Ozarks often moved inside the federal lines, and subsequently followed the troops as they moved around the region. Toward the end of the war, however, with the establishment of military farm colonies by the Union army, even Confederate-affiliated women, including the widow of one of the larger slaveholders in Washington County and four women with sons or husbands in Confederate service at the Union Valley Colony, were under the protection of federal troops.[35] Polly Clark and Nancy Carlisle, both of Madison County, were two women who traveled with Union troops as the wives of soldiers. Polly Clark was married to Reuben Clark and often took care of him and his fellow soldiers at a home in Fayetteville.[36] Nancy Carlisle married a soldier from Madison County at Cassville, Missouri, a wartime refuge for Arkansas Unionists, and resided with him in Fayetteville until his discharge. Clark and Carlisle probably knew each other: they were from the same part of Madison County, their husbands were childhood friends, and both men served in the First Arkansas Cavalry. Polly Ann Clark left no diaries or letters, but she did provide testimony in a number of pension files after the war. Injured veterans were eligible for a federal pension, and Clark's presence with the army, as well as her wartime care for the injured in her home, made her an ideal witness. Clark provided specific testimony about the health conditions of a number of men, and more than one mentioned their preference for her care over that of the hospital, as one was more likely to survive the former.[37] Clark's own husband was injured during a skirmish with Benton County guerrillas.[38] Her testimony illustrates her wartime experience: caring for soldiers in her home and moving with the First Arkansas between Missouri and Fayetteville as seasons and conditions changed, and later evacuating to Kansas with others from Madison County.

A unique story is Nancy Carlisle and her marriage, or perhaps "marriage," to Elisha McGinnis. In an attempt to gain access to the funds available in the pension system, Carlisle filed a fraudulent widow's pension claim after the war. She was denied when the Pension Office realized that McGinnis was still alive and filing an application of his own.[39] In June 1880, Nancy Carlisle McGinnis Kimball—she had accumulated a number of surnames—filed her claim. On the form, she stated she was married to Elisha McGinnis, formerly of Company L, First Arkansas Cavalry. She requested a pension for herself and her daughter Mary. The claim was "rejected on the grounds soldier is living and an applicant for pension."[40] Five years later, a special examiner sent to gather testimony on McGinnis for his claim of an injury during the war, as well as to clear up the issue of the fraudulent claim, spoke with Nancy, who by this time was Nancy Fox.

Nancy Carlisle Fox testified, and the Census corroborates, that she and McGinnis grew up near one another in Madison County.[41] She stated that she married him "in the winter or fall of 1863" at Cassville, Missouri. Many northwest Arkansas residents went to Cassville either to enlist or to seek aid throughout the war. Carlisle, however, was probably there because her father, formerly the captain of Company A of the First Arkansas, had been discharged from service for illness a year earlier. Ill former Union officers were wise not to return to northwest Arkansas, as Jane Lewis's experience illustrates. It is not unlikely that Carlisle and McGinnis could have been married at Cassville, though the two-season range she gave seems quite vague for an event as important as a marriage. Carlisle appears to have traveled with her husband to Fayetteville and lived there with him until he was discharged with a disability in the summer of 1864. She and McGinnis, along with a number of Madison County families, including the Clarks, then evacuated to Kansas. There, McGinnis "left her for another woman" in the winter of 1864–1865, and she "heard he obtained a divorce from her" sometime in 1865.[42] McGinnis married Reuben Clark's sister Catherine in 1867. Carlisle provided no documentation of either the marriage or the divorce. She was never charged for filing a fraudulent claim, perhaps because of her story that the man she was living with at the time had threatened to whip her to death if she did not file it.

These stories of Polly Clark and Nancy Carlisle reveal the experiences of women who are often lost in the usual historical record. They were in their late teens and early twenties at the time of the war, newly or recently married, and did not have established homes and families to maintain or protect. Both women were displaced by the conflict; they each mentioned living in at least three different places during the course of the war. Reuben Clark may have felt enlistment was the best way to feed and protect his family as conditions deteriorated in northwest Arkansas. Elisha McGinnis was already a soldier when he married Carlisle at Cassville in 1863. As a result, the women's experience of the war was shaped not just by displacement or violence, but by a direct relationship with the military—and in a typical northwest Arkansas fashion, both the Confederate and U.S. militaries. Reuben Clark and Elisha McGinnis were originally conscripted into the Confederate army. At some point in 1862, Clark left Confederate service. He enlisted with the First Arkansas Cavalry in Benton County in October of that year. McGinnis, who had agreed to one year of Confederate service in November 1861, left his Confederate unit on the march to the Battle of Prairie Grove in December 1862 and enlisted at Fayetteville with the U.S. Army on the tenth of that month. The two men received disability discharges from federal service on the same day in March 1864.[43]

As the wives of soldiers, Polly Clark and Nancy Carlisle McGinnis experienced occupation and war in a distinct way. For most of the war, their lives were controlled directly by Union commanders. They moved in relation to where their male relative chose to enlist and, later, in response to orders their husband received or because he was injured, discharged from service, and escorted to safer environs. Even after the war, the federal service of their husbands continued to shape their lives. Clark spent years testifying for men she had cared for during the conflict as well as fighting the pension system on behalf of her husband. Even divorced from McGinnis, Carlisle was drawn into the pension system and interacted with government authorities years after the war ended.

Women with sons in military service also had a distinct experience of the war, whether they were Unionist or Confederate. These women were in their late thirties or forties during the war and had homes and families to consider. The service of their sons was known in the community, although with the divided loyalties of the Ozarks, that could be a double-edged sword. Amanda Braly was a widow residing with her children in Newburg near Boonsboro, now known as Cane Hill, in Washington County. Her son William Carrick Braly served in the Confederate Thirty-Fourth Arkansas Infantry. Lucinda Sawyers had three sons serving in the Union army. Her eldest son, John, did not serve but was married in 1861 to Mary Jane Martin, daughter of the previously discussed Unionist Elizabeth Martin. The Sawyers family lived on a farm in Billingsley, Arkansas, about five miles from Elizabeth Martin and about ten miles east of Cane Hill and Amanda Braly.[44]

Braly's correspondence with Carrick, her eldest son, shows the experience of women among the upper class in the Ozarks. Braly's perspective is also interesting because she lived roughly ten miles east of the Hermann families, yet as a native-born, Confederate-affiliated woman, her experience was vastly different. Carrick Braly saw action outside of northwest Arkansas, but fortunately was able to keep his mother's letters safe during his service. The Braly Family Papers include extensive correspondence between the pair. A number of issues are relevant to Amanda Braly's perspective on conditions in northwest Arkansas. First, she was widowed in 1856, not during the conflict. While certainly missing the contribution of her eldest son, it was not an entirely new circumstance for her to act independently during the war. In terms of how she related the news and information about conditions at home, the fact that she was writing to her twenty-year-old son colored her tone and perhaps affected the type of information conveyed. She often expressed that she missed Carrick and requested visits along, of course, with motherly admonitions to write more often, but she rarely demanded aid and appears to have minimized the danger in northwest Arkansas. Despite these caveats, the Civil War experience revealed by her letters is a wrenching one.

Braly's early letters conveyed wartime information but more about the reality of running a home and farm. In an October 1862 letter, she mentioned her work on securing proper clothing and supplies for Carrick and told of speaking to a neighbor about gathering corn and sowing wheat.[45] By November 1862, at the same time the Hermann women noted the hostile presence of Hindman's Confederate troops, Braly related the first movements of federal troops in the area and expressed concerns about the food supply and theft. "If the army does not come up soon," she worried, "I fear we will have nothing left."[46] Yet in early 1863, by which time the Hermanns had evacuated the area, she reported that things had calmed with the passage of the federal troops and the family was well supplied. Throughout 1863, however, as the fighting season wore on, conditions in Braly's area became more unstable. In nearly every letter, she mentioned the destruction of homes, barns, or churches, as well as the deaths of neighbors and friends. This too resonates with the experiences of the other women I have discussed. Yet, as late as June, she still spoke of an adequate food supply and a variety of crops.[47] She specifically noted the fact that a number of the federal troops appeared to be Arkansans, an important observation of the divided nature of the area. In August 1863, she lamented the return of federal troops and stated, "I fear we will see hard times."[48] She was correct.

From the fall of 1863 onward, Braly chronicled the harassment and violence of both federal troops and Indians. The family made it through the winter of 1863–1864 but dealt with searches and the scavenging of supplies by federal troops. In the summer of 1864, she tempered her usual request for a visit with the admission that she would not be able to rest if her son were present in the area. "It is awful to think how this war is carried on here," she stated.[49] In November 1864, she related the worst news to date: "Our dear old houses are burnt to ashes." The family spent two days and a night in the open air.[50] Even a woman of Braly's means faced displacement and hardship. She interacted with troops, both friendly and unfriendly, as the situation demanded. She expressed both frustration and resignation about her situation, but above all, she managed the survival of her family despite the conditions. While Braly had the means to maintain herself and her family, other women relied on the financial support of their sons. Carrick Braly survived the war and returned to Washington County to help his mother rebuild.[51] Lucinda Sawyers, however, would face a loss that ultimately threatened the livelihood of the family.

While Sawyers was of more modest means than Amanda Braly, she and her husband, James, owned their farm and did well. But James was in his fifties and may have been in ill health; they relied on their sons' assistance.[52] As Union soldiers, the Sawyers sons, Henry Addison (known as Add), Jeptha Jefferson (JJ), and Alonzo, often sent a portion of their pay home to their parents. In May 1864, Add was shot in the left wrist by Confederates near Little Rock, nearly severing his hand.[53] In June of that year, Lucinda Sawyers received a letter from JJ from Van Buren, Arkansas. "Dear father and mother," he began, "I this morning take the opportunity of writing you a few lines to let you no [sic] that I am well at present. I just got here last night. Add was doing as well as could be expected. I think he will get well pretty soon. I am going to try to come home when we draw money. You said you was coming down here, we wrote for you to come, you needant come till we draw money."[54] This letter highlights two subjects important to many mothers of soldiers. First, it is clear that Lucinda Sawyers already knew of Add's injury before June 10, when JJ wrote, so communication was not severely hampered by the war, at least not for those on the Union side. Further, that JJ told his mother to stay in Washington County, at least until they got paid, indicates that travel was possible for civilians. Second, some sons were sending a portion, if not all, of their pay to their parents, suggesting that the monetary situation for the family back in Washington County at least in part relied on the boys for support. Unfortunately, it is unclear if Lucinda ever saw JJ again. He was captured by Confederate guerrillas and found shot in the back of the head on August 11, 1864. The war left Lucinda Sawyers with one son disabled and another murdered. Alonzo was the only one who survived the war physically unscathed. She eventually applied for and received a mother's pension from the federal government as compensation for the lost support of JJ.[55]

Though the outcomes were different, the stories of both Braly and Sawyers illustrate that the concerns of many northwest Arkansas women were focused not simply on the volatility of the Ozarks homefront but also on the experience, safety, and support of their sons directly participating in the war effort outside the immediate area. Furthermore, Braly and Sawyers were older than Carlisle and Clark and lived on well-established farms. They were not destabilized by the abrupt loss of the head of their household, like High, Harris, Lewis, and Buttram, nor were they faced with the quandary of freedom in the middle of a war, like Myhand, Blakely, and Maxey. Braly and Sawyers, as white mothers, represent yet another way the experience of northwest Arkansas women was shaped by the nuances of their identity and means.

Twenty-first-century observers, enmeshed in a culture at least slightly more advanced in terms of equality of the sexes, may too easily take for granted that women could and did face the hardships of war with independence and strength. The viewpoint of a male contemporary of these Ozarks women, however, shows how extraordinary their actions were to some people in the 1860s. Confederate sympathizer Robert W. Mecklin of Washington County chronicled the experiences of the Confederate-affiliated women in his neighborhood in letters to his sister in 1863 and 1864. Mecklin was sixty-eight years old in 1863 and, except for his slave Wesley, was surrounded by women in his area of Washington County near Mt. Comfort.[56] Women, in Mecklin's view, were compelled to execute too many decisions with limited and often-contradictory information. His wife and daughter interacted far more often with those who stopped by their farm than he did. Upon hearing men in the yard one day, his daughter, Louisa, "ran to her room, stuck her hatchet in her belt and was back by the time they had reached the north window," before recognizing the visitors as friendly.[57] In another incident, Mecklin related how robbers went through the area and took items from a number of homes, including his own. But at the McCormack place, where four men had stopped for the night on the way back to Cincinnati in the western part of the county, the robbers were confronted by the woman of the house as she protected her visitors. "Miss Margaret ... placed herself between [the visitors] and the muzzle of [the] robbers' pistols ... sprang to the middle of the pallet, claimed the soldier's blankets as her property and dared them to touch them, brandishing her fist in the faces of those who approached and set the hair of one of them on fire with her candle. They left, carrying off what they had already gotten. ... Hurrah for Miss Mag."[58] Mecklin was proud of what women did to ensure their survival and protect their homes. His observations illustrate the extreme circumstances under which Ozark women abandoned nineteenth-century social mores. The war created a space for white women where previously unadmirable, if not completely unacceptable, behavior was suddenly valued. In the final assessment, that a nineteenth-century patriarch had such a positive view of that change, going so far as to credit his survival to women — "perhaps to their wise counsel and kind care I am indebted for the safety of my own noggin from Federal sabers and balls"[59] — reveals the remarkable situation in the Arkansas Ozarks.

Whether occupied by outside troops, threatened by guerrilla fighters, facing constant news of, if not direct experience with, the deaths of friends and family, or welcoming emancipation and the possibilities of freedom under the pall of war, all northwest Arkansas women faced challenging experiences. As a result, for a brief time, the war created a space where the usual expectations of gender and race were in flux. The conflict ultimately left their homes, lives, and communities transformed and left the women with the challenge of determining how much of their changed status to take into rebuilding war-ravaged northwest Arkansas in the years to follow.

NOTES

1. For the purposes of this chapter, northwest Arkansas is defined as Benton, Carroll, Madison, and Washington counties as they existed in 1860.

2. Northwest Arkansas is part of a broader region that scholars define as having experienced guerrilla warfare — conflict among civilians, irregular troops, and formal armies — for much of the Civil War. The critical role of guerrillas and guerrilla warfare in the Civil War has been well established. Though much of the scholarship has been focused on Appalachia, one of the earliest and most influential works is Michael Fellman's exploration of violence and hardship, *Inside War: The Guerrilla Conflict in Missouri during the American Civil War* (New York: Oxford University Press, 1989), which examines the war in the nearby Missouri Ozarks. Fellman's work was one of the first studies of the Civil War to see irregular warfare as just as critical to the final outcome as the traditional battles between the major armies. By the late 1990s, several similar studies had followed. Most crossed the border, however, and combined studies of Unionism in Confederate states with examinations of the irregular fighting that aberrant affiliation inspired. Examples include Brian McKnight's *Contested Borderland: The Civil War in Appalachian Kentucky and Virginia* (Lexington:

University Press of Kentucky, 2006); Jonathan Dean Sarris's northeast Georgia study, *A Separate Civil War: Communities in Conflict in the Mountain South* (Charlottesville: University of Virginia Press, 2006); John Inscoe and Gordon McKinney's examination of the mountains of North Carolina in *The Heart of Confederate Appalachia: Western North Carolina in the Civil War* (Chapel Hill: University of North Carolina Press, 2000); the east Tennessee study of Noel Fisher in *War at Every Door: Partisan Politics and Guerrilla Violence in East Tennessee, 1860–1869* (Chapel Hill: University of North Carolina Press, 1997); and W. Todd Groce's *Mountain Rebels: East Tennessee Confederates and the Civil War, 1860–1870* (Knoxville: University of Tennessee Press, 1999). Combined, these works brought guerrilla warfare, and often southern Unionism, to the forefront of scholarship on the Civil War in the upland South. This trend culminated with the publication of Daniel Sutherland's award-winning *Savage Conflict: The Decisive Role of Guerrillas in the American Civil War* (Chapel Hill: University of North Carolina Press, 2009). The book won acclaim because it combined a synthesis of two decades of scholarship on guerrillas, irregular warfare, Unionism, and civilian suffering with Sutherland's own research and analysis to make the provocative and ultimately convincing argument that guerrilla warfare was not merely a sad and brutal subset of the broader fight; it *was* the fight. Guerrilla fighting shaped all aspects of the Civil War and was essential to its end result. That could not be truer than in Arkansas.

3. LeeAnn Whites, *The Civil War as a Crisis in Gender* (Athens: University of Georgia Press, 1995); LeeAnn Whites and Alecia P. Long, eds., *Occupied Women: Gender, Military Occupation, and the American Civil War* (Baton Rouge: Louisiana State University Press, 2009); Victoria Bynum, *The Long Shadow of the Civil War: Southern Dissent and Its Legacies* (Chapel Hill: University of North Carolina Press, 2010); Drew Gilpin Faust, *Mothers of Invention: Women of the Slaveholding South in the American Civil War* (Chapel Hill: University of North Carolina Press, 1996) and *This Republic of Suffering: Death and the American Civil War* (New York: Vintage, 2008).

4. For more on the political influence of southern women, see Stephanie McCurry, *Confederate Reckoning: Power and Politics in the Civil War South* (Chapel Hill: University of North Carolina Press, 2011).

5. Joseph Beilein, *Bushwhackers: Guerrilla Warfare, Manhood, and the Household in Civil War Missouri* (Kent, Ohio: Kent State University Press, 2016).

6. "U.S. Demography, 1790 to Present," *Social Explorer*, https://www.socialexplorer.com/a9676d974c/explore (accessed October 5, 2017).

7. Berryville became the county seat of a newly drawn Carroll County after the Civil War.

8. Examples of these family settlement patterns can be found in a number of northwest Arkansas townships in the 1850 and 1860 Censuses, such as the Clarks and Drakes of Richland Township in Madison County or the Cartwrights and their neighbors in Brush Creek Township in Washington County. Statistics about the enslaved population were drawn from manuscript Census returns. See U.S. Census, 1860, Slave Schedules, Washington County, Ark.

9. Whites and Long, *Occupied Women*, 3.

10. Michael A. Hughes, "Wartime Gristmill Destruction in Northwest Arkansas and Military-Farm Colonies," *Arkansas Historical Quarterly* 46 (Summer 1987): 180–86.

11. For more on guerrilla fighting in Arkansas, see Wendell P. Beall, "Wildwood Skirmishers: The First Federal Arkansas Cavalry," MA thesis, University of Arkansas, Fayetteville, 1988; Robert Mackey, "Bushwhackers, Provosts, and Tories: The Guerrilla War in Arkansas," in *Guerrillas, Unionists and Violence on the Confederate Home Front*, ed. Daniel E. Sutherland (Fayetteville: University of Arkansas Press, 1999), 171–85 (and the entire volume edited by Sutherland); Jay A. Prier, "Under the Black Flag: The Real War in Washington County, Arkansas, 1861–1865," MA thesis, University of Arkansas, Fayetteville, 1998.

12. For more on material conditions in the area during the war, see John F. Bradbury, "Buckwheat Cake Philanthropy, Refugees and the Union Army in the Ozarks," *Arkansas Historical Quarterly* 57 (Autumn 1998): 233–64; and Hughes, "Wartime Gristmill Destruction," 167–86.

13. For more information on the phenomenon of shifting affiliation, see Rebecca A. Howard, "Civil War Unionists and Their Legacy in the Arkansas Ozarks," Ph.D. diss., University of Arkansas, 2015, ch. 2.

14. Elizabeth Martin (Washington County, Ark.), claim no. 10861, Settled Case Files for Claims Approved by the Southern Claims Commission, 1871–1880, Records of the Accounting Officers of the Department of the Treasury, 1775–1978, RG 217, National Archives and Records Administration (hereafter NARA), reproductions at www.Fold3.com (accessed January 1–7, 2013) (hereafter Settled Case Files); manuscript Census returns, U.S. Census, 1870, Population Schedules, Washington County, Ark.; manuscript Census returns, U.S. Census, 1880, Population Schedules, Washington County, Ark. The inscription on James's headstone indicates he may have been ill before his death, so perhaps the couple reconciled when he returned home to the care of his family. Maybe they never reconciled, and Victorian era propriety overrode private squabbles and placed them side by side. It is worth noting, however, that an archaeological survey of the cemetery documented a child's grave between the two headstones. See John Riggs, field notes from the investigation of the Bryant/Martin Cemetery (3WA1468), 2010, Arkansas Archeological Survey, Fayetteville.

15. "U.S. Demography, 1790 to Present."

16. Both of these sources have their weaknesses. The slave narratives were recorded seventy years after the Civil War, which makes accurate details hard to come by and difficult to trust. However, the first-person impressions of the war offered by the interviewees do reveal a personal side to the conflict. In claims with the Southern Claims Commission, the individuals are trying to convince the federal government to give them money, which may have tainted some testimony.

17. "Mary Myhand, Benton County," in *Bearing Witness: Memories of Arkansas Slavery, Narratives from the 1930s WPA Collections*, ed. George E. Lankford (Fayetteville: University of Arkansas Press, 2003), 45. Myhand did not list her owners nor her maiden name in her narrative. She stated only that she stayed with her previous owners on the southern border of Benton County for more than twenty years after the war, before moving to Clarksville, Arkansas, where she was interviewed. A widowed Mary Myhand appears in the Census in Johnson County in 1900, living with the white Dunlap family as a servant, and in 1920 living with an elderly black man as a "helper." A woman by the name Mary Farley married Dan Myhand on May 6, 1891, in Johnson County, where Clarksville is located. In the 1870 Census, Mary Farley is listed as a housekeeper in the home of Eliza Farley, seventy years old, in Flint Township on the southern border of Benton County. In the 1880 Census, Mary Farley appears in the home of William Farley as a servant, along with Eliza Farley, seventy-nine years old, in the same area. Eliza Farley was married to W. T. Farley and appears with him in the 1860 Census, when they were both about sixty years old, again in the same area of Benton County. Also listed in the home that year was a William Farley, twenty, and James Farley, fifteen. James Farley could have been the owner's grandson whom Myhand mentioned when describing her master's evacuation to Texas. William Farley served in the Thirty-Second Regiment, Arkansas Infantry (Confederate). No Farleys in Benton or Washington counties are listed as slaveholders in 1860. However, Mary indicated in her narrative that there may not have been a large number of slaves in the household since she and her siblings appear to have lived with their owners in the same dwelling. Work with the 1860 slave schedules for northwest Arkansas has revealed that it was not uncommon for enslaved children to go uncounted. Myhand spoke with great affection for her mistress. Considering Eliza Farley's advanced age in 1880, it is probable that Eliza's passing precipitated

Myhand's move to Clarksville. Manuscript Census returns, U.S. Census, 1900, Population Schedules, Johnson County, Ark.; manuscript Census returns, U.S. Census, 1920, Population Schedules, Johnson County, Ark.; "Mary Farley Marriage to Dan Myhand," in *Arkansas Marriages, 1851–1900*, comp. Jordan Dodd, reproductions at www.ancestry.com (accessed October 22, 2013); manuscript Census returns, U.S. Census, 1880, Population Schedules, Benton County, Ark.; manuscript Census returns, U.S. Census, 1870, Population Schedules, Benton County, Ark.; manuscript Census returns, U.S. Census, 1860, Benton County, Ark.; William Farley, private, Thirty-Second Regiment, Arkansas Infantry, Compiled Service Records of Confederate Soldiers Who Served in Organizations from the State of Arkansas, RG 109, NARA, reproductions at www.Fold3.com (accessed June 2012 and August 22, 2015) (hereafter Civil War Service Records).

18. "Adeline Blakely, Washington County," in Lankford, *Bearing Witness*, 387–81.

19. Bean owned forty slaves, making him one of a few northwest Arkansas slaveholders with planter status. Manuscript Census returns, U.S. Census, 1860, Slave Schedules, Washington County, Ark.

20. Ran Maxey (Crawford County, Ark.), claim no. 16328, Settled Case Files.

21. Caesar Bean (Crawford County, Ark.), claim no. 17418, Settled Case Files. The story of the removal of Mark Bean and his family and slaves to the Arkansas River is also related in the slave narrative of Joe Bean. He recalled that the war caused them to move around and that the "first move" was to Dardanelle on the Arkansas River, which is the same general area related by Caesar Bean. Joe Bean never said what the subsequent moves were. "Joe Bean, Washington County," in Lankford, *Bearing Witness*, 382.

22. Fannie Maxey testimony, Caesar Bean claim, Settled Case Files.

23. Manuscript Census returns, U.S. Census, 1870, Population Schedules, Crawford County, Ark.

24. Manuscript Census returns, U.S. Census, 1880, Population Schedules, Crawford County, Ark.

25. Manuscript Census returns, U.S. Census, 1860, Population and Manufacturing Schedules, Washington County, Ark.

26. W. J. Lemke, "The Romantic Story of Old Hermannsburg, Now Dutch Mills," *Flashback* 9 (July 1959): 3.

27. Ibid., 5.

28. Ibid.

29. Ibid., 6.

30. Clarence Evans and Karl Friedrich Hermann, "Memoirs, Letters, and Diary Entries of German Settlers in Northwest Arkansas, 1853–1863," *Arkansas Historical Quarterly* 6 (Autumn 1947): 225–49.

31. After her husband was murdered in 1864, Margaret Champlin married W. Harris in 1866. Margaret M. Harris (Carroll County, Ark.), claim no. 18085, Settled Case Files.

32. Elizabeth High (Carroll County, Ark.), claim no. 21769, Settled Case Files.

33. Jane Lewis (Washington County, Ark.), claim no. 9626, Settled Case Files.

34. Eliza Buttram (Benton County, Ark.), claim no. 5780, Settled Case Files.

35. Hughes, "Wartime Gristmill Destruction," 183; Destitute Roll of Union Valley Colony, n.d., signed by Captain J. R. Rutherford, Rutherford Collection, Special Collections, Mullins Library, University of Arkansas, Fayetteville.

36. Soldier's Certificate no. 361530, Reuben Clark, private, Company L, First Arkansas Infantry, Case Files of Approved Pension Applications of Veterans Who Served in the Army and Navy Mainly in the Civil War and the War with Spain (Civil War and Later Survivors' Certificates), 1861–1934, Department of the Interior, Bureau of Pensions, 1849–1930, RG 15, Records of the Department of Veterans Affairs, 1773–2007, NARA (hereafter Pension Files).

37. Elisha McGinnis, deposition, Soldier's Certificate no. 366430; Elisha McGinnis, private, Company L, First Arkansas Calvary, Pension Files.

38. Reuben Clark, deposition, Reuben Clark file, Pension Files.

39. Elisha McGinnis file, Pension Files.

40. Nancy Kimball's denied widow's claim was eventually combined with McGinnis's approved pension file. Nancy Kimball, widow's pension claim, to Pension Office, June 16, 1880, Elisha McGinnis file, Pension Files.

41. Manuscript Census returns, U.S. Census, 1860, Population and Manufacturing Schedules, Madison County, Ark.

42. Nancy Fox, deposition, June 23, 1885, Elisha McGinnis file, Pension Files.

43. Reuben Clark does not appear in Arkansas Confederate service records, but he mentioned his prior Confederate service in his pension file. McGinnis's Confederate service record is brief: a one-year commitment that began on November 22, 1861. His departure from Confederate service and subsequent enlistment in the Union army is related in his pension file. Elihu [sic] McGinnis, private, Company G, 17th (Griffith's) Arkansas Infantry, Civil War Service Records; Elisha McGinnis deposition, Elisha McGinnis file, Pension Files; Reuben Clark, private, Company C, First Arkansas Cavalry, Civil War Service Records; Elisha McGinnis, private, Company L, First Arkansas Cavalry, Civil War Service Records.

44. Amanda Malvina Fitzallen McClellan Braly Family Papers, 1841–1920, Special Collections, University of Arkansas Libraries, Fayetteville; Henry Addison Sawyers, private, Company L, First Arkansas Cavalry, Civil War Service Records; Jeptha Jefferson Sawyers, private, Company A, First Arkansas Infantry, Civil War Service Records.

45. Amanda Braly to William Carrick Braly, October 1862, Braly Family Papers.

46. Braly to Braly, November 15, 1862, ibid.

47. Braly to Braly, June 8, 1863, ibid.

48. Braly to Braly, August 16, 1863, ibid.

49. Braly to Braly, August 20, 1864, ibid.

50. Braly to Braly, November 21, 1864, ibid.

51. The Braly Family Papers indicate that Carrick returned to northwest Arkansas after the war, rebuilt his mother's house, and took up the life of a country gentleman. He was named a trustee of Cane Hill College in 1873 and was elected to the state legislature later in the 1870s, going on record as a critic of the high level of public debt left over from "carpetbag rule." *Fayetteville Democrat*, December 28, 1920, and August 12, 1876.

52. Manuscript Census returns, U.S. Census, 1860, Population and Manufacturing Schedules, Washington County, Ark.

53. Henry Addison Sawyers, private, Company L, First Arkansas Cavalry, Civil War Service Records.

54. J. J. Sawyers to Lucinda Sawyers, June 10, 1864, and Mother's Pension Certificate no. 245021, both in Lucinda Sawyers file, Pension Files.

55. Jeptha Jefferson Sawyers, private, Company A, First Arkansas Infantry, Civil War Service Records.

56. W. J. Lemke, ed., "The Mecklin Letters Written in 1863–64 at Mt. Comfort, by Robert W. Mecklin, the Founder of the Ozark Institute," *Washington County Historical Society Bulletin* 10 (1955): 10.

57. Ibid., 7, 12.

58. Ibid., 41–42.

59. Ibid., 7.

Freda Hogan
(1892–1988)

A Socialist Woman in Huntington, Arkansas
MICHAEL PIERCE

Huntington, Arkansas, a small coal-mining town in the Ouachita Mountains near the Oklahoma border in southern Sebastian County, produced four of the nation's most prominent Socialist women in the first decades of the twentieth century. There was Mabel Hudson, who left Huntington to work at the Socialist Party of America (SPA) headquarters in Chicago, where she held a variety of posts, including the party's top position—executive secretary—for a brief time in the late 1920s.[1] Ida Hayman Callery moved from Huntington to study the law, and she became an attorney for the Socialist-led United Mine Workers of America (UMWA) District 14 in southeast Kansas before her untimely death in 1917.[2] Bertha Hale Brown White, the former wife of a Huntington coal miner, in 1924 was the first woman to head a national political party's presidential campaign when she served as the executive secretary of the SPA.[3] Later, White—then married to public power advocate Judson King—became an instrumental behind-the-scenes figure in the movement that brought electricity to rural residents all over the nation, including much of Arkansas, in the 1930s and 1940s.[4] Freda Hogan cut her journalistic teeth at her father's Socialist newspaper in Huntington before moving to Oklahoma City, where she kept that state's Socialists together, helped put out the influential *American Guardian*, worked with UMWA Socialists as they battled the leadership of John L. Lewis, and even received serious consideration for the SPA's presidential nomination in 1928.[5]

In this chapter, I use the biography of Freda Hogan, the only one of these women to leave an extensive written record of her Socialist roots in Arkansas, to argue that it was not mere coincidence or happenstance that these four women came from an Arkansas coal-mining town with a population that never exceeded 1,700.⁶ Mining towns have traditionally provided expanded opportunities for women to demand economic and civil rights and to engage in radical political activity. The nature of mining (teams of men working underground in a dangerous environment with few prospects for social mobility) and the geography of mining towns (relatively isolated, compact communities with populations overwhelmingly working class) made these communities places with well-defined class dynamics and worker solidarity. Distinctions between one's family and those of other workers often blurred, and women, who made up a large percentage of the people above ground on workdays, expanded their traditional roles as defenders of home and family to include the entire class. Freda Hogan explained the activism of women in mining towns by noting, "No woman has ever felt the keenness of the class struggle more, or knows better that there is a class struggle, than does the miner's wife."⁷

Huntington was home to the state's Socialist Party headquarters and its longtime leader, Dan Hogan, who also practiced law and published the *Huntington Herald*. Hogan served as something of a mentor to each of these women. As Hogan's daughter, Freda Hogan Ameringer, later recalled, "Our home and office were modest but their influence extended far beyond that little mining town.... It was there Ida Hayman Callery was encouraged to read law. Mabel Hudson began her work and interest in the Socialist Party in Papa's office, going from there to work in the National Socialist Party office as secretary to J. Mahlon Barnes.... Bertha [Hale] Brown, a sister, also began work in Papa's office." Dan Hogan's support was crucial for the careers of these women. He provided an avocation, initiated them into Socialist culture, and connected them to the Socialist world outside of Huntington.⁸

But the accomplishments of these women cannot be understood simply by their relationships to Huntington and Hogan. The women themselves participated in a larger network of Socialist women that connected them to activists across the nation and the globe. This community provided role models, nurtured friendships, opened opportunities beyond the borders of Arkansas, and encouraged women's participation in the public sphere. Perhaps most important, this network formed the core of a distinctively female Socialist culture that sustained the women in their political work, providing a cohesive community, a set of values, a worldview, and a mission that ultimately promoted greater activism. These women were so devoted to the work of the party that Freda Hogan Ameringer later characterized their commitment to the movement as "more like a religion than a political faith."⁹

The zeal with which women took to the Socialist cause was crucial to the success the SPA had in Arkansas and the nation. As evidenced by Bertha Hale

Brown White and Mable Hudson Barnes's service as the party's executive secretary and the consideration that Freda Hogan received in 1928 for the party's presidential nomination, women exercised more power, commanded more respect, and found greater opportunity in the SPA than they did in either the Democratic Party or the Republican Party. Though the SPA never truly lived up to its egalitarian ideas, it offered unprecedented opportunities for Arkansas women to participate in partisan politics in the first decades of the twentieth century. Women rallied the faithful on the lecture circuit, mobilized in the wake of women's suffrage, and performed the unheralded behind-the-scenes tasks that were necessary for the functioning of the party.

Freda Hogan came into the world on November 17, 1892, probably in Mansfield, a mining town a few miles from Huntington. Her mother, the former Charlotte "Lottie" Yowell, had met Dan Hogan in the Scott County town of Waldron, where he was reading law and she was living with a sister while attending school. In many ways, it was an odd match—a daughter of one of western Arkansas's most prominent families and the son of Irish immigrants—but the marriage lasted until his death in 1935. The couple moved to Mansfield, where at the time of Freda's birth Dan Hogan was practicing law and publishing the *Alliance Patriot*, a small paper affiliated with the Farmers' Alliance and the People's Party. For much of Freda Hogan's early life, Lottie Hogan's health problems limited her ability to perform many of the domestic functions, and Dan and Freda conspired to relieve her of many burdens, especially after she gave birth to three more children—Hazel in 1900, Alice in 1904, and Daniel Jr. in 1908. Although Lottie's health improved in the years before World War I, Freda continued to take up much of the slack by helping her father with his law practice, publishing efforts, and work for the Socialist Party.[10] This closeness led Freda to idolize her father, and she devoted herself to becoming an activist and community leader like him. Recalling her father's influence on her life, she declared: "His faith, his hopes, his problems, and his friends—as well as his enemies—became mine. . . . I wanted to be as Papa wanted me to be, to be worthy of him, to measure up to his fine ideals."[11]

It is unclear when the family moved the few miles from Mansfield to Huntington, but in the first years of the twentieth century Dan Hogan dedicated himself to building the Socialist Party of Arkansas, which was formally established in 1903. He worked closely with several other men, including Thomas Hagerty, a Van Buren, Arkansas, priest who played a central role in the founding of the Industrial Workers of the World, and Wells LeFevre, who went on to establish the Working Class Union. Arkansas Socialists, like those in nearby Oklahoma and Kansas, were never orthodox party members. Instead they blended populist ideas about the dangers of concentrated wealth and religious revivalism with the teachings of Karl Marx to produce what one historian called "grass-roots Socialism." The Socialist Party's founding platform included calls for the collective ownership of the means of production; reduction of work hours; an old-age pension; free, compulsory, and nonsectarian public education; direct legislation; public health insurance; and "equal political, civil, and religious rights [for] all men and women." But Freda Hogan Ameringer later explained the Arkansas Socialist Party's appeal more simply: the members, who were mostly trade unionists and middling farmers, were "people who were moved by the great ideal that they would have a cooperative commonwealth."[12]

The Hogans always lived on the edge of poverty. Income from party activism, a radical small-town newspaper, and legal work for unions was never enough to meet the family's needs and was always subject to the vagaries of the political environment. When Freda Hogan was six years old, her father helped in the UMWA's unsuccessful attempt to organize the local mines and lost his newspaper and small printing plant as a result. It wasn't until 1907—after the UMWA's successful organizing of the area's mines had brought in steady legal work and Dan Hogan had secured another printing plant—that the family was able to purchase its first home, a rather simple four-room frame house with two bedrooms added on later. The mortgage was just $10 a month, later increasing with the additional bedrooms, but the family could still barely afford the payments. To make ends meet, Lottie Hogan (like most wives in Arkansas towns) kept a large garden, chickens, pigs, and a milk cow to provide the bulk of the family's sustenance.[13]

While he was building the party, Dan Hogan traveled throughout the state and region and often took Freda with him, introducing her to the world beyond Huntington and to activists with whom she would work throughout her career. After a meeting with Dan Hogan in Fort Smith, Eugene Debs wrote, "It was a great joy to me to see you and your fresh, sweet daughter and I shall always see you hand in hand, a beautiful picture, fine to look upon and full of inspiration." The pair became so inseparable that party activists began referring to them as "old Dan and little Freda."[14]

Traveling with her father exposed Freda Hogan to Socialist luminaries like Eugene Debs, and prominent Socialists—including the party's most articulate and inspiring women—came to Huntington, where they gave public speeches, met with miners, interacted with townspeople, and stayed at the Hogan home. Freda Hogan Ameringer remembered Mary "Mother" Jones coming to visit. Although Jones "shocked certain elements in the town with her profanity," the people of Huntington "seemed to glory in the spirit of the frail-looking woman."

May Wood Simons, widely considered the party's foremost female intellectual, made a quite different impression in Huntington: "Her appearance, smartly tailored suit, in perfect taste, beautifully correct English, scholarly bearing, a speech showing perfect knowledge of her subject and well organized in every detail were all but stunning." Freda Hogan first met Kate Richards O'Hare, whom she considered to be "at the very top among Socialist women—able, well-informed speaker, fearless crusader and aggressive for standing up for her opinions in Socialist party organizations," when she visited Huntington.[15] These women—and other visitors like Lena Morrow Lewis, Anna Maley, and Caroline Lowe—modeled the type of life that Freda Hogan aspired to, provided her with a network of contacts, and introduced her to a wider female Socialist culture.[16]

Although traveling the country preaching the gospel of Socialism did not conform to early twentieth-century female ideals, women on the Socialist lecture circuit did not directly challenge traditional gender roles when speaking in Arkansas. Quite the contrary, they often reinforced the idea that women's primary responsibilities were domestic, and they usually conformed to conventional notions of femininity.[17] Emma Langdon, an organizer for the radical International Union of Mine, Mill, and Smelter Workers, told a Sebastian County audience, "If the government of the country were turned over to me to manage, my first act would be to send the women and the children home, where they should be—out of the stores and factories and away from the grind of industry." Likewise, Kate Richards O'Hare, who traveled the nation and left the care of her children to others, convinced one Arkansas newspaper that she was "an ardent lover of the home life." Even activists like Mary Jones, whose language and rough manner departed from the feminine ideal, took nicknames like "Mother," which underscored their role as protectors of the family. These women tended to see gender discrimination as arising from class exploitation and focused their attention on economic issues. To do otherwise would be akin to treating a disease's symptoms rather than its underlying cause.[18]

Like these others, Freda Hogan drew on the traditional idea of the woman as protector of home and family to claim a right to speak in the public sphere. She insisted that the capitalist system exploited all workers but especially women and children in its never-ending search for cheaper and cheaper labor. This exploitation threatened the very fabric of the nation's families because it forced "an unthinkable number" of women "to enter the scarlet ranks" and compelled children to leave the protection of home and school for mills, mines, shops, and factories. The only way to protect the home and family, Freda concluded, was to eliminate the capitalist system and replace it with the collective ownership of the means of production.[19]

Although she attended the public school in Huntington, which like most small-town Arkansas schools of the era only went through the eighth grade, Freda Hogan Ameringer never mentioned her formal education in her reminiscences. But she described a home environment in which learning was an integral part of life. The family dining table was the site of much of her education. Not only did the family members take turns reading aloud in the evenings, but frequent guests transformed the dining room into something of a debating hall, where discussions of political events, history, poetry, and literature could last for hours. The family's collection of books—usually housed at Dan Hogan's law office—was an asset not only to Freda but to the entire community. Freda Hogan Ameringer remembered: "Many a young miner boy or girl owes his first taste for good reading to that little frame office. For there was no public library in Huntington and most folks considered books and magazines as luxuries. How I remember our battered volumes of Shakespeare, Dickens, and other classics which made the rounds."[20]

Freda Hogan's life as an activist began in 1907, when she was just fourteen. That year, a member of the Arkansas General Assembly representing Monroe County, far from the coalfields, proposed a bill to repeal the state's mine-run law, which required that mine operators pay miners for all of the marketable coal that they dug. Freda heard about the bill and began going door to door asking residents to sign a petition demanding that the legislature leave the law alone. Local UMWA officials heard about her efforts and invited her to travel to Little Rock to lobby on the miners' behalf. She later recalled, "I got a pretty good hearing, and I remember telling them that counting idle days, when mines did not work, miners made only $1.25 a day." Legislators must have been impressed with the arguments of Hogan and others, because the bill failed to make it out of committee.[21]

As Freda became a teenager, her father began devoting more time to the Socialist Party, running for office on the state slate and serving on several national committees. His first run for governor was in 1906, when he received just 2,165 votes. But as the party grew, so did the number of votes he received. Dan Hogan garnered 9,196 votes (6.1 percent) in 1910 and 10,798 (8 percent) four years later. In 1908, he began representing Arkansas on the party's national council, and four years later he joined the SPA's executive committee. The high point of Hogan's prominence in the SPA came in 1912, when the party's left wing supported him for the vice presidential nomination that ultimately went to former Milwaukee mayor Emil Seidel.[22]

By her sixteenth birthday, Freda Hogan had ceased accompanying her father as he was spending more time campaigning and traveling to party functions. Instead, Freda became the family's main breadwinner, writing for the *Huntington Herald*, editing the paper, and running the printing business during her father's long absences. In fact, while Dan Hogan was conducting his 1910 gubernatorial campaign, seventeen-year-old Freda formally took charge of the *Herald*. The younger Hogan's stewardship of the paper so impressed editors throughout the region that one of them exclaimed, "That girl is a genius, a printer, a writer, and takes after her father, even to being Irish."[23]

Around this time, Freda Hogan also began taking advantage of her contacts with Socialist women to launch her journalist career outside of Huntington. Most of her early writing concerned traditional women's issues—family life, marriage, child labor, and the experiences of young women on their own—and was in the didactic style common to the era. Some of the work was fictionalized, like "Mary and John—Up to Date," an account of an overworked and beleaguered young married couple who are transformed into a contented and happy pair through work for the party. In other pieces, Hogan wrote about people in Huntington. "One Boy I Know—and His Ma" tells of a local young boy who was forced by poverty to leave school to join his father in the mines. Freda Hogan transformed his life by giving him some SPA literature. Not only was he converted to Socialism, but he also converted his mother, whose natural concerns about children and the home allowed her to see the benefits of a cooperative commonwealth. The son and mother, though, had no luck converting the father, whom Hogan presented as too stuck in the old ways of doing things to see the benefits of the collective ownership of the mines. Freda Hogan's point was that Socialism's hopes were tied to women and young men rather than to older men.[24]

The 1911 arrival of Ida Callery in Huntington transformed Freda Hogan's life. Unlike Mabel Hudson and Bertha Hale Brown, who became Socialists while living in Huntington, Callery arrived a devoted Socialist. Dan Hogan had convinced her to move to Huntington from nearby Bonanza, another Sebastian County mining town where she taught school, to serve as the secretary of the state's Socialist Party. She was married to Phillip Callery, who lived in Schenectady, New York, where he served as secretary to the Socialist mayor. Freda Hogan Ameringer later recalled, "For me a large gap in my life was filled by Ida. I had become so engrossed with my work and the Socialist cause, I no longer had ties to my former school friends and other Socialist women with whom I had contacts were much older. Ida and I became the best of friends, sharing our dreams and problems." Callery even helped Hogan get to the 1912 Socialist convention in Indianapolis, where she watched her father battle for the vice presidential nomination and where she first met her future husband,

Oscar Ameringer, a nationally prominent journalist who had earned a reputation as the "Mark Twain of the Socialists." For Freda Hogan and most female Socialists, distinctions between one's personal life and one's life as an activist were nonexistent.[25]

Ida Callery filled a void in Freda Hogan's life, and Arkansas Socialists credited Callery with the enormous growth of the party experienced in the years before World War I. An Arkansan described Callery's efforts in the *New York Call*: "She is small and wiry and can pound the typewriter all day and into the night with nervous prostration. She has literally reached out into the mountains and valleys and led the people in to organizing and maintaining locals. As a result there are now locals in the state reaching into nearly every county."[26] When Ida Callery left Huntington in 1914 to study law, Freda Hogan took over her duties as party secretary, determined to be every bit as successful. Callery had set a high standard, and Hogan thought that failing to meet that standard would not only let down the party but also betray her friendship with Callery. Under Hogan's stewardship, the party continued to flourish, at least until the crackdown on Socialists that came with World War I.[27]

By 1912, one publication had identified Freda Hogan as "among [the] most active women in Arkansas in furthering [suffragist] propaganda." In addition to working on suffrage issues in Socialist circles, Hogan served as the secretary of the women's suffrage organization in southern Sebastian County. But unlike some middle-class suffragists, who talked in a language of individual rights, Hogan and Arkansas's Socialist women saw the vote as a means to an end—elimination of the economic exploitation of industrial and agrarian workers. Arkansas's Socialist suffragists insisted: "Women, being slaves to men, men slaves to their employers and employers slaves to the system, thereby makes the female half of the race slaves three times over." Hogan explained that women were "exploited [by their employers] more ruthlessly than men. Always they work for lower wages and under poorer conditions." The expansion of the franchise to women, Hogan insisted, promised to end these three types of slavery. The vote would help make women equal to men. But more important, women—whose maternal instincts make them the natural enemy of economic exploitation—would use the franchise to challenge the economic system from which all forms of exploitation sprang. For Freda Hogan, the fight for women's suffrage became the main front in the larger battle for a more just economic system.[28]

Freda Hogan's work on suffrage and women's issues extended beyond Arkansas. In 1914, she joined the SPA's Woman's National Committee (WNC). Formed in the middle of the twentieth century's first decade, the WNC initially existed, in the words of historian Mari Jo Buhle, as an "educational service." It produced literature designed to attract sympathizers and to educate the converted in "the materialist conception of history as related to women's status." The WNC flourished under the leadership of Anna Maley and Caroline Lowe, two women whom Freda Hogan had come to know and respect from their frequent trips to Huntington and meetings on the Socialist lecture circuit in Arkansas.[29] Both Maley and Lowe served as mentors to Hogan, who was a generation younger, and they probably helped her secure a place on the committee.[30]

During Hogan's tenure, the WNC provoked a messy debate within the party over approaches to women's issues. Hogan and three other committee members advocated that the WNC move beyond its educational work and launch an aggressive campaign to organize women in anticipation of the extension of the vote. The WNC called for special organizers and the publication of a newspaper dedicated to women's issues. If the party failed to act, the committee warned, the two major parties would organize women and use their votes to strengthen capitalists' grip over the nation's political system. But many in the party—including some of its most prominent women—objected to the program and called for the elimination of the WNC altogether. For them, discrimination against women arose out of class exploitation, and the campaign for women's suffrage and the mobilization of women were so integral to the party's existence that they should not be segregated as women's work. The debate was not resolved to anyone's liking; the WNC was not eliminated, but it also did not launch its proposed campaign.[31]

Most of Freda Hogan's early activism and journalism focused on what had traditionally been seen as women's issues, but that changed in 1914 when she found herself at the center of a dispute between local members of the United Mine Workers and the Bache-Denman Coal Company. In April of that year, Bache-Denman's principal owner, Franklin Bache, abrogated the company's contract with the union and announced that its area mines would operate on a nonunion basis. The company recruited scab miners from Tennessee, expelled some union miners from company housing, and brought in heavily armed guards from the notorious Burns Detective Agency. When the citizens of southern Sebastian County held a rally to protest these moves, Freda Hogan was the featured speaker. She told the crowd of two thousand that they should not allow the company's actions to stand. After her speech, Hartford's Socialist town constable and a brass band led the crowd to one of the company's mines in an attempt to convince the nonunion miners and the guards to leave the area. But after one of the guards struck a boy with the butt of a gun, a huge melee ensued with the crowd forcing nonunion members to take flight and guards to surrender their weapons. The crowd then flooded the mine and hung from the tipple an American flag and a banner declaring, "This Is Union Man's Country." For the next three months, an armed struggle raged with the miners, citizens, local law enforcement officials, and the UMWA on one side and, on the other, Bache-Denman's hired thugs and U.S. marshals trying to enforce a federal labor injunction.[32]

Freda Hogan chronicled each twist and turn of the confrontation in Socialist and labor periodicals like the *International Socialist Review*, *Railway Carmen's Journal*, *New England Socialist*, and *Woodrow's Monthly*. The story she told was of a greedy and unscrupulous out-of-state mine owner disrupting life in the coalfields of Sebastian County and a community united in defense of UMWA members. Not only did Franklin Bache import armed guards who "insulted the wives and daughters of miners, [and] shot into their homes," but he also manipulated federal bankruptcy laws to have himself appointed as the receiver of his own indebted property. He then used his authority as receiver to secure a federal injunction against any interference with company property and U.S. marshals to enforce the injunction. After miners and local law enforcement officers routed Bache's private army in a series of gunfights, Bache convinced President Woodrow Wilson to send federal troops to protect his mines and federal prosecutors to arrest ten UMWA officials, who had sent miners weapons to defend their homes. More than anyone else Freda Hogan made the arrest and subsequent imprisonment of the UMWA officials a cause célèbre in Socialist and labor circles.[33]

As the Bache-Denman conflict receded from the headlines in 1915, when the UMWA officials were released from their imprisonment, Hogan tried to stop the United States from entering the world war that had begun in Europe in the late summer of 1914. Like other SPA members, she blamed those "reaping a harvest of dollars from the wholesale murder in Europe" for the increasing pressure on the United States to enter alongside England and France. She explained that "capitalists in the manufacture and shipment of munitions to the belligerents" had made a mockery of U.S. claims of neutrality and had ended up costing American lives on the high seas. Munitions makers—anxious to see more orders—had then used this loss of life to justify U.S. entry. These capitalists, Freda Hogan concluded, "desire that we make a breastwork of our bodies that this manufacturing may go on; that others of our class stand ready to go to war that still larger orders and profits may be theirs."[34]

Dan Hogan agreed with his daughter's assessment of the causes of U.S. involvement in the war. After U.S. entry in April 1917, he served on the SPA's Committee on War and Militarism and signed the committee's July 1917 resolution condemning the war as "a crime against the people of the United States." During the committee's debates, Dan Hogan proposed that the SPA demand that the federal government "conscript" income over $5,000 to pay for the war effort, declaring, "The capitalists involve us in war and they ought to be compelled to pay for it." The real purpose of such a tax, though, was not to increase government revenue but to remove what the Socialists saw as the real cause of the war: profits. Without the prospects of profit, Dan Hogan thought, those who clamored loudest for the United States to enter would lose interest in sustaining the conflict.[35]

The onset of the war disrupted the lives of the Hogans and like-minded Socialists. The SPA's opposition to the war and the government's implementation of the draft provoked a harsh response from the Wilson administration and Congress. Passage of the Espionage Act (1917) and Sedition Act (1918) essentially made it a crime to speak out against the war or the draft, and Freda Hogan feared that her father would be sent to prison. Although Dan Hogan avoided prosecution, some of the Hogans' friends were not so lucky. For example, a federal court sent Kate Richards O'Hare to prison for violating the Espionage Act. The court determined that she had willingly obstructed military enlistment, citing a speech in which she denounced the war, warned that soldiers would become fertilizer on the fields of France, and called mothers who proudly sent their sons off to war "brood sows." In Oklahoma's Canadian River valley, federal authorities arrested some four hundred members of the Working Class Union—founded by the Hogans' friend and former Huntington resident Wells LeFevre—for resisting the draft. Not even the nation's most prominent Socialist was spared. A federal judge sentenced Eugene Debs to twenty years in a federal penitentiary for declaring that in all wars the working class fights to benefit the elite.[36]

Soon after U.S. entry into the war, the family's financial straits and health problems forced Freda Hogan to leave Huntington. Oscar Ameringer, whom she married in 1930, later explained: "What with hard work, close confinement in a stuffy print shop, and worry about paper and ink bills, Freda got herself down to 96 pounds. The doctors pronounced her condition as incipient T.B. [tuberculosis], and urged her to seek health and livelihood in God's fresh air." Ameringer offered Freda a job raising capital for the *Oklahoma Leader*, a Socialist daily newspaper he was planning that would be modeled after and subsidized by Victor Berger's highly successful *Milwaukee Leader*. Not only did the job allow Freda Hogan to enjoy "God's fresh air," but the commissions she made on the sale of shares helped her family through some rough times back in Huntington. Ameringer saw his enlistment of Freda as the first step toward convincing the entire Hogan family to "leave the God-forsaken state of Arkansas and come to Oklahoma" to run the paper. Moving to a bigger city and a paper with greater resources promised the family not only a larger stage for its political work but also the type of economic security that it could never have in Huntington.[37]

Traveling around Oklahoma in a beat-up Model T, Freda Hogan and Oscar Ameringer had little trouble raising the necessary funds, but the federal government's harassment of Milwaukee Socialists interrupted the start of the paper. Federal authorities charged Victor Berger, who had been the first Socialist to serve in the U.S. House of Representatives, with violating the Espionage Act, citing antiwar editorials in the *Milwaukee Leader*. The authorities also revoked the paper's second-class postage permit and prevented the paper and Berger's local Socialist organization from receiving mail. Oscar Ameringer rushed to Wisconsin to mobilize support for Berger's fight, and Freda Hogan soon followed. Although she remembered being "lonely and a bit homesick" while in Milwaukee, Hogan kept busy collecting funds for the *Leader*, campaigning for women's suffrage, and, most important, helping the Socialists get around the postal service's sanctions. Ameringer later explained with his usual sarcasm: "No one would suspect that slip of an Arkansas girl—with the non-German name of Hogan—of trying to stop the World War. We installed her near one of the main branches of the Milwaukee post office, where she carried on her subversive activity as our underground depository of whatever mail our friends among the post employees could snitch and deliver after working hours." Although Ameringer, Hogan, and Milwaukee's Socialists could not stop the prosecution of Berger, they won in the court of public opinion. Milwaukee voters sent Berger back to Congress as he was appealing his conviction.[38]

Even though the war had brought women's suffrage, Freda Hogan could see little good coming from the conflict—just a "world of heartbreaking pain and sorrow." Not only had it been fought to advance the interests of munition makers and bankers, but also authorities had prosecuted those whom she held in the highest esteem. Kate Richards O'Hare sat in a Missouri prison, Eugene Debs was in the Atlanta penitentiary, and Victor Berger was appealing his conviction and twenty-year prison sentence. The movement that she and her father had worked so hard to build was in shambles. She confessed that the "war was too much [even] without the incarceration of our comrades. When I think about it all, it would be easy to lose my socialist faith."[39] Of course, Freda Hogan did not lose her socialist faith.

But Hogan did do something that Bertha Hale Brown, Mabel Hudson, Ida Callery, and countless other ambitious, politically active women had already done: she left Arkansas in hope of a brighter future. Freda and the whole Hogan family moved to Oklahoma City in late 1919 or early 1920 to start the *Oklahoma Leader*. While living in Oklahoma, Freda Hogan finally moved out of her father's shadow. She teamed up with Oscar Ameringer and UMWA Socialists to fight against John L. Lewis's corrupt leadership, was considered for the SPA's presidential nomination in 1928, helped produce the influential *American Guardian* and other political newspapers, and remained a vital part of Oklahoma City's left into the 1980s. Hogan's activities in Oklahoma prompted the great jurist Alfred P. Murrah to call her "the finest person I ever knew."[40]

The departure of Freda Hogan and her family for Oklahoma City coincided with the end of the Socialist Party's heyday in Arkansas. The reasons for the party's decline are many, but the Wilson administration's wartime persecution of Socialists and the postwar "red scare," which labeled party members as subversive, rank among the most important. The party limped through the 1920s, led by a cadre of activists at Commonwealth College in Polk County, some thirty miles south of Huntington, and members of the UMWA, but it never again attracted the followers in Arkansas and much of the rest of the region that it had before the war.

The Socialist Party's collapse in 1920s Arkansas did not mean the end of its ideas. Many of the items that the Socialist Party placed on the political agenda in the state—direct legislation, wage and hour regulation for women, and women's suffrage—were enacted during the party's heyday. Other party planks—old-age pensions, public power, abolition of child labor, regulation of employee hours, and government health insurance—were taken up by New Dealers in the 1930s or became part of Lyndon Johnson's Great Society program in the 1960s. Though the nation never became the cooperative commonwealth that young Freda Hogan hoped for, important pieces of the Socialist platform have eased the lives of many Arkansans, making the state a better place to live and work.

The collapse of the Socialist Party did, however, curtail the partisan political activities of Arkansas women. The party had offered women unprecedented opportunities in the political and public sphere—not as clubwomen or auxiliary members or tokens or widows of elected officials but as full-fledged members and leaders—and its distinct female culture had nurtured and sustained the women as they entered the political sphere. Bertha Hale Brown White and Mabel Hudson Barnes availed themselves of these opportunities, and each of them ascended from Huntington to the SPA's top post. Likewise, the Socialist Party contemplated nominating Freda Hogan for president in 1928. The passing of the party and its female culture closed doors for politically active women that would not be opened again until the 1970s or 1980s. Freda Hogan died on October 4, 1988.

NOTES

1. David A. Shannon, *Socialist Party of America: A History* (1955; repr., Chicago, Ill.: Quadrangle, 1967), 202; fragment of unidentified newspaper clipping, April 14, 1912, box 3, folder 1, Oscar and Freda Ameringer Papers, Oklahoma Historical Society, Oklahoma City (hereafter Ameringer Papers).

2. Biographical sketch, Phil and Ida Hayman Callery Collection, Pittsburg (Kans.) State University, http://library.pittstate.edu/spcoll/ndxcallerys.html (accessed August 9, 2010); Eugene V. Debs, "Sad Death of Ida Callery," *Social Revolution* (May 1917).

3. "Bertha Hale White," in *American Labor Who's Who*, ed. Solon DeLeon with Irma C. Hayssen and Grace Poole (New York: Hanford, 1925), 248; manuscript Census returns, U.S. Census, 1910, Population Schedules, Diamond Township, Sebastian County, Ark.; Freda Hogan Ameringer's Reminiscences, box 3, folder 13, Ameringer Papers, reprinted in Michael Pierce, "Great Women All, Serving a Glorious Cause: Freda Hogan Ameringer's Reminiscences of Socialism in Arkansas," *Arkansas Historical Quarterly* 69 (Winter 2010): 294–324; Nick Salvatore, *Eugene V. Debs: Citizen and Socialist* (Urbana: University of Illinois Press, 1982), 338.

4. Bertha Hale Brown White King's activism on behalf of public power can be traced through the Clyde Ellis diary, box 1, folder 8, Clyde Taylor Ellis Papers, Special Collections, University of Arkansas Libraries, Fayetteville; and the Judson King Papers, Library of Congress, Washington, D.C.

5. "Freda Hogan," in *American Labor Who's Who*, 107; Oscar Ameringer, *If You Don't Weaken: The Autobiography of Oscar Ameringer* (New York: Holt, 1940); Pierce, "Great Women All," 294–324; John Thompson, "She Never Weakened: The Heroism of Freda Ameringer," in *An Oklahoma I Had Never Seen Before: Alternative Views of Oklahoma History*, ed. Davis Joyce (Norman: Oklahoma University Press, 1994), 17; Vaughn Davis Bornet, *Labor Politics in a Democratic Republic: Moderation, Division, and Disruption in the Presidential Election of 1928* (Washington, D.C.: Spartan Books, 1964), 85.

6. Huntington's population waxed and waned with the health of the state's coal industry. It rose quickly with the coal boom that began at the end of the nineteenth century, reaching 913 in 1890 and 1,298 ten years later. The population peaked in 1910 with 1,700 inhabitants before declining after World War I, falling to fewer than 900 by 1930. *Thirteenth Census of the United States*, vol. 2: *Population* (Washington, D.C.: U.S. Government Printing Office, 1913), 106; *Sixteenth Census of the United States*, vol. 1: *Number of Inhabitants* (Washington, D.C.: U.S. Government Printing Office, 1942), 108.

7. *United Mine Workers' Journal*, February 8, 1912, cited in John Hinde, *When Coal Was King: Ladysmith and the Coal-Mining Industry on Vancouver Island* (Vancouver: University of British Columbia Press, 2011), 254 (quotation); Freda Hogan, "One Boy I Know—and His Ma," *Progressive Woman* (June–July 1913): 6; Bertha Hale Brown, "All's Right with the World," *Progressive Woman* (October 1912): 8.

8. Pierce, "Great Women All," 313–14. It is unclear if Freda Hogan Ameringer meant that Mabel Hudson and Bertha Hale Brown were biological sisters. I have been unable to locate either of them in the manuscript Census before 1910 because Hudson and Brown were the names of their first husbands.

9. Pierce, "Great Women All," 320.

10. Ibid., 310–11; Fred W. Allsopp, *History of the Arkansas Press for a Hundred Years and More* (Little Rock, Ark.: Parke-Harper, 1922), 440. The domestic arrangements of the Hogan family, including Lottie's infirmities, can be traced through the letters of Freda Hogan's grandmother: Alice I. Hogan to Fannie Carnall, January 27, 1895, February 21 and November 18, 1896, January 6 and April 30, 1897, all in box 1, folder 4, Emma Stevenson Black Collection, Special Collections, University of Arkansas Libraries, Fayetteville.

11. Pierce, "Great Women All," 310–11; Freda Hogan Ameringer, "Tribute to Dan Hogan by Daughter," *American Guardian* (Oklahoma City), January 25, 1935.

12. James R. Green, *Grass-Roots Socialism: Radical Movements in the Southwest, 1895–1943* (Baton Rouge: Louisiana State University Press, 1978), xi–xxi; G. Gregory Kiser, "The Socialist Party of Arkansas, 1900–1912," *Arkansas Historical Quarterly* 40 (Summer 1981): 119–53 (platform quotation, 130; cooperative commonwealth quotation, 152).

13. Pierce, "Great Women All," 312. The success of the UMWA not only brought a little economic stability to the Hogan family, it also transformed the lives of the local miners and their families.

Freda Hogan Ameringer recalled: "Before they had the Union, the miners all had these company houses which were very depressing to look at, just about as plain and unattractive as you could make them. Then as the Union was organized, these miners were able to build their own little cottages with vegetable gardens in the back yard and flowers in the front yard" (Green, *Grass-Roots Socialism*, 197n24).

14. E. V. Debs to Dan Hogan, July 10, 1908, box 3, folder 11, Ameringer Papers (first quotation); Fred W. Holt to Eugene V. Debs, February 23, 1915, in *Letters of Eugene V. Debs*, ed. Robert Constantine (Urbana: University of Illinois Press, 1990), 2:131–33 (second quotation); Brownie [probably Bertha Hale Brown] to Freda Hogan, March 31, 1915, box 3, folder 2, Ameringer Papers.

15. Pierce, "Great Women All," 315–19.

16. The contributions of these women to the SPA can be traced through Mari Jo Buhle, *Women and American Socialism, 1870–1920* (Urbana: University of Illinois Press, 1981), esp. 152–66.

17. When communicating with other Socialist women through the SPA's *Progressive Woman*, Arkansas women sometimes challenged the notion of separate spheres. See, for example, Jessamine S. Fishback, "The Legal and Actual Status of Women," *Progressive Woman* (October 1913): 8; Bertha Hale Brown, "Love and the Woman," *Progressive Woman* (November 1912): 7.

18. *Southwest American* (Fort Smith, Ark.), September 2, 1917; Peter H. Buckingham, *Rebel against Injustice: The Life of Frank P. O'Hare* (Columbia: University of Missouri Press, 1996), 52.

19. Freda Hogan, "Women Socialists of Arkansas," unidentified newspaper clipping, April 14, 1912, box 3, folder 1, Ameringer Papers.

20. Pierce, "Great Women All," 312–13; Ameringer, "Tribute to Dan Hogan by Daughter."

21. Pierce, "Great Women All," 313; *Journal of the Senate of Arkansas, 1907* (Hot Springs, Ark.: Sentinel-Record, 1907), 129–30, 185; *Arkansas Gazette*, March 3, 1907. On the mine-run law in Arkansas, see A. A. Steel, *Coal Mining in Arkansas* (Little Rock, Ark.: Democrat Printing and Lithographing, 1910–1912), 243–96.

22. Melvyn Dubofsky, *We Shall Be All: A History of the Industrial Workers of the World*, rev. ed. (New York: Quadrangle/New York Times Books, 1973), 83; Kiser, "Socialist Party of Arkansas," 119–53; Ira Kipnis, *The American Socialist Movement, 1897–1912* (1952; repr., Chicago: Haymarket, 2004), 406.

23. *Fort Gibson Post* (Okla.), March 3, 1910; Pierce, "Great Women All," 311; Allsopp, *History of the Arkansas Press*, 439.

24. Mary E. Marcy to Freda Hogan, May 7, 1913, box 3, folder 2, Ameringer Papers; Freda Hogan, "Mary and John—Up to Date," *Detroit Emancipator*, March 23, 1912, clipping in box 3, folder 1, Ameringer Papers; Hogan, "One Boy I Know," 6. Also see Hogan, "The Baby," and Hogan, "Inspiration in Lowly Places," both clippings in box 3, folder 1, Ameringer Papers; Hogan, "To the Girl," *Railway Carmen's Journal* 19 (June 1914): 354–55.

25. Pierce, "Great Women All," 322–23. Bertha Hale Brown and Mabel Hudson also married men who had devoted their lives to the party. Brown married Dan White, a Socialist leader in Massachusetts, and Hudson married J. Mahlon Barnes, who served as the SPA's executive secretary from 1905 until 1911 (ibid., 313–16).

26. Green, *Grass-Roots Socialism*, 233.

27. Pierce, "Great Women All," 322–23.

28. Ibid., 310; Freda Hogan to Mamey, February 9, 1917, box 3, folder 11, Ameringer Papers; unidentified clipping, April 14, 1912, box 3, folder 1, ibid. (first and second quotations); Hogan, "Women Socialists of Arkansas" (third quotation). Also see Hogan, "One Boy I Know," 6.

29. Buhle, *Women and American Socialism*, 152–60.

30. In her reminiscences, Freda Hogan Ameringer fondly recalled Maley's and Lowe's visits to Arkansas: "Anna had grown up and worked in the great Minnesota Socialist movement, which had

elected [Thomas] Van Lear mayor of Minneapolis. Her speaker's appeal, a fund of information, and delightful sense of humor, were irresistible. She attacked the subject with body blows and had our crowds laughing and cheering to the end. Caroline, on the other hand, was a gentle soul, one of the dearest most considerate women who ever lived. She appealed to the heart and the conscience of her hearers, showing them a Socialist world of love and beauty, with happiness and plenty for all. Crowds instantly loved and trusted her" (Pierce, "Great Women All," 318–19). For more on Maley's and Lowe's visits to Arkansas, see Anna Maley to Freda Hogan, February 12, 1917, box 3, folder 2, Ameringer Papers; advertisement in *Harrison Times* (Ark.), August 5, 1916.

31. Report of the Woman's National Committee, May 1915, box 3, folder 1; circular letter from Woman's National Committee to Socialist Editors, n.d., box 3, folder 1; Brownie to Freda Hogan, March 31, 1915, box 3, folder 2, all Ameringer Papers.

32. *United Mine Workers' Journal*, April 16, 1914; *Arkansas Gazette*, April 6, 1914; *Southwest American* (Fort Smith, Ark.), April 8, 1914; Samuel Sizer, "'This Is Union Man's Country': Sebastian County, 1914," *Arkansas Historical Quarterly* 27 (Winter 1968): 306–29; Stephen H. Norwood, *Strikebreaking and Intimidation: Mercenaries and Masculinity in Twentieth-Century America* (Chapel Hill: University of North Carolina Press, 2002), 154–63.

33. Freda Hogan, "Arkansas to Repeat Colorado Mine War? Trouble Is Brewing," *New England Socialist* (Fitchburg, Mass., and Boston), November 27, 1914, clipping in box 3, folder 1, Ameringer Papers; Hogan, "Fine and Jail Sentences for Revolting Coal Miners," *Woodrow's Monthly* 1 (March 1915): 24–26, ibid.; Hogan, "The Struggle in Arkansas," *Railway Carmen's Journal* 19 (December 1914): 766–68; Hogan, "The Miners of Arkansas," *International Socialist Review* 13 (January 1915): 438–40 (quotation).

34. Freda Hogan, "Only for Ourselves," clipping, n.d., box 3, folder 1, Ameringer Papers. The article was reprinted from the *Appeal to Reason* (Girard, Kans.).

35. J. Louis Engdahl, "Party Demands Capitalists Pay Expense of the Conflict," *Milwaukee Leader*, April 14, 1917, 1, 12.

36. Freda Hogan to Seigfried Ameringer, March 21, 1918, box 3, folder 9, Ameringer Papers; Bertha Hale White, "The Green Corn Rebellion in Oklahoma," *New Day* (Milwaukee), March 4, 1922, 68; Sally Miller, *From Prairie to Prison: The Life of Social Activist Kate Richards O'Hare* (Columbia: University of Missouri Press, 1993), 190–91; Green, *Grass-Roots Socialism*, 357–68; Ameringer, *If You Don't Weaken*, 347–56. The Socialists were not the only ones to oppose U.S. entry into the war. Antiwar sentiment was widespread throughout the rural South and Plains. Jeannette Keith, *Rich Man's War, Poor Man's Fight: Race, Class, and Power in the Rural South during World War I* (Chapel Hill: University of North Carolina Press, 2004); James F. Willis, "The Cleburne County Draft War," *Arkansas Historical Quarterly* 26 (Spring 1967): 24–39.

37. Ameringer, *If You Don't Weaken*, 313 (first quotation); Seigfried Ameringer to Freda Hogan, September 5, 1917; Oscar Ameringer to Dan Hogan, November 13, 1917 (second quotation); Seigfried Ameringer to Dan Hogan, October 19, 1917, all box 3, folder 8, Ameringer Papers.

38. Pierce, "Great Women All," 319–20 (first quotation); Ameringer, *If You Don't Weaken*, 325 (second quotation); Sally Miller, *Victor Berger and the Promise of Constructive Socialism* (Westport, Conn.: Greenwood, 1973), 191–219; Oscar Ameringer to Freda Hogan, June 13 and December 20, 1919, box 3, folder 3, Ameringer Papers.

39. Freda Hogan to Theodore Debs, December 26, 1919, box 3, folder 1, Ameringer Papers.

40. Ibid.; Thompson, "She Never Weakened"; Alfred P. Murrah to Freda Hogan, December 13, 1954, box 1, folder 7, Ameringer Papers.

Senator Hattie Caraway
(1878–1950)

A Southern Stealth Feminist and Enigmatic Liberal

SARAH WILKERSON FREEMAN

In December 1935, national newspapers noted that the voting record of Arkansas senator Hattie Caraway was "one of the most consistently liberal in Congress." Yet "Silent Hattie," as the press dubbed her, had not addressed the Senate during the four years since she took office in 1931.[1] This changed in 1936 when President Franklin Delano Roosevelt sought a second term. Caraway vociferously defended New Deal relief programs, insisting that if FDR's administration "had done nothing else in the three years it has functioned, it would have justified the change of administration, as well as the radical departure from what was the conventional—nay, the old and ultraconservative way of dealing with these problems."[2] Caraway swiped at FDR's conservative Republican and Democratic critics while she maintained her independence from the president, for she was more liberal than he in her support of women's rights, old-age pensions, wealth redistribution, and federal aid for public education. For the most part, Caraway supported Depression-era New Deal legislation and received the honor of seconding FDR's nomination at the 1936 Democratic National Convention. She earned this distinction through hard work and dedication. As she told a reporter in 1937, "Chivalry's all right in the parlor, but mighty dangerous when carried into politics."[3]

Hattie Caraway's life and political career enable historians and others to see more clearly how southern populist and progressive agendas, coming out of Tennessee and Arkansas, survived, evolved, and prepared the ground for liberal and feminist social and political reforms while simultaneously perpetuating racial injustice and white supremacy. During the New Deal, some populist or quasi-socialist principles found new traction in the form of liberal legislation and programs. Hattie Caraway was instrumental in that transformation. She saw her southern liberal reform opportunity in the rise of FDR, and she took it. But her thirteen years on a rough and chauvinistic political main stage, facing the greatest challenges of the twentieth century, have remained somewhat in shadow. While biographies by Diane Kincaid, Nancy Hendricks, and David Malone provide information regarding her life and career, little attention has focused on Caraway's southern liberalism and "stealth feminist" political style.[4] This examination also reveals critical information regarding the surprising close to Caraway's career when, in the 1944 Democratic primary, the young, even more liberal, and newly elected Congressman J. William Fulbright made an extraordinary decision to run for the Senate and defeated her.

Hattie Wyatt Caraway's personal background sheds some light on her development as a southern white liberal and feminist in the 1930s. She was born in February 1878 and grew up in Tennessee fifty miles west of Nashville, where multiple wild rivers created rich, isolated bottomlands. Her father, William C. Wyatt, was born in 1817, owned two enslaved women in 1860, and ran a farm and dry goods business. Wyatt was sixty and married to his third wife, Lucy Burch (twenty-five years his junior), when his fifteenth child, Hattie, named after Wyatt's first wife, was born. A sixteenth child, a son born a few years later, completed the family. Lucy Burch was born in 1842 in North Carolina and grew up near Centerville, Tennessee, where her father owned a grain mill.[5] As Wyatt aged, Lucy took in boarders, and she and the children shouldered increasing responsibilities for the farm and store. As a youngster, Hattie clerked at the dry goods store, a gathering place for local farmers, and absorbed cracker barrel political discourse. The Wyatts, white Dickson County folk of some means and property, depended on southern farm-based economies and the resources of an aging patriarch.

A bright child, Hattie briefly attended nearby Ebenezer College and at age fourteen enrolled with her older sister Mozella ("Mosie") at Dickson Normal School, where she met Thaddeus Caraway, a fellow student ten years her senior.[6] Their meeting at the white public coed college suggests some explanations for Hattie's progressive-to-liberal feminist ideology. During her formative years in the 1880s and 1890s, Tennessee had large, organized movements of women who fought hard and in the open to pass laws to restrict the sale of alcohol, raise the female age of consent above the age of ten, and establish public schools. Many of these women became leaders in national women's rights and suffrage movements. Tennessee produced a number of particularly "audacious white feminists" in this period and led the South in that regard.[7] Feminists and female teachers joined forces to fight for equal pay for equal work for educators in Shelby County, Tennessee, where women served as school superintendents beginning in 1884. That year, Tennessee legislators named Julia Doak to serve as the interim state superintendent of public instruction.[8] Pressure from east Tennessee feminists pushed open the doors of the University of Tennessee, which admitted women students in 1892.

The Woman's Christian Temperance Union, Farmers' Alliance, populists, and other reform organizations in the 1880s and 1890s prodded southern legislators to establish white coed public normal schools, which gave women options for self-support, especially as schoolteachers. In 1895, during Hattie's and Thad's last year at Dickson, a young local widow, Agnes Ann Work Shipp, ran for county superintendent of schools (with her toddler daughter in tow) and won.[9] After graduating, Hattie taught in Dickson County schools under Shipp, who had proven that women could overcome gender prejudice to achieve public office. Also, just north of the Wyatt farm was Ruskin Colony, a utopian socialist egalitarian cooperative established in 1894. Public talks at Ruskin regularly featured internationally known radicals, such as Charlotte Perkins Gilman, a socialist feminist author who visited in 1898. Hattie Caraway's 1930s politics took shape as a natural extension of her education and local feminist practices in 1890s Tennessee. In later years, Senator Hattie Caraway supported temperance and voted against FDR's 2.75 beer bill, but she did not come out of Dickson County, Tennessee, with a closed mind or a predilection for Bible thumping. Quite the contrary, she emerged with a ready wit and a fairly irreverent sense of humor, especially regarding men and power.[10]

Hattie's father died in 1901, and she and Thad married. She joined him in Mississippi County, Arkansas, where he was teaching while studying law. The couple bought and rented out rich Delta land near Big Lake, Arkansas, and Thad opened a law office in Jonesboro. By 1908, he had earned a reputation as a bombastic, sometimes shirt-ripping prosecuting attorney for the Second Judicial District. They had two sons, Paul and Forrest, the latter named for the founder of the Ku Klux Klan in Tennessee, Nathan Bedford Forrest.

Beginning in 1912, Thad was elected as a Democrat to the U.S. House of Representatives. He served four terms, which coincided with Woodrow Wilson's presidency, the resegregation of federal offices, World War I, passage of the federal income tax, Prohibition, and the women's suffrage amendment—all of which Thad supported. Hattie and the boys made occasional visits during congressional sessions to D.C., where a third son, Robert Easley, was born in 1915. In Jonesboro, Hattie belonged to the local women's, music, and bridge clubs but was not directly involved in the women's suffrage movement even though she worked hard in Thad's political campaigns.[11]

Arkansas, like Tennessee, had a strong and powerful network of women suffragists and feminists, such as Florence Cotnam. Like Hattie Caraway, Cotnam was educated in Tennessee in the 1880s, and her teachers in Monteagle were inspired feminist leaders who encouraged Cotnam to hone her oratorical skills.[12] She married, settled in Little Rock, and became a founder of the Arkansas Federation of Women's Clubs. Cotnam also emerged as an outspoken leader of the Arkansas Equal Suffrage Central Committee, affiliated with the National American Woman Suffrage Association (NAWSA), and joined the more militant National Woman's Party.[13] In 1913, NAWSA tapped Cotnam to serve as a national speaker, sending her to twenty-five states. Women suffragists scored their first victory in the South when Arkansas's legislature passed a bill in 1917 that allowed white women to vote in the primaries. Cotnam led a delegation of Arkansas women suffragists in December 1917 to the White House, where President Woodrow Wilson granted the women a unique private interview.[14]

According to NAWSA's 1918 *Handbook*, it was "a big year politically for the women of Arkansas.... A number of primaries have been held in the several counties and cities, and always the women's votes have been a big factor in deciding the election."[15] Governor Charles Brough and Thad Caraway publicly supported the women's suffrage cause, and several county governing bodies elected women as members. Little Rock's Pulaski County, where Cotnam was most active, elected six women to office. Cotnam also addressed the Tennessee legislature in February 1919 on behalf of that state's women's suffrage bill. The legislation passed, marking another critical inroad for women suffragists in the South. At NAWSA's 1919 national convention, Florence Cotnam led discussions about how women could improve election methods.[16] Recognizing her influence, male Democratic leaders named her as a delegate-at-large to the Democratic National Convention in June 1920, and Arkansas sent a contingent of women to serve as alternate delegates. Of the southern states, only Tennessee, Texas, Kentucky, and Arkansas sent women delegates.[17] Before the women's suffrage amendment passed in August, Cotnam had organized the Arkansas League of Women Voters and the Arkansas Democratic Women's Clubs. In Congress, Thaddeus Caraway stood apart from most southern Democrats as a stalwart advocate of white women's suffrage and an original supporter of the Equal Rights Amendment proposed by feminists in the National Woman's Party.[18]

Thad also distinguished himself in Congress as a virulent racist. He introduced legislation to arrest offenders of Washington, D.C.'s Jim Crow laws, to impose strict racial segregation in housing, and to outlaw interracial marriages.[19] In July 1916, he introduced a bill to prohibit men of the "colored races" from enlisting or reenlisting in the armed forces. One African American editorialist sarcastically dismissed Caraway as a "great(?)" "statesman(?)" who pandered to his white southern constituents. Thad Caraway's racist proposals were politically timely considering the recent release of the film *The Birth of a Nation* and the rise of the second Ku Klux Klan.[20] In August 1919, after thousands of African American men had fought in the First World War, Thad introduced a bill to prohibit the peacetime enlistment of black men and to bar them from enrolling in military academies (all three Caraway boys would attend West Point). The *Washington Bee* referred to Caraway as one of the southern Democrats' "cheap country jakes," but African American newspapers outside Washington, D.C., treated him as a serious threat.[21] After the murder of untold numbers of black people by white mobs in Phillips County, Arkansas, in the fall of 1919, Thad read into the *Congressional Record* a diatribe against the National Association for the Advancement of Colored People (NAACP) and castigated the black farmers who defended themselves during the massacre.[22]

In 1920, Thad Caraway threw his hat into the ring for a Senate seat and turned his barbed prosecutor's tongue on his Democratic primary opponent, incumbent senator William Kirby. Thad had been a strong supporter of Wilson, the war, the League of Nations, farm aid, and low tariffs.[23] Kirby had famously opposed Wilson's war policies. Arkansas women voted in that primary battle. While Hattie later recalled, "After equal suffrage in 1920, I just added voting to cooking and sewing and other household duties," her statement masked her political activities in 1920.[24] Hattie worked at her husband's headquarters during that vicious primary battle and helped propel her husband into the Senate. The family moved from Jonesboro to D.C., Paul and Forrest entered West Point, and Hattie Caraway's ride on the Washington merry-go-round began.

The 1920s were critical years in Hattie's political development as the Republicans settled in for a decade of political dominance. "Caustic Caraway" (the press's nickname for Thad) spearheaded unrelenting attacks against Republican president Warren G. Harding's administration that brought to light the Teapot Dome scandal and forced the U.S. attorney general to resign. Caraway's Senate office was ransacked, and the senator demanded a formal investigation. Senate testimony revealed that the Caraway family had been under surveillance in 1921 and 1922. Gaston Means, a special agent for the Bureau of Investigation and the Justice Department, had hired former senator Kirby's Little Rock secretary, Laura Jacobson, to dig up dirt on the Caraways in hopes of blackmailing, and presumably silencing, the senator. In light of this abuse of federal power, the head of the Bureau of Investigation resigned.[25]

Back in Arkansas, women as a political force continued to gain momentum.²⁶ In April 1922, Congressman H. M. Jacoway announced his intention to resign. The national press reported that Florence Cotnam, supported by women voters, was vying to fill the remainder of Jacoway's term and positioning herself to be the first Arkansas woman to run for Congress.²⁷ But Jacoway delayed his resignation. In June, newspapers reported that Cotnam remained a candidate for Jacoway's unexpired term once he vacated his office, but she would not be a candidate in the primary.²⁸ Rather than resigning, Jacoway simply decided not to run again. Cotnam refocused her energies on building the political strength of Arkansas women to challenge male dominance in the state's Democratic Party leadership. Her work bore fruit with the elections of Hattie Caraway.

As the wife of a U.S. senator in the 1920s, Hattie Caraway became more worldly and somewhat glamorous, as her photos show. In 1926, she and Thad traveled to Europe, and he was reelected. During the 1927 inaugural season, Hattie playfully complained to her son Paul that she was "worn to a frazzle" after a week of card parties, Senate luncheons, and formal dinners.²⁹ Her convivial personality earned her the presidency of the Arkansas State Society, a social organization of Arkansans in D.C. But she also retained a very down-to-earth, commonsense quality. In advising Paul, she asked him to give his friends her love but tell them "hands off. I want you to use your own mind as to what you will do."³⁰ By this time, Paul was twenty-four years old, Forrest was eighteen, and Bobby was thirteen. With the heavy demands on Thad's time, Hattie devoted a great deal of her attention to Bobby, perhaps trying to compensate for the boy's politically riven childhood with the special advantages his father's success could afford. In the summer of 1928, mother and son sailed to Casa Blanca.

Meanwhile, back in Arkansas, the Great Flood of 1927 had left thousands in the region homeless and destitute. President Calvin Coolidge, who did not intend to run in 1928, sent Commerce Secretary Herbert Hoover to survey the devastation and work out programs purportedly to assist white and black farmers, but they accomplished little. The agricultural economy had been suffering throughout the 1920s, and many counties in Arkansas had closed their white public schools or had begun charging tuition to attend. The South was suffering, but the Republican, northern-based federal administrations did little to address the systemic decline.

The bombastic 1928 Democratic Convention nominated New York governor Al Smith, an Irish American and a "wet," to run against the Republican "Great Humanitarian" Herbert Hoover for the presidency. Thad Caraway had warned that women voters would not support Smith because of the Prohibition issue, but when Democrats chose Arkansas's senior senator, Joe Robinson, as the vice presidential nominee to balance the ticket, Caraway, who almost always stood with Robinson, had to support Smith too. The 1928 campaign quickly took on an ugly cast as superpatriots claiming to be "100% Americans" trained their sights on Smith, an Irish Catholic. Republican strategists focused on the South. The anti-Catholic, anti-immigrant Ku Klux Klan recruited white "Hoovercrats," traditional southern Democrats, and leaders in the Woman's Christian Temperance Union. Thad Caraway presumably had the Arkansas Klan in his pocket, or vice versa, as the state's KKK chapters had been extremely active during 1921–1926, which were years of railroad strikes, oil booms, and Prohibition violations. But as a junior senator, Thad Caraway joined Joe Robinson in defending Smith against the KKK's hate-filled campaign of anti-Catholic bigotry. Nonetheless, the Republican "southern strategy" worked. The Democrats lost much of the South, and the Republicans retained their hold on the White House.[31]

On November 19, 1928, just days after reelection to a tenth consecutive term in Congress, Arkansas representative William Oldfield, the House Democratic whip and the Democratic National Committee chair, died unexpectedly. The Arkansas Democratic Central Committee at first asked Oldfield's widow, Pearl, to run in the special election to complete the remainder of her husband's term but also nominated her to fill the House seat to which William Oldfield had been elected before he died. In January 1929, Pearl Oldfield was elected and sworn into office, becoming the first southern woman to serve in the U.S. House of Representatives, a position she held during the crisis-ridden years of 1929–1931.[32]

In this period, Hattie Caraway lived a full life of family and social obligations, but she also exhibited an increasing interest in the work of the Senate and sat in on important treaty deliberations in January 1929. By this time, she had spent the last seventeen years as the wife of a U.S. congressman and senator, nine of those years in Washington, D.C. She felt the need for a haven from the rough, pretentious, and chilly capital, a place where she could be close but not consumed by politics. In February 1929, she moved her family into Riversdale, a historic mansion in Maryland.[33] The 1801 mansion had been built for a Flemish aristocrat and passed into the Calvert family, descendants of the fifth Lord Baltimore. Hattie began to restore the home and its spacious grounds, where she raised chickens. She bought a collie puppy for fourteen-year-old Bobby and a loud but affectionate Siamese cat with the intention of raising and selling kittens. Society pages in the late 1920s depicted Hattie as a southern senator's wife ensconced in a white-columned mansion—the picture of gentility. Paul and Forrest hosted grand parties for their West Point friends in Riversdale's mirrored ballroom while Hattie used the mansion for political entertaining, such as hosting the Arkansas Parents and Teachers Association delegation that was in town to attend the national PTA convention.³⁴

As the Great Depression set in, Senator Thad Caraway championed the causes of labor, farmers, and Bonus Army veterans. He opposed Hoover's high tariffs and relief for the banks. When Hoover blocked aid to Arkansas drought victims in 1930, Hattie wrote off "Sir Erbert" as mean, arrogant, and small. She clearly had very strong views on the failure of politicians, especially Republicans, to attend to the desperate needs of millions in distress. Then, in October 1930, Arkansas representative Otis Wingo died from injuries incurred in an accident years before. His wife, Effiegene, had served as his unpaid assistant, and Congressman Wingo wanted her to succeed him. Before he died, Otis Wingo wrote to a top male contender for his office that for four years, Effiegene "has done most of the work. . . . This experience, her natural qualifications, her personality, and strong ties of friendship . . . will enable her to render splendid service."³⁵ Both the Arkansas Democratic and Republican central committees nominated Effiegene Wingo to run for her deceased husband's House seat. She won, and Wingo joined Pearl Oldfield in Congress. In 1930, Arkansas became the only state with two congresswomen in the U.S. House.

In the dark days of economic crisis, ideological divisions deepened and intruded into everyday relationships. In June 1930, Hattie and Bobby took another transatlantic voyage, this time to Spain, Portugal, and Greece. On the voyage, Hattie complained that other passengers snubbed her for no apparent reason. She felt "a subtle antagonism that makes me so self-conscious and stiff." Hattie was unable to make a "point of contact" and suspected she was being "hazed" because her husband was a senator. "I have been so spoiled by having people love me and laugh with me, and at me," Hattie wrote to Paul, "that I wilt under competition."³⁶

Back in the States, Hattie became more deeply involved in the serious business of solving the South's economic challenges and discussed with Thad how to deal with agricultural and infrastructural problems in the region. During the 1931 Cotton Convention in New Orleans, the Caraways spent time with Governor Huey Long and his wife, Rose. Federal government power could be used, they believed, to help the South by purchasing large quantities of cotton and/or limiting planting. The highly controversial Louisiana governor soon ran for a U.S. Senate seat on a quasi-populist platform of social and economic reform. Once elected, Long asked Thad Caraway to escort him to his Senate swearing-in ceremony. Thad accepted but did not live to perform the honor.³⁷ On November 6, 1931, Senator Thaddeus Caraway was in a Little Rock hospital recovering from a kidney stone operation and preparing to run for a third term. He did not recover, and his unexpected death shocked Hattie, his wife of thirty years, and their three sons. But there was little time for grieving as the Democrats held the majority in the Senate by only one vote. It was imperative that Arkansas governor Harvey Parnell quickly name a successor. The law required that an interim appointee be named and a special election held to determine who would serve the remainder of the term. The interim officeholder would have some advantage in the special election and in the 1932 primaries and election for a full Senate term. To avoid infighting among leading Democratic men, Governor Parnell discussed with Hattie and her sons if she would serve in Thad's place. Parnell assured her that she would be the chosen candidate for the special election, giving her the opportunity to be the first woman elected to the U.S. Senate.

Just days after Thaddeus's death, Hattie Caraway accepted the high office and began a career in the U.S. Senate that spanned the dark years of the Great Depression and World War II. As with Oldfield and Wingo, Arkansas's Democrats supported her in the special election. But as Caraway biographer Diane Kincaid noted, the Arkansas Women's Democratic Club (AWDC), under the leadership of Florence Cotnam and Laura Davis Fitzhugh, raised funds to hold the election in precincts that otherwise could not afford it and turned out a large women's vote for Caraway.[38]

Caraway's history-making victory in the special election inspired many Arkansas women to become politically active. The AWDC also encouraged women to enter the August primary as candidates for political office.[39] Fitzhugh had reinvigorated the flagging AWDC and became its president in 1932. She organized Democratic "study clubs" for white women throughout the state and worked to garner support for Caraway. Fitzhugh also became vice chair of the state's Democratic Central Committee in 1934 and continued to lead Arkansas women in Democratic political activism. Myrtle Price, the assistant manager of the *Glenwood Herald* (a newspaper owned by her husband, Charles), strongly supported Hattie Caraway during her controversial campaign with Huey Long.[40] On the basis of that experience, Price became chair of the Pike County Democratic Club in 1936 and an enthusiastic partisan operative on behalf of the New Deal. In August 1936, Vivian Lewis Sigmon of Monticello, Arkansas, represented Caraway at the Chicago Democratic Convention and began corresponding with Molly Dewson, the head of the Democratic Party's Women's Division and vice chair of the Democratic National Campaign Committee. Sigmon provided Dewson with materials sent to her by FDR's Republican enemies and detractors, most notably derogatory tracts sent by the former president general of the Daughters of the American Revolution. Sigmon was a DAR member but not a Republican. Dewson thanked her for the "succilous propaganda" and sent her sets of "rainbow flyers," multicolored sheets containing pertinent pro-Democratic facts and policy statements that the Women's Division used to spread its own propaganda.[41] Some county units of the AWDC hosted benefits to help women pay their poll taxes so they could afford to vote.[42] Throughout the New Deal, the AWDC remained a strong political force in the region.

Hattie's Senate diary for her first six months in office shows her hard at work. As she listened to arguments on the floor, she became increasingly disgusted by the displays of male egotism and inefficiency.[43] Privately, she wrote sarcastic poems criticizing senators for their pompous grandstanding while people suffered in need of government assistance. She quietly voted to tax large fortunes and increase income and inheritance taxes on the wealthy. Without bombast, she voted against sales taxes on candy, automobiles, and bank checks and voted to exempt low-paid federal employees from wage cuts.[44] She voted to protect labor from injunctions, supported tariffs on oil and lumber to help Arkansas industries, and secured the first federal loan through the Reconstruction Finance Corporation for a public college, a model later used by the New Deal. She also quietly endured nationwide embarrassment when in February 1932 newspapers reported that her brother Walter Wyatt had been charged in a Nashville federal court with illegally owning and operating a distillery near Waverly, Tennessee.[45] She said little to the press, which in turn called her "demure," "unsophisticated," and "silent." But her silence was strategic and deliberate. Hattie's quiet liberalism was such that she was deeply annoyed when a reporter "made me out to be a communist."[46]

Although she was a new senator, Caraway had a critical advantage in that Garrett Whiteside, Thad Caraway's secretary, had remained in harness to run the office and help Hattie manage affairs. Whiteside was the well-seasoned "dean of senatorial secretaries," who had come to Washington, D.C., in 1907 and served Arkansas representatives William Ben Cravens and Otis Wingo. He became Thad's secretary in 1921, when Caraway opened his Senate office—the office that was ransacked by federal operatives. After ten years of working with the irascible Thad, Whiteside had become a loyal friend of the Caraways.[47]

As primary season neared, Hattie experienced a crisis of conscience. None of the male candidates for her seat, she believed, would protect farmers and workers as she had. It saddened her to think of her political life as over, and she worried about spending years as a dependent, presumably taken care of by her boys. She wondered what it would be like to return to the simple life. On May 9, 1932, the day before the filing deadline, Hattie Caraway presided over the Senate at the request of Republican vice president Charles Curtis. Lifting the gavel, she became the first woman to preside, and then shocked everyone by announcing her candidacy for a full term in the U.S. Senate. Caraway seemed to make her decision on impulse, but when asked by reporters why she was running, she answered, "The time has passed when a woman should be placed in a position and kept there only while someone else is being groomed for the job."[48]

That evening, Hattie wrote in her diary: "Well, I pitched a coin and heads came three times, so because the boys wish and because I really want to try out my own theory of a woman running for office I let my check and pledges be filed. And now won't be able to sleep or eat."[49] Arkansas's Democratic leaders had pressured Pearl Oldfield and Effiegene Wingo not to run again after their terms ended in order to make way for new men. Wingo at first had resisted, but health issues convinced her to capitulate. Hattie Caraway was in new territory. As the reality of her situation set in, she noted, "Thank God (in all reverence) that I am able to eat and sleep and laugh at myself. If I can hold on to my sense of humor and a modicum of dignity I shall have had a wonderful time running for office, whether I get there or not."[50] One man, O. L. Bodenhamer, the former national commander of the American Legion and a friend of Thad, had visited Hattie Caraway in Washington earlier in the spring to tell her that if she decided to run, he would support her. She had insisted that she did not intend to run, and probably at that moment she did not. Bodenhamer returned to Arkansas to launch his own campaign using many of Thad's former managers and fundraisers.[51] Hattie Caraway would have to run her unprecedented campaign in an unprecedented way.

While Arkansas's Democratic leaders were dismissive of Hattie Caraway's candidacy, Senator Huey Long passionately endorsed Caraway on the Senate floor. "It would be a fatal error, a distinct loss, a march backward," he insisted, if Caraway was not returned to the Senate. "The common people of this country need that Caraway vote," Long proclaimed, because she voted a straight "progressive" humanitarian line.[52] She had also supported Long's "Share the Wealth" legislation, and she and Long had both voted differently from Arkansas's business-oriented senior senator, Joe Robinson, on key issues. Caraway gambled that Long's elite-bashing oratory would resonate with Arkansas voters and accepted his offer of a whirlwind one-week campaign tour. Together, they challenged big corporate interests and stood up for the "Have-nots and Have-littles."[53] She had sold Riversdale in February, but Long's machine depicted Caraway as a victim of foreclosure.[54] Wearing black, Hattie looked the picture of a matronly, down-to-earth, rural widow. Against the odds, she and Long beat her opponents, and with the Democratic landslide in 1932, Hattie Caraway's time had arrived.

Her years in the Senate reveal a woman with a liberal conscience. In the first hundred days and second hundred days of the New Deal, Caraway voted for emergency and unemployment relief, the five-day work week, farm aid, rural resettlement, federal housing, higher taxes on the wealthy and utilities, and the Tennessee Valley Authority, which brought electricity to millions of southerners. She initiated legislation to build levees for flood control and bridges that became critical links in national transportation networks. She voted against repealing Prohibition (and lost). Caraway fought for public works and protections for coal miners, and she strengthened an antipollution law to limit the discharge of corrosives. Tragically, in July 1934, in the midst of the launching of a myriad of critical New Deal programs, Hattie's eighteen-year-old son, Bobby, was killed when he was thrown from a horse while visiting relatives near Newbern, Tennessee.[55]

But, again, there was little opportunity for grief. New rounds of legislation, some designed to create long-lasting change and not just emergency relief, required her attention. Hattie Caraway not only supported the creation of Social Security, she wanted to guarantee all recipients a monthly payment of fifteen dollars even if states did not match the federal entitlements; the amendment lost. Then another tragedy occurred. Just when the political heat of Huey Long, Caraway's seatmate, was pressuring FDR to expand social programs, Long was assassinated. Senator Caraway delivered Long's eulogy on the Senate floor and then continued her work with Senator Rose Long filling the seat next to her. In January 1936, Caraway voted with Republicans to override FDR's veto and delivered long-promised payments to veterans. She also opposed FDR's 1937 U.S. Supreme Court packing scheme, parting company with Senator Joe Robinson, who expended himself so vigorously for the plan that he died in the midst of the ill-fated battle.[56]

Even though Caraway had enjoyed the support of Robinson's avowed archenemy Huey Long, after Long's assassination the Caraway-Robinson relationship improved. After Robinson was reelected in 1936, the petite woman senator from Arkansas, in a moment of playful gender-bending, and to the delight and laughter of her fellow senators, "firmly grasped the elbow of her bulky colleague Senator Robinson and escorted him to the dais" for his swearing-in.[57] After Robinson's death in 1937, Caraway abandoned her standard practice of silence on the Senate floor. She also became more openly supportive of the biracial Southern Tenant Farmers Union (STFU) in which many white farm women from northeastern Arkansas were active.[58]

Caraway also became more vocal in her support of the Equal Rights Amendment (ERA). One week after she dressed in black and sat next to Robinson's empty chair during the Senate's memorial ceremonies, both House and Senate subcommittees gave unanimous reports in support of the ERA. Caraway told the press she was delighted and hoped the amendment would soon be submitted to the states for ratification.[59] Simultaneously, the Business and Professional Women's Clubs (BPWC), which counted significant numbers of female federal employees as members, endorsed the ERA. The national presidents of the BPWC in 1937 and 1938 were fellow Tennessean Charl Ormond Williams and Mississippi postmistress Erline White. Hattie Caraway's work on behalf of women's rights earned her endorsements from the BPWC and the National Woman's Party, and in 1937 she introduced the ERA on the floor of the Senate.[60] White's support of Caraway and her close proximity to Arkansas would be factors in Caraway's 1938 campaign.

While Caraway supported programs that assisted women and white and black farmers, she drew the line at advancing the political rights of black Arkansans.[61] Thaddeus Caraway in 1922 had joined other southern senators to filibuster the Dyer Anti-Lynching Bill, arguing that "a [white] man will have to stand over his family with his gun" if the proposed antilynching legislation passed.[62] In 1938, Senator Hattie Caraway sided with her southern Democratic colleagues in "filibustering... to death" the Wagner–Van Nuys Anti-Lynching Bill. The black press castigated her. One editorialist wrote, "We have seen also, Southern white women stoop to the same shameful language of cheap southern white men.... Particularly of[f] key was the remark by Senator Hattie Caraway of Arkansas that she likes Negroes 'as servants.' Then why is Arkansas supporting a State College for Negroes at Pine Bluff, granting Liberal Arts degrees?... Senator Caraway is just a cheap Southern white woman following in the tradition of cheap Southern white men. Sad, but true."[63]

While Hattie Caraway defended white supremacy, in June 1938 she engaged in a dramatic fight in the Senate to pass a wage and hour bill being piloted by her female Democratic colleague in the House, Mary T. Norton of New Jersey.[64] Once again, Caraway's liberal attitudes toward federally guaranteed fair wages and working conditions set her apart from conservative Republicans and Democrats. After that vote, Caraway immediately returned to Arkansas to parlay her bona fides as a southern New Deal Democrat and feminist into a successful campaign for a second term in the Senate.

The Brotherhood of Railroad Trainmen and its women auxiliaries, the American Federation of Labor, the STFU, the American Legion, and the DAR all endorsed her. Talking with a reporter, while "darning a stocking and answering a persistent telephone," Caraway stated, "My record is there now to stand for itself." This time, there was no Huey Long to assist her, and three men stepped up to vie for her seat. While Caraway observed that "a woman senator isn't so much of a novelty as before," her principal opponent, Representative John McClellan, ran on the slogan "Arkansas Needs Another Man in the Senate."[65] Caraway appealed to feminist voters, appearing before the BPWC beside national president Erline White of Mississippi. Through the Women's Division of her campaign headquarters, Caraway deployed an army of women to speak on her behalf.[66] McClellan protested that women working in Arkansas's Works Progress Administration offices were actively campaigning for Caraway, and undoubtedly many were. In July, FDR visited Arkansas and personally, though tepidly, endorsed her.[67] She beat McClellan by eight thousand votes.[68]

Embarking on her second full term, Hattie Caraway assumed she would wield the power of a senior senator in controlling patronage appointments. But in early 1940, Congressman Wade Kitchen nominated Irene Bodenhamer, a McClellan supporter and the widow of O. L. Bodenhamer, to be the postmistress of El Dorado, Arkansas. Bodenhamer, a thirty-four-year-old widow, had two small children and was financially wiped out soon after her husband was killed in an accident.[69] Nonetheless, Caraway sharply communicated to one of Roosevelt's advisors that Irene Bodenhamer's nomination was "personally obnoxious" to her. The two women were "long-standing political enemies and very bitter."[70] Caraway insisted that Bodenhamer had walked out of an El Dorado meeting when the national BPWC president, Erline White, was complimenting Caraway.[71] Bodenhamer, who also served as an alternate delegate to the 1938 Democratic National Convention, defended herself before a Senate committee by explaining that she had been in the back of the room and slipped out quietly during the BPWC meeting to take care of her elderly father-in-law. Irene Bodenhamer had also worked as John Miller's assistant campaign manager in 1937, when he won the special election to fill the remainder of Joe Robinson's term, making Miller the junior senator.[72] Caraway refused to bury the hatchet, and the Senate committee tactfully allowed the nomination to die.[73] Bodenhamer's son Lee recalled that his family's situation "changed for the worse" when his mother did not receive the federal appointment, and a year later, loyal supporters appointed Bodenhamer to a paid position on the state's Oil and Gas Commission.[74] While Caraway again introduced the ERA on the Senate floor, her treatment of Bodenhamer made Hattie look mean and petty and tarnished her image as a feminist.

For the most part, Caraway continued to conduct herself in an understated manner even as her stature, with her seniority, grew. She was the first woman to chair a Senate hearing, earned coveted assignments on the Commerce Committee, and weighed in and asked questions during hearings, most particularly on arbitration law. She was especially dedicated to her work on the Agriculture and Forestry Committee since this enabled her to directly affect the lives of rural southerners. Her secretary, Garrett Whiteside, noted in a 1942 *Arkansas Historical Quarterly* article that Hattie Caraway's office served as a "sort of bureau of information regarding Arkansas" and that "the scope covered by the average volume of mail coming to [a] Congressional office is almost beyond comprehension."[75] He also praised her for preventing the loss of an Arkansas congressional seat through the passage of her Apportionment Act, calling it "the cleverest handling of a legislative measure of comparable importance I have ever seen."[76]

With the rise of Adolf Hitler, Nazism, and the fascist takeover of much of Europe, Hattie Caraway stepped squarely into the international spotlight at 9:30 p.m. on February 27, 1941, and delivered a stirring speech over a nationwide radio network in support of the Lend-Lease Bill. She noted how isolationists had played on people's fear of war to oppose both the Neutrality and Selective Service acts, neither of which drew the nation into war. They had been false prophets. She made it clear that Hitler was the enemy and called out the opponents of lend-lease as fearful cowards overly concerned with Hitler's wrath. "Why all this cringing before Hitler?" she challenged. "Why the fear that we may do something which would make the German dictator angry?" Caraway told her listeners that because she was the only woman in the Senate, she received a great deal of mail from opponents of lend-lease, detractors who seemed to think she and the women of the country would be frightened by the possibility of belligerent ramifications. While most letters were sincere, she also saw in this effort the "slimy hands of Nazi propagandists" and many who were "unwittingly being used as tools by the Hitler machine."[77]

Her response was to fight Hitlerism with feminism. She explained: "I stated when I entered the Senate that I saw no reason for differentiating between men and women who serve in legislative capacities. There should be equal responsibility among them with a new view toward equal service to achieve identical goals. . . . The history of this country shows that the women of America are just as loyal, just as courageous, and just as self-sacrificing as the men. I know that if war should come to us, the women would show equal courage with the men. In fact, I sometimes think they would have to show more, for long after war is over the women will still be fighting for American principles." To further illustrate the depth of her conviction, she stated, "I think that I have as much interest in keeping this nation out of war as anyone. I have two sons already in the military service. They entered military service because it was their wish to do so. I gave my consent. If they were civilians and there was a national emergency and they did not do their part, I would disown them." She did not want war, nor was she willing to allow the brutality of fascism and the devastation of Great Britain to continue with the tacit compliance of the United States.[78] Caraway's speech was printed in the *Congressional Record* at the request of a Senate colleague, and newspapers throughout the country reprinted versions of the text. Her speech was considered one of the most effective in the campaign for lend-lease, and the bill passed soon afterward.

While Hattie had written at the beginning of her Senate career that she would try to vote the way she thought Thad would vote, the challenges of World War II could not have been anticipated. In truth, her own lights guided her. Historian Rhodri Jeffreys-Jones noted that Caraway's support of the military helped Arkansas.[79] She supported the GI Bill and used her influence to establish in Arkansas five airbases, two incarceration and relocation camps for Japanese Americans, ordnance and aluminum factories, Camps Robinson and Chaffee, and a large veterans' hospital in Hot Springs.

But even as Caraway invoked the American beliefs in freedom, democracy, and self-government, she actively worked against the political advancements of racial minorities. In 1942, she filibustered to block a bill to eliminate the poll tax, although many southern white feminists, notably Florence Cotnam, had begun to fight for poll tax reforms. When Arkansas's freshman congressman, J. William Fulbright, entered the House in 1943, he supported anti–poll tax legislation. The war also inspired Fulbright to want to bridge the gaps between nations and races. In April, he proposed a resolution to put the House on record as supporting "the creation of appropriate international machinery with power adequate to prevent future aggression and to maintain lasting peace, and as favoring participation by the United States therein through its constitutional processes."[80]

In the summer of 1943, John Hughes Reynolds, the president of Hendrix College, a Methodist-affiliated school in Conway, Arkansas, began "urging" Fulbright to run for Caraway's seat.[81] Reynolds had been an outspoken and influential white supremacist academic in the early 1900s, but in 1942 he began to give speeches promoting a new internationalism, proclaiming: "We must recognize the brotherhood of man, remembering that the colored people constitute the majority of the human race. We must be prepared to get down off of our sense of racial superiority and feel and think in terms of all mankind."[82] Reynolds feared that Caraway and other candidates did not share his vision of a tolerant sweeping internationalism that meant also giving up their white racial superiority complex.[83] Fulbright had not planned to run for the Senate so early in his political career, but Reynolds would not take no for an answer. He lobbied senators to support the Fulbright resolution, which laid the groundwork for the United Nations.[84] After its adoption, Reynolds contacted other college presidents and began a campaign to solicit support for a Fulbright candidacy. He contacted local leaders in Caraway's own Jonesboro to assess her strength and persuade them to shift their allegiance to Fulbright. With great reservations, Fulbright finally threw his hat in the ring. Reynolds pulled out all the stops, using his substantial influence to undermine Caraway, whom he privately called a "good housemother."[85]

Caraway was thrown off by Fulbright's announced candidacy. She had vigorously supported military preparedness and strengthening international relations, but she could not depend on the younger generation of veterans to support her. As she prepared to run for a third term in 1944, the U.S. Supreme Court ruled that all-white primaries were unconstitutional.[86] The Arkansas Negro Democratic Association organized to get out the vote. The electoral ground had shifted.[87] Caraway sent FDR a desperate plea for his endorsement, but he was embarking on his own extremely controversial campaign for a fourth term. Aides counseled that Caraway's chances were not good and advised FDR to send a simple message of gratitude for their work together as old friends in the past.

The primary debates centered on the military records of the principal male contenders, Fulbright and Governor Homer Adkins. Caraway refused to engage this issue and spent little time campaigning in Arkansas, explaining that governing in the midst of war required her presence in Washington, D.C. Critically, the previous support she had relied on from women did not materialize. Fulbright's mother, Roberta, a powerful newspaperwoman and editorialist, was without question instrumental in electing her son to the Senate. But the early intervention of John Hughes Reynolds played a strong, perhaps decisive role in defeating Hattie Caraway in the 1944 Democratic primary.[88] Hattie Caraway placed last in the field of four in the first round of the primaries.

This loss marked the rise of a new sort of southern white liberal. In the August 1944 Democratic primary runoff between Adkins and Fulbright, twelve thousand African Americans purportedly voted and voted overwhelmingly for Fulbright, who had supported anti–poll tax legislation. Adkins had stated clearly that he did not want "a single nigger vote" and accused Fulbright of being a "nigger lover."[89] The press made a great deal of the role of black voters in Fulbright's victory.

When Caraway left the Senate in March 1945, her colleagues gave her a rare standing ovation. Roosevelt, before his death in April, appointed her to the Employees' Compensation Commission. President Harry S. Truman appointed her to the Employees' Compensation Appeals Board in 1946.

Senator Hattie Caraway participated in arguably the most important domestic and foreign policy decisions of the twentieth century. While her record on black civil rights in particular stands as a telling remnant of Old and New South racism, a great number of programs and policies she supported shaped and continue to define the liberal policies and agendas of the Democratic Party. Caraway's long career as a southern Democrat in the 1930s and 1940s demonstrates how the shifting ground of southern politics in those years made it possible for southern white women to gain unprecedented influence within the established system of white supremacy. It also demonstrates how difficult it would have been for her to continue to serve in the Senate beyond 1945. Her career began with a silent but determined dedication to increasing women's roles in government by inserting herself, to the great surprise of leading male Arkansas Democrats, into the political equation. It ended at the juncture recognized by scholars as a wartime transition toward respecting human rights and women's abilities—critical groundwork for the rise of a rather boisterous second wave of feminism.

But the first woman in history to be elected (and reelected) to the U.S. Senate would not live to see the world-changing domestic human rights movements of the 1950s and 1960s. Hattie Caraway, a progressive southern schoolteacher born in 1878 in the wild hollows of middle Tennessee, passed away after suffering a stroke in 1950. She was laid to rest in Jonesboro, Arkansas, next to her husband, Thaddeus, and son Robert, in a simple grave at Oaklawn Cemetery.

NOTES

I would like to express my gratitude to the dedicated and good-natured historians known as the Delta Women Writers, who critiqued drafts of this chapter.

1. *Logansport Pharos Tribune* (Ind.), December 9, 1935.

2. Senate Proceedings, sess. 72-2, *Congressional Record* 80, pt. 5 (April 14, 1936), 5474–77, highlights Caraway's emphatic support of the New Deal's "radical departure" and her simultaneous rejection of "conventional" and "ultra-conservative" approaches to the nation's problems.

3. George Creel, "The Woman Who Holds Her Tongue," *Collier's*, September 18, 1937, cited in Betty Marie Sneed, "Hattie Wyatt Caraway, United States Senator, 1931–1945," MA thesis, University of Arkansas, 1975, 13.

4. Diane D. Kincaid (Blair), ed., *Silent Hattie Speaks: The Personal Journal of Senator Hattie Caraway* (Westport, Conn.: Greenwood, 1979); David Malone, *Hattie and Huey: An Arkansas Tour* (Fayetteville: University of Arkansas Press, 1989); and Nancy Hendricks, *Senator Hattie Caraway: An Arkansas Legacy* (Stroud, UK: History Press, 2013). For an explanation regarding southern feminists who were not obvious in their ideology and practices, see Sarah Wilkerson Freeman, "Stealth in the Political Arsenal of Southern Women: A Retrospective for the Millennium," in *Southern*

Women at the Millennium: A Historical Perspective, ed. Melissa Walker, Jeanette Dunn, and Joe Dunn (Columbia: University of Missouri Press, 2003).

5. Lucy Burch had been previously married in the 1860s, but the fate of that union remains unknown. Single again by 1870, Lucy married William Wyatt in 1873.

6. Jill Knight Garrett, *A History of Humphreys County, Tennessee* (N.p.: N.p., 1963), 169.

7. See Sarah Wilkerson Freeman, "Tennessee's Audacious White Feminists, 1825–1910," in *Tennessee Women: Their Lives and Times*, ed. Beverly Greene Bond and Sarah Wilkerson Freeman (Athens: University of Georgia Press, 2016), 2:182–214.

8. For more on feminist activism among southern white women teachers, especially equal pay for equal work campaigns, see Kathleen C. Berkeley, "'The Ladies Want to Bring about Reform in the Public Schools': Public Education and Women's Rights in the Post–Civil War South," *History of Education Quarterly* 24 (Winter 1984): 45–58; and Sarah Wilkerson Freeman, "Pauline Van de Graaf Orr (1861–1955): Feminist Education in Mississippi," in *Mississippi Women: Their Histories, Their Lives*, vol. 1, ed. Martha H. Swain, Elizabeth Anne Payne, Susan Ditto, and Marjorie Julian Spruill (Athens: University of Georgia Press, 2005), 72–97.

9. Shipp remarried and strongly encouraged her children and grandchildren to get involved in politics. Her grandson Frank Clement was elected governor of Tennessee, and her granddaughter Anna Belle Clement O'Brien was elected to the Tennessee state senate. Steve Jacks, *Anna Belle Clement O'Brien: The First Lady of Tennessee Politics* (Wartburg, Tenn.: Morgan County Publishing, 1995), 20–23.

10. Among the first entries in Caraway's Senate diary was her response when she learned she had been assigned to the same desk previously occupied by Rebecca Latimer Felton, the first woman to serve in the Senate. Felton had been a token and temporary appointment, serving only one day. Caraway quipped about the desk, "I guess they wanted as few of them contaminated as possible." See Kincaid, *Silent Hattie Speaks*, 28.

11. In Jonesboro, Hattie Caraway was active in the Study Circle of the Woman's Foreign Mission Society of the First Methodist Church. *Craighead County Sun* (Jonesboro, Ark.), September 22, 1904. Also prominent in Jonesboro's Twentieth Century Club activities, Caraway frequently hosted meetings and large parties for the white women's organization. Club members studied and gave papers called "The Lives of Japanese Women" and "The Religions of Japan." *Jonesboro Evening Sun*, April 20, 1905. As part of the club's Education, Civic, and Philanthropy Committee, Caraway reported on the committee's work. *Jonesboro Daily News*, April 17, 1909. See also Creel, "The Woman Who Holds Her Tongue."

12. For more on the Monteagle, Tennessee, feminists, see Freeman, "Tennessee's Audacious White Feminists."

13. "Mrs. Cotnam Speaks at Aggie College," *Jonesboro Daily Tribune*, May 4, 1916; *Handbook of the National American Woman Suffrage Association and Proceedings of the Jubilee Convention, 1869–1919, Held at St. Louis, Mo., March 24–29, 1919*, National American Woman Suffrage Association Convention, National American Woman Suffrage Association Collection, Library of Congress; Dallas Tabor Herndon, "Florence Brown Cotnam (Mrs. T. T.)," in *Centennial History of Arkansas* (Chicago: S. J. Clarke Publishing, 1922), 3:1140–42.

14. Herndon, "Florence Brown Cotnam."

15. *Handbook of the National American Woman Suffrage Association*, 254.

16. Ibid., 57.

17. *New York Times*, June 27, 1920.

18. Kincaid, *Silent Hattie Speaks*, 3n2, 32.

19. *Washington Bee*, August 5, 1916, February 6 and August 23, 1919; *Savannah Tribune*, August 30, 1919.

20. *Washington Bee*, August 5, 1916.

21. *Washington Bee*, August 23, 1919; *Savannah Tribune*, August 30, 1919.

22. *Helena World*, November 26, 1919; *Congressional Record*, 58th Cong., November 19, 1919, 8818–21; J. W. Butts and Dorothy James, "The Underlying Causes of the Elaine Riot of 1919," *Arkansas Historical Quarterly* 20, no. 1 (Spring 1961): 95–104.

23. Thad Caraway also supported Wilson's progressive legislation (Clayton Antitrust Act, Federal Reserve Act, direct election of senators, etc.), but he was best known at home for securing a $50,000 federal appropriation to build a white girls reform school in Arkansas in 1918.

24. *Current Biography, 1945* (New York: H. W. Wilson, 1945), 89–92.

25. *New York Times*, March 5, 1922.

26. In 1922, Pulaski County boasted that it had a woman sheriff, Alice Clark, who carried a revolver and commanded the "healthy respect of law violators." *Bismarck Tribune*, April 3, 1922.

27. *Bemidji Daily Pioneer* (Minn.), May 16, 1922. I want to thank Amanda Milligan for bringing this source to my attention.

28. *Sunday Tulsa Daily World* (Okla.), June 25, 1922.

29. Hattie Caraway to Paul Caraway, February 28, 1927, box 38, Caraway Papers, William L. Clements Library, University of Michigan, Ann Arbor (hereafter Caraway Papers). In this period, the Caraways frequently socialized with Rhode Island senator Peter Gerry and his wife, Edith Stuyvesant Dresser. I am extremely grateful to Eeta Gershow and Judith Rose for obtaining copies of these letters for use in this chapter.

30. Hattie Caraway to Paul Caraway, n.d., box 38, Caraway Papers.

31. When Thaddeus Caraway campaigned for Smith and Robinson, he argued that superpatriots and religious bigots should have more trouble with Hoover's pacifistic Quakerism than Smith's Catholicism. For more on the Ku Klux Klan in Arkansas, see Charles C. Alexander, *The Ku Klux Klan in the Southwest* (Norman: University of Oklahoma Press, 1995); Kathleen Blee, *Women of the KKK: Racism and Gender in the 1920s* (Berkeley: University of California Press, 1991); Brooks R. Blevins, "The Strike and the Still: Anti-Radical Violence and the Ku Klux Klan in the Ozarks," *Arkansas Historical Quarterly* 52 (Winter 1993): 405–25; Donald Holley, "A Look behind the Masks: The 1920s Ku Klux Klan in Monticello, Arkansas," *Arkansas Historical Quarterly* 60 (Summer 2001): 131–50; Nancy MacLean, *Behind the Mask of Chivalry: The Making of the Second Ku Klux Klan* (New York: Oxford University Press, 1994); Rory McVeigh, *The Rise of the Ku Klux Klan: Right-Wing Movements and National Politics* (Minneapolis: University of Minnesota Press, 2009).

32. Pearl Oldfield followed the same path as Mae Ella Nolan (R-Calif.), who was elected in 1922 by special election to fill her deceased husband's seat; Florence Prag Kahn (R-Calif.), who in 1925 was elected to fill the vacancy created by the death of her husband; and Edith Nourse Rogers (R-Mass.), who in 1927 was elected in a special election to fill her deceased husband's seat. Nolan served only one term, but Kahn, the first Jewish woman in Congress, was reelected until 1936, when she was defeated in the FDR landslide. Rogers was elected to eighteen consecutive terms and shared many of the same interests in supporting veterans and the military as Hattie Caraway. Mary Teresa Norton (D-N.J.) was elected in 1924 and served until 1951. In light of the political success of these women and the Republicans' willingness to advance women into office in the 1920s through the "widow's succession," the Arkansas Democratic Central Committee's treatment of Oldfield

and Caraway (and Wingo, discussed later in the chapter) was not a great departure but part of a trend.

33. *Washington Evening Star*, February 16, 1926. Thad Caraway's desire to possess Riversdale conflicted with Hiram Johnson's presumption that he could occupy the home even after the Caraways purchased it. Consequently, it took years for the Caraways to move into Riversdale.

34. Hattie Caraway to Paul Caraway, May 11, 1929, box 38, Caraway Papers.

35. Quoted in Lindley C. Shedd, "Effiegene Wingo: An Early Congresswoman from Arkansas," *Arkansas Historical Quarterly* 67, no. 1 (Spring 2008): 27–53.

36. Hattie Caraway to Paul Caraway, June 17, 1930, box 38, Caraway Papers.

37. *Time*, November 16, 1931.

38. *Journal-Advance* (Gentry, Ark.), December 17, 1931.

39. Ibid.

40. Malone, *Hattie and Huey*, 62–63; Mrs. Charles [Myrtle] Price to Mary Dewson, September 24 and October 26, 1936, folder 32, Correspondence by State, Arkansas–Misc H–Z, 1934–1936, Women's Division, Democratic National Committee, Franklin Delano Roosevelt Library, Hyde Park, N.Y. (hereafter FDR Library).

41. Vivian Sigmon to James Farley, August 26, 1936; Sigmon to Molly Dewson, October 26, 1936; Dewson to Sigman [sic], October 27, 1936, all in box 13, Correspondence by States, 1933–1937, Women's Division 1933–1944, Democratic National Committee, FDR Library.

42. Mrs. C. Woodward Baughman to Mrs. James Wolfe, February 17, 1936, Democratic National Committee, Women's Division, Correspondence by State, Arkansas–Misc H–Z, 1934–1936, folder 32, FDR Library.

43. Kincaid, *Silent Hattie Speaks*. Hattie Caraway's style contrasted sharply with the press's depiction of her husband's methods. In 1930, *Time* had applauded one of Thad's Republican adversaries for standing up to the "arrogant," "pestiferous," "bumptious," "menacing" Senator Caraway and his "senile gabbling" and "gutter psychology." When Thaddeus Caraway died, *Time* noted that the Senate had lost "its foremost sarcastigator, the Democrat whose tongue was like the lash of an Arkansas snake whip." The "narrow-eyed" junior senator, *Time* eulogized, never made long formal speeches but drawled out bitter words that stung his adversaries and left scars. *Time*, January 6, 1930, and November 16, 1931.

44. Kincaid, *Silent Hattie Speaks*, 30.

45. *Reno Evening Gazette* (Nev.), February 23, 1932.

46. Ibid.

47. *Washington Times-Herald*, December 9, 1941, read by Senator Lister Hill of Alabama into *Congressional Record* 87, pt. 9 (December 11, 1941), sess. 77-1, A5539. See also Garrett Whiteside, "'Watching Washington' for Thirty-Five Years," *Arkansas Historical Quarterly* 1, no. 3 (September 1942): 235–43.

48. Susan M. Hartmann, "Caraway, Hattie Ophelia Wyatt," in *American National Biography* (New York: Oxford University Press, 1999), 4:369–70.

49. Kincaid, *Silent Hattie Speaks*, 121.

50. Ibid., 124.

51. Author's telephone interview with Lee Bodenhamer, August 19, 2014.

52. Kincaid, *Silent Hattie Speaks*, 22.

53. There are competing stories about how and why Louisiana senator Huey Long joined Caraway's campaign. One version is that Long, Caraway's seatmate, noticed that Caraway quietly but consistently voted along a progressive line. Other versions suggest that he simply took pity on

her and offered to help. His motives seemed to be, of course, political since he was able to use Caraway's support of "Share the Wealth" legislation to cast Senator Joe Robinson as a friend of the wealthy and big business. Long also saw the Arkansas campaign as an opportunity to flex his populist political muscle outside of Louisiana, perhaps as a dress rehearsal for a 1936 run for the White House. In yet another version, one of Caraway's campaign organizers, L. S. (Sharpe) Dunaway (an *Arkansas Gazette* editor), who knew Long when the young itinerant salesman from Louisiana peddled pencils and soap in the small towns of Arkansas, asked Long to help with the Caraway campaign. See Malone, *Hattie and Huey*; William Curtis Mears, "L. S. (Sharpe) Dunaway," *Arkansas Historical Quarterly* 13, no. 1 (Spring 1954): 77–85; Stuart Towns, "A Louisiana Medicine Show: The Kingfish Elects an Arkansas Senator," *Arkansas Historical Quarterly* 25, no. 2 (June 1966): 117–27.

54. *Washington Post*, January 9, 1932.

55. *Hope Star* (Hope, Ark.), August 1, 1934.

56. William E. Leuchtenburg, *The Supreme Court Reborn: The Constitutional Revolution in the Age of Roosevelt* (New York: Oxford University Press, 1996), 152.

57. *Billings Gazette* (Mont.), January 6, 1937.

58. See Donald H. Grubbs, *Cry from Cotton* (Fayetteville: University of Arkansas Press, 2000), 158–59n70. Grubbs noted that the STFU-style cooperatives in Arkansas received support from Caraway, who had been a "former enemy."

59. *Syracuse Herald*, July 25, 1937.

60. *New York Times*, June 24, 1937.

61. Hattie Caraway also blocked the appointment of Brooks Hays, whom FDR considered the most progressive Arkansas politician, to a federal judgeship in 1936 and tried to get Hays fired from his federal job working for Henry Wallace in the Department of Agriculture. Roosevelt intervened, and Hays kept his job. James Thomas Baker, *Brooks Hays* (Macon, Ga.: Mercer University Press, 1989), 58–59.

62. *New York Times*, March 5, 1922.

63. *Plaindealer* (Kansas City, Kans.), January 28, 1938.

64. *Reno Evening Gazette* (Nev.), June 15, 1938.

65. *Reno Evening Gazette* (Nev.), June 22, 1938.

66. *Northwest Arkansas Times*, July 28, 1938.

67. *Northwest Arkansas Times*, July 16, 1938.

68. *New York Times*, July 29, 1938; and J. B. Shannon, "Presidential Politics in the South: 1938," *Journal of Politics* 1, no. 2 (May 1939): 146–70.

69. Author's interview with Lee Bodenhamer. See also U.S. Census, 1940, El Dorado, Union County, Ark., roll T627_177, 6A, enumeration district 70-16.

70. James Rowe Jr. to FDR, April 19 and 29, 1940, PPF 5456, Franklin Delano Roosevelt Library, Hyde Park, N.Y.; *Hope Star*, April 19, 1940.

71. *Northwest Arkansas Times*, April 17, 1940.

72. *Northwest Arkansas Times*, October 2, 1937.

73. Senator Miller publicly stated that he would support the Bodenhamer nomination and, as newspapers reported, "some members privately expressed hope that a reconciliation of differences could be effected, but those close to the Arkansas senator [Caraway] are not optimistic." *Hope Star*, May 1, 1940.

74. Author's interview with Lee Bodenhamer.

75. Whiteside, "'Watching Washington' for Thirty-Five Years," 241.

76. Ibid., 238.
77. *Congressional Record*, 77th Cong., 1st sess., 1941, 87, pt. 10, appendix, A893-94.
78. Ibid.
79. Rhodri Jeffreys-Jones, *Changing Differences: Women and the Shaping of American Foreign Policy, 1917-1994* (New Brunswick, N.J.: Rutgers University Press, 1997), 95.
80. See Randall Bennett Woods, *Fulbright: A Biography* (New York: Cambridge University Press, 1995), 80-83.
81. Typed campaign speech, July 14, 1944, box "J. H. Reynolds Speech and Reports," John Hughes Reynolds Papers, Hendrix College Archives, Conway, Ark. (hereafter Reynolds Papers).
82. December 23, 1942, speech delivered at the Conway Rotary Club, box "J. H. Reynolds Speech and Reports," Reynolds Papers.
83. John Reynolds has been regarded by Arkansas historians as a leader in the Lost Cause movement to valorize the history of the Confederate states. See Fred Arthur Bailey, "The Free Speech and the 'Lost Cause' in Arkansas," *Arkansas Historical Quarterly* 55, no. 2 (Summer 1996): 143-66. Reynolds's extraordinary shift away from his earlier ideology and views on race are a fascinating aspect of the liberalization process in response to World War II.
84. Within days of the Senate concurring with the Fulbright resolution on September 21, 1943, John Hughes Reynolds met with Senator Harold Hitz Burton of Ohio and other internationalists in New York and Washington, D.C. See Concurrent Resolution 25, 78th Cong., September 21, 1943; typed notes from luncheon on September 24, 1943, Roosevelt Hotel, New York City, September 27, 1943, Reynolds Papers.
85. Reynolds to President Wiley Lin Hurie, College of the Ozarks, December 15, 1943, Reynolds Papers. Reynolds's letter followed up on a telephone conversation he had with Hurie the previous evening: "Mrs. Caraway, a good housemother, has been there long enough, if we were under obligation to her distinguished husband.... If we put Fulbright in now, he will have a distinguished career in the United States Senate for the next twenty years. Arkansas needs that. I believe the college men of Arkansas can exercise a powerful influence in this effort."
86. In 1930, the Arkansas Supreme Court had upheld the use of the all-white primary, and the U.S. Supreme Court had refused to hear an appeal. But in 1941 the tide turned in favor of voting rights when the U.S. Supreme Court ruled in *United States v. Classic* (a Louisiana case) that primary elections were subject to federal regulation. The constitutional test of the Texas Democratic white primary, *Smith v. Allright*, was argued before the U.S. Supreme Court on January 12, 1944, and decided in favor of the African American plaintiff, Lonnie Smith, on April 3. The Court ruled that Smith's federally guaranteed right to vote had been violated and, as Justice Stanley F. Reed argued, a state could not legally "permit a private organization to practice racial discrimination" in elections.
87. Caraway had received criticism in the national press as one of the "Senators who voted to deprive soldiers of their right to the ballot in 1944 by putting responsibility for creating election machinery in the hands of each of the 48 states." See the anonymously written "Lest We Forget," *Antioch Review* 3, no. 4 (Winter 1943): 618.
88. The critical role of Reynolds in Fulbright's 1944 campaign has been neglected by historians. Evidence in Reynolds's papers indicates that he approached Fulbright in June or early July 1943 to encourage him to run and began contacting others to similarly pressure Fulbright. Fulbright's biographer Randall Woods seemed unsure of the process by which Fulbright began to consider such a bold move and simply wrote: "Sometime that summer [1943] the thought crossed Fulbright's mind" to challenge Senator Caraway. Not until August 1943, after Reynolds began pressuring Fulbright,

did Roberta Fulbright, who had been a friend of Caraway, begin organizing meetings to garner support for her son's possible run for the Senate. Woods was mistaken about Caraway's relationship with Huey Long, whom she and Thad visited in New Orleans. Long was her seatmate after Thad's death. Woods, however, wrote that Long had not met Caraway until he offered to campaign for her in 1932. See Woods, *Fulbright*, 87–90.

89. *Plaindealer* (Kansas City, Kans.), August 18, 1944.

Hilda Kahlert Cornish
(1878–1965)

A Community Volunteer and Civic Leader: The Birth Control Movement in Arkansas

MARIANNE LEUNG

❀ ❀ ❀

Sally Ellis Benson, a married woman from Searcy, Arkansas, wrote a brief note to Hilda Cornish of Little Rock requesting reliable birth control information in February 1952. It is clear this was not Benson's first attempt to ask for such information because her note specifically requested not to be referred to a physician because "I have already inquired from several, and each just refers me to some one [sic] else." In her response to Benson, Cornish referred the woman to Dr. M. C. Hawkins and assured her that this physician was supportive and could be trusted. Predicting that the woman would be most reluctant to see the doctor, Cornish also invited Benson to visit Little Rock to see her in person, woman to woman. As if suspecting that the fifty-mile trip to Little Rock might be too cumbersome, Cornish even offered to make the trip to Searcy herself and "perhaps talk to a small group on the subject." When she had not received any response from Benson by April 20, Cornish sent another letter to check up on her. Again inviting Benson to visit her in Little Rock, she wanted to know if Benson ever saw Hawkins, as suggested. She ended the brief letter with "I want you to know that I am very much interested in helping mothers who need contraceptive advice & would be happy to see you at your convenience."[1] At the time of this correspondence, Hilda Cornish was seventy-four years old and at the end of a long career as a volunteer community organizer. Beginning in 1930, she devoted the next three decades to tirelessly rallying community support to assure that all women of Arkansas would have access to safe and effective birth control. Her goal was realized in 1966, the year after her death, when women in all counties of Arkansas finally gained access to safe and effective birth control through the state's public health care system.[2]

As a result of Cornish's leadership, women who sought birth control advice and could afford to see a private physician had by the early 1940s access to such services in Arkansas. Enough physicians by then had access to reliable knowledge, and they saw birth control as a legitimate medical issue. Cornish became most concerned about the many women who could not afford these services and who therefore were dependent on public health institutions or charity clinics. Through her volunteer work, Cornish learned that poor women would not likely be served by the privatized medical system. From her involvement in the field of social work, she came to believe that the key to solving many contemporary social problems was to aid women in limiting the number of pregnancies. Using the volunteer organization as a vehicle for change, she continuously allied with groups and individuals that would best accomplish these goals. Throughout, Cornish found inspiration and guidance from Margaret Sanger, the national leader of the birth control movement at the time.[3] She also found strength from and thrived amid the camaraderie she developed with a core group of Little Rock citizens who shared her values. From our vantage point today, we might expect that the Arkansas birth control advocates, working in a rather traditional southern community, would have met opposition when challenging both the traditional view of sexuality and the idea that birth control is primarily a private issue. However, the more serious obstacle turned out to be the fear of a government extending its powers by taking control of the privatized medical system.[4] At the end of her life, Hilda Cornish was a respected civic leader with a reputation for being genuinely concerned for those in need. What guided her work for so many years was her conviction that an individual's actions matter and that the larger community's responsibility for the needy is necessary for significant change to happen.

Cornish created for herself a social position from which she could aid others in the community. Her work is an example of an individual serving as a significant agent of change in the larger story of the American birth control movement. Her effort speaks not only to the complexity of the motives and actions of many community leaders across the nation but also to the power of volunteerism. The personal experiences of Hilda Cornish shaped her outlook and understanding of how society should work and the role of one's responsibility in it. By examining the voice of Cornish herself (found in her private correspondence) as well as the voices of those with whom she interacted, it becomes clear that she was a genuinely compassionate woman willing to work hard for her community. Her relatively humble background and early life experiences possibly contributed to her strong commitment to aid the needy, while her acquired connections among the elite Little Rock social circles clearly gave her the ability to build the community support needed to effect change.

Even though Hilda Cornish would become an influential member of Little Rock society, her upbringing differed from many of the community members she would attract to support her cause. Her parents, Rudolph and Sophie Kahlert, migrated to the United States from Germany in 1861 and eventually had eight daughters; Hilda, the seventh, was born in 1878. Settling on the south side of St. Louis, Missouri, they lived on the outskirts of the already established German neighborhood. By 1880 the family lived along the new extension of Chippewa Street, where most of the neighbors were immigrant families who had left various German states (e.g., Bavaria, Hanover, Wurttemberg) prior to the unification of Germany in 1871, but there were also a few households originating from England, France, and Scotland. Rudolph Kahlert supported his growing family as a carpenter, but struggled at times to find employment. At age forty-seven, he was without steady work for at least six months at a time when Hilda and her younger sister, Gertrude, were mere toddlers. Typical of a girl coming of age in the 1890s, Hilda did not have access to advanced schooling, but she managed to complete eight grades in the St. Louis school system. In her late teens, Hilda left St. Louis for Newark City, New Jersey, where she lived in a boardinghouse while working as a milliner at the turn of the twentieth century.[5]

When she arrived in Little Rock, Arkansas, in 1901, at age twenty-three, Hilda quickly embraced the community as her own. She soon made important connections that put her in a position to serve later as a liaison between various social groups in the community. While renting a room at a boardinghouse during her first year in town, Hilda met Edward Cornish, a widower since 1897 with a five-year-old daughter, Edith. At age twenty-six he had lost his wife and three children to illness.[6] Ed and Hilda married on July 2, 1902. Their first daughter, Hilda, was born two years later, and the family's first son, Ed Jr., was born in 1907. Hilda Cornish would give birth to four more children between 1912 and 1917. First came Sylvia in March 1912 and then Miriam in November 1913, born eighteen months apart. In 1915, the family experienced tragedy with the death of a newborn son, Jack. At age thirty-nine, in 1917, Hilda gave birth to her last child, Don. In addition, Ed's daughter from his previous marriage grew up in the household. Hilda, who was nicknamed "Bunny" by the family, certainly had a large family to keep her busy, and she and Ed also had the financial means to give each child a strong foundation for life.[7]

Hilda Cornish was able to devote the first twenty years of her marriage to watching over the children without the strain of economic hardship. Edward Cornish provided well for the family through real estate and banking ventures. The family could afford household help to assist Hilda with caring for the growing family. In 1910, for example, they employed a live-in domestic worker, Mabel

Smith, a seventeen-year-old African American woman, who helped care for little Hilda and Ed Jr., in addition to doing house work. The Cornish family built a substantial house with 8,200 square feet of living space, covering four residential lots. With plenty of room in the house, by 1920 the family had three household employees. By this time, the eldest child, her stepdaughter, Edith, had married Raymond Low, an insurance agent, and settled in Omaha, Nebraska. The Cornish family was economically secure, and life was good. They could afford to spend their summers in Ludington, Michigan, away from the pressing Arkansas heat.[8]

Because the family employed household workers, Cornish was often relieved of childcare responsibilities and was therefore able to join other middle-class women in developing a career as a volunteer in civic work.[9] Throughout the 1920s, she sought various positions of leadership in the community and, in the process, built a strong social network consisting of family members and friends. One significant civic project to which Cornish devoted time was the Little Rock playground movement. The goal was for the Community Chest to take over the financial responsibility to further expand and direct safe play environments for Little Rock children.[10] At the time, Hilda had three children under the age of ten, with her youngest child, Don, only three years old. Then in 1922, Governor Thomas C. McRae appointed Cornish to be a member of the board of managers for the State Farm for Women, a correctional institution a few miles outside Jacksonville in Pulaski County.[11] Her sincere interest in social work led her to accept the position. This interest would continue to be central to her life, and she would constantly seek solutions to perceived social problems by organizing and lobbying for institutional changes in Arkansas. Her long involvement with the existing Conference of Social Work attests to this approach to community activism. Another arena in which she developed leadership skills was through her involvement in the women's club movement. For example, by 1924 she chaired the Program Committee of the Arkansas Federation of Women's Clubs. The programs presented by the various clubs might not always have addressed the more significant social problems in the larger community, but through her active participation Cornish gained important social connections, and she developed a reputation for being both dependable and respectable.[12]

While the urban industrialized regions of the nation were enjoying economic prosperity for much of the 1920s, Arkansas still depended on an agriculture economy that experienced depressed crop prices throughout the decade. When the Mississippi River flooded in 1927, the state experienced a serious crisis. The situation demanded government interference, and Cornish led the voluntary personnel department for the flood relief program.[13] In this capacity, she experienced firsthand the difficulties that beset people during natural disasters, and she also understood the need for government intervention at times when individuals are unable to access resources on their own. Personal disaster shook the family a year later: Edward Cornish committed suicide in a New Orleans hotel room in November 1928 when his banking ventures faced financial trouble and he saw no solutions. In two notes left for Hilda, he expressed his love for her, assured her that she would be financially secure, gave instructions concerning whom to trust with financial investments, and warned about those who might prey on her under these circumstances. Ed also let her know that he wished for the money left behind to be used to educate the children. Despite his business losses, Ed Cornish had left his widow financially secure.[14]

At the time of her husband's death, Hilda was fifty years old and her youngest child, Don, was then eleven years old. This was, of course, a severe shock for Hilda and the family. After a time of adjustment to her new life situation, Hilda Cornish embarked on an intense career in the world of unpaid volunteer work.[15] While Ed and Hilda each had completed only eight years of formal schooling, their children would all eventually enroll at prestigious universities. Agreeing with her husband's wishes, she would see to it that three of the girls—Hilda, Miriam, and Sylvia—attended Bryn Mawr College in Pennsylvania; that Edward Jr. attended Yale University in Connecticut; and that Don had the opportunity to enroll at both the Massachusetts Institute of Technology and Yale University.[16]

While the Cornish family was well established financially, other Arkansans faced economic hardships due to the economic crash in 1929 and the deepening of the Depression that followed. The average per capita income for the nation was $705 in 1929, while the Arkansas per capita income was a mere $305.[17] In addition to a depressed national economy, the rural population had been struggling to recover from the 1927 flood and, in addition, would experience a severe drought in 1930–1931. Therefore, rural communities were hit the hardest, and poverty became an overwhelming reality to many. As a result, people desperate to feed their families staged a number of demonstrations in several locations across the state. Farmers responding to Red Cross officials' announcement that aid could not be distributed until administrative formalities had been resolved initiated a well-noted outbreak in the rural town of London, located eighty-five miles northwest of Little Rock. Bread lines were organized by local merchants, who feared more serious trouble if food was not somehow distributed immediately.[18] It was in this context that Cornish became an advocate of universal access to safe and effective birth control for women in Arkansas.

Cornish became interested in the issue of birth control when her oldest son, Ed Jr., and the son of Margaret Sanger, Stuart, were roommates at Yale University.

Sanger was at the time diligently working to build a national network of activists to demand the dissemination of safe and effective birth control to all women. Meeting Sanger, Cornish was introduced to the various facets of running a local birth control clinic. During the summer of 1930, Cornish visited New York for the purpose of observing Sanger's work of running a clinic at the Birth Control Clinical Research Bureau. Sanger had built this clinic, which opened in 1923, into an impressive organization that served more than ten thousand clients a year by 1930; the clinic also trained physicians and medical students in various methods of contraception. During her stay in New York, Cornish learned much in conversations with Margaret Sanger, and as a result of their mutual interests, a friendship between the two women developed that would last throughout their lives.[19] The course charted for the local Little Rock birth control movement by Cornish for the next three decades closely reflected this relationship. Gaining support for such a potentially controversial issue in the larger community would seriously test the leadership abilities of Cornish.

Social activists in local communities across the nation built support for the birth control cause in various ways depending on their respective local cultures.[20] Hilda Cornish shrewdly approached Little Rock leaders and rallied support from a relatively broad spectrum of citizens. The individuals whom Cornish targeted knew of her through religious fellowship, organized community activities, or business relations. A group of twelve men and women met for a luncheon at the Cornish house in November 1930 to make plans, and they decided to appoint Cornish as their leader. The Arkansas Eugenics Association (AEA) was created in that meeting with the intention of promoting "the eugenic development of the human race under favorable physical, economic, and social conditions," as stated in the second article of its constitution.[21] There is no clear evidence to suggest that the group in Little Rock focused their work on pursuing a truly eugenic agenda, judging from their reports and other public information generated by the AEA. The group, however, chose to focus on poor married white women and made use of eugenic rhetoric in their attempt to establish support for disseminating contraceptives to the population at large. Rather than officially affiliating with the Sanger-led movement, the group selected a name for their organization they felt would draw the widest support and the least controversy. As one of the founding members recalled, "It was suggested that because the [birth control] movement might evoke criticism on the part of a rather orthodox and staid community, that we call it the Arkansas Eugenics Association on the grounds that nobody would object to being well born."[22] Margaret Sanger was at this particular time in a new phase of her efforts to direct and organize a national birth control movement. By opening the first birth control clinic in 1916 in Brooklyn, New York, she had seriously challenged moral expectations of women's primary roles as mothers. Her ideas were for the time both radical and controversial as she suggested women could express their sexuality more freely without the consequence of pregnancy. During the 1920s, however, Sanger slowly had changed her tactics to increase sympathy for her cause. By 1930, she allied with the more conservative segments of society, although she still had the reputation with the general public as a radical.[23]

It was important to couch the birth control topic in a way to educate those who could potentially support the establishment of a birth control clinic. Indicative of her leadership ability, Cornish carefully selected a group of individuals to form the leadership core of the AEA. Her intent was to neutralize a potentially controversial cause by assembling respected community members who would be able to bring the message to their various constituents and friends. Half of the members of the organizing meeting in November 1930 were women. Most of them were involved in unpaid volunteer work, but at least one had a career in public service: Lillian Dees McDermott.[24] Highly educated, she was instrumental in creating the Pulaski County Juvenile Court and served as its referee from 1927 to 1942. As an influential woman in the community, she was a welcome addition to the ranks of the AEA. McDermott was born a year prior to Cornish, and the two women were close friends and supported each other's causes over several decades. Other women recruited for the birth control cause by Cornish were respected members and leaders of various women's clubs or the relatives of such. All three of her daughters, Hilda, Sylvia, and Miriam, would be intimately involved and highly supportive of their mother's agenda. In other words, Cornish shrewdly utilized the connections she had developed throughout the years as a volunteer in groups advocating for civic improvement.[25]

Cornish also recruited individuals anchored in the business world. Graham Roots Hall, for example, assisted the AEA in legal matters. His attempts to influence local public attitudes about birth control were not always conventional, however. He is known to have shocked guests at formal dinner parties by pulling a diaphragm (a contraceptive device) out of his vest pocket.[26] That he could get away with such a stunt suggests that the topic of effective birth control soon became accepted in the social circles of the well-to-do community members.

Cornish's carefully selected group of AEA founders also included individuals who had faced controversy in the past. Rabbi Ira E. Sanders of Temple B'nai Israel was already involved in numerous civic organizations and was an early proponent of civil rights. Cornish and Sanders had met while serving on the Little Rock Public Library's board of trustees, and over the years they developed a strong friendship that lasted until Cornish's death in 1965.[27] In 1929, Sanders had insisted that two African American women students be enrolled in the Little Rock School of Social Work, started by Sanders in 1927, over the strong objections of others. At the time, the school was a unit of the University of Arkansas Extension Department. As a result, the school was briefly racially desegregated, until Sanders was forced to give in to the official segregated policy of the university. That Cornish selected such a man as a close friend, and continuously supported his work throughout the years, suggests that she was, indeed, a woman who did not mind challenging the status quo on behalf of those less powerful.

Other religious leaders from the community were included in the group of organizers. While Hilda Cornish did not formally belong to a religious institution, she had supporters in several of the Little Rock churches. Dr. Hay Watson Smith, the minister of the Second Presbyterian Church, had been involved in a controversy of his own during the 1920s because he was teaching evolution in the schools. He was publicly criticized for interpreting the Bible inaccurately and for leading his parishioners to follow a road that led them astray. Between 1929 and 1934, Smith faced charges of heresy by the Arkansas Presbytery (four times), the Arkansas Synod (three times), and the General Assembly of the Presbyterian Church in the United States (four times). Despite this criticism of Smith, the increase in church membership during his twenty-eight years of leadership, to more than 2,300 people, testifies to the fact that his views were acceptable to a great extent.[28]

With a core group of supporters established by 1930, Cornish set out to convince the Little Rock community that a birth control clinic for poor white women was indeed a worthwhile cause. In order to build support, she emphasized that educating Little Rock citizens about the benefits of contraceptives and child spacing was essential at a time when the community was experiencing hardship due to the severity of the Depression. Information disseminated by the AEA was constructed in a way to appeal to a large variety of people. For those unfamiliar with the benefits of safe and effective contraceptives, the AEA facilitated opportunities to learn the scientific facts by offering printed materials and lectures. For those who feared that the number of poor and economically dependent people was increasing, information was presented that suggested effective solutions. To those who had moral doubts about liberalizing access to birth control for the general public, the association presented lectures and discussions at which religious leaders promoted a morally acceptable context for birth control. Those who blamed men for women's suffering also found support for their views in the ideas and information promoted by the AEA. In other words, it was possible for people of quite diverse opinions to find something appealing in the work of the AEA. Reports were composed and distributed to prospective supporters of the movement, including civic clubwomen, individuals involved in a broad range of social work, physicians, insurance companies, and others who were either in a position to contribute economically or likely to be in contact with prospective clients.[29]

By the time Little Rock birth control advocates joined the larger birth control movement in 1930, activists in the Sanger-led branch had developed two strategies to accomplish the main goals of opening physician-controlled clinics in order to disseminate information and dispense contraceptive devices to women, and influencing the legislative process in order to successfully remove all legal obstacles to the dissemination of birth control information. The Birth Control Clinical Research Bureau in New York was the model for the clinic movement, and the National Committee on Federal Legislation for Birth Control, Inc., was the vehicle created by Sanger to influence the laws. Hilda Cornish served as the liaison between these national organizations and the local Arkansas birth control movement. At the time, national leaders quarreled about strategies, and Sanger in 1928 had broken away from the American Birth Control League, the organization she had originally created.[30] Even though Cornish was a friend of Sanger and was aware of this schism, she elected to affiliate with both organizations on paper throughout the 1930s. The official stationery designed and used by the Arkansas group listed the National Committee on Federal Legislation for Birth Control on top in all capital letters and the American Birth Control League below in lowercase letters. This suggests that Cornish and her Little Rock advocates adopted the strategies that were most useful to their local circumstances.

Modeled on the work of the Birth Control Clinical Research Bureau in New York and under the leadership of Cornish, the Arkansas Eugenics Association organized and then directed the Little Rock Birth Control Clinic from 1931 until 1940. When examining the number of women served by the clinic, it is important to realize that it was only open one and a half to three hours per week over the years. Overall, the record shows that approximately 1,650 women were directly served. The vast majority of the women included in the clinic statistics were indigent white women (1,500 of the 1,650 clients), since African American women were not invited until October 1937. Additional women were either informed of the clinic or visited without actually completing the procedure of the initial interview, physical examination, and instructions for methods.[31]

The women who approached the clinic clearly desired to limit the size of their families, but had been unable to acquire an effective method to do so. Poor and working-class women in Arkansas did have some access to birth control information before the AEA opened its clinic in 1931: they learned from other women and possibly from advertisements and sales by the contraceptive industry. Because the main challenge for women was to gain access to information about the most harmless and reliable methods, those who sought the advice of the AEA seemed unconcerned with why Arkansas birth control advocates had turned their attention to the poorest segment of the population at this particular time. Letters from these poor women demonstrate that they had their own reasons for seeking reliable birth control, no matter where the information originated.[32]

By the mid-1930s, the word was out that Hilda Cornish and the AEA were in command of birth control information, and both poor and middle-class Arkansans wrote letters requesting help. Most letter writers lived in areas outside Little Rock and were unable to visit the clinic in person. The letters testify to both the needs of the individual families and their gratitude for the services rendered by the Little Rock Birth Control Clinic. While some women had little knowledge about reliable and safe contraceptive methods, many were eager to share what they learned to help others. A woman from Gassville, a town 150 miles north of Little Rock, desperately wanted information, since she believed that having four or five children was too much for poor people. "I was told that salt water douche was reliable but it failed. . . . I have been told that Lysol douches, permanganate or potach [sic] and etc. would do but I was afraid of them. . . . Would be very glad if you could help me by telling me some sure and safe method."[33] In another case, a friend of a destitute young woman living in Cisco wrote to Hilda Cornish. On behalf of her friend, the letter writer described the circumstances of the family in question where the husband was considered irresponsible and the young mother was desperate for information to help prevent further pregnancies. This thirty-year-old mother already had four children, and Cornish was informed that "the 3 older children have not had as much milk nor other foods as they need. . . . If there is anything that can be done to prevent this woman having more children it will be a blessing beyond comfort to her and the children she has. I am now financially unable to do more than help them with groceries and clothes."[34]

Even though the AEA publicly addressed the need to prevent poor women from reproducing, middle-class individuals also sought out the clinic for advice. In some cases, letters addressed to Margaret Sanger's clinic in New York by people living in Arkansas were forwarded to Cornish. One such letter writer was from Camden and requested contraceptive information for his fiancée. As they were soon to be married, he requested the names and addresses of physicians "qualified to make a thorough pre-marital examination for my fiancée, and fit her with a dependable contraceptive device for use after our marriage. . . . My fiancée wishes to have this matter attended to at as early a date as possible, and she is particularly anxious to have the examination made by a woman." In her response to the request, Cornish referred the couple to specific physicians affiliated with the local birth control movement, and she suggested that it would be unlikely that other doctors would be willing to give contraceptive advice to an unmarried woman. Cornish closed her letter by stating that she wished "that more men and women contemplating marriage would adopt the procedure that you and your fiancée have."[35]

During the many hours she spent reading and responding to these letters, Hilda Cornish developed a sincere compassion for the women's needs. Her kind and informative responses testify to the genuine respect she had for these women. Various reasons for seeking out birth control advice included life-threatening physical conditions, economic hardships, abusive husbands, sickly children due to too frequent pregnancies, and a general lack of knowledge about reproductive health. As in the case with Mrs. Benson from Searcy in 1952, Cornish would respond to the letter writers and either give the women the information they sought, refer them to a physician willing to aid, or maybe even set up a meeting to discuss the individual's concerns. The AEA developed a list of physicians willing to assist women in the various counties, and Cornish would draw from this list and pass on the names and contact information of physicians to the letter writers. In effect, she served as a liaison between the women and the physicians.[36]

Hilda Cornish also observed firsthand some of the economic struggles women experienced in the midst of the Great Depression and how government programs could make a difference in the lives of individuals. In 1934 Cornish accepted a position offered by the Federal Emergency Relief Administration (FERA) as the director of the Division of Women's Work. This program was especially designed to assist farm wives and widows in order to alleviate some of the severe economic hardships experienced by these particular groups. Her responsibilities included serving as a consultant on projects tailored to women and acting as a facilitator of communications with other New Deal agencies and programs. Cornish began the work in the summer of 1934, and by the fall she oversaw 161 different FERA projects involving 5,663 women. That Cornish was by this time known in the community for her promotion of birth control is obvious by the humorous teasing at the "follies" program performed on the last day of a three-day meeting with the Conference of Social Work in mid-May 1935. In a song led by Miss Evalyn Powell titled "Nothing Wrong with the FERA," several Federal Emergency Relief Administration officials were targeted. One of the verses acknowledged Cornish's work with the following creative lyrics: "Said Mrs. Ed Cornish to the little red hen, 'you haven't laid an egg in I don't know when.' Said the little red hen, 'Why, how droll, I thought you believed in birth control.'" This song was published in the *Arkansas Gazette* for all the readers to enjoy.[37] This was the only paid position Cornish would hold during her life. An indication that perhaps the extra income was a necessity at this time was the sale in 1934 of the large family house; it had cost $60,000 to build in 1919, but sold for a meager $10,000 to a real estate agent.[38]

In addition to directing the birth control clinic and reaching out to women in need of contraceptive information, the AEA also followed the lead of Sanger's movement and lobbied for changes in the laws. The aim of these initiatives was to encourage legislation that would give physicians the freedom to disseminate birth control information, since it was believed that this would add legitimacy to the issue and therefore bring respectability to the cause. Because of this focus on the medical control of contraceptives, physicians' participation in the individual local movements was essential. What no nationally governed organization could assist with, however, was how to approach physicians in various local communities steeped in their own unique cultures and traditions.

Early in her quest to ensure access to reliable contraceptives, Hilda Cornish realized that she faced three main obstacles in gaining the support of Arkansas physicians. First, many were confused about the legality of administering birth control advice to women. Other physicians were supportive, but did not have adequate knowledge or the experience to confidently aid the women who sought their advice. The most serious obstacle, however, was many physicians' lack of interest in birth control. This issue was not high on their list of priorities at a time when the federal government, led by Franklin D. Roosevelt, was suggesting changes to the medical system that were perceived as threatening to the autonomy of the medical profession.

The physicians who agreed to serve at the Little Rock clinic were not considered radical, nor were they on the margins of their profession; they were leaders in the local professional medical community.[39] While other local clinics across the nation often relied on women physicians and public health nurses, Hilda Cornish did not seek the support of either group. Female physicians in Arkansas were very few at the time. According to Census figures, there were 7 female and 235 male physicians in Little Rock in 1930, and none of those women specialized in obstetrics and gynecology.[40] A different issue explains the lack of involvement by public health nurses. Whether or not Cornish was aware of the struggle between physicians and public health practitioners during the previous decade, she was wise to select one group over the other as her ally.[41]

While not philosophically opposed to aiding women with contraceptives, some physicians did not always have enough knowledge about reliable birth control methods. Their training in medical school had not prepared them to serve in this role.[42] The Arkansas School of Medicine in Little Rock (now the College of Medicine of the University of Arkansas for Medical Sciences) did not offer any such instruction, but Charles R. Henry took his own initiative in 1931 while enrolled there as a senior. He had heard about Hilda Cornish and the AEA-sponsored Little Rock Birth Control Clinic and decided to spend some time learning by observation. Gaining this knowledge was of primary importance to Henry because his medical interest was in obstetrics and gynecology. Henry would later be an important ally for Cornish, and his future contributions would greatly increase Arkansas women's access to reliable birth control.[43]

As early as 1931, Cornish and the AEA had urged the medical school to include teaching about contraceptives in the curriculum. They initiated letter-writing campaigns to lobby for Arkansas physicians to embrace the study and dissemination of birth control information. It would not be until the mid-1930s, however, that birth control advocates would see enough significant change to propel the birth control movement forward. In March 1934, the AEA sent letters to the secretaries of each county's medical society inquiring about its members' views on birth control. In order to build support, Cornish offered a copy of *The Technique of Contraception: An Outline* by Eric M. Matsner. Most of the local societies that responded requested this information. In this context, the Arkansas Medical Society adopted a resolution in support of birth control at its annual meeting in 1935. Present at this meeting were Hilda Cornish and Enid Branner, the Arkansas representative for the National Committee on Federal Legislation for Birth Control, Inc. Arkansas birth control advocates had lobbied the state medical society for some time, and their work eventually paid off. Nine other state medical societies also responded in support of birth control, and the 1935 annual meeting of the American Medical Association decided to study the matter.[44] A year later, the AMA made an even stronger commitment when requesting clarification concerning the legal rights of physicians in relation to contraceptives.[45]

Also in the mid-1930s, the final legal obstacle to disseminating birth control was removed in the verdict issued by the U.S. Court of Appeals for the Second Circuit in the case of *United States v. One Package of Japanese Pessaries* (1936). This ruling established that physicians could legally disseminate contraceptives. Margaret Sanger had orchestrated this case in order to facilitate a change in the law. It would take another year, until 1937, before the AMA would "officially approve of birth control as having a definite place in medical practice."[46] As a result of these events, the support and cooperation of physicians became a central issue for birth control advocates like Hilda Cornish.

It is important to note that relative to other state medical associations, the Arkansas Medical Society was quite willing to engage its member physicians in the debate. This state society joined a small group of other medical societies to pressure the larger membership of the AMA to at least study birth control issues. In general, individual Arkansas physicians were supportive of the agenda promoted by Cornish and the AEA. That the Little Rock Birth Control Clinic was able to stay open between 1931 and 1940, when many other clinics around the nation could not, testifies to the effective leadership of Cornish in calling people into action at a time of economic hardships. It is clear that in the larger context, physicians as an organized profession were rarely at the forefront of this lengthy process of assuring the availability of safe and effective contraceptives. Instead, they trod in the footsteps of women reformers like Hilda Cornish, who were acting in the interests of women and their families.

By the end of the 1930s, Cornish could look back with satisfaction at the community's acceptance of birth control as a respectable topic of public discourse and as worthy of support. In 1930, when Cornish had called together a group of influential community members for the purpose of launching the Arkansas birth control movement, the consensus had been that the mentioning of Margaret Sanger and the larger birth control movement might be too controversial. They therefore had opted for affiliation with eugenics instead. By the time Sanger visited Arkansas in 1937, local communities seemed to embrace her with open arms. This change in public opinion was in response to the effective campaign to educate people about birth control and the ability to frame the topic in ways that were comfortable to the local culture at the time.[47]

The much more challenging goal for Cornish to accomplish, however, was to convince the Arkansas community to include reliable contraceptives in statewide public health facilities. From her perspective, this would ensure that all women, regardless of economic abilities, would benefit. While she continued to ally with those she perceived could aid in this goal, larger forces influenced by the context of the time would overpower her individual contributions in this phase of her efforts. Cornish continued to look for guidance from her friend Margaret Sanger and opted to follow the lead of the Committee on Public Progress, initiated by Sanger in early 1938. The purpose of this organization was to make the public aware of the importance of reliable birth control information as a cure for many contemporary problems. This, of course, resonated with Cornish's goals for the Arkansas scene. The nationwide network of activists developed during the earlier phase of the larger movement was now efficiently linked and utilized. In January 1938, Hilda Cornish officially joined the Committee on Public Progress and agreed to the required membership commitment of writing one letter per month to agencies suggested by the leaders of the committee. The strategy was to entice concerned citizens to produce a large number of letters in support of birth control and then bombard selected agencies with these letters. Cornish would again serve as the link between a national organization and the Arkansas community by supplying the names of influential local citizens who were then, in turn, approached by the national office.[48]

In this campaign, Cornish went much beyond the requested "one letter per month" and even added her own selection of recipients to the official list issued by the committee. For the month of May, Sanger suggested that letter writers inundate the editors of four popular magazines widely read by women, encouraging the magazines to publish articles informing women about birth control. Cornish composed a letter to the editor of the *Farmer's Wife Magazine* in St. Paul, Minnesota, in which she stated, "Some recent articles on birth control in several periodicals caused such a favorable comment by the members of the Arkansas Eugenics Association that they have suggested that a similar article might interest the rural subscribers."[49] She chose to write not as an individual, but as a person backed by a group of concerned citizens. That Cornish chose a magazine targeting the rural population was not a coincidence. She had firsthand knowledge about the personal lives of these women both through her work with the FERA project in 1934 and through information relayed in the many letters that women wrote explaining their reasons for wanting to prevent additional pregnancies. Based on these experiences, she told the editor, "We find it difficult to serve the rural woman and she is greatly in need of information of the program as it is carried out today." The editor of the magazine, F. W. Beckman, responded that the magazine was not contemplating publishing such an article.[50] He perceived the topic as too controversial and was unwilling to risk offending the readers.

Locally, Cornish continued to utilize the AEA as a vehicle of change in her quest for reliable birth control services for poor women in Arkansas. The stated goal in the annual reports of the Arkansas Eugenics Association beginning in 1938 was for the outpatient departments of hospitals and public health clinics across the state to assume the task of issuing contraceptive advice and devices. The Little Rock Birth Control Clinic, directed by the AEA, was now considered by Cornish to be a "demonstration clinic" and therefore only served a limited number of women. Clinics directed and operated by volunteers, such as this one, did not have the potential to serve a large number of women, and it might fail once the current group of advocates retired from their efforts.[51] Therefore, Cornish looked to advance the program by seeking out institutions that could possibly sustain a larger program over time. The Little Rock Birth Control Clinic finally closed its doors in 1940 when prospective clients were given the opportunity either to visit the "University Clinic," a part of the medical school in Little Rock, or to be referred to physicians in their respective communities who were willing to assist. The clinic affiliated with the medical school was only offered to married women who were unable to afford a physician in private practice. Charles Henry, the young medical student who in 1930 had learned by observation at the clinic initiated by Cornish, was now instrumental in organizing the clinic at the medical school. At this point, he was a professor in the Gynecology and Obstetrics Department and arranged for these clinics to be held every Friday at 3 p.m. in connection with the already existing postpartum clinics. As of 1939, there were seven cities in Arkansas where birth control advice was available. There were 507 functioning clinics in 1940, and most of those clinics were initiated and directed by volunteers, similar to the one in Little Rock.[52]

To continue the educational aspects of the AEA, Cornish made good use of her connections with other organizations in the community. Serving alternately as a regular member and as a member of the executive board, she had a long-standing relationship with the Arkansas Conference of Social Work. Her good friend Lillian Dees McDermott was also a leader of this organization and served as the president in the 1940s. Among other strategies, Cornish made sure to arrange for educational exhibits of family planning topics to be included in the annual meetings, which often lasted three days. These conferences attracted individuals who would likely be in contact with families in need of reliable birth control information.[53]

The Birth Control Federation of America changed its name to the Planned Parenthood Federation of America in 1942. Again, following the lead of the national scene, Little Rock birth control advocates changed the name of the Arkansas Eugenics Association to the Planned Parenthood Association of Arkansas that same year. Cornish was now sixty-four years old and a grandmother of children ranging from infants to teenagers. This could have been a good time for Cornish to hand over the leadership to the next generation, but instead of retiring, she turned her focus to lobbying for the public health system to include safe and effective birth control among its services.[54]

While various community groups supported this effort, the organized community of physicians turned out to be too serious of a challenge for Cornish this time. While the Arkansas Medical Society actually had spearheaded the campaign among physicians in support of considering contraceptives a legitimate medical issue in the 1930s, in the 1940s it now refused to endorse the goal of including birth control services in public health facilities. The strategy Cornish elected to reach her goal was again based on the directives of the national parent organization, the Planned Parenthood Federation of America. After all, being connected to other local clinics and sharing information about strategies had served her well in the past. Utilizing her position as the chair and state representative of the Planned Parenthood Association of Arkansas, Cornish embarked on the suggested letter campaign to target county medical societies and individual physicians known to be supportive of the birth control cause. To encourage the letter recipients to act, copies of model resolutions were enclosed. The model for a county society partially stated, "Be it resolved: That the Pulaski County Medical Society go on record as favoring the introduction of birth control for the indigent, and medically determined deserving cases, as a public health activity of the Arkansas State Board of Health."[55] At none of the three occasions that the Arkansas Medical Society voted on such a resolution (1941, 1944, 1950) did they endorse the proposed changes.[56] Clearly, their collective objection to government interference in the highly privatized medical system was at the root of these outcomes.

Cornish might have miscalculated a bit this time. Just as she had followed her affiliate organization's directives and disseminated its propaganda, the physicians did the same. When legislation was introduced that threatened the autonomy of the medical profession, the American Medical Association effectively counteracted these efforts and instructed its members to comply. Influences beyond the control of Hilda Cornish's best intentions set the stage for the Arkansas Medical Society's rejection of the resolution in 1944. A U.S. House of Representatives bill proposing an extension of the government-controlled Social Security program was presented in 1943, the Wagner-Murray-Dingell Bill. In response, the AMA called a special meeting with the result of thrusting the professional medical organization into the world of political lobbying in Washington, D.C. The Council for Medical Services and Public Relations was created by the AMA and was charged to direct a public debate against efforts to nationalize any aspect of the medical system.[57] By this time, U.S. citizens had for a decade endured a federal government that had asserted an extraordinary amount of power over local communities—not that Hilda Cornish seemed to mind, as long as it benefited those in need.

Not giving up on getting the Arkansas physicians onboard, Cornish in 1949 again embarked on a campaign to get the Arkansas Medical Society to support the public health resolution.[58] She used the same strategy as in 1944, but when the resolution was up for a vote by the Arkansas physicians in 1950, even stronger political forces worked against Cornish and her fellow birth control advocates. President Harry S. Truman had called for national health insurance in his State of the Union address in 1948. He proposed that the government should ensure that all citizens have access to adequate health care services. As historian Melanie

Kay Welch has argued in her study of these events in Arkansas, the national health insurance program that Truman proposed was highly controversial and quite threatening to many physicians.[59] But it was the action the following year by the national representative of the physicians, the AMA, that possibly caused several Arkansas physicians to reject the public health resolution once again.

The previously proposed Wagner-Murray-Dingell Bill was again introduced in 1949, adding to physicians' anxiety about the future status of the medical system. In reaction to the bill, the AMA actually hired a public relations firm, Whitaker and Baxter. The firm initiated an intensive campaign to "educate" both physicians and the general public on the evils of "socialized" medicine.[60] While it is clear that many individual members of the Arkansas Medical Society were in support of women gaining access to reliable birth control service, they were collectively more concerned with the perceived threat to the structure of the medical system and therefore voted not to endorse the public health bill in 1950. This must certainly have been a serious disappointment to Cornish, and it would take until the political winds eventually turned in the 1960s, with Lyndon B. Johnson's War on Poverty and the Great Society reform legislation, for Arkansas women of all economic groups to have their needs met. It would take until 1964, the year before Hilda Cornish passed away, for the Arkansas public health system to initiate birth control services in public health departments, and until 1966 before women in all Arkansas counties had access to safe and effective contraceptives and other much-needed family planning services.[61]

Hilda Cornish was finally ready in 1951 to retire from publicly leading the community. Her friend Rabbi Sanders agreed to take over the helm.[62] The Planned Parenthood Association of Arkansas struggled with support at the time, and in 1955 Sanders informed the national Planned Parenthood office that the local leadership had decided to dissolve the Arkansas group, due to a lack of financial means to carry on the program in accordance with the federal group's requirements. He asked that "all cases that might come to the organization" be referred to Cornish.[63] Even at age seventy-seven, Cornish was unwilling to abandon those women who might seek her out for birth control advice. Not willing to leave the scene of action completely, Cornish traveled with Margaret Sanger on a tour of ten nations and participated at the International Conference on Planned Parenthood in Tokyo, Japan, that same year. She had previously joined Sanger on a similar tour in 1952, when the two participated at the International Birth Control Conference in Bombay, India. It was at this conference that the International Planned Parenthood Federation was created. It is quite remarkable that these two elderly women, Sanger at seventy-six and Cornish at seventy-seven years old in 1955, still had the passion and energy to be engaged.[64]

Hilda Cornish spent the last decade of her life in her own home after suffering complications during spinal surgery, which left her dependent on nurses and housekeepers. With her daughter Hilda Cornish Coates living just down the street, Cornish stayed close to family. She passed away on November 19, 1965, at age eighty-seven, and at her request her good friend Ira E. Sanders gave the eulogy at the funeral.[65]

Hilda Cornish is often remembered today as the "Birth Control Lady" in the Little Rock community, and rightfully so. She should be given the credit for demanding that those in a position to control access to safe and effective birth control take the appropriate steps to make it available to all women in Arkansas. While believing this to be a civic duty, Cornish and her fellow advocates had to combat organized physicians, who resisted relinquishing control of the contemporary medical system for the sake of the larger community. Based on the strategies she adopted, Cornish must have understood that when individuals organize together on a voluntary basis and collectively utilize their combined resources, positive change happens in society. Her motive was not to suggest that government agencies take full responsibility for the health of the individual; rather, she recognized that the obstacles for poor women to be able to control their own reproduction could only be overcome if government powers were used to facilitate access to information and services that women simply could not get on their own.

NOTES

1. Sally Ellis Benson to Cornish, February 27, 1952; Cornish to Benson, March 1, 1952; Cornish to Benson, April 20, 1952, all in Ira E. Sanders Papers, UALR.MS.0098, box 1, file 17, Center for Arkansas History and Culture, Arkansas Studies Institute, University of Arkansas, Little Rock (hereafter UALR-CAHC).

2. For a detailed discussion of the Arkansas birth control movement between 1942 and 1980 and the significance of the political climate of the time, see Melanie Kay Welch, "Politics and Poverty: Women's Reproductive Rights in Arkansas, 1942–1980," Ph.D. diss., Auburn University, 2009.

3. For a comprehensive overview of Margaret Sanger's relationship to local community advocates, see Cathy Moran Hajo, *Birth Control on Main Street: Organizing Clinics in the United States, 1919–1939* (Urbana-Champaign: University of Illinois Press, 2010).

4. Welch, "Politics and Poverty," 127–44.

5. Information about the early life of Cornish was derived from her grandson Edward Coates, letter to author, June 23, 1995. Information concerning neighborhoods and households, including the Cornish household, was derived from the U.S. Census, 1880, St. Louis County, Mo., and U.S. Census, 1900, Newark City, N.J.

6. For the death of Edward Cornish's first wife and three of their children, see "A Terrible Blow," *Arkansas Gazette*, September 28, 1898, 3:3; letter from Annabelle Lambert Crandall to Edith Cornish

Low (Edward Cornish's daughter), October 5, 1951, in the possession of Julie Low Morin (Edith Low's granddaughter).

7. Information concerning the Cornish family life was derived from her daughter Hilda Cornish Coates, interview with author, July 12, 1989, transcript, 2 and 6, Oral History Research Office, University of Memphis, Tennessee; Hilda Cornish Coates, letters and conversations with author, 1989–1995; Edward Coates, letter to author, June 23, 1995; U.S. Census, 1890, 1900, 1910, 1920, 1930, 1940; *Little Rock City Directory*, 1890, 1893, 1897, 1902, 1907, 1926, 1928, 1930, 1934, 1940; Alex Nichols, "Cornish House," in *Encyclopedia of Arkansas History and Culture*, http://www.encyclopediaofarkansas.net/encyclopedia/entry-detail.aspx?entryID=7594.

8. Julie Low Morin, emails to author, June 2013.

9. For overviews of the significance of women's volunteer work, see Anne Firor Scott, *Natural Allies: Women's Associations in American History* (Urbana-Champaign: University of Illinois Press, 1991); and Robin Muncy, *Creating a Female Dominion in American Reform, 1890–1935* (New York: Oxford University Press, 1991).

10. "Mrs. Ed Cornish Dies: Led in Birth Control," *Arkansas Gazette*, November 20, 1965, B10:2. Evidence of Cornish's volunteer work was also found in various documents in the records of the Arkansas Eugenics Association and the Little Rock Clinic, housed at the Historical Research Center, University of Arkansas for Medical Sciences Library, History of Public Health in Arkansas Collection, boxes 5 and 6 (hereafter BC-UAMS). See also Arkansas Federation of Women's Clubs, UALR.MS.0056, UALR-CAHC.

11. "Annual Report of the State Farm for Women, Jacksonville, Arkansas: 1922," pamphlet.03224, UALR-CAHC. Also see "Pulaski County Grand Jury Report, 1926," Arkansas History Commission, Small Manuscript Collections, box 48, no. 5.

12. See Mrs. Frederick Hanger and Clara B. Eno, "The Story of the Arkansas Federation of Women's Clubs, 1897–1934," Arkansas Federation of Women's Clubs, UALR.MS.0056, UALR-CAHC.

13. Nancy Hendricks, "Flood of 1927," in *Encyclopedia of Arkansas History and Culture*, http://www.encyclopediaofarkansas.net/encyclopedia/entry-detail.aspx?search=1&entryID=2202; "The Toll of the Flood," *New York Times*, August 31, 1927. For the role of Cornish, see "Mrs. Ed Cornish Dies."

14. Hilda Cornish Coates, interview with author, 14. The following newspaper clippings are in the possession of Julie Low Morin: "Found Dead with a Pistol Wound through His Head: Edward Cornish Takes His Own Life," *Arkansas Gazette*, November 6, 1928; "Ed Cornish's Body Will Be Brought Here," unidentified clipping, November 6, 1928.

15. Community activities included serving as executive secretary of the Goodfellows Club for twelve years; vice president and president of the Council of Social Agencies; and president of the Woman's City Club (1934–1935). She served on the following boards: the Family Service Agency, the Little Rock Public Library, and the Pulaski County Welfare Commission. See "Mrs. Ed Cornish Dies."

16. Hilda Cornish Coates, letter to author, May 27, 1995.

17. David E. Rison, "Arkansas during the Great Depression," Ph.D. diss., University of California, Los Angeles, 1974, 5.

18. Forty people in Conway raided a store. Other outbreaks took place at Pine Bluff and Fort Smith. See Rison, "Arkansas during the Great Depression," 5, 20; and Gail Murray, "Forty Years Ago: The Great Depression Comes to Arkansas," *Arkansas Historical Quarterly* 29 (Winter 1970): 296.

19. Hilda Cornish to "Secy. Nat. Com. on Fed. Leg. for Birth Control," July 24, 1930, Margaret Sanger Papers, reel 84, Manuscript Division, Library of Congress, Washington, D.C. (hereafter MS-LOC); Hilda Cornish Coates, interview with author, 2. See also untitled newspaper clipping, box 5, file 4, BC-UAMS. For an overview of the Sanger-led organizations, see "Birth Control Or-

ganizations," Margaret Sanger Papers Project, https://www.nyu.edu/projects/sanger/aboutms/bc _organizations.php (accessed October 24, 2017).

20. A great overall discussion of local birth control advocates can be found in Cathy Moran Hajo, *Birth Control on Main Street: Organizing Clinics in the United States, 1916-1939* (Urbana-Champaign: University of Illinois Press, 2010).

21. For a more detailed analysis of the formation and goals of the AEA, including a discussion of the group's interpretation of eugenics, see Marianne Leung, "'Better Babies': The Arkansas Birth Control Movement during the 1930s," Ph.D. diss., University of Memphis, 1996, 38-71.

22. Rabbi Ira E. Sanders, interview by Charlotte Gadberry, January 18, 1978, Little Rock, Ark., transcript, UALR.MS.0218, box 9, file 17, Oral History Collection, UALR-CAHC.

23. Concerning this change in Sanger's approach, see Joan M. Jensen, "The Evolution of Margaret Sanger's 'Family Limitation' Pamphlet, 1914-1921," *Signs* 6 (1981): 548-57; and Helen Chesler, *Woman of Valor: Margaret Sanger and the Birth Control Movement in America* (New York: Simon and Schuster, 1992), 269-309.

24. Unlike Cornish, McDermott had formal educational credentials, having studied at the University of Arkansas Law School and the University of Southern California, where she focused on social work. For additional information, see Leung, "Better Babies," 42-43; and Julienne Crawford, "Lillian Dees McDermott," in *Encyclopedia of Arkansas History and Culture*, http://www.encyclopediaofarkansas.net/encyclopedia/entry-detail.aspx?search=1&entryID=1710.

25. Hilda Cornish Coates, telephone conversations with author and letters to author, July-October 1989.

26. Raida Pfeifer, interview with author, June 17, 1992, transcript, 9-10, Oral History Research Office, University of Memphis, Tennessee.

27. For the friendship between Cornish and Sanders, see Hilda Cornish Coates, interview with author, 5. For other information about Sanders, see Claire N. Moody, "Rabbi Sanders Is an Advocate of the Brotherhood of Man," *Arkansas Democrat*, June 2, 1951, magazine section, 1; Matilda Tuohey, "Rabbi Will End 37 Years at B'nai Israel August 31," *Arkansas Gazette*, October 22, 1961, A1-2; Carolyn Gray LeMaster, *A Corner of the Tapestry: A History of the Jewish Experience in Arkansas, 1820s-1990s* (Fayetteville: University of Arkansas Press, 1994), 64.

28. For a more detailed discussion of Hay Watson Smith, see Leung, "Better Babies," 39-42.

29. Records of the Arkansas Eugenics Association, BC-UAMS, boxes 5-6.

30. About Sanger's leadership and the politics concerning various national birth control organizations, see Chesler, *Woman of Valor*; and Hajo, *Birth Control on Main Street*.

31. This information is derived from annual reports of the Arkansas Eugenics Association and from the correspondence found in the records of the clinic at BC-UAMS, boxes 5-6.

32. See Angus McLaren, *A History of Contraception: From Antiquity to the Present* (Cambridge: Blackwell, 1990).

33. Letter to "State Hygenics [sic] Department" from unidentified woman in Gassville, Ark., May 7, 1939, BC-UAMS, box 6. Numerous individual letters are among the documents pertaining to the AEA and the Little Rock Birth Control Clinic, BC-UAMS. For a more detailed discussion of this topic, see Leung, "Better Babies," 146-53.

34. Letter to Mrs. Hilda Cornish from unidentified woman in Cisco, Ark., March 29, 1939, BC-UAMS, box 6.

35. The earliest letter in this particular string of communication by the man in Camden was dated December 19, 1937. See letter to Emira Coutant, American Birth Control League, Inc., New York City. The writer was informed that his letter had been forwarded to the AEA in a letter dated

December 28, 1937. For the quotes, see letter to Arkansas Eugenics Association by unidentified man from Camden, Ark., January 4, 1938; letter by Cornish to unidentified man in Camden, January 5, 1938, all at BC-UAMS.

36. See correspondence between Hilda Cornish and leaders of various county medical societies in the collection for the AEA and the Little Rock Birth Control Clinic, BC-UAMS.

37. Holly Hope, *An Ambition to Be Preferred: New Deal Recovery Efforts and Architecture in Arkansas, 1933–1943* (Little Rock: Arkansas Historic Preservation Program, 2006), 20–21; untitled newspaper clipping, Arkansas Conference of Social Work, UALR.MS.0097, box 11, file 21, UALR-CAHC.

38. Nichols, "Cornish House."

39. My analysis is based on information in the *Journal of the Arkansas Medical Society* and the *American Medical Directory: A Register of Legally Qualified Physicians*. I looked for evidence of medical expertise as well as leadership initiatives in the professional medical community in the 1920s and 1930s. For a more detailed discussion, see Leung, "Better Babies," 103–39.

40. Leung, "Better Babies," 125.

41. See Elissa L. Miller, "From Private Duty to Public Health: A History of Arkansas Nursing, 1895 to 1954," Ph.D. diss., Case Western University, 1989, 112–28.

42. A 1933 study conducted by Abraham Stone and published in *Human Fertility* suggested that only twenty-eight of sixty-two medical schools surveyed offered any instruction about contraceptives. While a larger number of medical schools demonstrated evidence of addressing the topic by 1942, the instruction was "adequate in only a few schools; in most schools it is still desultory and there is definitely too little clinical training." Abraham Stone, "The Teaching of Contraception in Medical Schools," *Human Fertility* 7 (August 1942): 108–11.

43. Charles R. Henry Sr., interview with author, September 26, 1989, transcript, 2–3, Oral History Research Office, University of Memphis, Tennessee.

44. Branner reported about the meeting in a letter to Hazel Moore, the national field secretary for the national committee, that "the state Medical Society gave us the privilege of the floor (it was darn hard to get)." Branner to Moore, April 19, 1935, reel 84, MS-LOC. For the AMA decision, see "Resolutions on Contraception," American Medical Association, House of Delegates Proceeding, annual session, June 10, 1935, 34 and 45, http://ama.nmtvault.com/jsp/viewer.jsp?doc_id=ama_arch%2FHOD00001%2F00000026&query1=&recoffset=0&collection_filter=All&collection_name=1ee24daa-2768-4bff-b792-e4859988fe94&sort_col=publication%20date&CurSearchNum=-1.

45. "Report of Committee to Study Contraceptive Practices and Related Problems," *Journal of the American Medical Association* 106 (May 30, 1936): 1911.

46. William L. Laurence, "Birth Control Is Accepted by American Medical Body," *New York Times*, June 9, 1937, 1:1. For more information about the Arkansas Medical Society and the process of soliciting its support, see Leung, "Better Babies," 125–39.

47. Leung, "Better Babies," 191–96.

48. See letter to "Dear Friend" from Margaret Sanger, January 1938, BC-UAMS, box 5, file 5; and correspondence between Cornish and the national office of the committee, BC-UAMS, box 6.

49. Cornish, letter to the editor, *Farmer's Wife Magazine*, May 2, 1938, BC-UAMS, box 5, file 5.

50. Letter to Cornish from F. W. Beckman at *Farmer's Wife Magazine*, May 6, 1938, BC-UAMS, box 5, file 5.

51. This was a common experience for other clinics directed by volunteers. See Hajo, *Birth Control on Main Street*, 19–27.

52. See draft of the 1939 annual report for the Little Rock Birth Control Clinic, prepared by Miriam Phillips (one of Cornish's daughters and a clinic volunteer), BC-UAMS, box 6, file 4.

53. Copies of annual conference programs, 1935–1945, Arkansas Conference of Social Work, UALR.MS.0098, box 6, UALR-CAHC.

54. Jerry Dean, "1930s Birth Control Clinic Featured in Health History," *Arkansas Gazette*, March 9, 1983. Also see Hilda Cornish correspondence with various community members on stationery labeled Planned Parenthood Association of Arkansas in 1942 and thereafter, BC-UAMS, box 6.

55. Mrs. Ed Cornish to Dr. Joseph O. Boydstone (Hot Springs, Ark.), April 14, 1944, BC-UAMS, box 6, file 7. As Welch demonstrated in her study, representatives of the state Department of Public Health had objected to assuming birth control services as an additional responsibility on the grounds of lack of personnel. Welch, "Politics and Poverty," 57–66.

56. Welch, "Politics and Poverty," 34, 57–66; "Proceedings of the Sixty-Ninth Annual Session: Arkansas Medical Society, April 17 and 18, 1944," *Journal of the Arkansas Medical Society* 41 (June 1944): 29.

57. Edward R. Annis, "Towards Socialized Medicine (Part I): A Historic Chronology," *Hacienda Publishing*, http://www.haciendapub.com/medicalsentinel/towards-socialized-medicine-part-i-historic-chronology (last modified 2016).

58. Letters to various physicians and county medical societies urging support, copied and exchanged between Sanders and Cornish, kept the two closely informed about the community events taking place. Ira E. Sanders Papers, UALR.MS.0098, box 1, file 18, UALR-CAHC.

59. Welch, "Politics and Poverty," 61–63.

60. Jill Lepore, "The Lie Factory: How Politics Became a Business," *New Yorker*, September 24, 2012, http://www.newyorker.com/reporting/2012/09/24/120924fa_fact_lepore?currentPage=all&mobify=0&utm_source=buffer&buffer_share=24a19.

61. Welch, "Politics and Poverty," 136.

62. Letter to Dr. Ira E. Sanders from Mrs. Fifield Workum of Planned Parenthood Federation of America, Inc., June 18, 1951, Ira E. Sanders Papers, UALR.MS.0098, box 1, file 16, UALR-CAHC.

63. Sanders corresponded using Temple B'nai Israel stationery, rather than the Planned Parenthood Association of Arkansas stationery previously used by Cornish. Letter to Planned Parenthood Federation of America, Inc., New York, from Sanders, October 14, 1955, Ira E. Sanders Papers, UALR.MS.0098, box 1, file 17, UALR-CAHC.

64. Hilda Cornish Coates, interview with author, 11. The travel itinerary for October 13–December 14, 1955, was prepared by Anita Schutze Travel Service, Austin, Texas, for the trip to the Fifth International Conference on Planned Parenthood, Tokyo, Japan. BC-UAMS, box 5, file 2.

65. Information concerning living arrangements and the health of Cornish at the end of her life was derived from several conversations and correspondence with Hilda Cornish Coates, March 1996.

Adolphine Fletcher Terry

(1882–1976)

Seventy-Five Years of Social Activism in Arkansas

DIANNA OWENS FRALEY

On September 10, 1958, Adolphine Fletcher Terry phoned Vivion Brewer and asked, "Are you ready to do something about Little Rock?"[1] Days earlier, Governor Orval Faubus had closed the Little Rock schools for the 1958–1959 school year and effectively displaced 3,655 black and white students.[2] The previous year, Faubus had blatantly defied the federal mandate to integrate public schools and brought Little Rock, a mostly moderate sleepy southern capital, into the racially charged national spotlight. In the fall of 1957, Central High School was forced to integrate nine black students under federal protection, but in 1958, Faubus moved to deny free public education to the city's youth as a ploy to uphold segregation. Even though many of the white students during that year found alternative education, many of the black students were left without such options. Terry was emotionally undone after the first year of the Central High School integration crisis. In recalling the events of 1957–1958 to Brewer, she stated, "When the governor saw a chance to further his political career and caused all that trouble at Central High School, I wanted to die. It felt [like] my life was completely washed out, and I sank back in misery, trying to forget the world."[3] She, like so many other southerners, both black and white, watched in horror as the events played out in the national media.

Prior to the making of that fateful phone call, Terry had retreated to the East Coast (as she regularly did) during the summer of 1958. However, the receipt of some unexpected correspondence refocused her priorities upon her return to Little Rock. According to Brewer, Terry said, "'We here in Arkansas are [the] most hospitable, the kindest, the most generous people on earth, but we have to admit it,' after screaming crowds and an opportunistic governor made her beloved home internationally infamous, 'we are just plain ignorant.'"[4] A letter she received from Velma Powell, the wife of a vice principal at Central High School, drew her into the integration crisis on a personal level. Powell had lived at the Fletcher-Terry mansion, the family home in Little Rock, for a year while attending college and was a dear friend of the family, so it was not surprising that her letter had a profound impact on the elderly social activist, challenging her understanding of current events and prompting her to action. Powell's letter read something like this: "In the past whenever problems have had to be faced in Little Rock, you have taken a lead in solving them. Why are you silent now? Where are you?"[5] At seventy-six years old and after a lifetime of progressive activism, few would have begrudged Terry the choice of silent anonymity now, but instead of resting on her laurels, she acted on these questions and made that pivotal phone call to Vivion Brewer. This resulted in the formation of a women's movement in the Little Rock community to reopen the schools. She cofounded an organization, the Women's Emergency Committee to Open Our Schools (WEC), which held its first meeting in Terry's dining room on September 12, 1958.[6] Terry, Brewer, and Powell decided that their goal was simple—reopen the schools—but the process proved to be much more complex. To start, they were going to openly oppose the governor's segregationist agenda and promote racial harmony in the city, no small order even in the twilight of Jim Crow.

This begets the question, who was Adolphine Fletcher Terry? How could she motivate the white upper-middle-class women of Little Rock to openly defy both the political and societal norms of the day? How had she obtained so much political clout and social influence in a southern city dominated by a "good ol' boy" political system? Historian Stephanie Bayless contends that Terry "was in many ways a stereotypical southern aristocrat, but she was also a strong and intelligent woman who was committed to creating a more egalitarian world for those Arkansans who were not in a position to help themselves."[7] To accomplish this, Terry became a champion of social causes for more than fifty years in Arkansas and impacted society in ways that would not have been thought possible in such a white patriarchal setting. As a woman of means and influence, Terry helped her native state accept the changes of an ever-evolving nation by bringing the message of integration through a body of familiar, socially acceptable local women.[8] According to her friend Vivion Brewer, "Terry has left her mark on almost every charitable organization and on all the public welfare agencies in the state of Arkansas."[9] The WEC is often considered the most memorable of her many contributions in large part because it demonstrated the power of white women in the South concerning race relations.

Adolphine Fletcher was on born on November 3, 1882, in the capital city of Little Rock, Arkansas. As the first surviving child of John Gould and Adolphine Krause Fletcher, Terry was adored by both parents, and in particular her father. The Fletchers were members of the small elite society of Little Rock, which exposed Terry to a mixture of privileged and Victorian social standards and culture. Though some of John Gould Fletcher's business ventures could be connected to New South ideology, the bulk of his wealth was tied to cotton trading. Though her unpublished memoir describes a somewhat frugal and rural lifestyle throughout her childhood, summer trips to the East Coast and Chicago point to a much more opulent life than most Arkansans were accustomed to at the turn of the twentieth century. While the traditions, customs, and racist tenets of the New South marked Terry's early childhood, she witnessed only a few examples of social justice in these early years; each had a profound impact on her ideological development. In her memoir, Terry did not describe her mother as loving or affectionate, but she was aware of the strength of her mother's convictions. One of the most powerful memories of Terry's youth centered on the actions of her mother, which not only imparted a glimpse into the commonness and acceptability of false and malicious accusations toward African Americans during this time period but also emphasized the importance of speaking up for those who could not. While a cousin was visiting the family in Little Rock, her diamond ring disappeared, and according to Terry, "[she accused] Fred, the black boy who worked for us . . . and she wanted my mother to send for the police and have him arrested. My mother refused. . . . Fred, she felt, was entirely honest, or, if he wasn't entirely honest, at least he wouldn't steal from us, and the ring must be on the place somewhere."[10] The cousin eventually found the ring in the folds of her skirt, but refused to acknowledge her mistake.[11] Terry never forgot this incident and stated that she "had already come to recognize the fact that black people had very little chance to hold their own in an argument with a white person."[12]

Education beyond the borders of Arkansas was probably the gateway to Terry's transformation. Initially, her mother provided her educational instruction until she entered school at the age of nine. She subsequently went to a neighborhood school before attending Frederick W. Kramer School, a public institution; she graduated from Peabody High School on June 2, 1898. Her mother had read about the opening of Vassar College in Poughkeepsie, New York, and believed that was the school her daughter should attend.[13] Due to poor test scores, Terry was initially denied admittance to the institution, but after a visit from her father, she was accepted without any probationary period. Vassar was the leading institution for women's higher education at the turn of the century, and the lessons learned there became the cornerstone of Terry's social activism.

During her time at Vassar, Terry solidified her belief system concerning race relations in the South, which led her to dedicate her life to improving the social circumstances of those affected by racial and economic inequality in her home state. At an informal roundtable discussion with Vassar classmates, Terry related an epiphany she had had about her life and what she should do:

> One evening we got off on the subject of the Negro problem in the South and I made the statement, which I had heard all of my life, although not from my father, that if a black man assaulted a white woman he should be lynched on the spot. Lucy Burns, who came from Brooklyn and had more experience than I, looked at me with perfect horror, and I can still remember her exact words: "For the sake of taking revenge on one poor wretch, would you destroy the very foundations of law and order in your community?" Well, I just sat back and thought about that. I knew she was right, and it really has affected my entire life. It gave me an entirely different look, an adult look, at the situation which we faced here in the [S]outh, or for that matter, anywhere. I think that was the beginning of my spiritual education and the beginning of wisdom, and learning not to accept a thing because everybody in the community was saying it.[14]

Sufficiently challenged by her peers and exposed to the ideas of liberal Progressivism and the immorality of segregation in the South, Terry's experiences at Vassar forever influenced her life of advocacy for those less fortunate. According to historian Joan Marie Johnson, "Few [white] southern women were as brave as Virginia Durr and Adolphine Terry or as interested in challenging southern race mores."[15] Terry graduated in 1902, and upon returning to Little Rock she viewed the culture differently and questioned the values of the status quo. She reflected in her memoir, "My life would have been entirely different if I had not gone to a good eastern college, and met the kinds of people I did."[16]

Despite her freethinking spirit, Terry was still a wealthy young lady, and thus at the urging of her mother she was formally introduced into Little Rock society as a debutante. "When we returned from New York," she wrote after graduation, "I felt that that phase of my life was over, but had no ideas about what I would do next. I came back to an entirely different life.... I had never been to real parties before, since I wasn't quite sixteen when I went away to college, but I was twenty when I came home, and ready to join the social life of Little Rock."[17] To appease her mother, Terry attended parties and gatherings and participated in the traditional courtship rituals of Little Rock society. Even though this led to her meeting her future husband, David Dickson Terry, she made a rather poor showing during her time as a debutante. She looked back on this youthful period of her life as wasted time and a "waiting period."[18]

In reality, the network of influential friends and acquaintances she acquired during this time later became instrumental in helping her accomplish many of her Progressive reforms. Through the women's clubs that were common in the Progressive era, Terry and many other southern white women found an avenue for activism while playing the part of the southern lady for the white political establishment.[19] In this spirit of civic engagement, Terry cofounded in 1905 the Southern Association for College Women, which she called the College Club. She stated that before she married, "her only useful contribution [to society] was to help start the College Club, a forerunner of the Little Rock Branch of [the American Association of] University Women."[20] Though the ostensible purpose of the club was to encourage women to attend college, it instead became a network of women whose intelligence challenged the static traditions of Arkansas society; many members of the College Club later became the grassroots activists who changed their state for the better.

In 1908, during the brief tenure of Governor X. O. Pindall (1907–1909), Terry and her friend Blanche Martin, another Vassar graduate, were asked to serve on a national committee to investigate the needs of Arkansas education and make recommendations. Being one of the few college-educated women in the state, Terry readily accepted the appointment. "In the middle of all the parties and other entertainments, I took part in the first really serious project of my life."[21] In conjunction with recommendations made by the Arkansas Teachers Association, Terry and Martin's committee reviewed the current school infrastructure, as well as the "lack of revenue" and "lack of efficiency through a useless multiplication of school districts."[22] Terry, upon reflection, said, "We took our appointment very seriously and after some discussion and research found that the schools around the state had no adequate supervision. Each school was a law unto itself; there were no county superintendents and no supervision of the teacher except by the local school board which appointed them. The majority of the schools were one room country schools which had remained the same since they were established, and there was no thought of consolidating the schools or transporting children to other schools."[23]

Terry and Martin realized that teachers best understood the educational deficits in the state, and so they wrote to a number of teachers asking them to submit a three-hundred-word essay on either transportation or consolidation for publication. "Since we didn't have the vote yet, we wrote only to men because we felt what they had to say would have more influence," Terry noted.[24] Everyone they wrote to responded. This type of activism—working within the system to create change—became Terry's trademark for the remainder of her life. She always tried to find ways to maneuver within the power structure of the state and society to alter them both for the better. Terry also found through her College Club connections that county newspapers had no objections to running a weekly article on education, "especially since it would not cost them anything. We did all the work and paid for our materials."[25] In an inversion of the typical gender roles of the era, "Dave [Terry], who was then in law school, typed the articles for use each week."[26]

Success quickly came with the consolidation of the first school in Scott County in 1908. Soon legislation was passed for all schools statewide to consolidate when needed. In the 1908 annual report on Arkansas education, the superintendent of instruction, George B. Cook, conveyed the need for progressive reform in the public schools: "No longer are the public schools looked upon as merely supply houses for stored book knowledge, but these schools are expected to train the youth for citizenship and life work."[27] Also outlined in the report were the recommendations made by Terry and Martin's committee: "the consolidation of weak school districts into strong centralized districts, a Compulsory School Attendance Law, professional training of teachers, the election of County Superintendents, and the creation of a State Board of Education."[28]

In response to Terry's newspaper crusade, the legislative successes, and public sentiment, Governor George W. Donaghey created the twenty-two-member Arkansas Education Commission in 1910. Adolphine Terry stated, "It was such an obvious need at the time that it really went over big, and we very soon retired from printing our articles because the idea had caught on. I think we worked on it for two years and I have never worked on anything that was more pleasant or easier to do because the time was ripe for it to happen and, although we helped a little, centralization would have come anyway."[29] Though Terry considered this her "waiting period," it had obviously been a productive time. She fully participated in the project of streamlining the educational system in Arkansas and witnessed measurable progressive reform.

As Arkansas addressed its educational needs, Adolphine dealt with life-changing events. After the death of her father in 1906, her mother had been diagnosed with cancer and did not want her to marry as long as she was living. "I think she would have forgiven me had we gone ahead [and married]," she wrote of her relationship with David Terry, "but I just couldn't take that chance because she was a very stubborn woman and I didn't want to hurt her. John [Terry's brother] had been a heartache to her because he had left Harvard and got to Europe against her wishes."[30] Adolphine Krause Fletcher died in May 1909. On July 7, 1910, Adolphine Fletcher married David D. Terry after a four-year engagement.[31] Shortly after becoming a wife, she also became a mother of sorts, when David's half sister, Mary Louise, came to live with them after the death of her mother.[32] "She was very smart and like me, and we became great friends. . . . for many years she was part of the family, and when she graduated high school she also went to Vassar College," Terry wrote.[33]

Terry gave birth to her first child, David, in June 1911.[34] Terry stated that she purposely raised David differently than she had been reared: "Reacting to my own upbringing, I raised David not to be afraid of anything. He was never told to avoid large dogs or not to climb trees, and he could have slept on the grass if he had wanted to."[35] Terry had been raised in a strict Victorian fashion, in which children were dressed warmly even during the summer months to prevent illness and were not allowed to get dirty or play rough in case of injury.[36] Her desire to raise her son differently reveals her iconoclastic personality: she disregarded tradition for tradition's sake. She wanted her children to experience life, both the good and the bad, and to become self-reliant and knowledgeable of the world around them. In many respects, her hopes for her children were the same as her hopes for Arkansas.

Arkansas, like many southern states, was late in adopting the ideas of Progressivism, which strove for economic, social, and political justice. Though most Progressives, who were white upper-middle-class individuals, did not agree on the specific solutions to the problems facing society, all agreed that more government involvement was necessary to address the ills of the nation. In Arkansas in particular, the Progressives' efforts were continually challenged by the adverse feelings toward the federal government since the Reconstruction era.[37] Regardless of the challenges, the reform spirit informed the social consciousness of people like Terry for the next fifty years. A trio of Arkansas governors, Jeff Davis (1901–1907), George Donaghey (1909–1913), and Charles Brough (1917–1921), attempted to implement Progressive measures in the state.[38] As a result, new legislation increased the government's participation in the lives of Arkansas citizens like never before.[39] Terry quickly and unexpectedly became involved with Progressive legislation concerning the juvenile justice system in Arkansas. In 1911, the Woman's Christian Temperance Union appointed her and other members to investigate the juvenile court system in Arkansas and to visit with Judge Joseph Asher, who was in charge of appointing a probation officer and a juvenile court board. The team was to report back to the organization on the status of his endeavors. After visiting with Judge Asher, Terry was surprised to learn that he had appointed her as chair of the juvenile court board in Arkansas.[40] She was unsure of her ability to lead or to serve on the committee because she knew virtually nothing about the juvenile court system. Asher responded that "he knew nothing about it either, since it was a new idea."[41] With little direction Terry set about creating a juvenile court system to meet the growing demands of the state.

Regardless of her lack of qualifications for the job, Terry attempted to do the best for the underserved children of Arkansas. The first major obstacle for the juvenile board centered on housing. At first, members of the board brought the wards to their private homes; later, after a failed attempt at renting a house primarily for them, the temporary use of a building in downtown Little Rock was secured.[42] Passed in 1905, Act 199 decreed that the state reform school was to be managed by the state board of penitentiary commissioners with the goals of rehabilitation and providing a useful trade or skill for its inmates, in a segregated setting.[43] In reality, the school did not focus on rehabilitation, but rather used the children for cheap labor; only three months of the year were spent on education, and for the remaining months the children were used as laborers at the state reform school.[44] Terry's tenure on the board witnessed a significant change in this agenda. The Boys and Girls Industrial School of the State of Arkansas was created in 1917 to replace the penal-type state reformatory established in 1905.[45] The Girls Industrial School was relocated to Alexander, Arkansas, and by 1925, it housed seventy-five girls.[46] Terry was proud of her work with the juvenile court board, but eventually became disillusioned with the lack of qualified personnel, inadequate authority, and cronyism of the patronage system.[47] As she explained in her memoir: "a man was elected Governor who never should have been, and he regarded the school as one of the places to which he could appoint people who had done him favors and who need[ed] jobs."[48] She never shied away from the ugly side of the culture, noting, "I am always amused when people try to shield me from knowledge of the sins of the world, because I learned everything about human beings years and years ago. During the nineteen years I was chairman of the juvenile court board I was exposed to everything from robbery to incest, and if I could have been shocked, I would have been shocked long ago."[49]

During her tenure on the juvenile court board, Terry gave birth to two daughters, Mary in 1914 and Sally in 1916. Mary was born with a rare disorder that broadened Terry's compassion for the human condition. "Osteogenesis Imperfect" caused Mary's bones to break easily, and she required special medical attention her entire life.[50] A decade of trips to Chicago for medical treatments, summers on the East Coast, and winter visits to the desert Southwest to aid Mary's health taxed the endurance of mother and daughter alike. Terry depicted her daughter's struggles in the book *Courage!*, which she wrote under the pseudonym Mary Lindsey.[51] Terry had formerly viewed the birth of a mentally or physically handicapped child as "the worst grief which could befall a human soul."[52] Her experiences with Mary informed her view on how handicapped individuals were denigrated by both society and government. In her unpublished autobiography, she told the story of a young disabled boy on the train going to see specialists for the first time after his father's coworkers had taken up a collection: "If I had to look at my child every day and know we didn't have the money to help him, I would have become an anarchist."[53] Raising Mary seems to have increased Terry's confidence in her own moral authority. More than ever, doing what she felt was right and necessary regardless of what others thought was paramount: "However difficult, I have always preferred to meet a circumstance actively, rather than passively wait for something, whether good or bad, to transpire."[54] While her views on race had changed at Vassar, her experience with Mary gave her the confidence to address the wrongs of society in any given situation.

In 1916, as America edged toward joining the Allied war effort, anti-German sentiment swept the country. Witnessing firsthand the discrimination toward people of German descent in Little Rock, Terry wrote, "My cousins, the Hotzes ... were under suspicion even though Clara was running the work room for the Red Cross and was engaged to an Army officer. They had all been born in this country and had never thought of being anything other than loyal citizens."[55] The daughter of proud German immigrants, Terry took a rather ominous view of the war and wrote, "Murder had suddenly become not only respectable, but heroic and glamorous. I walked around as if I were in a complete daze. I felt as my world had washed away and I had nothing to stand on."[56] Terry's state of mind at this time was remarkably similar to the deflated emotions she would experience in the wake of the first year of school desegregation in Little Rock. Both occasions seem to have caught her by surprise, as if she underestimated the power of societal prejudice to override individual reason. Despite the similarities between the discrimination faced by people of German descent during the war and the discrimination that people of African descent faced at all times, Terry gave no indication that one experience informed the other. However, as the child of German immigrants, the anti-German hysteria of the war years likely gave her a glimpse of what life was like for African Americans in the South. In a personal way, the ethnocentric discrimination of World War I connected Terry to a better understanding of the long-standing segregation in the South.[57]

While the war raged in Europe, American women were fighting for equal voting rights, and Terry had some limited participation in this struggle as well. Terry's younger sister Mary Fletcher was more involved with the women's suffrage movement than Terry was. Mary Fletcher had created in 1911 the Political Equality League of Little Rock, which replaced the defunct Equal Suffrage League (formed in 1888). The Political Equality League is considered the real beginning of the statewide suffragist movement in Arkansas.[58] Though the organization was very active, the legislature did not pass any bills set forth by the Political Equality League. Undeterred, Terry lent a hand at rallies and marches and encouraged other women to join the movement in Little Rock. Reflecting on her time in the movement, Terry stated: "We acted like complete hellions to get the vote. We of the 'lady' class had always been on a pedestal . . . beauteous womanhood, all that kind of junk. The men had looked up to us, idolized us. They had changed their attitude when we tied ourselves to telephone poles and did the unseemly and unladylike things to attract attention to our cause. The Negroes and the college students are using the same tactics today. It's funny but you just have to do it. 'Ladies' and 'Uncle Toms' don't get anywhere."[59] After the passage of the Nineteenth Amendment in 1920, Terry served as a founding board member of the League of Women Voters in Pulaski County.[60] "To me, the vote represents more than just saying how a person feels about an issue or a candidate, it represents human dignity and the fact that a citizen can express his or her opinion on any subject without fear of reprisal. That, I think, is what real human dignity consists of."[61]

While working as part of the suffragist movement, Terry had another formative experience that opened her eyes to the existence of, and possible alliance with, elite black women who shared her Progressive outlook. The unique connection occurred during her service on an advisory committee to establish an African American branch of the Young Women's Christian Association (YWCA) in Little Rock, a crusade that began in March 1918 and had the support of the African American community. The funds necessary to begin construction were available by 1919.[62] Terry understood perfectly well that she was defying societal expectations of southern white women, yet she maintained her support. She knew that "the members of the board of directors of the white YWCA wouldn't touch the whole project with a forty foot pole," yet Terry acknowledged that some white participation was necessary for the project to be successful.[63] Explaining how her time on the advisory board changed her, Terry stated:

> The women who served as director of the club were all well educated and leaders of their community, and they had plenty of ideas of their own. We advisers got more out of the experience than we gave, because we made friends among these black women who since the Civil War had never been thought of as possible friend[s] of ours, and who had lived in a world apart. They were the wives of professional

men, and they provided us with an education. We, the daughters of Confederate veterans, who had heard a great deal about the white side of [the] war, now learned of the suffering of the black population, before, during and after the war, and of the lacks from which they still suffered.[64]

Despite her support for this project, it would be many years before Terry accepted equality for all people. Terry did not protest in the streets or openly defy the laws of segregation, but her involvement with the YWCA challenged her ideas about racial equality. As she worked side by side with African American women, with whom she developed lasting friendships, she began to realize that true equality was not the paternalistic relationship of Progressive reform.[65] The Phyllis Wheatley YWCA opened to the public in 1921, the only recreational facility for black people in Little Rock.[66] Although Terry's involvement was limited, she took away from her experience the fact that the African Americans in Little Rock desired racial equality. In reaching across established racial boundaries, Terry discovered that the compartmentalization endemic to the Jim Crow South was even more artificial than she had realized.

By the early 1920s, Terry was a married woman and a mother of three, soon to be five, children (she would give birth to her fourth child and adopt another during the 1920s). Like the majority of women in Arkansas at the time, she worried more about her home and family than anything else. Unlike the majority of women in Arkansas, her class and status afforded her the time and opportunity to continue her social reform endeavors.[67] She continued her work with the YWCA advisory board, the League of Women Voters, and the juvenile court board, while raising her young family.

In the 1930s Terry embraced the emerging political career of her husband. David Terry served four terms in the House of Representatives as a Democrat from 1934 until 1943.[68] Terry committed herself to her husband's campaigns and cultivated the family image by making "as many friends as possible."[69] To help further his political career, Terry joined many clubs and organizations and sat on as many boards as possible. Like many political wives, Terry thought the sacrifice was worth it, but she did not always feel comfortable with her role: "many times in my life I have felt as if I were teetering on the brink of a volcano."[70] Nor did she always think highly of her colleagues: "These women's organizations are strange things—clothes seem to be the main consideration."[71] Most members talked, but few acted, and Terry was first and foremost about action.

During this time Terry advocated for perhaps her most well-known cause outside of the Central High desegregation crisis: improving the public library system in Arkansas. Terry apprehensively accepted an appointment as chair of the

Committee on Americanism of the local American Legion Auxiliary, which at the time promoted "community involvement and advancement."[72] Given Terry's experiences with anti-German prejudice during World War I, she was understandably ambivalent about promoting "Americanism": "The word was not popular with me and I had no idea what would be involved, but I accepted and went to my first meeting with many misgivings. I opened the pamphlet which was given to me and found that our first and chief duty was to get books into the hands of our young people; in other words, to establish libraries. That was the thing I most wanted to do. Reading is only a tool; to teach children to read and not give them something worthwhile to read is a waste of time and money."[73] Terry elaborated in her diary in 1934, "I casually accepted a position last summer as chairman of the Americanism Committee of the local Auxiliary—again the wife of a politician, for I had never been to a meeting of the organization—and found that the committee had been asked by the national [organization] to put on a library program. Nothing could have pleased me more."[74]

According to Terry, the Depression had caused the state to shutter all but three libraries. She also reported that the American Legion considered Arkansas "the most bookless state in the union."[75] Terry spearheaded a separate library committee that secured Federal Emergency Relief Administration funds to reestablish the free library system in Arkansas. Cities with populations of more than five thousand were eligible for a library, and a state librarian was also appointed.[76] Now, Terry needed books. She approached her friends, distinguished members of the community, and the American Legion, all of which donated books. She recalled, "The whole thing was a glorious success."[77] During the summer of 1934, Terry's committee helped to open several state libraries and used all available funds in support of the state library system.[78] Terry served as a trustee of the Little Rock Public Library system until her retirement in 1966, and as a tribute to her hard work and dedication to the library system in Arkansas a branch in Little Rock was given her name.[79]

While her husband conducted business in Washington, D.C., Terry remained in Arkansas raising their children and securing federal funds for several state projects. Some of her efforts included cofounding the Pulaski County Tuberculosis Association, the Little Rock Housing Authority, and the Arkansas Federation of Women's Clubs; she continued to work on the juvenile court board and for the library system in Little Rock.[80] In 1939, she and nine others founded the Little Rock Housing Association "with funds from the 1937 United States Housing Act in an effort to combat slum housing in Little Rock."[81] Through Terry's persuasive lobbying and the eventual passage of state legislation, "the City of Little Rock incorporated the Little Rock Housing Authority in 1940."[82] At the same time, Terry became a founding board member for the Urban League of Greater Little Rock, which formed in 1937 and consisted of both black and white citizens who were dedicated to improving the circumstances of local African Americans.

By the early 1940s, the United States was again at war. With her husband in Congress and both sons serving in the military, Terry continued dealing with issues on the homefront and working for social reforms. Using her network of upper-class women, Terry organized a women's auxiliary committee of the Urban League. Having served with her on numerous committees and campaigns, white women of her social class readily accepted her call to arms for a new cause. The committee encouraged voters to approve programs in "slum clearance and low-rent housing [and] . . . a solution to health problems among the poor."[83] Not all citizens of Little Rock were happy with this plan, especially those whose homes would be relocated.[84] As with most urban renewal projects, these early efforts did not always benefit those in need.

Terry also worked with the Arkansas Federation of Women's Clubs on improving the arts throughout the state by promoting artistic endeavors.[85] When Terry was appointed the chair of fine arts, she attended "a number of artistic productions[,] an opera, an art show, a symphony and many others."[86] Even though they were all quite good, attendance was low, so she planned to incorporate several artistic events into a "festival of the arts" to promote attendance and continuity.[87] As a member of the United Nations branch of the Arkansas Federation of Women's Clubs, Terry organized a trip to New York City and a meeting with First Lady Eleanor Roosevelt, as well as a tour of Washington, D.C. She continued to focus on historic preservation and the arts for the remainder of her life, even donating her family home, which was built by Albert Pike, a famous Confederate officer and newspaper owner, to the Arkansas Arts Center for use as a decorative arts museum.[88]

One of Terry's greatest accomplishments involved her work with the library board of trustees to integrate the public libraries of Little Rock during the 1950s. Although the library board had decided to partially integrate the library system in 1951, according to Terry the board members were not unanimous in their desire to change: "When we decided that we would open the library up to all the adults of town, black, white and red, one of the members of the Board who didn't want to do it, suggested that we send notices around to the black churches telling people that they should behave like ladies and gentlemen in the library. I asked him who on earth he thought was coming and what the people were coming for. I felt they were coming to read and take out books, and not to disturb anything or anybody."[89] The libraries were quietly integrated, with no major incidents reported. Terry was optimistic that perhaps this was a sign that Little Rock had become a more open society. Hindsight painfully exposed that such a low-profile strategy might have been more prudent during the Central High School desegregation crisis:

> We opened the library before there was any real attempt at integration in the community, and we did it very gradually. We said nothing in print about what we were doing, but just did it. I had discovered that if you want to do anything that is different, the people who are most vocal are those who object. You can beat them out of it if you say nothing in public, but just go ahead.... As it was, there were no major objections to opening the library, but if we had put a notice in the paper, there doubtless would have been. We did it quietly and I can't remember getting any letters or phone calls objecting to what we had done.[90]

Prior to the desegregation crisis of 1957, both Little Rock and the state of Arkansas were on a gradual path to integration. Several schools in Arkansas had successfully desegregated after the 1954 *Brown v. Board of Education* decision with only minor incidents.[91] In fact, in the South, only Texas had more desegregated schools than Arkansas by 1957.[92] When the Little Rock school board adopted the Blossom Plan, it met the minimal compliance with gradual integration. Supporters quietly believed that their optimism about more change was warranted.[93] Terry later realized that she had been too hopeful in her assessment: "I had looked back on the year before [1956] and been greatly encouraged by the cultural and economic progress of Little Rock. The junior college had become Little Rock University and a new symphony orchestra had come into being with the backing of the Chamber of Commerce. The Museum of Natural History and the Fine Arts Museum had both acquired experienced curators, and the Junior League had decided to devote its energies to cultural affairs.... we thought that a new day for our city and state had arrived and nothing could stop our progress."[94]

The Blossom Plan seemed like just another progressive step, albeit a small one, when it called for nine African American students to integrate Central High School in 1957.[95] In an effort to stop school integration, Governor Orval Faubus, under the guise of protecting the nine students, ordered the Arkansas National Guard to keep them from entering the building.[96] Daisy Bates, an NAACP leader, had organized the students who were integrating the school and was in constant contact with the national NAACP office in New York regarding the growing crisis.[97] After reading a *U.S. News and World Report* article that stated that one of the nine students had been expelled for breaking the pledge that she would not "retaliate," regardless of the actions of the white students toward her, Terry "decided to come out of my lethargy and see if I could help in the situation."[98] She spoke with teachers who said that discipline had completely broken down and that "the Negro students were persecuted daily and when they complained the principal remonstrated with the white boys and girls and nothing happened."[99] Terry also interviewed Daisy Bates, who "thought the high school authorities should have stronger discipline."[100]

As the crisis unfolded, Terry continued to seek out people who could assist her; Herbert Thomas was one such individual. Thomas was the founder and president of First Pyramid Life Insurance Company and president of the University of Arkansas board of trustees. Thomas had led the integration of both the medical and law schools at the university ten years earlier with little fanfare.[101] Terry wanted Bates to meet Thomas, who had devised a plan to withdraw the African American students in 1957–1958, but then create an interracial commission to develop a blueprint for integration. Terry was optimistic about the meeting and felt that "if the two of them sat down together without any other desire than to work out a solution to the problem they would probably come up with an acceptable answer."[102] However, Bates and the NAACP did not accept Thomas's plan because it did not immediately follow the federal law, and they felt that segregationists should not determine how the law was implemented for African Americans.[103]

Terry had voted for Faubus in the two previous elections because of his moderate stance on segregation and had met with his wife, Alta Faubus, socially on several occasions. It was through this connection that Terry tried to reach a compromise on the crisis. Terry suggested to Mrs. Faubus that "since the problems of integration would ultimately be solved by adults, it would be a good idea if the Governor expressed himself in favor of law and order in the schools. She agreed with me and promised to discuss the matter with him, but nothing seemed to come of it."[104] Terry's pleas fell on deaf ears. Faubus continued his defiance of federal authority by closing the public high schools to prevent further desegregation. His plan was to put the matter to a public vote in late September before the November 1958 election. In response to the governor's plan, and as a result of a letter between two friends and a phone call with another, a group of upper-class white women in the city organized the Women's Emergency Committee to Open Our Schools in September 1958. They were confident in their abilities to bring positive solutions to the growing educational problems in Little Rock. Modeling their group after the Association of Southern Women for the Prevention of Lynching, this was the first white organization to oppose segregation in Little Rock.[105] The goal of the WEC was to "get the four free public high schools re-opened; to get students back in their classes; to retain our staff of good teachers; and to regain full accreditation by the North Central Association."¹⁰⁶ In her memoir, WEC cofounder Vivion Brewer described the feelings of the women at the first meeting: "Believing without reservation that all people are far more alike than they are different and that hatred is insanity, we pooled our anxieties. We agreed that it was useless to continue our stunned silence of the past year during which we had waited for the men of affairs to do something."¹⁰⁷ To achieve these goals Terry felt that the organization needed to appeal to the greatest number of people in Little Rock. To this end she, Brewer, and Powell decided that they must appeal to the white voter by making their organization "whites only" and that they would not take a stand for either segregation or integration, but rather for education. The WEC was "dedicated to the principle of free and public school education, to law and order and stand[s] neither for integration nor for segregation, but for education."¹⁰⁸

Even with these concessions, not everyone who attended the first meetings of the WEC was eager to embrace the ideas it set forth. Several women left meetings or asked that their names be removed from the roster. Though Terry was no stranger to biracial activities and organizations, the WEC had chosen not to include African Americans. According to historian Grif Stockley, "A lily-white organization was tactically necessary, though it did not sit well with blacks who were initially sympathetic" to its cause.¹⁰⁹ Daisy Bates later recalled that Terry asked her not to attend the meetings.¹¹⁰ Upset by this apparent snub, Bates wrote an article against the WEC, but did not publish it out of respect for Terry; however, she still felt that the "[WEC] were working *for* the Negros, not *with* them."¹¹¹

Faubus set the election to decide the integration question for September 27, 1958. The time constraint gave the WEC little time to organize, but the women quickly mobilized and began phoning eligible voters, organizing to drive people to the polls, lobbying members of the state legislature, and even hosting two televised discussion panels. Faubus argued that private schools were the only answer to the lower educational standards and violence that would occur if integration passed.¹¹² One member of the television broadcast panel argued against these ideas and tried to convince voters that they were not voting for immediate integration, but instead for the gradual introduction of the Blossom Plan, regardless of the ballot language.¹¹³ Terry stated, "If people had asked any of us if we were for integration, we would probably have told them no, we hadn't come to that point yet. But we were for integrating the schools because there had never been enough money in Arkansas for one good school system, let alone two."¹¹⁴ Again, Terry knew she would have to work within the white southern political system to obtain her ultimate goal of integration. By telling whites that the WEC was not supporting integration for integration's sake, but for the betterment of the overall school system, she could placate radicals and sway moderates toward the desired reform.

Even though the WEC made a concerted and valiant effort, its strategies did not work. The majority of the voters opposed integration, and the Little Rock schools remained closed for the remainder of the 1958–1959 school year. Though all Little Rock public school students were displaced, approximately six hundred seniors, both black and white, wondered how they would obtain a high school diploma without a school system. Most white students found alternative modes of education: attending private schools, moving in with relatives in other parts of the state, or starting college without a diploma. African American students in Little Rock did not fare as well, and most went a year without any education.[115] Upset by the vote, Terry argued, "All the disturbances at Central High, I felt, had been created by Faubus solely to re-elect himself, and he had succeeded probably beyond his own wildest dreams. I felt he was doing exactly what he would do if he were a communist: fomenting dissension between groups of people and causing intolerance to breed more intolerance. He was working in one of the poorest and most ignorant states, and his influence was radiating in all directions."[116] In a final attempt to keep the schools open, she appealed directly to the governor prior to the election in November 1958: "I believe you can be a second Lincoln, but you are now on the wrong path. Lincoln was looking towards the future; you are still looking in the past. The South has no chance of ultimately winning in this matter of segregation. With the election of all the progressive new Democrats there is less chance now than ever before. Whether we like it or not, Segregation around the world is as dead in 1958 as slavery was in 1858. The South cannot afford to fight for lost causes."[117]

Faubus was reelected in November, carrying all seventy-five counties.[118] Terry, who did not hold an office and was mostly an advisor to the members of the WEC, and other members were harassed for their role in the integration crisis. After a photo of her appeared in *Time* magazine, she received several hostile letters and phone calls. One of her relatives was fired from his job and eventually took his own life because he could not find another. Ministers who worked with her and the WEC lost their congregations and were forced to leave the city.[119] Even though the ballot measure was defeated, the WEC was not deterred from its mission and continued to work at the grassroots level to reopen the schools. Terry and Brewer were both independently wealthy and were not affected by the whims of the populace concerning money or business, but many local businesspeople were. They soon found that segregation was affecting their bottom line, and their traditional role in politics no longer worked. The fact that they did not promote any radical change to the political process but supported the status quo only allowed the standoff over school integration to last longer than necessary. Personally, most supported segregation, but in time they finally realized just how much it was costing them to keep segregation in place.[120] In May 1959, businesspeople and other civic community members eventually took a stand against the segregationists and formed a group, Stop This Outrageous Purge, in response to the firing of a large number of school employees. With the backing of the WEC, a recall election of the school board members was held within a month: three moderate board members were retained and three additional moderate members were elected. The new board had a moderate majority and set a goal of gradual desegregation.[121]

Having met its goal, the WEC disbanded in November 1963, and the eighty-one-year-old Terry successfully passed the torch of social activism to a new generation of women. Terry retired from the spotlight after the WEC disbanded, but seven years later, in 1970, she again tried to influence the leaders of Little Rock regarding the ongoing issue of desegregation of the public schools. She recalled, "I cannot bear to see my town ruined by the stupidity (or is it the cupidity?) and indifference of its citizens."[122] The indifference on the part of both political leaders and the public by 1970 had allowed members of the white elite to create a distinct racial line in the Little Rock school system that fell within the parameters of federal law. By 2003, private schools had become the norm for wealthy white students and public schools were predominantly populated by African American students, not unlike other areas of the South.[123]

Following a series of strokes, Terry died on July 25, 1976, at the age of ninety-three. She is buried at Mount Holly Cemetery in Little Rock.[124] Adolphine Terry is most well known for her involvement in the Little Rock integration crisis in the late 1950s, but she had served her community long before the civil rights era. Her lifelong social activism in Arkansas and her desire to help those in need are her lasting legacy. She began her social activism as a Progressive with a paternalistic obligation to help others, but as she worked alongside the marginalized populations of her community, her attitudes expanded and evolved. "I see no reason to pay any more attention to the color of a person's skin than to the color of his eyes. It's so much easier to speak to a person merely as another person than to put on a different voice and different face for someone of another color," she wrote.[125] Terry's ability to motivate and inspire people to improve their environment regardless of societal expectations made her a pivotal leader during some of the most trying times in Arkansas history. She played a significant role in the social history of Arkansas during the first half of the twentieth century, and her personal story reflects the role of prominent white southern women in the broader civil rights movement throughout the South.

NOTES

1. Vivion Lennon Brewer, *The Embattled Ladies of Little Rock: The Struggle to Save Public Education at Central High, 1958–1963* (Fort Bragg, Calif.: Lost Coast Press, 1999), xxii, 6–9; Elizabeth Jacoway, *Turn Away Thy Son* (New York: Free Press, 2007), 268; Sara Alderman Murphy, *Breaking the Silence: Little Rock's Women's Emergency Committee to Open Our Schools, 1958–1963* (Fayetteville: University of Arkansas Press, 1997), 79.

2. Sondra Gordy, *Finding the Lost Year: What Happened When Little Rock Closed Its Public Schools* (Fayetteville: University of Arkansas Press, 2009), xii.

3. Brewer, *Embattled Ladies*, 5.

4. Ibid., 290.

5. Ibid., 7. This is a recollection of the letter from Powell to Terry.

6. Adolphine Fletcher Terry, "Life Is My Song, Also," unpublished manuscript, 237, Fletcher-Terry Papers, University of Arkansas at Little Rock Archives, Arkansas Studies Institute, Little Rock ; Brewer, *Embattled Ladies*, 8.

7. Stephanie Bayless, *Obliged to Help: Adolphine Fletcher Terry and the Progressive South* (Little Rock, Ark.: Butler Center Books, 2011), 15.

8. Ibid., 17–18. Adolphine Fletcher Terry's father, John Gould Fletcher, was a wealthy businessman in Little Rock. The Fletcher family were long-time residents of Saline County, Arkansas. Colonel Fletcher, as he was called, was considered an honest and hardworking individual, and he and his partner, Peter Hotze, became prominent cotton brokers.

9. Brewer, *Embattled Ladies*, 290.

10. Terry, "Life Is My Song, Also," 38–39; Bayless, *Obliged to Help*, 19.

11. Terry, "Life Is My Song, Also," 57; Bayless, *Obliged to Help*, 23–24.

12. Adolphine Fletcher Terry, *Charlotte Stephens: Little Rock's First Black Teacher* (Little Rock: Academic Press of Arkansas, 1973); and Terry, *Cordelia: A Member of the Household* (Fort Smith, Ark.: South and West, 1967).

13. Terry, "Life Is My Song, Also," 57. "No one from here [Little Rock] had been to Vassar when I was a little girl, but my mother had read an article about the college when it opened, and she felt that was the place for me to go, and Harvard was the place for my brother [John Gould Fletcher] to go, and by heavens, we went."

14. Ibid., 60–61.

15. Joan Marie Johnson, *Southern Women at the Seven Sister Colleges: Feminist Values and Social Activism, 1875–1915* (Athens: University of Georgia Press, 2008), 108.

16. Terry, "Life Is My Song, Also," 59.

17. Ibid., 72.

18. Ibid., 95–96.

19. Gail S. Murray, ed., *Throwing Off the Cloak of Privilege: White Southern Women Activists in the Civil Rights Era* (Gainesville: University Press of Florida, 2008). Marcia G. Synnott's essay in that volume, "Crusaders and Clubwomen: Alice Norwood Spearman Wright and Her Women's Network," gives good insight into the role of women's clubs in the South during the civil rights era. See also Francis Mitchell Ross, "The New Woman as Club Woman and Social Activist in Turn of the Century Arkansas," *Arkansas Historical Quarterly* 50 (Winter 1991): 317–51; Shannon Frystak, "Rosa Keller," in *Know Louisiana*, ed. David Johnson (New Orleans: Louisiana Endowment for the Humanities, 2010–), http://www.knowla.org/entry/846.

20. *Arkansas Gazette*, July 26, 1976.

21. Terry, "Life Is My Song, Also," 81.
22. Stephen Weeks, *History of Public Education in Arkansas* (Washington, D.C.: U.S. Government Printing Office, 1912), 78.
23. Terry, "Life Is My Song, Also," 82.
24. Ibid.
25. Ibid., 83.
26. Ibid.
27. George B. Cook, *Syllabus of the Twentieth Biennial Report of the Department of Public Instruction, 1907–1908* (Little Rock, Ark.: N.p., 1908), 4.
28. Ibid., 7–14.
29. Terry, "Life Is My Song, Also," 84.
30. Ibid., 96. According to Terry, "During his fourth year at Harvard, as the time approached to graduate, John decided that he really owed nothing to the school. My mother had dominated his education decisions and had picked out his course of study. For this reason, he didn't take the courses that would have meant the most to him, and he came to feel that his real education came from the libraries, art galleries and concert halls of Boston, for that is where he spent most of his time. My mother had a fit about it, but he left Harvard and bought himself a ticket to Europe where he traveled and ultimately married for the first time. My mother never lived to see his success as a poet."
31. David Terry and Adolphine Fletcher marriage license, Fletcher-Terry Papers, University of Arkansas at Little Rock Archives, Arkansas Studies Institute, Little Rock. See also Terry, "Life Is My Song, Also," 94.
32. Mary Louise Terry was born in 1901. She attended Vassar College after high school just like Terry. Letter from David D. Terry to William L. Terry, March 30, 1915, Fletcher-Terry Papers, University of Arkansas at Little Rock Archives, Arkansas Studies Institute, Little Rock.
33. Terry, "Life Is My Song, Also," 101.
34. Ibid., 102.
35. Ibid.
36. Ibid., 118.
37. Bayless, *Obliged to Help*, 48.
38. C. Fred Williams, S. Charles Bolton, Carl Moneyhon, and LeRoy T. Williams, eds., *A Documentary History of Arkansas* (Fayetteville: University of Arkansas Press, 1984), 161.
39. Michael Dougan, *Arkansas Odyssey: The Saga of Arkansas from Prehistoric Times to Present* (Little Rock, Ark.: Rose Publishing, 1994), 331.
40. Ross, "New Woman," 342.
41. Terry, "Life Is My Song, Also," 103. Nationally, juvenile courts were a recent development; the first was established in 1899 in Illinois. This juvenile court operated under the idea that "children differed from adults" and that they needed to have separate provisions under the law.
42. Bayless, *Obliged to Help*, 52.
43. Public Acts of Arkansas 199 (1905).
44. Ross, "New Woman," 343.
45. H. P. Hargis, *Out of the Woods: The Story of the Arkansas Boys' Industrial School* (Pine Bluff, Ark.: N.p., 1947), 2.
46. Terry, "Life Is My Song, Also," 108.
47. Ibid., 108–10.
48. Ibid., 109. Terry is referring to Tom Jefferson Terral, the governor of Arkansas from 1925 to 1927.

49. Ibid., 109–10.
50. Ibid., 111.
51. Mary Lindsey, *Courage!* (New York: Dutton, 1938).
52. Ibid., 9, 20.
53. Terry, "Life Is My Song, Also," 117–18.
54. Lindsey, *Courage!* 92.
55. Terry, "Life Is My Song, Also," 122–23.
56. Ibid., 119–20.
57. John C. Williams, "David Dickson Terry (1881–1963)," in *Encyclopedia of Arkansas History and Culture*, http://www.encyclopediaofarkansas.net/encyclopedia/entry-detail.aspx?entryID=4660.
58. Carl H. Moneyhon, *Arkansas and the New South, 1874–1929* (Fayetteville: University of Arkansas Press, 1997), 118.
59. *Arkansas Gazette*, June 22, 1969.
60. Ibid.
61. Terry, "Life Is My Song, Also," 133–34.
62. Peggy Harris, "'We Would Be Building': The Beginning of the Phyllis Wheatley YWCA in Little Rock," *Pulaski County Historical Review* 43 (Winter 1995): 72–75.
63. Terry, "Life Is My Song, Also," 130.
64. Ibid., 130–31.
65. Murray, *Throwing Off the Cloak of Privilege*, 3–4.
66. Harris, "We Would Be Building," 76.
67. Her fourth child, William (Bill) Terry, was born very healthy in 1922; Joseph Terry was adopted in the early 1920s.
68. David D. Terry left Congress after an unsuccessful bid for a seat in the U.S. Senate in 1942.
69. Adolphine Fletcher Terry diary, 1934, Fletcher-Terry Papers, University of Arkansas at Little Rock Archives, Arkansas Studies Institute, Little Rock (hereafter Terry diary).
70. Ibid., 19.
71. Ibid., 60.
72. Terry, "Life Is My Song, Also," 159; American Legion Auxiliary, http://www.alaforveterans.org (accessed October 24, 2017).
73. Terry, "Life Is My Song, Also," 159.
74. Terry diary, 5.
75. Terry, "Life Is My Song, Also," 159.
76. Terry diary.
77. Terry, "Life Is My Song, Also," 162.
78. Terry diary.
79. Bayless, *Obliged to Help*, 99.
80. Peggy Harris, "Adolphine Fletcher Terry," 2, in *Encyclopedia of Arkansas History and Culture*, http://www.encyclopediaofarkansas.net/encyclopedia/entry-detail.aspx?entryID=1779.
81. Guide to Little Rock Housing Authority Scrapbooks, 1, Archives and Special Collections, University of Arkansas Library, Little Rock.
82. U.S. Department of Housing and Urban Development, "HUD History," http://portal.hud.gov/hudportal/HUD?src=/about/hud_history; Martha Walters, "Little Rock Urban Renewal," *Pulaski County Historical Review* 24 (March 1976): 13.
83. Directory, 1958–1960, Arkansas Federation of Women's Clubs Collection, University of Arkansas at Little Rock Archives, Arkansas Studies Institute, Little Rock.

84. Bayless, *Obliged to Help*, 106.
85. Convention minutes, April 27, 1955; and Directory, 1954–1955, Arkansas Federation of Women's Clubs Collection, University of Arkansas at Little Rock Archives, Arkansas Studies Institute, Little Rock.
86. Terry, "Life Is My Song, Also," 226.
87. Ibid.
88. Harris, "Adolphine Fletcher Terry," 1.
89. Terry, "Life Is My Song, Also," 228.
90. Ibid., 228–29.
91. David Appleby, dir., *Hoxie: The First Stand*, California Newsreel, 2003.
92. David Chappell, *Inside Agitators: White Southerners in the Civil Rights Movement* (Baltimore, Md.: Johns Hopkins University Press, 1994), 101.
93. John A. Kirk, *Redefining the Color Line: Black Activism in Little Rock, Arkansas, 1940–1970* (Gainesville: University Press of Florida, 2002), 25–35.
94. Terry, "Life Is My Song, Also," 230.
95. Todd E. Lewis, "Virgil Tracy Blossom," 1, in *Encyclopedia of Arkansas History and Culture*, http://www.encyclopediaofarkansas.net/encyclopedia/entry-detail.aspx?entryID=5610. The Blossom Plan was created by Little Rock (Pulaski County) superintendent of schools Virgil Tracy Blossom in answer to the *Brown v. Board of Education* Supreme Court decision. His plan was for a gradual integration of the school system. At first, he wanted to integrate the elementary schools starting with six-year-olds, but outrage from parents that this was too young and fear that students would not learn proper social norms led him to change his plan and integrate at the high school level. His original plan was to integrate four high schools in Little Rock, including Central High School. Voting on a more rigid plan, the school board decided to only integrate Central High and only with nine African American students (down from the original two hundred eligible students).
96. Kirk, *Redefining the Color Line*, 25–35.
97. Grif Stockley, *Daisy Bates: Civil Rights Crusader from Arkansas* (Jackson: University Press of Mississippi, 2005), 148–59.
98. Terry, "Life Is My Song, Also," 232.
99. Ibid.
100. Ibid.
101. Murphy, *Breaking the Silence*, 55.
102. Terry, "Life Is My Song, Also," 233–34.
103. Bayless, *Obliged to Help*, 118–19.
104. Terry, "Life Is My Song, Also," 232.
105. Murphy, *Breaking the Silence*, 17–20; Bayless, *Obliged to Help*, 122.
106. Undated flyer, "Policy and Purpose," Women's Emergency Committee Papers, Arkansas History Commission, Little Rock; Bayless, *Obliged to Help*, 122.
107. Brewer, *Embattled Ladies*, 8–9.
108. "Policy and Purpose"; Bayless, *Obliged to Help*, 122.
109. Stockley, *Daisy Bates*, 185.
110. Murphy, *Breaking the Silence*, 72–73; Bayless, *Obliged to Help*, 123.
111. Brewer, *Embattled Ladies*, 9–12, 71–72; Murphy *Breaking the Silence*, 72–73, 75; Stockley, *Daisy Bates*, 185.
112. "Governor Tells Plan for Private Schools," *Arkansas Gazette*, September 19, 1958; Bayless, *Obliged to Help*, 124–26.

113. Terry, "Life Is My Song, Also," 239–40; Brewer, *Embattled Ladies*, 24–30; Murphy, *Breaking the Silence*, 88–90; Bayless, *Obliged to Help*, 125–26.

114. Terry, "Life Is My Song, Also," 238.

115. Bayless, *Obliged to Help*, 127–28.

116. Terry, "Life Is My Song, Also," 236–37.

117. Letter from Adolphine Terry to Orval Faubus, November 12, 1958, Fletcher-Terry Papers, University of Arkansas at Little Rock Archives, Arkansas Studies Institute, Little Rock; Bayless, *Obliged to Help*, 119.

118. Bayless, *Obliged to Help*, 119–20.

119. Terry, "Life Is My Song, Also," 240–43.

120. Henry Alexander, *The Little Rock Recall Election* (New York: McGraw-Hill, 1960), 4–6; Chappell, *Inside Agitators*, 110.

121. Alexander, *Little Rock Recall Election*, 8–11; Brewer, *Embattled Ladies*, 56–59, 155; Murphy, *Breaking the Silence*, 172–73, 181–82; Bayless, *Obliged to Help*, 130–31; Brent E. Riffel, "Stop This Outrageous Purge (STOP)," 1, in *Encyclopedia of Arkansas History and Culture*, http://www.encyclopediaofarkansas.net/encyclopedia/entry-detail.aspx?entryID=715.

122. Adolphine Fletcher Terry to William H. McLean, March 9, 1970, ser. 1, box 2, file 6, Fletcher-Terry Papers, University of Arkansas at Little Rock Archives, Arkansas Studies Institute, Little Rock; *Arkansas Gazette*, March 11, 1970; Ben F. Johnson III, "After 1957: Resisting Integration in Little Rock," *Arkansas Historical Quarterly* 66, no. 2 (Summer 2007): 258–83.

123. In 2003, Little Rock was in the top ten of metropolitan areas with a large percentage of white private school enrollees. For example, only 1 black student (of 102 graduates) graduated from the private Pulaski Academy in 2003, and only 43 of the 283 graduates at Hall High School (a public school) were white. Johnson, "After 1957," 281; Ben F. Johnson III, *Arkansas in Modern America, 1930–1999* (Fayetteville: University of Arkansas Press, 2002).

124. Harris, "Adolphine Fletcher Terry," 3.

125. *Arkansas Gazette*, July 26, 1976.

Sue Cowan Morris

(1910–1994)

An Educator and the Little Rock, Arkansas, Classroom Teachers' Salary Equalization Suit

JOHN A. KIRK

In 1942, schoolteacher Sue Morris filed suit for the equalization of black and white teachers' salaries in the Little Rock School District with the assistance of the National Association for the Advancement of Colored People (NAACP). Although the Arkansas courts denied her claim, she finally won the case in the Eighth Circuit Court of Appeals in St. Louis, Missouri, which ordered the district to equalize teachers' pay. An NAACP historian, Mark Tushnet, described the case as one of the "most important salary suit[s] of the 1940s."[1] Morris's stand came at a cost. Her actions led to her contract with the school district not being renewed. It was many years before she was rehired by the district and only then after being forced to apologize for filing the suit in the first place. Nevertheless, the teachers' salary lawsuit had an important impact on the evolving black activism in the state. The suit attracted attention from the NAACP national office and laid the foundations for that organization's expansion in Arkansas. In 1945, the Arkansas State Conference of NAACP Branches was formed. The growing strength of the NAACP in the state was crucial to the ability of another black woman activist, Daisy Bates, to provide leadership during the 1957 Little Rock school desegregation crisis. The school crisis, which made national and international headlines, proved to be a turning point in the civil rights movement in Arkansas and nationally.

Sue Morris was born Sue Cowan on May 29, 1910, in the small town of Eudora in southeast Arkansas near the Louisiana border and the Mississippi River. She was the only child of J. Alex Cowan, a school principal, and Lelia Roberts Cowan, a schoolteacher. Morris's mother died soon after Sue's birth. She was raised by her maternal grandmother in Texas before returning to be with her father in Eudora at the age of four. With a keen understanding of the value of a good education, Sue's father and stepmother made the necessary financial sacrifices to send her to the best southern schools available to African Americans at the time. Sue attended a private Congregational Church school in Clinton, Mississippi, for the fifth and sixth grades, before moving to Spelman College in Atlanta for the seventh and eighth grades. She completed her schooling in Alabama at Tougaloo High School and at Talladega College. In 1935, Sue Cowan started teaching at Paul Laurence Dunbar High School in Little Rock and became chair of the English Department. At some point between starting to teach at Dunbar and appearing as the plaintiff in the teachers' salary suit in 1942, Cowan was apparently married, since her name changed to Sue Morris, although there is little information about her husband in the historical record. In preparation for the salary lawsuit, over the summer of 1941 Morris attended a graduate program at the University of Chicago and made straight A's in the course Methods of Teaching English. As Morris explained, "I decided to go to the University of Chicago because it [was] a prestigious institution.... And after the suit was filed, I wanted to prove that I was capable of being the test case."[2]

The determination of Sue Morris and other black Little Rock teachers to file suit came against the backdrop of increasing national interest in teachers' salary equalization cases in the late 1930s and early 1940s. Thurgood Marshall, NAACP special counsel, was the chief legal champion of the cause. Marshall had firsthand experience of the discrimination faced by African American educators: his mother, Norma Williams Marshall, was a teacher. Indeed, Marshall's biographer Juan Williams claimed that Marshall "took it personally that his mother's work was valued less than a white teacher's."[3] Certainly, Marshall believed, "One of the most glaring inequalities was the gap between white and colored teachers."[4] In his home state of Maryland, Marshall won the first out-of-court settlement to equalize black and white teachers' salaries in the case of Montgomery County teacher William Gibbs in 1937. The first successful court ruling in favor of equalization came in the case of Anne Arundel County teacher Walter Mills in 1939.[5] After these victories, Marshall looked to pursue similar lawsuits across the South. However, although there were inquiries from teachers' groups in Florida, Alabama, Kentucky, and Louisiana, no significant breakthroughs came. In some places, teachers withdrew from the case because their jobs were under threat. In others, the school district managed to string out the case in the courts in an attempt to dishearten and intimidate the teachers through delaying tactics. Another ploy used by school districts was to offer out-of-court settlements on the condition that teachers drop their lawsuits first. This removed the prospect of legal redress on the basis of what often turned out to be empty promises of equalization.[6]

Nevertheless, Marshall persevered, and he was finally rewarded with his first southern victory in 1940 when Melvin O. Alston, president of the Norfolk Teachers Association in Virginia, won a claim for equal pay on appeal.[7] Alston had replaced the original plaintiff chosen for the case, Aline Black, after the school district refused to renew her contract in 1939. The *Alston* case had a direct bearing on the decision by teachers in Little Rock to take similar action. In 1940, Little Rock's African American population stood at 22,098, accounting for 25.1 percent of the city's 88,039 residents. The city was a major hub of African American business, professional, political, civic, and cultural affairs in the state. It was also Arkansas's main center for African American education. Three African American denominational institutions, Philander Smith College (Methodist Episcopal Church), Arkansas Baptist College, and Shorter College (African Methodist Episcopal Church), located across the Arkansas River in North Little Rock, provided access to higher education. The other main African American college of note in the state was the land-grant institution Arkansas Agricultural, Mechanical and Normal College (AM&N), located in Pine Bluff, forty-five miles southeast of Little Rock.[8]

There were eight African American public schools in Little Rock with an enrollment of 4,324 students. By far, the most important of these was Paul Laurence Dunbar High School. Built in 1930, Dunbar High was known as "the finest high school building in the South for Negro boys and girls."[9] A smaller-scale model of the white Little Rock (later renamed Central) High School built in 1927, Dunbar High's construction was, in part, funded by the Rosenwald Fund and the General Education Board. Julius Rosenwald, a successful Jewish businessman and a co-owner of Sears, Roebuck and Company, established the Rosenwald Fund in 1917. Much of its early activities focused on building schools in black communities in the South.[10] John D. Rockefeller, the founder of Standard Oil, and his business and philanthropic advisor Frederick T. Gates had established the General Education Board in 1902. One of its main areas of focus was building public high schools in the South.[11] The impressive brick structure of Dunbar boasted thirty-four classrooms; physics, chemistry, and biology laboratories; shops for carpentry, woodworking, plumbing, electricity, automobile mechanics, bricklaying, and printing; an auditorium; and a large library. Students could take classes in English, mathematics, social sciences, science, Latin, French, and American history, government, and economics. The school building also housed Dunbar Junior College, which was mainly used as a center for

African American teachers' training. In 1941, Dunbar High had an enrollment of 1,607 students, and Dunbar Junior College had 142 students.¹²

The eighty-six African American teachers who taught in Little Rock's segregated public schools belonged to a professional association, the Little Rock Classroom Teachers Association (CTA), an affiliate of the Arkansas Teachers Association, which, in turn, was the state affiliate of the national African American professional organization the American Teachers Association. It was the CTA that coordinated the campaign for a teachers' salary equalization suit in Little Rock. Solar M. Carethers, a teacher at Capital Hill Elementary School and a CTA member, had watched the teachers' salary cases develop from Maryland to Virginia with keen interest. Carethers had been active in instilling pride in African American achievements by establishing Negro History Week at Capital Hill School and Stephens School in Little Rock. The Carethers Award went to the three best-performing students in a test at the end of Negro History Week. After the U.S. Supreme Court ruled in favor of equal teachers' salaries in Norfolk, Carethers suggested that Little Rock teachers take similar action. The teachers agreed to form a Salary Adjustment Committee, with Carethers as its secretary, to investigate further.¹³ In February 1941, Carethers wrote to Melvin Alston and Walter White, NAACP secretary, asking for advice about "the method of procedure and techniques of bringing about equal salaries for teachers."¹⁴

Following recommendations from Alston and White, the Salary Adjustment Committee conducted research to determine the precise disparities that existed between African American and white teachers' salaries in Little Rock. They discovered that in the city, as in the rest of the state—which already had the lowest rates of pay in the South for both African American and white teachers—large gaps in pay existed because of race.¹⁵ There were 320 white teachers in the Little Rock public school system. White elementary school teachers in Little Rock received an average annual salary of $526, while African American elementary school teachers received only $331. White high school teachers received an annual salary of $856, while African American high school teachers received only $567. This was despite the fact that white and African American teachers did virtually the same work in the same public school system.¹⁶ The African American teachers drew up a petition for the equalization of salaries and presented it to the recently appointed Little Rock superintendent of schools, Russell T. Scobee. He passed the petition to the Little Rock school board, which chose to table the matter indefinitely. In fact, over the summer of 1941, unequal pay raises administered by the school district increased the pay disparity between African American and white teachers. Infuriated by this, the African American teachers began to contribute to a fund for a salary equalization suit and retained local lawyers Scipio A. Jones, Joseph R. Booker, and Myles A. Hibbler in preparation for the case.[17]

Sue Morris recalled of the process, "When we would go to faculty meetings there would be a discussion of how we could alleviate this condition, since we knew that we were not getting the same salary as white teachers.... The white teachers were better paid.... So there were several teachers who were able to go forward with this, and after the faculty meeting, the general faculty meeting citywide, they would call for a meeting of the committee, and that meant those teachers who were interested in taking this to the nth degree would stay and the others would leave. So at this particular meeting the motion was made that we would file suit against the Little Rock School District."[18]

The determination of the CTA to press ahead took Thurgood Marshall by surprise. Ignoring his advice to wait until they received their salary schedules for the 1942–1943 school year, an adamant CTA insisted that they were ready to go to court immediately since they feared that any delay might lead to a weakening of their members' resolve. The school authorities had got wind of their intention to file suit for equal salaries, and the teachers were worried that clauses were going to be inserted into their new contracts that would prevent them from taking legal action. Like teachers in many other southern states, teachers in Arkansas did not have tenure, and they were appointed only on annually renewable contracts. The NAACP Legal Defense Fund agreed to lend its support. Marshall arrived in Little Rock in February 1942 to assist the local attorneys.[19]

In Little Rock, Marshall attended a meeting of the CTA and watched its members adopt a final resolution to go ahead with the action. Marshall noted with interest that the teachers insisted on voting individually on the matter and performing a roll call of the votes to ensure complete unanimity. All of the teachers present at the meeting voted to file a lawsuit. A suitably impressed Marshall wrote to the assistant executive secretary of the NAACP, Roy Wilkins, "these Southern Teachers have acquired new backbones." Marshall noted that all of the members of the CTA had enthusiastically pledged themselves as NAACP members "and not just for one dollar memberships either."[20]

Thurgood Marshall studied the qualifications of the CTA members and drew up a short list of three possible candidates to head the lawsuit. Sue Morris was chosen because of her impeccable credentials. On February 28, 1942, Judge Thomas C. Trimble heard the CTA lawsuit, which had been filed against the chair of the Little Rock School District, Robert M. Williams, along with several members of its board of directors, and superintendent of schools Scobee, in the U.S. District Court at Little Rock. The CTA alleged that the school district had "consistently pursued and maintained a policy, custom and usage of paying colored teachers and principals less salary than white teachers." Such a disparity, the CTA attorneys contended, violated Morris's Fourteenth Amendment rights to equal protection and due process under the law.[21]

Attorneys for the school district disagreed. They denied that racial discrimination existed in the district's policy on teachers' pay at all. Rather, they claimed, the criteria that the district used to determine salaries were based on a wide range of factors, including the "special training, ability, character, experiences, duties, services and accomplishments" of teachers. The implication was that African American teachers were inferior to white teachers for a host of reasons and not solely because of race. By implying this, the school district's attorneys both dodged the issue of racial discrimination and justified the existing inequalities. Trimble upheld the school district's argument by refusing to rule on the issue of Fourteenth Amendment rights. Moreover, he dismissed the case on the technicality that the CTA was an unincorporated organization that could not sue in a federal court. Trimble did not kill off the suit completely, however, since he agreed to hear the case with Sue Morris serving as an individual plaintiff.[22]

The salary equalization suit also received a hostile reception from white school officials. The state's education commissioner, Ralph B. Jones, decried the "strong-arm methods" of the teachers in taking their case to court. "We believe the only real solution to the problem is a cooperative discussion and agreement," he added, although discussions had failed to bring any such action in the past. Jones questioned the teachers' loyalty to the United States: "It is regrettable when any group takes advantage of an emergency such as faces the nation to bring pressure to bear on the problem." The board of directors of the Little Rock School District declared the suit "untimely and ill-advised" and echoed Jones's sentiment that "at this particular time of national crisis an effort is being made to accelerate advantages which are already far ahead of the vast majority of situations elsewhere." The *Arkansas State Press*, the state's leading African American newspaper, based in Little Rock, disagreed. The owner and editor of the paper, Lucious Christopher (LC) Bates, who was a staunch supporter of the NAACP, declared himself fully behind the teachers' cause. "The day of idle talk is over," he editorialized. "Your steps have been taken in the right direction; in the direction of liberalism and Americanism." Bates warned against bending to white pressure: "To grow weary because of possible slurs which are bound to come from sources unfamiliar with progress will disintegrate a highly desirable movement."[23]

It took a full nineteen months after the suit had been filed before the case eventually came to trial. In the meantime, Morris lost her job at Dunbar. In the spring of 1943, the school district declined to rehire her for the following academic year "because I had filed that suit," Morris later reflected. "But that was never put in writing. The letter stated that I would have no further contract. It never said why." She continued, "And as some people said, when I decided that I would be the test case, that I knew that I was going to get fired. Which I did. And it was just one sentence that my contract would not be renewed for another year. Nothing about the case. The contract would not be renewed. . . . And I went to the superintendent's office, and he said he was sorry, that it wasn't his decision, he was just sorry that it happened." Morris was offered a position teaching at Arkansas AM&N College in Pine Bluff (today the University of Arkansas at Pine Bluff) by college president Laurence A. Davis. She accepted, but only stayed a couple of weeks, since she was homesick for Little Rock. "I'd see the bus coming to Little Rock [and] I was always wanting to come home," Morris remembered. "I had been away from home a lot, but [Little Rock] was too near home not to be at home." Morris moved back to Little Rock, and a friend, J. D. Scott, suggested that she apply to work at the Arkansas Ordnance Plant in Jacksonville, just north of Little Rock. Morris worked testing ammunition there until the end of the war. After World War II, when the plant closed, she took up a post teaching English at Arkansas Baptist College in Little Rock.[24]

Morris had the opportunity to reflect on her role in the wartime struggle for freedom and equality in a piece called "The Woman in the War Effort," which she wrote for the *Bulletin of the Arkansas Teachers Association* in December 1943. In it, Morris declared, "It is a privilege to be a woman today, an American woman, and an American Negro woman." She continued:

> Negro women have upon their shoulders the responsibility for careful planning toward real racial emancipation. This is not a time for action that will cause undue racial friction, but it is a time for the Negro to choose objectives and techniques which will accomplish social and economic progress with a minimum of racial conflict. Racial relations never stand still. Since pressures are always active, forward or backward, we can not call a moratorium on the social and economic advancement of the Negro. This is a time when people "all over the world" are affirming the concept of equality of opportunity and the Negro, too, in America must affirm with a strong voice that the rights fundamental to all men must no longer be denied to him.[25]

While Morris dealt with the repercussions of the case, Thurgood Marshall slogged on through the court delays. "What do I have to do to get the transcript on the Teachers Case?" he asked local attorneys Joseph R. Booker and Scipio A. Jones in exasperation. "Do I have to come to Little Rock and bring my pistol?" In part, the delay was due to the vast amount of material that needed to be collated. "The record in the case," according to Marshall, "consist[ed] of 832 printed pages in two volumes, [which] contained all the salaries of all the teachers [in the school district], minutes of the school board, and other material." All this documentation had to be transcribed by the court stenographer to enter into the trial record. When the hearing was finally held between September 28 and October 2, 1943, Marshall continued to take the line that inequality in teachers' salaries violated Morris's Fourteenth Amendment rights. He noted that the school district employed only white supervisors to visit African American schools to observe teachers, to advise them on their work, to assist them in improving their teaching methods, and to report back to the school superintendent with observations and suggestions for improvement. The supervisors rated teachers against the qualifications and abilities laid out on a merit rating sheet. These ratings were then used in determining teachers' salaries. The principal of Dunbar High, John H. Lewis, testified that in his opinion Morris "ought to be a Group 1 [highly rated] teacher." Indeed, this was Lewis's recommendation to the principal of the white Garland High School, Charles R. Hamilton, who was in charge of setting the salary ratings for Dunbar High teachers. Lewis held a master's degree from the University of Chicago and a divinity degree from Yale, and he had done graduate work at the University of California. He was a former president of Morris Brown College in Atlanta and a qualified expert on rating teachers. By contrast, Hamilton held only a bachelor's degree and admitted to the court that he based his salary ratings on only "three or four" visits to Dunbar High every year. Superintendent Scobee maintained that Morris was "a very poor teacher," although he conceded that his evaluation was based only on watching her teach for ten minutes after the case had been filed.[26]

Despite gaining the early upper hand, Marshall's anxiety that the school district had hired "top flight lawyers . . . determined to fight this out" proved well justified. The school district's attorneys from Little Rock's Rose law firm, J. Fairfax Loughborough and William N. Nash, hammered on the argument that their client judged teachers not by the color of their skin but rather on a transparent merit-based system. They then produced what Marshall referred to as their "trump card": a merit rating sheet for 1941. Other southern school districts had drawn up similar merit rating sheets to justify unequal pay on what they claimed to be objective criteria. As elsewhere, the merit rating sheet aimed to show that most African American teachers in the Little Rock school system were, as Marshall put it, "lousy."[27] Of the 86 African American teachers in the school system, 50 did not have degrees from and had not conducted work at accredited schools or colleges, while all 320 white teachers held degrees from or had conducted work at accredited schools or colleges.[28] Next, the school district's attorneys propped up their argument by calling Annie Giffey to the stand. Giffey, the white supervisor of primary school teachers in Little Rock, was a well-known and well-respected woman with thirty-one years of teaching experience. Giffey testified that "regardless of college degrees and teaching experience no white teacher in Little Rock is inferior to the best Negro teacher." From finely argued points of law to blatant racism, the school district's attorneys covered all the ground that they thought might sway the court. The trial left Marshall depressed. "This has been one of the hardest cases so far," he reported, "and we are all quite tired of it."[29]

While Trimble deliberated over his ruling, African American educators in Little Rock found out that school officials were prepared to take the fight beyond the courtroom. "They made conditions intolerable for all of our witnesses so that they eventually had to leave the system," explained Marshall. The principal of Dunbar High, John H. Lewis, left his job. In a letter of resignation to the superintendent of schools, Lewis stated that it was the "definite dissatisfaction" shown over his part in the teachers' salary suit that had forced him to leave his post. "I definitely told them that if they did not want me, I did not want them and if I was called as a witness a thousand times I would take the same position," Lewis wrote to Marshall. Soon, Lewis was appointed president of Shorter College in North Little Rock. Shortly afterward, John H. Gipson, head of the CTA and a teacher at Dunbar High, left his job and joined Lewis at Shorter.[30]

When Judge Trimble finally announced his verdict on January 5, 1944, it was, as Marshall had suspected it would be, in favor of the school district. The case, Trimble declared, came down to three questions of law.[31] First, was there a salary schedule that discriminated against African American teachers? Trimble ruled that there was not. When Morris and her attorneys had been given access to the school district minutes, they had discovered that such schedules carefully avoided any mention of race. Morris did have a document titled "Special Adjustment Plan, Negro Teachers, 1940," which had been mysteriously delivered to her mailbox at Dunbar High. However, there was no clear sign that this actually came from the school district and thus, Trimble said, it could not be admitted as evidence.[32]

Second, was there "a policy, custom or usage to pay colored teachers and principals less salary and compensation solely on account of race and color"?[33] Trimble did not explicitly address this point, but rather focused on Morris's contention that teachers should be paid in relation to their qualifications and experience. He said that teachers' pay could not be decided by such a "mathematical formula" since a number of different factors affected the performance of a teacher. These might include things such as "character, interest, efficiency, ability to teach, loyalty, or any of those intangibles that enter into the personality of the individual teacher and affect his value to the system." Members of the school district's board of directors were empowered, Trimble said, to exercise "judgment and discretion," and this should indeed play a role in how teachers' salaries were determined.[34]

The process of hiring teachers and fixing their salaries was based on a wide range of criteria. The standard application form asked for a large amount of information as a basis for assessment, including age, race, religious affiliation, marital status, number of children, general health, condition of eyesight and hearing, amount of education and professional training, courses taken and grades attained, degrees held, teaching experience, subjects and grades taught, amount of salary in any previous posts, and amount of salary acceptable if hired. Applications often required a photograph of the applicant to be attached. This application was looked at by the superintendent of schools, who sometimes called in the prospective teacher for an interview. References from former work colleagues were also sought. The superintendent then relayed this information and his recommendation to the board of directors. More often than not, they accepted his recommendation, but they also had the power to overrule him. At the end of this process a decision about employment and salary was finally taken.[35]

Trimble, essentially acting as a character witness for the defendants, expressed his confidence that the system was administered fairly. He reported that he was "very much impressed" by Scobee, the superintendent of schools, who had exhibited "sincerity, frankness [and] fairness [in] his demeanor upon the stand."[36] As for the school district's board of directors, Trimble noted that they were "men and women of high standing in the community," and declared that "many of the individual members have been known to the Court personally for many years, and others of them a like period by reputation. All of them are men and women of the highest caliber, civic minded, desiring to serve their community."[37]

Trimble concluded that "the defendants have a right to fix the salary of each individual teacher in the system, according to their real worth and value to the system as teachers, and are not required to set up and adhere to some arbitrary standard of college degrees and years of experience teaching, some mechanical method or means of determining salaries."[38] Although mistakes may be made as, Trimble pointed out, Scobee and members of the board of directors were happy to admit had been the case at times, the merits of such a system outweighed its shortcomings. It was not the job of the court to review such individual errors, but to make sure that the actual processes governing the determination of pay were sound and nondiscriminatory. Trimble was satisfied that they were.[39]

Finally, did the case raise a constitutional question? Having dismissed Morris's two main contentions, Judge Trimble decided that it did not. In dismissing

Morris's case, Trimble ordered her to pay the court costs since she had failed to meet the burden of proof required.[40]

Morris and her attorneys were successful in overturning Trimble's decision before the Eighth Circuit Appeals Court at St. Louis. The case on appeal included another African American woman teacher, Frances B. Hibbler, the wife of attorney Myles A. Hibbler, who acted as an intervener in the case on behalf of the CTA membership. This was to ensure that a plaintiff was listed who was currently employed by the Little Rock School District at the time of the hearing. One significant advantage that African Americans in Arkansas had in appealing lower court decisions was the fact that, through a quirk of political geography, Arkansas was the only southern state that belonged to the Eighth Circuit federal court district. The other states in the district were all from the North or the Midwest. Judges sitting on the appeals court therefore tended to be less steeped in southern racial mores, and there was a much greater likelihood of an impartial ruling.[41]

The school district's advocates became increasingly nervous about the outcome of the case on appeal. While still defending their existing practices, they also sought to reach an out-of-court settlement with the teachers. Attorney J. Fairfax Loughborough and school district director Murray O. Reed met with the teachers' attorney Joseph R. Booker in an attempt to broker a deal. They offered equal pay to African American and white teachers at the entry level, equal pay to teachers from accredited institutions according to experience and educational qualifications or training, and equal pay to teachers from nonaccredited institutions in accordance with their professional status. In return, they wanted to reserve the right to use the character and personality of teachers as factors in determining pay, and they wanted the teachers' salary equalization suit to be dropped. When Thurgood Marshall responded to the suggestion with a point-blank refusal to drop the suit, based on similar empty promises and double-dealing of school officials he had encountered in the past, the school district unilaterally raised all teachers' salaries equally. Although this made both African American and white teachers better off, it continued the disparity. Loughborough then tried to arrange a meeting with the NAACP attorneys to use this latest move as leverage for calling off the lawsuit. In the middle of these negotiations, Loughborough suffered an embolism and died. "I am thinking that this was super induced by cogitation over the brief filed by you and yours," Booker reported to Marshall. Loughborough's replacement, Archibald F. House, continued to press for a settlement. As the date of the appeal drew closer, the efforts of the school district's attorneys became more desperate. Booker reported a few weeks before the appeal hearing, "Mr. House has just called me again. . . . he stated . . . he is fearful that 'somebody will be hurt' if we wait too long. These are his words."[42]

On June 19, 1945, appellate judges John Benjamin Sanborn, Joseph William Woodrough, and Seth Thomas reversed Judge Trimble's ruling. The legal team for Morris was again led by Marshall, who was joined by the chair of the NAACP national legal committee, William H. Hastie, and NAACP assistant special counsel Edward R. Dudley, with local attorneys Booker and Hibbler assisting (Scipio A. Jones, another of the local lawyers, had died in 1941). Also in attendance were American Civil Liberties Union attorneys Luther Ely Smith and Victor B. Harris of St. Louis, Missouri, and Nanette Dembitz of Washington, D.C., acting as friends of the court.[43]

The appeals judges returned to the two questions that had already been raised in the case: the existence of a salary schedule and whether there was a "policy, custom or usage" to pay African American teachers less than white teachers. On the existence of a salary schedule, the appeals court upheld the finding of the lower court that there was no evidence to suggest one existed. The case hinged, the judges said, solely on the "policy, custom or usage" of pay discrimination. To determine this, the court carefully scrutinized the evidence, which included "pay rolls, the qualifications of teachers, their years of experience, their positions, and the minutes of the Board" in the school district from as far back as 1926. The court found that over a period of almost twenty years new African American teachers entering the school system were routinely paid less than their white counterparts. In 1928, 1929, and 1936, pay raises were awarded to African American and white teachers at different rates—again, consistently lower for African American teachers—and they were, therefore, clearly based on racial factors. Moreover, in 1941 and 1942, the school district had a surplus of funds that it had agreed to distribute among the teachers. A committee composed solely of white teachers decided on a formula to distribute the money on an unequal basis that used racial considerations as a determining factor. Based on this evidence, the appeals judges concluded that "very substantial inequalities have existed between the salaries paid to colored teachers and those paid to white teachers and that such inequalities have continued over a period of years." The ruling of the lower court was reversed and the case was remanded back to the district court with the direction to enter a declaratory judgment for the plaintiffs with jurisdiction reserved to make sure that the school district abandoned its discriminatory pay policy.[44]

Victory in the Little Rock suit undoubtedly had its limits. Although the case proved that African American teachers could take on figures of white authority in the courts and win, it also illustrated the potential pitfalls of litigation and black teachers' precarious job status in a white-controlled public education system. The case cost the jobs of the plaintiff, Sue Morris; the principal of Dunbar

High, John Lewis; and the head of the CTA, John Gipson. Moreover, the white school district successfully demonstrated that it could still exercise control over African American teachers' pay. In line with other southern school districts, Little Rock adopted the National Teacher Examination, which was used to provide a standardized and allegedly objective test to legitimate African American and white teachers' unequal pay.[45] The decision in the Morris case affected only the salaries of Little Rock teachers and not those of other teachers in the state, some of whom faced even worse discrimination. Neither did the case tackle the other myriad problems facing African American educators in Arkansas.[46]

But the teachers' salary lawsuit did have a profound impact on the African American struggle for freedom and equality in Arkansas, as it did in other states, which went well beyond its original scope and intentions. Importantly, it helped to forge links between local African American activists and the NAACP. Thurgood Marshall's presence in Little Rock energized the previously reluctant African American population there to embrace the organization's agenda for racial change. "He sure did shoot them some straight dope as to their part and membership to be played in the NAACP cause," reported Little Rock's NAACP branch secretary, Mrs. H. L. Porter, of one meeting that Marshall attended. "Then and there at that meeting we collected $68.50 in membership.... Little Rock is 'agog' over him."[47] In response to this rising local interest, the national NAACP headquarters began to show more interest in organizing in the state. In 1945, the Arkansas State Conference of Branches was founded. In 1952, Daisy Bates, the wife of newspaper editor L. C. Bates and co-owner of the *Arkansas State Press*, was elected its president.[48]

Soon after Bates's election the paths of local African American activists and the national NAACP crossed again. After the *Brown* decision, Bates spearheaded state and local efforts to implement school desegregation. When Little Rock's NAACP branch determined that school officials in Little Rock were not moving forward with desegregation plans quickly enough, with the assistance of regional and later national NAACP lawyers it launched the *Aaron v. Cooper* (1956) lawsuit. The case, on appeal as *Cooper v. Aaron* in 1958, delivered another landmark victory for the NAACP when the U.S. Supreme Court ruled that school districts could not use the threat of violence to delay school desegregation implementation plans. The legal battle formed the backdrop to the dramatic events that unfolded in the city in September 1957 when attempts to desegregate Central High School were blocked by Arkansas governor Orval Faubus, who called out National Guard troops, preventing the entry of nine African American students. The situation was only resolved when President Dwight D. Eisenhower federalized the National Guard and sent in U.S. soldiers to ensure the safe passage of the students into Central High.⁴⁹ The *Cooper* case had a direct lineage from the earlier success of the *Morris* suit in a number of ways, including the development of the NAACP's legal strategy at a national level and the impact that the case had on the growth of the NAACP at the state and local levels. There were also direct personal links between the two cases: the mother and an aunt of one of the Little Rock Nine, Ernest Green, were both teachers, and both had been involved in the teachers' salary equalization suit in Little Rock in the 1940s.⁵⁰

Sue Morris married a Little Rock pastor, Booker T. Williams, in 1946, after which she went by the name of Sue Cowan Williams.⁵¹ In 1952, she was rehired at Dunbar High from Arkansas Baptist College, where she had taught since the mid-1940s. Dr. Leroy M. Christophe, who was appointed Dunbar's principal in 1945, had placed the school district under constant pressure to reinstate her. Christophe, a personal friend of Sue Cowan Williams and a fellow alumni of Talladega College, made the case for her rehiring each year after his appointment. Finally, ten years after she had initially pursued her claim for equal pay, the school district relented. The superintendent of schools, Harry Little, called Williams "and asked me if I had learned my lesson." She reluctantly admitted that she had—"The lesson was not to file suits and—you know, don't do that any more"—in order to pursue her vocation as a high school teacher. Christophe was "very upset over that person['s request]," Williams recalled. "He said he didn't know how I was going to answer." But she "said, 'Yes' . . . which [she] didn't want to say." Her desire to be back in the Little Rock school system and back at Dunbar High where she belonged proved too strong for her not to swallow her pride. When Horace Mann High School was built and opened as a segregated (black) high school in Little Rock in 1956, which involved staffing changes at Dunbar, Williams was promoted back into her old role as chair of the English Department, a position she held until she retired in 1974. After her retirement from Dunbar, Williams went back to Arkansas Baptist College and taught English there and also worked part time for the Little Rock School District in the reading-testing program for elementary students.⁵²

Throughout her life, Williams played an active role in community affairs. As a member of Little Rock's Mount Zion Baptist Church, she belonged to the Modern Priscilla for Girls, Youth in the Choir, the Sanctuary Choir, the Maids, the Matrons, and the Ministers', Deacons' and Wives' Trustees Club. She was also a youth director, director of several church pageants, chair of the Fred T. Guy Memorial Fellowship Hall dedication, and second vice president of the Woman's Missionary Union. Outside of church, she was president of Delta Sigma Theta, Inc., president of the Phyllis Wheatley YWCA, president of four city committees, and a member of the NAACP, the Urban League, the National

Council of Negro Women, and Little Rock Retired Educators. Among numerous awards she received was a Bicentennial Graphic Tribute to Women in Education from the National Education Association.[53] In 1979, Williams was honored at a Dunbar alumni gathering in Little Rock's Robinson Auditorium, where she told more than one thousand former students, "you must be bold enough to change the present, when circumstances demand it; nostalgic enough to restore that part of the old that never changes; and futuristic enough to dream of a community where human rights and justice prevail."[54] Williams died in 1994 at the age of eighty-four, preceded in death by her second husband. In 1997, the tenth library in the Central Arkansas Library System, which serves the Dunbar High School area, was dedicated as the Sue Cowan Williams Library in her honor.[55]

Sue Morris's 1942 lawsuit was an important landmark in Arkansas civil rights history. It was the first successful suit by an Arkansan to challenge African American inequality in the state that led to a permanent structural change: the abolition of unequal wages for black teachers in Little Rock. It paved the way for the establishment of the NAACP as a force in Arkansas, which in turn laid the groundwork for more legal challenges in the state. The NAACP formed a statewide infrastructure, supported by the New York office, upon which later civil rights activism built. Though Morris's activism has been largely overlooked in Arkansas history, since headlines tend to gravitate toward the internationally known events of the 1957 Little Rock school crisis and the NAACP activism of Daisy Bates, Morris played a crucial role by taking the first steps that laid a foundation for the later episode. As historians have discovered in other southern states, the struggle for black freedom and equality predated and outlasted the more familiar civil rights movement activism of the 1950s and 1960s. A closer look at those longer struggles reveals the vital role that black women like Sue Morris often played at the local level, gaining early traction for later movement successes. In that sense, Arkansas's civil rights history resembles the events elsewhere in the South—even though, so far, that story has been explored in far less detail and scope. Stories like Morris's help to highlight the history of the civil rights struggle in Arkansas and its intrinsic connection to other regional and national developments.

NOTES

1. Mark V. Tushnet, *The NAACP's Legal Strategy against Segregated Education, 1925–1950* (Chapel Hill: University of North Carolina Press, 1987), 90–92.

2. Thurgood Marshall to Walter White and William H. Hastie, September 30, 1942, group II, ser. B, container 174, folder "Teachers Salaries—Arkansas—Little Rock—Morris v. School Board

(General) 1941–1943," National Association for the Advancement of Colored People Papers, Manuscript Division, Library of Congress, Washington, D.C. (hereafter NAACP Papers); Sue Cowan Williams (née Morris), interview with author, Little Rock, Ark., January 8, 1993, Special Collections, University of Arkansas Libraries, Fayetteville (hereafter Williams interview); *Arkansas Democrat-Gazette*, June 2, 1994.

3. Juan Williams, *Thurgood Marshall: American Revolutionary* (New York: Times Books, 1998), 90.
4. Langston Hughes, *Fight for Freedom: The Story of the NAACP* (New York: Norton, 1962), 135.
5. Mills v. Anne Arundel County Board of Education, 30 F. Supp. 245 (1939).
6. Tushnet, *NAACP's Legal Strategy*, 20–26, 116–22.
7. Alston et al. v. School Board of City of Norfolk et al., 112 F.2d 992 (4th Cir. 1940).
8. Writers' Program of the Work Projects Administration in the State of Arkansas, *Survey of Negroes in Little Rock and North Little Rock* (Little Rock, Ark.: N.p., 1941), 38–43, 171, Special Collections, University of Arkansas Libraries, Little Rock. On African American education in Arkansas, see William H. Martin, "The Education of Negroes in Arkansas," *Journal of Negro Education* 16 (Summer 1947): 317–24; Thomas E. Patterson, *History of the Arkansas Teachers Association* (Washington, D.C.: National Education Association, 1981); and C. Calvin Smith and Linda Walls Joshua, eds., *Educating the Masses: The Unfolding History of Black School Administrators in Arkansas, 1900–2000* (Fayetteville: University of Arkansas Press 2003).
9. On Dunbar High School, see James D. Anderson, *The Education of Blacks in the South, 1860–1935* (Chapel Hill: University of North Carolina Press, 1988), 206–11; Faustine C. Jones, *A Traditional Model of Educational Excellence: Dunbar High School of Little Rock, Arkansas* (Washington, D.C.: Howard University Press, 1981); Work Projects Administration, *Survey of Negroes*, 38–40; "History of Dunbar High," National Dunbar Alumni Association website, based on the traveling exhibit *The Finest High School for Negro Boys and Girls: Dunbar High School in Little Rock, Arkansas, 1929–1955*, http://www.mosaictemplarscenter.com/traveling-exhibits/dunbar-traveling-exhibit (accessed October 3, 2017).
10. On the Rosenwald Fund, see Stephanie Deutsch, *You Need a Schoolhouse: Booker T. Washington, Julius Rosenwald, and the Building of Schools for the Segregated South* (Evanston, Ill.: Northwestern University Press, 2015); Mary S. Hoffschwelle, *The Rosenwald Schools of the American South* (Gainesville: University Press of Florida, 2014); and Alfred Perkins, *Edwin Rogers Embree: The Julius Rosenwald Fund, Foundation Philanthropy, and American Race Relations* (Bloomington: Indiana University Press, 2011).
11. On the General Education Board, see John Ensor Harr and Peter J. Johnson, *The Rockefeller Century: Three Generations of America's Greatest Family* (New York: Scribner, 1988).
12. Work Projects Administration, *Survey of Negroes*, 38–40.
13. Tushnet, *NAACP's Legal Strategy*, 119–20; Williams interview. The full text of the *Alston* ruling was published in *Bulletin of the Arkansas Teachers Association* 12, no. 4 (December 1940): 10–12, 16 (available at University of Arkansas Libraries, Pine Bluff). On Carethers, see Lois Pattillo, *Little Rock Roots: Biographies in Arkansas Black History* (Little Rock, Ark.: Parkhurst, 1981), 28–35.
14. Solar M. Carethers to Melvin O. Austin [sic], February 20, 1941; Solar M. Carethers to Walter White, February 22, 1941, both in group II, ser. B, container 174, folder "Teachers Salaries—Arkansas—Little Rock—Morris v. School Board (General) 1941–1943," NAACP Papers.
15. Leander L. Boykin, "The Status and Trends of Differentials between White and Negro Teachers' Salaries in the Southern States, 1900–1946," *Journal of Negro Education* 18 (Winter 1949): 45.
16. "Memorandum Brief for the Plaintiff," in *Morris v. Williams* (1942), Civil Docket no. 55, District Court of the United States, Western Division of the Eastern District of Arkansas, 9. See

appendix, tables 1-18, for a breakdown of individual teacher's pay. Copy in author's possession courtesy of Sue Cowan Williams.

17. Scipio Jones to Thurgood Marshall, August 12, 1941; Frank D. Reeves to Scipio A. Jones, August 15, 1941; J. L. Wilson to Thurgood Marshall, December 9, 1941, all in group II, ser. B, container 174, folder "Teachers' Salaries—Arkansas—Little Rock—Morris v. School Board (General) 1941–1943," NAACP Papers. For profiles of the local lawyers, see the website Arkansas Black Lawyers, http://www.arkansasblacklawyers.com (accessed June 25, 2008).

18. Williams interview.

19. Thurgood Marshall to J. L. Wilson, February 11, 1942; J. L. Wilson to Thurgood Marshall, February 16, 1942; Thurgood Marshall to Roy Wilkins, February 28, 1942, all in group II, ser. B, container 174, folder "Teachers' Salaries—Arkansas—Little Rock—Morris v. School Board (General) 1941–1943," NAACP Papers.

20. Thurgood Marshall to Roy Wilkins, February 28, 1942, group II, ser. B, container 174, folder "Teachers' Salaries—Arkansas—Little Rock—Morris v. School Board (General) 1941–1943," NAACP Papers.

21. Morris v. Williams, 59 F. Supp. 508 (E.D. Ark. 1944); *Arkansas Gazette*, March 1, 1942.

22. *Arkansas Gazette*, May 21, 1942.

23. *Arkansas Gazette*, March 8 and 13, 1942.

24. Williams interview; *Arkansas Democrat-Gazette*, June 3, 1994.

25. Sue Cowan Morris, "The Woman in the War Effort," *Bulletin of the Arkansas Teachers Association* 15, no. 4 (December 1943): 9–11 (quotations, 11) (available at University of Arkansas Libraries, Pine Bluff).

26. Thurgood Marshall to Walter White and William H. Hastie, September 30, 1942, and Thurgood Marshall to Friends (J. R. Booker and Scipio Jones), November 1, 1942, both in group II, ser. B, container 174, folder "Teachers' Salaries—Arkansas—Little Rock—Morris v. School Board (General) 1941–1943"; memorandum from Thurgood Marshall to Consuelo Young, June 21, 1945, group II, ser. B, container 174, folder "Teachers' Salaries—Arkansas—Little Rock—General, 1942–1946," all in NAACP Papers; *Bulletin of the Arkansas Teachers Association* 15, no. 4 (December 1943): 3; *Arkansas Gazette*, October 3, 1942; *Arkansas State Press*, May 28, 1943.

27. Thurgood Marshall memorandum to Walter White, William H. Hastie, and [Prentice?] Thomas, September 19, 1942, group II, ser. B, container 174, folder "Teachers' Salaries—Arkansas—Little Rock—Morris v. School Board (General) 1941–1943," NAACP Papers.

28. Morris v. Williams, 508.

29. Thurgood Marshall to White and Thomas, October 3, 1942; Thurgood Marshall to Consuelo Young, June 21, 1945; Thurgood Marshall, "Memorandum Re: Little Rock Teachers' Case," September 22, 1942, all in group II, ser. B, container 174, folder "Teachers' Salaries—Arkansas—Little Rock—*Morris v. School Board* (General) 1941–1943," NAACP Papers; *Arkansas Gazette*, October 3, 1942; *Arkansas State Press*, October 9, 1942; Mark V. Tushnet, *Making Civil Rights Law: Thurgood Marshall and the Supreme Court, 1936–61* (New York: Oxford University Press, 1994), 120.

30. Thurgood Marshall to John H. Lewis, July 16, 1943; John H. Lewis to Thurgood Marshall, July 19, 1943; Thurgood Marshall to J. R. Booker, May 29, 1945, all in group II, ser. B, container 174, folder "Teachers' Salaries—Arkansas—Little Rock—Morris v. School Board (General) 1941–1943," NAACP Papers; *Arkansas State Press*, May 28, 1943; Patterson, *History of the Arkansas Teachers Association*, 90.

31. Morris v. Williams, 59 F. Supp. 508 (E.D. Ark 1944), 508.

32. Ibid., 508–12.

33. Ibid., 510.

34. Ibid., 513.
35. Ibid., 513–14.
36. Ibid., 514.
37. Ibid., 515.
38. Ibid.
39. Ibid., 515–16.
40. Ibid., 516–17.
41. Patterson, *History of the Arkansas Teachers Association*, 90; *Bulletin of the Arkansas Teachers Association* 18, no. 1 (January–March 1946): 13 (available at University of Arkansas Libraries, Pine Bluff). The U.S. Eighth Circuit district covers Arkansas, Iowa, Minnesota, Missouri, Nebraska, North Dakota, and South Dakota.
42. J. R. Booker to Thurgood Marshall, May 18, August 21, and October 21, 1944, March 13, May 23, and May 28, 1945; Thurgood Marshall to J. R. Booker, May 20 and October 27, 1944, all in group II, ser. B, container 174, folder "Teachers' Salaries—Arkansas—Little Rock—Morris v. School Board (General) 1941–1943," NAACP Papers; *Arkansas Democrat*, September 21, 1944.
43. *Morris v. Williams*, 149 F.2d 703 (8th Cir. 1945).
44. Ibid.; *Arkansas Gazette*, January 6, 1944; press release, June 21, 1945, group II, ser. B, container 174, folder "Teachers' Salaries—Arkansas—Little Rock—Morris v. School Board (General) 1941–1943," NAACP Papers; Tushnet, *NAACP's Legal Strategy*, 90.
45. Scott Baker, "Testing Equality: The National Teacher Examination and the NAACP's Legal Campaign to Equalize Teachers' Salaries in the South, 1936–1963," *History of Education Quarterly* 35 (Spring 1995): 49–64; *Arkansas Democrat*, September 21, 1944.
46. Xavier Zinzeindolph Wynn, "The Development of African American Schools in Arkansas, 1863–1963: A Historical Comparison of Black and White Schools with Regards to Funding and the Equality of Education," EdD thesis, University of Mississippi, Oxford, 1995, 209–43.
47. Mrs. H. L. Porter to William Pickens, June 9, 1940, group II, ser. C, container 9, folder "Little Rock, Arkansas, 1940–1947," NAACP Papers.
48. John A. Kirk, *Redefining the Color Line: Black Activism in Little Rock, Arkansas, 1940–1970* (Gainesville: University Press of Florida 2002), 70–74.
49. On the *Cooper v. Aaron* case, see Georg Iggers, "An Arkansas Professor: The NAACP and the Grassroots," in *Little Rock, U.S.A.: Materials for Analysis*, ed. Wilson Record and Jane Cassells Record (San Francisco, Calif.: Chandler, 1960), 283–91; Tony A. Freyer, *Little Rock on Trial: Cooper v. Aaron and School Desegregation* (Lawrence: University Press of Kansas, 2007).
50. Ernest Green, interview in "Teachers Worked behind the Scenes," American Federation of Teachers website, https://www.aft.org/periodical/american-educator/summer-2004/teachers-roles-ending-school-segregation (accessed October 3, 2017).
51. I am grateful to Rhonda Stewart at the Butler Center for Arkansas Studies, Little Rock, for this information. See Stewart, "Sue Cowan Williams," in *Encyclopedia of Arkansas History and Culture*, http://www.encyclopediaofarkansas.net/encyclopedia/entry-detail.aspx?search=1&entryID=4063.
52. Williams interview; Patterson, *History of the Arkansas Teachers Association*, 90–91; Smith and Joshua, *Educating the Masses*, 78; *Arkansas Gazette*, July 27, 1979.
53. *Arkansas Gazette*, June 2, 1994.
54. *Arkansas Gazette*, July 22, 1979.
55. Sue Cowan Williams Library, https://www.cals.org/about/locations/williams.aspx (accessed October 3, 2017).

Daisy Lee Gatson Bates
(1913?–1999)

The Quest for Justice

ELIZABETH JACOWAY

On May 4, 1956, Daisy Bates burst into the white consciousness in Little Rock.[1] As president of the Arkansas State Conference of Branches of the National Association for the Advancement of Colored People (NAACP), Bates provided testimony in a deposition for a case challenging the Little Rock school board to commence desegregation immediately.[2] The school board's attorney, Leon Catlett, known as the best trial lawyer in the state, questioned Bates at length about her intentions and those of the NAACP, always addressing her as "Daisy." Bates finally interrupted the questioning to say that her first name was acceptable only when used by "my intimate friends and my husband and I haven't met you before today, so I want you to refrain from calling me Daisy. My name is Mrs. Bates." Obviously shocked by Bates's bold departure from his region's customary racial etiquette, which denied African Americans the courtesy titles of Mr. and Mrs. and mandated that they be called by their first names, Catlett replied, "I won't call you anything then." Bates responded, "All right. That will be fine."[3]

Daisy Lee Gatson Bates had spent a lifetime preparing herself for this moment.[4] Born in 1913 or 1914 in the south Arkansas sawmill town of Huttig to fifteen-year-old Millie Riley and seventeen-year-old Hezekiah "Babe" Gatson, Bates learned at the age of nine that her mother had been raped and murdered by three white men when Daisy was an infant and that her father had then abandoned her.[5] Taken in by friends of her parents, Susie and Orlee (or perhaps Oralee) Smith, Daisy had experienced a happy childhood until she first encountered racism at the age of seven or eight and then learned of her parents' fates a year or so later. This new knowledge filled the little girl with a rage and a hatred of white people that never left her. As she recalled, "There was so much hate inside me, but somehow, that hate prepared me for what came later in my life. It gave me the strength to carry it all out. I don't think anything prepared me more than my anger."[6]

In addition to the anger and bitterness that drove her, Bates realized years later that her status as a virtual orphan was a major factor in her psychological makeup. "Even though nobody in Huttig called me an orphan," she reflected, that was, in fact, what she was. "I was given away by my one living parent, and never adopted by those good foster parents, the Smiths. They never gave me their name . . . and that always bothered me."[7] In response, she decided, "I would spend my life making my life worth something. Orphans come here with the feeling that they're in this world alone, even if we have lots of people who love us. The people who mean the most are not there to confirm that." Whether consciously or not, she decided "to fight for what I thought was rightfully mine . . . my sense of worth as a human being, my rights, justice, equal opportunities."[8]

By 1956, Daisy Bates had become a leader in Little Rock's African American community. Married to the owner and editor of a crusading black newspaper and serving as executive secretary of her state's Fair Employment Practices Commission and, most recently, as president of the Arkansas NAACP, Daisy had risen from obscurity in the fifteen years since she had moved to Little Rock.[9] Undoubtedly her ascent had been helped by her stunning good looks, her outgoing personality, her stylish clothes, and her air of sophistication. One biographer described her as "full of life, charismatic, charming, and very beautiful."[10] Daisy and L. C. Bates's rise, however, had not been without difficulty. They had alienated many of the African American community's traditional leaders—mostly clergy—by calling them pawns of the white community.[11] They had also taken hardline stands on black voting rights and police brutality, stands that had made many of Little Rock's African Americans feel that the Bateses were pressing too hard for change to occur too fast. Bates's biographer Grif Stockley wrote that many black people in Little Rock were unwilling to challenge the status quo, and their "lack of aggressiveness was continually a problem for Daisy Bates and the NAACP."[12] Bates told photographer Brian Lanker that "there were blacks that didn't understand what was happening to them. This disturbed me an awful lot. There were not enough people who wanted to change, not enough of them to fight for a change."[13]

A more significant impediment to the Bateses' assumption of leadership positions was their less-than-respectable past. Daisy Lee Gatson fell in love with L. C. Bates when she was fifteen and he was twenty-seven, and she moved with him to Memphis not long after that.[14] Unfortunately for Daisy, L. C. was married and had two children.[15] The Memphis years are a blank in Daisy's autobiography and in her later interviews, and the narrative always resumes in 1941 when she and L. C. moved to Little Rock. In 1942 they slipped away to a small Arkansas town and married.[16]

Another obstacle to Daisy Bates's rise to respectability in Little Rock's black community was her lack of education. The town of Huttig did not have a high school, and it is likely that Daisy's formal education ended at the eighth grade.[17] Though she later claimed to have taken courses at Little Rock's Philander Smith College and Shorter Business College and at LeMoyne College in Memphis, no records of her attendance have survived.[18] Little Rock's black elite valued education highly, and college sororities played a major role in the social lives of the women of that community.[19] The principal of Paul Laurence Dunbar High School had the only earned doctorate in the Little Rock school system, and more than half of his faculty either held or were in the process of earning master's degrees.[20] Many years after her heroic service to her city during the Little Rock desegregation crisis of 1957–1959, Bates told a young friend that her "lack of education and finesse made me uncomfortable many times."[21]

Apparently, by the time she and L. C. moved to Little Rock, Daisy had realized that she could not have children, which she had wanted desperately, and she had tired of the vacuous life of being a kept woman.[22] L. C. had always encouraged her to develop her interests and talents, so when he purchased the *Arkansas State Press*, she began to get involved in its day-to-day operations. She soon discovered that she was fascinated by the newspaper world and especially by L. C.'s passionate dedication to the pursuit of civil rights for black Americans.[23] By her mid-thirties, Bates was going out to cover stories on her own, though she did not write them herself but dictated them to members of the staff. Her insecurity about her writing skills lasted throughout her life.

Toward the end of her life, Bates reflected: "The truth is, it was because of Daddy and L. C. that I ever got into the business of civil rights work, in the first place. I think I always had the courage, Daddy gave me that; but I needed the forum, and L. C. gave me that."[24] Her foster father, Orlee Smith, had been a member of the NAACP almost from its inception, and he paid dues for his wife and for his little daughter Daisy.[25] After she became aware of the racism that existed in Huttig, Smith often talked to her about the need to correct the racial inequities in their world and his hope that the NAACP would be able to do so. He told her "how hard educated black people [were] working to get laws changed, to bring equality to the South for colored folks."[26] L. C.'s passionate devotion to racial justice was one of the things that made him attractive to the much younger Daisy; as she remembered it, "We had fallen in love first, but after that, it was our passion for justice that made us soul mates."[27]

In 1942, L. C. wrote a series of outraged articles about the killing of a black serviceman, in uniform, by a white policeman before a large crowd of onlookers in the African American business district.[28] White businesspeople immediately tried to pressure L. C. through economic reprisal by canceling their advertising.[29] The president of the Little Rock Chamber of Commerce offered to make him "one of the biggest Negroes in the South," if he would soften his tone.[30] From that day forward, L. C. said, he "never solicited an advertisement from a white business."[31] One of Daisy Bates's biographers called this "a watershed moment" for the *Arkansas State Press* because it raised the newspaper's profile in the African American community, but it also alienated some of the local black elites who were accustomed to following the dictates of Little Rock's white leaders.[32] Even before this, L. C. had launched a campaign on the front page of his newspaper calling for new leadership in the black community.[33] In the ensuing years, L. C. mentored his wife in his brand of militant racial politics and then made her the city editor of his newspaper; increasingly, the two of them began to be recognized as a team.

Acutely conscious of her image, Daisy Bates developed a persona that radiated command and confidence, but her affected self-assurance often masked a looming sense of inadequacy. In public she appeared unfailingly in stylish clothes, high heels, heavy makeup, and a flawless coiffure, and her fun-loving, effervescent manner completed the picture of a woman who expected agreement and acceptance. Grif Stockley wrote that during the 1940s, Daisy "had absorbed the lesson that how one was perceived was more than half the battle of civil rights."[34] Biographer John Adams wrote that the projected image of middle-class respectability was another source of Bates's influence and power.[35] By the time she found herself called on to serve as a mentor to the Little Rock Nine in their quest to integrate Central High School, Bates had perfected her self-presentation, but the cost to her would be high in terms of self-doubt and stress, which ultimately played havoc with her health. This insecurity may have been the source of her tendency to place herself center stage whenever possible and to exaggerate the roles she played at key moments in her life. As Grif Stockley wrote, "Beneath her lovely clothes and effusive manner she possessed a will of steel, energy to match, and an ego, as she became famous, that increasingly put herself at the center of the universe. . . . She was not like her friend Rosa Parks—humility was not Bates's long suit. Had it been, she would have been washed away as a historical footnote in the tidal wave of pressure of 1957."[36]

In 1952 Daisy Bates served as a tour director and chaperone for the Spirit of Cotton tour, an event the National Council of Negro Women sponsored in conjunction with the annual Memphis Cotton Makers Jubilee, the black counterpart to the all-white Memphis Cotton Carnival.[37] Bates chaired the National

Council of Negro Women's Citizenship Education Committee in Little Rock, and she had worked for two years as the Little Rock chair for the jubilee. The tour had stops in Memphis, Washington, D.C., Baltimore, New York, Philadelphia, Pittsburgh, Cleveland, and Chicago. In each city, the women met with community leaders on both sides of the color line. Adams called this her "formal coming out in the national black press," suggesting that black reporters exhibited a "level of fascination" with the fair-skinned, beautiful young chaperone from Little Rock.[38] The *Pittsburgh Courier* referred to her as "a new personality."[39] The stylish, petite Bates was experiencing many of the same reactions in Little Rock, and the extensive press coverage of the tour enhanced her image as an attractive and effective black leader.

Upon her return to Little Rock, the thirty-nine-year-old Bates achieved the presidency of the NAACP's Arkansas State Conference of Branches, largely because that organization was at a low ebb financially and organizationally; she and L. C. were able to engineer her elevation from vice president to president at a poorly attended conference where other candidates did not offer themselves.[40] The national office had expressed increasing concern about the dearth of leadership in Arkansas, and Daisy and L. C. had long railed against the influence of the black clergy who opposed the NAACP.[41] Daisy soon proved up to the task, increasing memberships from 201 to 720 in her first year as president.[42] She threw herself into the work with the zeal of a person who has finally found her calling, and she was a dynamic and positive leader. She resurrected languishing branches around the state, while L. C. promoted her work in the *Arkansas State Press*. The lawyers in the national office were delighted, and they discovered that they liked her.[43] Bates was equally thrilled to be proving her mettle.

Following the lead of the national NAACP, Daisy and L. C. focused their attention on educational equality after the ruling in the *Brown v. Board of Education* case in 1954, which outlawed segregation in the schools. As Janice Kearney wrote, they used the *Arkansas State Press* "to educate the local black community about the importance of school integration to racial progress"; the result was that they were able to build "an informed black community that not just expressed unity against segregation in 1957, but, more important, understood the national implications inherent in the outcome of what began as a local conflict."[44] One of her future lieutenants would later describe Daisy as "having no skills," and he believed that L. C. was the brains behind the operation.[45] The Central High School vice principal for girls, Elizabeth Huckaby, thought otherwise, writing in her memoir: "I could see why Mrs. Bates was successful as president of the state NAACP. She was a good infighter, persistent, intelligent, and unintimidated—a woman who had made a choice of this career fully aware of its dangers to her person and also its rewards in prestige and in service to her people."[46] As would in time become clear, Daisy Bates was also a master of public relations, and a part of her persuasiveness in that role was her unwavering attention to how she presented herself to the world. Possessed of a large ego and confident of her beauty and charm, Bates worked tenaciously to maintain a public façade that must have been as exhausting as it was effective.

In the year after *Brown*, while the nation waited for implementation orders from the Supreme Court (a directive in 1955 that would come to be known as *Brown II*), Little Rock school superintendent Virgil T. Blossom spoke to hundreds of parents in dozens of meetings all over the city.[47] His school board had announced the week after *Brown* that they would comply, and he set about educating his patrons and formulating a workable plan.[48] Daisy Bates made it her business to attend as many of these meetings as possible, and she quickly realized that the superintendent was saying different things to white and black audiences.[49] She called him on it, asking pointed questions in front of large groups of people. It soon became apparent that her presence at a meeting left him visibly flustered. She informed Thurgood Marshall in the national NAACP office that she did not trust the superintendent.[50]

Shortly before *Brown II* came down on May 31, 1955, Virgil Blossom announced the Little Rock School District's meager proposal, which came to be known as the Blossom Plan. It involved a gradual, phased program of integration that openly called for "minimum compliance" with the *Brown II* directive and specified no date for implementation.[51] Bates immediately began to recruit students to participate in the desegregation process; many of them were members of the youth chapter of the NAACP that she had organized in 1954.[52] Increasingly she was recognized as the African American community's spokesperson on integration and its most zealous advocate, and the national black press began to view her as a rising star in the civil rights movement.[53]

In February 1956 the Little Rock NAACP, despairing of receiving fair treatment from the Little Rock school board, filed suit in federal district court demanding full and immediate integration in a case styled *Aaron v. Cooper*.[54] Daisy Bates's stunning exchange with Leon Catlett occurred while he was taking depositions in that case. The federal judge ruled in favor of the school board, arguing that they had made a "prompt and reasonable start" toward desegregation.[55] The NAACP attorneys appealed the decision to the Eighth Circuit Court of Appeals, which upheld the district judge's decision but also ordered him to retain jurisdiction in the case and set an implementation date of September 1957.[56] Now it was definite that integration, however limited, *would* proceed in Little Rock.

By this time the forces of white resistance to integration throughout the South—soon to be called "massive resistance"—had begun to gain momentum, and the *Arkansas State Press* and the Little Rock NAACP came under increasing attack. In the February 1957 session of the Arkansas General Assembly, segregationists introduced and passed four bills designed to cripple the integration effort in Arkansas.[57] The most serious of these created the State Sovereignty Commission whose purpose was, according to NAACP lawyer Wiley Branton, "to require members of the NAACP and other civil rights organizations to register with a state agency and to report their various activities and finances."[58] Increasingly militant, L. C. Bates refused to moderate his tone in the face of this assault, and both he and Daisy seemed to draw strength from the charge into battle. It was, however, a decision that would cost L. C. his newspaper and Daisy her health.

During the spring of 1957, Virgil Blossom initiated a "screening" process, using the black principals, to determine which black children would be eligible to participate in integration. When Daisy Bates learned of this through some of the members of the NAACP's youth council, she contacted the black principals, who then suggested that Blossom should meet with Bates to explain his procedures.[59] The meeting occurred in May, and Bates took with her several members of the Little Rock NAACP's executive committee, as well as L. C. Blossom dismayed the assembled group by stating, "I feel that for this transition from segregation to integration in the Little Rock school system, we should select and encourage only the best Negro students to attend Central High School—so that no criticism of the integration process could be attributed to inefficiency, poor scholarship, low morals, or poor citizenship." The Bates group responded to Blossom's suggestions by saying that the process of screening students "seemed only to instill a feeling of inferiority, fear, and intimidation, and that the procedure should be discontinued." Blossom demurred.[60]

Through the summer, Bates felt fairly confident that integration would proceed in September without incident, but a week before the school year was to begin, white segregationists threw a rock through a window of her new "dream" home and burned a cross on her lawn.[61] She wrote to Gloster Current in the national NAACP office that "there is a real campaign of terror going on down here.... We have set up the flood lights in front of my home and it is being guarded around the clock."[62] This was just the beginning of what would become two years of unremitting threats of violence and venomous personal insults that rabid white segregationists hurled at Daisy and L. C. Bates. The complicated legal maneuvers undertaken by a beleaguered school board, the encouragement of the segregationists by an opportunistic governor, and especially the danger of harm to the black children who desegregated Central High School—all turned Daisy Bates into a warrior. From this point forward, Bates became uncompromising in her demands for racial justice.

On the evening of September 2, 1957, in a surprise move, Governor Orval E. Faubus stationed a contingent of the Arkansas National Guard around Central High School. Speaking in a televised address later that evening, Faubus claimed that he had given the soldiers the responsibility to maintain law and order when school started the next day.[63] Neither Virgil Blossom nor Daisy Bates knew whether the governor intended to prevent integration or protect it. Blossom immediately called the black parents and asked them to keep their children out of school and bring them to a meeting in his office in the morning. The parents called Bates and asked her to be present. While a mob of angry whites gathered in front of Central High the next morning, the black children, their parents, and Bates met in the superintendent's office. They were dismayed to hear him suggest that the children should approach the school the next day unaccompanied by their parents. He thought it would be easier to protect them if the adults were not present. One of the students, Carlotta Walls (later LaNier), remembered in her memoir that "the room was so still, it felt as if no one even breathed."[64]

In conversations that day with the national NAACP office, Bates admitted that she did not know why the National Guard had been stationed at Central High. Thurgood Marshall told her that in order to proceed legally against the governor (if indeed he was obstructing the students' entry), someone would have to force a statement from the National Guard that they were there to prevent the black students from entering the school.[65] Through a harried afternoon and evening, Bates dealt with the concerns of worried parents, the demands of her own organization, and the presence of a growing contingent of the African American press, which had decided to use her home as their headquarters.[66]

Bates could not free herself from the horrifying images of what could happen to the black children if they approached Central High School unprotected.[67] Late in the evening she hit on the idea of having the students escorted to the school by an integrated group of ministers.[68] After a number of frantic phone calls, she received a few commitments, and after midnight she began to call the parents of the black students (at this point, seventeen had been selected to attend), telling them to gather a couple of blocks from the school so they could be escorted in safety.[69] Unable to find a number for Elizabeth Eckford, she fell into bed exhausted about 3 a.m., intending to contact her in the morning. Bates had begun the habit of taking a sleeping pill with scotch, and when she awoke after only two hours of sleep, she forgot to call Elizabeth's parents.[70]

On Wednesday morning, September 4, Daisy and L. C. were in the car headed to the designated rendezvous point when they heard on the radio that a young girl was being mobbed in front of Central High School. "Oh my God I forgot Elizabeth!" she screamed in horror.[71] L. C. jumped from the car, a gun in his pocket, and ran to find Elizabeth, while Daisy drove on to meet the other students. After a harrowing, life-scarring thirty minutes, Elizabeth made it onto a city bus and left the scene.[72] The other eight children who showed up walked with four ministers as far as the National Guard blockade, where a soldier told them that he could not admit them on orders from the governor.[73] Now Thurgood Marshall had the evidence he needed to proceed legally against the state of Arkansas for obstruction of a federal mandate.

When the group left Central High after being turned away on that first day, Bates took nine of the courageous students to Virgil Blossom's office, hoping he would be able to come up with some course of action. He was not in, so she then took them to the office of the U.S. attorney, who greeted them with a "deer in the headlights" look and clearly did not know what to do. Confusion reigned in all quarters.[74] The courageous students, soon to be dubbed the "Little Rock Nine"—Minnijean Brown, Elizabeth Eckford, Ernest Green, Thelma Mothershed, Melba Pattillo, Gloria Ray, Terrence Roberts, Jefferson Thomas, and Carlotta Walls—stayed the course through a lonely, damaging year, earning the right to pass into history as civil rights warriors.[75]

The school board appealed immediately to the federal judge for further instructions.[76] The judge who earlier had retained jurisdiction in the case had recused himself (to preserve his political viability), and the visiting judge, Ronald Davies, was from North Dakota and had demonstrated in an earlier ruling that he had little sympathy for the school board's dilemma.[77] Three days later he ordered the board to proceed with integration immediately.[78] Governor Faubus had created a constitutional crisis by pitting state against federal power, and the administration of Dwight D. Eisenhower did not know what to do next.[79] Neither did Judge Davies. On September 10 he issued an order directing the U.S. attorney general and the U.S. attorney in Little Rock to enter the case as friends of the court, thereby authorizing them to advise and assist him in this convoluted situation.[80] The NAACP lawyers in Little Rock also filed a pleading asking for an injunction against Faubus. Davies set a trial date of September 20, giving himself time to attend the wedding of his youngest daughter.[81]

During the interim, "four plane loads" of FBI agents continued an investigation they had begun a week earlier in an effort to substantiate or disprove Governor Faubus's claim that great potential for violence existed in Little Rock.[82] A summary of their report, which was leaked to favored journalists, claimed that no such threat existed; the full report, however, which historian Tony Freyer obtained years later through the use of the Freedom of Information Act, detailed extensive threats and dangers of violence.[83] The FBI agents also investigated Daisy Bates in an attempt to ascertain if she had any ties to the Communist Party.[84]

In this period, while the black students were out of school, they received many invitations from around the country offering them opportunities to leave Little Rock and pursue their education elsewhere. Bates called them together and gave them the letters and invitations, explaining to them that it was their decision to make. They discussed the possibilities of making up time if they transferred to another school, but finally one of them said thoughtfully, "You know we cannot go anywhere, for if we do, the entire fight would be lost." When Bates called the parents to inform them of their children's decision, they told her that "they had already been informed that the children had decided to remain and added, 'We are with you 100%.'"[85]

In the meantime, Arkansas congressman Brooks Hays had arranged a meeting between Governor Faubus and President Eisenhower at the president's vacation retreat in Newport, Rhode Island. Though their meeting was amicable, it was inconclusive, and Faubus returned to Arkansas increasingly aware that his stance was at odds with the thinking of the federal government, the Little Rock school board, and his state's leading newspaper. At the trial on September 20, Judge Davies directed Faubus to stop interfering with the orders of the court. Faubus withdrew the National Guard from their posts around Central High School and flew off to a meeting of the Southern Governors' Conference in Sea Island, Georgia.

Over the weekend, Virgil Blossom, Brooks Hays, Harry Ashmore (editor of the *Arkansas Gazette*), Mayor Woodrow Mann, former Arkansas governor Sid McMath, and Edwin Dunaway (a white, liberal lawyer and close friend of Daisy Bates) worked frantically to prepare for the violence at Central High School that they had said publicly would not happen. They secured a commitment from the Little Rock Police Department that its officers would turn out in force to preserve the peace when the nine black children attempted once again to enter the school.[86] They asked Daisy Bates to secure commitments from the nine students' parents that their children would brave the mob one more time, even though Faubus had asked the NAACP to withhold the students through a "cooling off period."[87] Bates recalled: "The kids were so courageous. They were ready to go and they wanted to go. The whites didn't want them and it made them want to go more."[88] Ernest Green remembered later, with characteristic teenage invincibility, that he never dreamed he could be hurt. Terrence Roberts thought the white kids would like him once they got to know him. Only Daisy Bates had the sickening feeling that something could go terribly wrong.[89]

Bates reported to Gloster Current at NAACP headquarters in New York that she spent all day on Sunday, September 22, working with Ashmore, Dunaway, and Mann, trying to get the federal government to provide some kind of protection for the black children when they entered Central High. The Justice Department refused.[90] Late on Sunday night Virgil Blossom called Bates and told her to have the nine students at her house on Monday morning and then await instructions on how to proceed. The scene at her house that morning was frenzied, with the students, their parents, and a swarm of national reporters crowding the small home. In the two weeks that the children had been out of school, they had had frequent interviews with the national black press. Bates recalled a few years later: "I would always be present so they couldn't put words in the children's mouth. . . . Whenever they would ask a loaded question I would say you are not being fair with us. . . . Finally we won most of the reporters. . . . It was important that the reporters themselves understood the children . . . they [the students] weren't handpicked by me."[91]

The radio at the Bates home blared frequent reports about the huge and growing crowd outside Central High and the threatening comments many of the emotional segregationists were making.[92] Finally, the assistant police chief, Gene Smith, called to say that plans were in place to allow the children to enter the school through an out-of-the-way door on the south side of the building.[93] Most of the white reporters dashed to their cars as soon as the phone call came through, but several of the black reporters waited to hear the full details, and as an unintended consequence they functioned as a diversionary tactic—and suffered severe beatings—while the black students scurried into the school.[94] When the white mob realized that the black children had gotten inside, they set up a howl that lasted for hours; the school librarian described it as sounding like an earthquake or storm, "a steady, deep roar all the time."[95] The rioters lashed out at the white policemen who guarded the perimeter of the campus, many of whom were segregationists themselves. *New York Times* reporter Claude Sitton wrote later that what kept the police lines from breaking during the rioting was that "those policemen were more afraid of big Gene Smith than they were of the mob."[96] As Smith told Harry Ashmore from a pay phone at the scene, he had walked inside the police line from one end to the other, over and over, and "I've told those sons of bitches if any of them step back I'd shoot them in the back of the head."[97]

Back at the Bates home, the anxious parents listened to the continuing radio reports. Many white students left the school as soon as the black children went in, and they gave lurid reports to the eagerly waiting reporters. One claimed that he had seen several fights between black and white students in the corridors and "three Negroes with blood on their clothing."[98] After each report, Daisy Bates secured an assurance from Gene Smith that the rumors were false, but a frightened Oscar Eckford spoke for the assembled parents when he screamed at Bates, "Well, if it's not true, why would they say such things on the air?"[99] By noon, Smith, Blossom, and Mann had concluded that the mob could not be controlled and the black children were increasingly at risk, and the trio decided to remove the black students from the school, to the consternation of the school principal and the black kids themselves, who all thought that the situation inside the school was under control.[100] Bates announced to the reporters gathered at her home that afternoon: "The children will not return to Central High School until they have the assurance of the President of the United States that they will have protection against the mob."[101] By suppertime that night, Eisenhower had issued a proclamation calling on the citizens of Little Rock to refrain from their "willful obstruction of justice" and disperse, but there was no mention of federal protection for the children.[102]

The Little Rock police guarded the Bates home and each of the homes of the nine children that night, and a cadre of well-armed friends and neighbors also gathered at Daisy and L. C.'s house. The segregationists felt they had won a victory at the school, and the Bateses' telephone rang constantly with whites hurling crude insults and vicious threats. Much of the national black press corps had gathered at the small frame house, including Alex Wilson, who had been beaten that day at the high school. The atmosphere was tense and expectant, because there had been rumors of a caravan of segregationists descending on Little Rock from east Arkansas. About 10:30 p.m., one of the guards ran in and reported that police had stopped a caravan of about one hundred cars just two blocks from the Bates home and that the cars had been loaded with guns, ammunition, and dynamite.[103] That report proved to be exaggerated, but it was quite alarming at the time.

About 2 a.m., the phone rang. When Daisy answered a white voice announced: "We just had our first killing in Little Rock and you are responsible." That report also turned out to be false, but as Bates recalled three years later: "I was absolutely at the breaking point because this is what we didn't want. This is what Faubus had predicted, this is what we had worked so hard against."[104] Daisy walked into her bedroom and cried, "God how much can a person stand?" She felt that she just could not take any more. "The way I felt at that moment if I could have lifted the cotton curtain and walk[ed] behind the iron curtain I would have told America to go straight to hell. Because, I felt absolutely there was no justice anywhere in America." Bates thought it was terrible "for children and adults to be subjected to this kind of treatment with no help forthcoming and we had begged the president and I had begged for relief. And these children had gone into two mobs. What can you expect in America? And so I cried. . . . I hated everything and everybody at that moment."[105]

No one slept very much that night. The next morning about 7:30, Bates received a telephone call from a man who told her, "We didn't get you last night, but we will. And you better not try to put those coons in our school!"[106] In her conversation with Gloster Current at the NAACP office in New York that morning, Daisy said: "The children are at home where they are going to stay. We cannot subject these children to that mob violence."[107]

Across town, Mayor Woodrow Mann sent a frantic and wildly exaggerated telegram to President Eisenhower, requesting federal troops. Much discussion and preparation in Little Rock and Washington, D.C., had preceded the sending of that telegram, and the president was ready.[108] Shortly before noon Eisenhower ordered units of the famed 101st Airborne Division of the U.S. Army to Little Rock; he also federalized the Arkansas National Guard, thereby taking those troops out of Faubus's control.[109] By late afternoon an integrated force of 856 soldiers had landed at the Little Rock Air Base, and by nightfall 319 of these men, all white, had taken up stations around Central High School. Another 99 men arrived by land the next day.

At first Bates was relieved when she learned the federal troops were coming. People were asking her why she didn't just give up and whether the price was worth it. At times she wondered. She remembered: "I just didn't see how I could win. With the bickering in Washington . . . the background check, whether I was being directed by Russia or what. This was a great decision for me to make whether I should continue."[110] Bates realized that she held the lives of nine children in her hands, and in a rare moment of quiet and reflection she asked herself, "Why am I the person to have to do this? . . . What have I done? Have I done the right thing? . . . In the final analysis I had to make the decision. If one child died I would be blamed for it and this is what hit me right between the eyes."[111]

In a typescript that did not make it into her published memoir, Bates asked herself at this point, "Had I made the right decision? In my quest for justice, had I helped my people? Or was this day the result of a vendetta I made against all white people at the age of six years?"[112] Bates felt an overwhelming exhaustion, and she realized that "I had been fighting all my life."[113] Feeling she was nearing mental and physical collapse, she wanted to give up.[114] She was so tired that she could barely lift her feet, but she answered the ringing telephone to hear someone cursing at her: "You are bringing in these damn integrated troops. . . . if you think this is going to stop us you have another goddamn thing coming . . . you black bitch."[115] Bates knew then that she could not give up, but she decided it was time for "a scotch and a sleeping pill."[116]

About 1:00 a.m. Virgil Blossom called to say that the children should plan to go into the school that morning. Bates responded: "I can't do it. I just called nine parents and told them tomorrow not today. . . . I just can't do it . . . you've got to do it. . . . How am I going to do it? He said I don't know . . . you have to do it . . . [and I said] I certainly am not driving around this city alone tonight." So Blossom called the black principals, both men, to go with her, and she "went and took a bigger scotch."[117] The three African American adults drove around to the homes of all nine children and told the parents to have the kids at her house the next morning at 8:30. Gloria Ray's father met them at the door with a shotgun in hand and refused their request, saying, "I don't care if the President of the United States gave you those instructions! . . . I won't let Gloria go. She's faced two mobs and that's enough."[118] Bates recalled later that she was thinking as "we eased on down the steps . . . Lordy are we going to have this at every one of them?"[119] The three had breakfast about 4 a.m. and then went to bed. All the children were at her house the next morning at 8:25 when an army station wagon pulled up to drive them to school.[120] Gloria Ray's father had delivered his daughter and said, "Here, Daisy, she's yours. She's determined to go."[121]

Surrounded by soldiers, the Little Rock Nine climbed the imposing, curving staircase outside Central High School and marched triumphantly through the huge front doors. The helmeted troops guarding the school's perimeter, with bayonets affixed to their guns, made short work of the slight resistance outside the school. The army's analysis of the first day was that its initial show of force was "an unqualified success."[122] The parents of the nine students sent a letter to President Eisenhower saying, "We the parents of the nine Negro children who have enrolled at Little Rock Central High School want you to know that your actions in safeguarding their rights have strengthened our faith in democracy. Now as never before we have an abiding feeling of belonging and purposefulness."[123] Inside the school, without soldiers to protect them in the classrooms, the nine young heroes engaged in a new kind of battle, one that escalated as the year progressed, one for which they had no preparation.

In the ensuing weeks, the nine youngsters gathered frequently after school at Mrs. Bates's home, where they would decompress in the room downstairs she called her "rumpus room."[124] They would share their stories of the mistreatment they were receiving inside the school, they would drink Cokes, and they would dance. Daisy Bates coached them on all sorts of things: how to hold their books so they couldn't be knocked out of their arms, how to walk so they looked dignified and proud, and how to interact with the reporters who always pressed for details on life inside the school. She also tried to prepare them for the real possibility of injury or death. As she remembered two decades later, "So I told them that one of us might die in this fight. And I said to them, 'If they kill me, you would have to go on. If I die, don't you stop. If Jeff died...' He said, 'I ain't going to die' (laughs)."[125] Daisy Bates began to think of them as "her" children, and they would soothe a yearning she had long felt.[126] She told one of her biographers near the end of her life, "All my children... I mean... the ones I called mine... the nine, those sweet children who sacrificed so much, lost so much, ... they would call me 'Miss Daisy.' And I knew that was a real sign of respect."[127]

Fairly precipitously, the army began to reduce its presence in Little Rock. The NAACP had encouraged the nine black students to report incidents of harassment, such as shoving in the halls, name calling, close following that made their heels bleed, and the throwing of sharpened pencils, but some of the nine felt that most of the school authorities seemed to resent their reporting, and the kids grew increasingly reluctant to do so. The NAACP field secretary, Clarence Laws, had reported to his superiors that this reluctance, combined with "the failure of the Army and the school to make known the actual situation in the school, gives the impression of a peace and quiet which does not actually exist," and he feared that this incorrect impression could "cause the untimely withdrawal of all troops."[128] He was right. On November 27 the army withdrew the last of its men, leaving the protection of the black students to the Arkansas National Guard.[129] The attacks inside the school escalated.

About this time, Daisy and L. C. received word that someone had offered $10,000 to any person or organization who could get the nine out of Central High School. Thelma Mothershed's mother called Bates to tell her that a local black politician, I. S. McClinton, had come to her home and said, "I would not risk my child's life." Other parents reported that Reverend Wesley E. Hayes, the pastor of Mount Pleasant Missionary Baptist Church, told them that "we were just tearing up the town; the town would never be the same again." L. C. put an article on the front page of the *Arkansas State Press* saying that they had heard about the $10,000 and that "some people" had tried to collect, promising that the next time he heard such stories, he was "going to print names." That stopped the problem.[130]

Bates settled into a demanding schedule of giving speeches every weekend all over the country for the NAACP.[131] Thousands of letters arrived at her house during this period, some vicious and hateful, some filled with praise for her and the nine students.[132] Financial contributions also began to arrive, and Bates created a scholarship fund for "her" young students' college educations.[133] The

Ku Klux Klan printed cards declaring "Open season on Daisy Bates" and listed her address.[134] Fire bombs and stones continued to be hurled at her house. Her front door was riddled with bullet holes.[135] One woman called every morning at 3:00 a.m. to harass her.[136] Daisy Bates had become the face of integration in Little Rock, and it was an exhausting, exhilarating time in her life.[137]

Bates reflected a decade after the crisis: "We were determined they were not going to chase us out of town. Had they chased us out of town, the movement would have died."[138] This was a characteristic overstatement from Bates, who always placed herself at the center of the action. In interviews and in her autobiography she frequently exaggerated her role, as when she told this interviewer that she had marched with the students up to the line of the National Guardsmen, when the abundant photographs from that day show she was not there.[139] This is perhaps understandable, given the high emotion of the period, but it was a pattern that opened her to severe criticism, especially from some of the Little Rock Nine, who felt that they and their parents should have received more of the credit for keeping "the movement" alive.[140]

In February 1958 the Little Rock school board went back to the federal courts and asked for a delay of two and a half years so passions and tempers could cool.[141] As soon as Judge Harry Lemley granted the requested delay, the NAACP appealed his decision to the Eighth Circuit Court of Appeals in St. Louis. The Eighth Circuit reversed Lemley, and the Little Rock school board appealed that decision to the U.S. Supreme Court. In an unusual called session of the Court, that body ruled in *Cooper v. Aaron* that the presence of violent resistance was an insufficient reason to deprive black citizens of their rights, and the justices ordered the school board to proceed with the plan of integration it had initiated the year before.[142] In preparation for just such a decision, a special session of the Arkansas legislature had passed a series of anti-integration laws, one of which allowed the governor to close the schools in the event of "forced integration."[143] On September 12, 1958, Orval Faubus closed all the high schools in Little Rock.[144]

Daisy Bates flew into action, of course, attempting to find tutors for the seven remaining students (Minnijean Brown had been expelled in February and Ernest Green had graduated with his class in May).[145] Fairly quickly, the families of Terrence Roberts and Gloria Ray moved away from Little Rock, but the remaining five enrolled together to take correspondence courses through the University of Arkansas, with the national office of the NAACP footing the bill.[146] That organization had decided it needed the remaining children to stay in Little Rock, explaining, "Obviously if the Negro students currently enrolled in Central High School should leave the state for education elsewhere, there would presumably be no immediate reason why the high school could not be re-opened on an all-white basis."[147] Bates continued her grueling routine of raising money for the students' college scholarship fund, running interference with visiting reporters, speaking around the country for the NAACP, and supporting her increasingly frantic husband as his newspaper foundered (despite significant infusions of cash from the national NAACP office) as a result of his militant championing of desegregation in Little Rock.[148]

During the school year of 1958–1959, remembered in Little Rock as "the lost year," the school board resigned, new school board elections produced a split board with three strong segregationists and three businessmen who advocated reopening the schools on an integrated basis, the all-white Women's Emergency Committee to Open Our Schools emerged as a new force in Little Rock politics, the split school board fired forty-four of the city's best teachers (accusing them of being integrationists), and the business community found its voice with a campaign called Stop This Outrageous Purge, which ousted the segregationist school board members and elected three "moderate" members who rehired the fired teachers. White students moved to neighboring towns to attend school, went off to the prestigious prep schools that had recruited them heavily, or attended one of the private schools that opened during the year. Most black high school students remained out of school, and many never went back.[149]

By the fall of 1959, the city's white leaders had learned the high cost of maintaining segregation and had decided that industrial and business growth depended on providing public education for their youth. Jefferson Thomas and Carlotta Walls enrolled again in Central High School, and the school year started without much fanfare.[150] The months of unrelenting stress had taken their toll on Daisy Bates, however, and when the David McKay Publishing Company offered her a contract to write a book about her experiences, she jumped at the opportunity and moved to New York. She told friends that "she needed to leave the scene of the war, to save her own self."[151] As she told one biographer, "The Crisis had placed every part of her life in jeopardy; her marriage, her health, her sanity and certainly hers [sic] and L. C.'s financial stability."[152] Daisy and L. C.'s marriage had suffered as she had moved out from under his wing and onto center stage. Their business had suffered as advertising and subscriptions fell off sharply at the *Arkansas State Press* in response to a concerted campaign by segregationists.[153] The newspaper closed in 1959, and L. C. went to work for the NAACP as a field secretary under Daisy Bates's leadership (she was still president of the Arkansas State Conference of Branches), a reversal of roles that undoubtedly increased their marital stress.[154]

From 1960 to 1962, Daisy lived in New York, with frequent trips back to Arkansas to check on the situation there.[155] She also continued her schedule of speaking around the country for the NAACP, and she joined that organization's national board.[156] She found herself unable to write her memoir, however, in part because of its searing emotional nature, in part because she had no confidence in her writing abilities. Thrown into a glamorous world of celebrity and high living where she was the star of the moment, she found a thousand excuses to avoid the rigors of writing. The names in her address book included Lena Horne, Harry Belafonte, Alex Haley, Maya Angelou, Lorraine Hansberry, Miles Davis, Charles Diggs, Jackie Robinson, Arthur Spingarn, and, of course, Roy Wilkins and Thurgood Marshall.[157] Bates began to dream about making a movie of her life, with her friend Lena Horne starring as Daisy.[158] Rumors made their way back to Little Rock that she was having an affair with a white man, and of course L. C. suffered.[159] Finally, with the assistance of at least four ghostwriters, including Alex Haley and Benjamin Fine, Bates finished her book and saw it published.[160] She returned to Little Rock and divorced L. C. in 1963.[161]

Daisy and L. C. remarried within six months, but their brief divorce indicated the extreme nature of Daisy's stress and exhaustion.[162] (They remained married until L. C.'s death in 1980.) Also in 1963, Daisy spoke at the March on Washington, the only woman invited to do so, and she continued work she had been doing for President John F. Kennedy: registering voters in several northern cities.[163] After Kennedy's assassination, Bates went to work for President Lyndon Johnson; as she said in an interview ten years later, "it was simply because we had to eat. We couldn't get a job in Little Rock. We had to make payments on our house."[164] In 1965, the frantic pace of Daisy Bates's life caught up with her, and she suffered a debilitating stroke that impaired her speech and her gait.[165] Determined to continue to make her mark, she moved to Mitchellville, a tiny, impoverished town in south Arkansas, and for six years applied all the tools she had acquired working in the War on Poverty to bring the little town back to life.[166] The fiery crusader just could not yield to the demands of age and a lifetime of stress, and she was determined to keep going, to keep making a difference.

In 1976, this author interviewed Daisy Bates for the Southern Oral History Program at the University of North Carolina. A few months later, she called to ask if I could bring two professors to meet her, and Bates agreed. The obligatory niceties out of the way, Bates asked if they would like something to drink, such as a cup of tea. The two northern gentlemen, not wanting to put their impaired hostess to any trouble, declined. As a southern girl, she understood what was being offered, and she accepted. Bates disappeared briefly and then returned carrying a silver tea service and lovely bone china, and she served her guests with as much confidence and elegance as any lady in an English country manor. She was indomitable, and she was determined to show these three white professors that she knew "how to do." It was classic Daisy, with an impressive ego and a lot of brass. They could all see how the little girl from Huttig had made her way to the top of the civil rights elite.

After a long decline, Daisy Bates died in 1999 at the age of eighty-six. She was the first and only woman to lie in state in Arkansas's capitol rotunda, and a thousand people came to pay their respects.[167] In the following years, the street that runs beside Central High School was renamed for her; a day honoring her was added to the Arkansas calendar; and her home became a civil rights shrine.[168] Aside from these tributes, Bates has never received the widespread recognition her leadership and sacrifices should have brought.

Although Daisy Bates was superseded in the civil rights pantheon by heroes who took a more militant stance and made larger demands, none were more courageous, or more determined, or more glamorous. At the time of her death, an editorial in the *Arkansas Democrat-Gazette* said that "Daisy Bates demonstrated . . . that some things never go out of style: courage, candor, honor, character, simple human dignity."[169] As one of her biographers reflected, "The most prolific of writers could have never created a story as incredible as the life that Daisy Bates lived," and this is undoubtedly true.[170] Near the end of her life Bates suggested that despite the battle scars, she had no regrets about any of her involvement. She had long ago concluded that "I was put here to make a difference."[171] She did that, in spite of her doubts and insecurities, and the nation is in her debt.

NOTES

I thank the Delta Women Writers symposium for their rigorous and generous critiques of this chapter.

1. Charles Allbright, "Leaders of NAACP Declare They Want Desegregation Now," *Arkansas Gazette*, May 5, 1956, 1A.

2. John Aaron v. William G. Cooper, Eastern U.S. District Court, Eastern District of Arkansas, Western Division, Depositions of the Witnesses, Rev. J. C. Crenshaw and Mrs. L. C. Bates, Taken at Instance of Defendants, May 4, 1956, box 6, folder 1, 89, Daisy Bates Papers, Wisconsin Historical Society, Madison (hereafter cited as WHS).

3. John Lewis Adams, "'Time for a Showdown': The Partnership of Daisy and L. C. Bates, and the Politics of Gender Protest and Marriage," Ph.D. diss., Rutgers University, 2014, 359. For another interesting treatment of the influence of gender in Daisy Bates's life, see John Kirk, "Daisy Bates, the National Association for the Advancement of Colored People, and the 1957 Little Rock School Crisis: A Gendered Perspective," in *Gender and the Civil Rights Movement*, ed. Peter Ling and Sharon Monteith (New York: Garland, 1999), 17–40. For an excellent discussion of the southern region's

"racial etiquette," see David R. Goldfield, *Black, White, and Southern: Race Relations and Southern Culture* (Baton Rouge: Louisiana State University Press, 1990).

4. Bates reflected late in life: "I always felt as if life had prepared me for the role I played in Little Rock." Janis F. Kearney, *Daisy: Between a Rock and a Hard Place* (Little Rock, Ark.: Writing Our World Publishing, 2013), 103. For the most comprehensive and scholarly Bates biography, see Grif Stockley, *Daisy Bates: Civil Rights Crusader from Arkansas* (Jackson: University Press of Mississippi, 2005).

5. Daisy Bates, *The Long Shadow of Little Rock: A Memoir by Daisy Bates* (1962; repr., Fayetteville: University of Arkansas Press, 1987), 10–15; Kearney, *Daisy*, 120–24. See also Judith Bloom Fradin and Dennis Brindell Fradin, *The Power of One: Daisy Bates and the Little Rock Nine* (New York: Clarion, 2004), 8. Two of Bates's biographers, Grif Stockley and John Adams, have argued that much of her autobiography is unreliable, if not outright fictionalized. Adams suggested that "the construction of her early years is consistent with an African-American autobiographical writing tradition that uses the power of individual narratives to reflect the general experiences of the race" (Adams, "Time for a Showdown," 96).

6. Kearney, *Daisy*, 125. On his deathbed Orlee Smith begged Daisy to turn her hatred and bitterness into a positive force, fearing that otherwise it would destroy her (Bates, *Long Shadow*, 29).

7. Kearney, *Daisy*, 108.

8. Ibid., 109. Bates was always disturbed when the public misunderstood her motives: "It bothered me so much when people would look at me as if I was just doing something to get attention, or to make a name for myself" (126).

9. Adams, "Time for a Showdown," 235.

10. Ibid., 139. White civil rights advocate Reverend Will D. Campbell of the National Council of Churches called her "the beautiful and indomitable Daisy Bates" (Fradin and Fradin, *Power of One*, xi).

11. "Who Is to Blame?" *Arkansas State Press*, December 18, 1942. Daisy was also very outspoken; as she told biographer Janis Kearney, "I never was able to keep my mouth closed, and never cared about putting things nicely so people could stomach them. L.C. used to get so mad at me about that, but he also was very proud of how brave I was" (Kearney, *Daisy*, 156).

12. Stockley, *Daisy Bates*, 44; Adams, "Time for a Showdown," 181–82. Bates later recalled that many in Little Rock's African American community felt that she was an outsider who was "stirring up trouble." See Daisy Bates interview with Elizabeth Jacoway, October 11, 1976, 54, Southern Oral History Program, University of North Carolina, Chapel Hill (hereafter SOHP).

13. Brian Lanker, *I Dream a World: Portraits of Black Women Who Changed America* (New York: Stewart, Tabori and Chang, 1989), 73.

14. Linda S. Caillouet, "Daisy Lee Gatson Bates," *Arkansas Democrat-Gazette*, January 12, 1992; Stockley, *Daisy Bates*, 24–25; Kearney, *Daisy*, 160–62; Bates, *Long Shadow*, 32–33.

15. Adams, "Time for a Showdown," 140.

16. Stockley, *Daisy Bates*, 27; Adams, "Time for a Showdown," 8. For some interesting insights on this period in her life, see Fradin and Fradin, *Power of One*, 30–31.

17. Kearney, *Daisy*, 113; Leroy Matthew Christophe, *The African American Hall of Fame* (Little Rock, Ark.: National Dunbar Alumni Association of Little Rock, 1993), 71. A childhood friend believed that Daisy might have attended high school while she lived with her grandmother in another town for two or three years (Fradin and Fradin, *Power of One*, 29).

18. Caillouet, "Daisy Lee Gatson Bates." Bates claimed in her autobiography that she had taken some correspondence courses at Philander Smith and at Shorter, where she "took courses in Busi-

ness Administration, Public Relations, and other subjects related to the newspaper field" (Bates, *Long Shadow*, 38–39). In an interview with this author, she noted that she took flying lessons at Philander Smith (Bates interview with Jacoway, 15, SOHP). One of her childhood friends thought she had taken some college courses while in Memphis (Fradin and Fradin, *Power of One*, 31).

19. Grif Stockley interview with Annie Abrams, in Stockley, *Daisy Bates*, 281.

20. Faustine C. Jones-Wilson and Erma Glasco-Davis, *Paul Laurence Dunbar High School of Little Rock, Arkansas: "Take from Our Lips a Song, Dunbar to Thee"* (Virginia Beach, Va.: Donning Company, 2003), 31–32, 42.

21. Kearney, *Daisy*, 105.

22. Ibid., 127. Daisy Bates told Kearney: "The one thing that haunted [me] more than the desire to see our people freed in every way ... was my desire to have a child to call my own. I know how people gossiped that I was too busy running around the world, being a civil rights queen and [too busy] with the newspaper to really have time to care for a child" (ibid.).

23. Irene Wassell, "L. C. Bates: Editor of the *Arkansas State Press*," MA thesis, University of Arkansas, School of Journalism, Little Rock, 1983.

24. Kearney, *Daisy*, 156.

25. Bates interview with Jacoway, 4, SOHP.

26. Kearney, *Daisy*, 120.

27. Ibid., 150, 160.

28. For example, "City Patrolman Shoots Negro Soldier, Body Riddled while Lying on Ground, White Military Police Look On," *Arkansas State Press*, March 27, 1942.

29. Bates, *Long Shadow*, 36–37.

30. Wassell, "L. C. Bates," 36–37.

31. Ibid.

32. Adams, "Time for a Showdown," 214.

33. *Arkansas State Press*, January 16, 1942.

34. Stockley, *Daisy Bates*, 58.

35. Adams, "Time for a Showdown," 361.

36. Stockley, *Daisy Bates*, 58.

37. "Woman Editor Escort for Jubilee Queen," *Chicago Defender*, March 15, 1952; Adams, "Time for a Showdown," 279–80. See also Cynthia Sadler, "'On Parade': Race, Gender, and Imagery in the Memphis Mardi Gras, Cotton Carnival, and Cotton Makers' Jubilee," in *Tennessee Women: Their Lives and Times*, ed. Beverly Greene Bond and Sarah Wilkerson Freeman (Athens: University of Georgia Press, 2015), 2:125–51.

38. Adams, "Time for a Showdown," 288. Bates's father, Hezekiah Gatson, was said to have been light-skinned enough to pass for white. According to Bates's biographer Janis Kearney, his mother was German (Kearney, *Daisy*, 98).

39. Adams, "Time for a Showdown," 20.

40. Ibid., 283–86. Adams wrote that the Arkansas State Conference of Branches "was on the brink of extinction."

41. Kearney, *Daisy*, 63.

42. Ibid., 295.

43. Ibid., 285.

44. Ibid., 304.

45. Chris Mercer interview with Grif Stockley, January 17, 2002, in Stockley, *Daisy Bates*, 50. Roy Wilkins, executive secretary of the NAACP, disagreed, writing to Pauli Murray: "No one can repay

Mrs. Bates for the magnificent job she did in Little Rock. Personally I do not believe any other person had just the right mixture of skills and the exact temperament for success that were the possession of Daisy Bates" (Wilkins to Murray, July 18, 1958, Daisy Bates Papers, carton 2, WHS). See also Stockley, *Daisy Bates*, 149.

46. Elizabeth Huckaby, *Crisis at Central High: Little Rock, 1957–1958* (Baton Rouge: Louisiana State University Press, 1980), 94.

47. Virgil T. Blossom, *It HAS Happened Here* (New York: Harper, 1959).

48. Ibid., 25.

49. Bates interview with Jacoway, 14–16, SOHP.

50. Ibid., 15.

51. Blossom, *It HAS Happened Here*, 21–22.

52. Adams, "Time for a Showdown," 296. In the final analysis, the students "selected themselves" (Bates interview with Jacoway, 12). See also Elizabeth Jacoway, "Not Anger but Sorrow: Minnijean Brown Trickey Remembers the Little Rock Crisis," *Arkansas Historical Quarterly* (Spring 2005): 7; Terrence Roberts, *Lessons from Little Rock* (Little Rock, Ark.: Butler Center Books, 2009), 11, 15; Carlotta Walls LaNier, *A Mighty Long Way: My Journey to Justice at Little Rock Central High School* (New York: One World, 2009), 51.

53. Adams, "Time for a Showdown," 327.

54. For a brief treatment of this case as it proceeded all the way to the U.S. Supreme Court, see Elizabeth Jacoway, "Richard C. Butler and the Little Rock School Board: The Quest to Maintain 'Educational Quality,'" *Arkansas Historical Quarterly* 65, no. 1 (Spring 2006): 24–38.

55. "Aaron v. Cooper," *Race Relations Law Reporter* 1 (October 1956): 859–60.

56. Tony A. Freyer, *Little Rock on Trial: "Cooper v. Aaron" and School Desegregation* (Lawrence: University Press of Kansas, 2007), 75–76.

57. Stockley, *Daisy Bates*, 93–94; Elizabeth Jacoway, *Turn Away Thy Son: Little Rock, the Crisis That Shocked the Nation* (New York: Free Press, 2007), 59; Bates, *Long Shadow*, 53.

58. Wiley A. Branton, "Little Rock Revisited: Desegregation to Resegregation," *Journal of Negro Education* 52 (Summer 1982): 251.

59. Jacoway, *Turn Away Thy Son*, 101; Stockley, *Daisy Bates*, 97.

60. Frank Smith, "Report of the Conference between the Little Rock School Superintendent and NAACP Representatives, May 29, 1957," ser. III, container A, box 98, folder 2, NAACP Papers, Library of Congress, Washington, D.C.

61. "Oral Interview with Mrs. Bates concerning 1957 Crisis, June 21, 1960," Daisy Bates Papers, Manuscript Collection MC582, ser. 6, subser. 1, box 12, tape 1, University of Arkansas, Fayetteville (hereafter Bates interview, UA); Stockley, *Daisy Bates*, 112–13.

62. Memorandum to Miss Geier from Mr. Current, August 29, 1957, ser. III, container A, box 98, folder 2, Library of Congress, Washington, D.C.

63. "Faubus Calls National Guard to Keep Schools Segregated," *Arkansas Gazette*, September 3, 1957, 1A. For a full discussion of Faubus's decision to use the National Guard, see Jacoway, *Turn Away Thy Son*, 119–27.

64. Bates, *Long Shadow*, 63; LaNier, *A Mighty Long Way*, 60.

65. Bates interview with Jacoway, 13, SOHP.

66. In an interview three years later, Bates recalled: "At this time there were 300 reporters around the clock[.] They ... stayed at the house[,] they ate up my steaks" (Bates interview, UA, 5).

67. Kearney, *Daisy*, 135.

68. Stockley, *Daisy Bates*, 122–23; Bates, *Long Shadow*, 64.

69. Kearney, *Daisy*, 136–37; Bates interview, UA, 3; Bates, *Long Shadow*, 65.

70. Bates interview, UA, 11.

71. Ibid., 4.

72. Years later, Bates would reflect: "I know that my mistake changed Elizabeth's life . . . but, in many ways it changed mine as well. I have relived that terrible nightmare so many times" (Kearney, *Daisy*, 136). Bates claimed that the National Guardsmen made no effort to protect Elizabeth Eckford (Bates, *Long Shadow*, 71–73).

73. Stockley, *Daisy Bates*, 125.

74. Ibid., 127.

75. Apparently the Pulitzer Prize–winning journalist Relman Morin crafted the phrase the "Little Rock Nine" in Morin, "In This Hurricane's Eye? Calm Settles on City," *Arkansas Democrat*, October 7, 1957, 3.

76. Jacoway, *Turn Away Thy Son*, 126–27.

77. For an explanation of Judge John Miller's recusal, see ibid., ch. 5.

78. Lawrence Brooks Hays interview with Ronald A. Tonks, 26, in Southern Baptist Convention Presidents, Southern Baptist Historical Library and Archives, Nashville, Tenn.

79. See Jacoway, *Turn Away Thy Son*, 132–46, for a discussion of the confusion prevailing in Washington, D.C.

80. Ray Moseley, "U.S. Begins Move to Enjoin Faubus, 2 Guard Officers; [North Little Rock] Negroes Turned Back," *Arkansas Gazette*, September 10, 1957, 1A.

81. "U.S. Course Plotted to Give Governor His Day in Court," *Arkansas Gazette*, September 11, 1957, 1A.

82. Kearney, *Daisy*, 144.

83. Warren Olney III to Herbert Brownell, September 13, 1957, "Summary of FBI Report in Little Rock Difficulty," box 5, folder 2, Arthur Brann Caldwell Papers, Mullins Library, University of Arkansas, Fayetteville; "F.B.I.—Little Rock Crisis Reports," Butler Center for Arkansas Studies, Little Rock.

84. Federal Bureau of Investigation, Daisy Bates file, Grif Stockley Papers, ser. II, Butler Center for Arkansas Studies, Little Rock.

85. Daisy Bates speech, n.d., Daisy Bates Papers, carton 2, WHS; Bates interview, UA, 5.

86. Gene Foreman, "City Will Maintain Order at School, Mayor Says; Ike Bids for Acceptance," *Arkansas Gazette*, September 22, 1957, 1A.

87. Relman Morin, "Get Negroes Out, Faubus Peace Formula," *Montgomery Advertiser*, November 18, 1957, in Southern Education Reporting Service Papers, Vanderbilt University Special Collections and University Archives, Nashville, Tenn.

88. Lanker, *I Dream a World*, 73.

89. Ernest Green interview with John Pagan, January 26, 1973, 5, Elizabeth Jacoway Little Rock Crisis Collection, Butler Center for Arkansas Studies, Little Rock (hereafter EJC); Walter Lister Jr., "Police Guard Negroes if They Go to School in Little Rock Today," *New York Herald Tribune*, September 23, 1957, in Southern Education Reporting Service Papers, Nashville, Tenn.; Daisy Bates interview with John Pagan, August 23, 1957, 2, EJC.

90. Transcript of telephone conversation between Daisy Bates and Gloster Current, September 23, 1957, group III, ser. A, container 98, Library of Congress, Washington, D.C.

91. Bates interview, UA, 5.

92. Jacoway, *Turn Away Thy Son*, 169; Bates, *Long Shadow*, 89.

93. Jacoway, *Turn Away Thy Son*, 169.

94. Ibid., 172; Stockley, *Daisy Bates*, 143, 145; Bates, *Long Shadow*, 91.

95. Lola Alice Dunnavant, "Inside Central High School: Little Rock, Arkansas, 1957–1958," 9–11, EJC.

96. Claude Sitton, "U.S. Marshalls Would Keep Order in Little Rock, Backed by Police," August 24, 1958, *Chattanooga Times*.

97. Harry Ashmore interview with Elizabeth Jacoway, November 17, 1976, 78, EJC.

98. Robert Troutt, "Growing Violence Forces Withdrawal of 8 Students at Central High," *Arkansas Democrat*, September 23, 1957, 1; Bates, *Long Shadow*, 91.

99. Bates, *Long Shadow*, 91.

100. Caillouet, "Daisy Lee Gatson Bates."

101. "Negroes Out until Ike Acts," *Arkansas Democrat*, September 23, 1957, 1.

102. "Obstruction of Justice in the State of Arkansas by the President of the United States of America: A Proclamation," September 23, 1957, box 6, folder "Integration—Little Rock, 1957," Dwight David Eisenhower Papers, Eisenhower Presidential Library, Abilene, Kans. (hereafter DDE).

103. Stockley, *Daisy Bates*, 145–46.

104. Bates interview, UA, 8.

105. Bates, *Long Shadow*, 96; Bates interview, UA, 8.

106. Bates, *Long Shadow*, 96.

107. Stockley, *Daisy Bates*, 146.

108. See Jacoway, *Turn Away Thy Son*, 176–78, for a discussion of the maneuvering behind the telegram.

109. Executive Order 10730: Providing Assistance for the Removal of an Obstruction of Justice within the State of Arkansas, September 24, 1957, box 6, folder "Integration—Little Rock (2)," DDE.

110. Bates interview, UA, 9; Daisy Bates FBI file, Grif Stockley Collection, ser. II, box 1, folder 5, Butler Center for Arkansas Studies, Little Rock.

111. Bates interview, UA, 11.

112. Bates typescript, Daisy Bates Papers, carton 3, WHS.

113. Bates interview, UA, 11.

114. Kearney, *Daisy*, 142.

115. Bates interview, UA, 1.

116. Ibid., 11. Kearney wrote of this moment: "While there comes a time in the midst of the '57 Crisis that she questions her role, and the sanity of it all, more often, she accepts with fortitude and conviction that this was an opportunity that fate or God, or both presented to her; and she dare[d] not pass it up" (Kearney, *Daisy*, 73).

117. Bates interview, UA, 12.

118. Bates, *Long Shadow*, 101–2. Gloria Ray was a straight-A student who wanted to become an atomic scientist; her father had attended Tuskegee Institute. See "Program for the Citizens National Scholarship Dinner," January 31, 1958, Daisy Bates Papers, carton 12, WHS.

119. In her memoir Bates attributed this comment to Leroy Christophe, one of the principals, but in characteristic fashion, in a later interview she claimed it for herself. Bates, *Long Shadow*, 103.

120. Bates interview, UA, 12.

121. Bates, *Long Shadow*, 103.

122. Robert W. Coakley, *Operation Arkansas*, Monograph no. 158M (Washington, D.C.: Office of the Chief of Military History, 1967), 80.

123. Parents to Eisenhower, September 30, 1957, Daisy Bates Papers, carton 12, WHS.

124. Bates interview with Jacoway, 26, SOHP. In a characteristic attempt to inflate her role, Bates claimed in her memoir that the children met at her house every afternoon (Bates, *Long Shadow*, 131); the nine students remembered it differently (Stockley, *Daisy Bates*, 163).

125. Bates interview with Jacoway, 20, SOHP.

126. Caillouet, "Daisy Lee Gatson Bates"; Kearney, *Daisy*, 146.

127. Kearney, *Daisy*, 94.

128. Clarence Laws statement, November 14, 1957, Daisy Bates Papers, carton 2, WHS.

129. Jacoway, *Turn Away Thy Son*, 220–21; Shawn A. Fisher, "The Battle of Little Rock," Ph.D. diss., University of Memphis, 2013, 294.

130. Bates interview with Jacoway, 31, SOHP.

131. Stockley, *Daisy Bates*, 152, 180. Daisy's white friend Fred Darragh, who had "flown the hump" in World War II, flew her in his own plane on many of these assignments; see Elizabeth Jacoway interview with Fred Darragh, ser. I, box 35, folder 6, EJC.

132. Most of the hate mail contained in the Daisy Bates Papers, WHS, came from Texas, Louisiana, California, and northern states; very little came from Arkansas. In her standard response to the positive mail, which was sent to many northern and foreign supporters, Bates wrote: "When this Little Rock school problem has been resolved and the city is permitted to return to its former peace and tranquility, I doubt that those of us who have been close to this problem will recall too much the words and deeds of the bigots and the misguided. Rather, I believe that we will remember most those fine persons like yourself, who spoke or wrote words of praise and encouragement. In our most trying hours these words have been the source of abiding strength and solace." See, for example, Daisy Bates to Grace Paton, February 14, 1958, Daisy Bates Papers, carton 2, WHS.

133. The national NAACP helped with the creation of this scholarship fund; Stockley, *Daisy Bates*, 166.

134. "Keeping an Eye on Daisy Bates," *Arkansas Democrat-Gazette*, October 15, 2000.

135. Caillouet, "Daisy Lee Gatson Bates."

136. John Pagan telephone interview with Daisy Bates, August 23, 1972, EJC.

137. The vice principal for girls at Central High School, Elizabeth Huckaby, wrote in her memoir: "The devil himself could not have been more abhorred by the segregationists than Daisy Bates" (Huckaby, *Crisis at Central High*, 200).

138. Bates interview with Jacoway, 19, SOHP.

139. Ibid., 13. Bates told Linda Caillouet she had entered Central High School with the nine students on September 25, but she did not (Caillouet, "Daisy Lee Gatson Bates").

140. Stockley, *Daisy Bates*, 224, 226. Bates recognized the problem, but told Janis Kearney, "I know some people didn't like it . . . that I got the attention while L.C. and others in the struggle worked just as hard, but got half the attention. But, that's just the way things work" (Kearney, *Daisy*, 156). In an interview with Grif Stockley, Terrence Roberts recalled, "I would have perhaps wanted her to have a more balanced perspective about that—to see herself more in a service role than the role of occupying the spotlight" (Stockley, *Daisy Bates*, 224). Stockley concluded that the heart of the issue was that the nine students felt that "their parents' contributions have not been properly recognized" (226).

141. "School Board Cites Inability to Enforce Compliance; Asks U.S. Court to Halt Integration," *Arkansas Democrat*, February 21, 1958, 1.

142. Jacoway, "Richard C. Butler and the Little Rock School Board."

143. Ernest Valachovic, "All Faubus Bills Sail Through; House Acts Rapidly to Outstrip Court," *Arkansas Gazette*, August 28, 1958, 1A.

144. "Faubus Closes CHS after Court Denies Delay of Integration," *Arkansas Gazette*, September 13, 1958, 1A. The Little Rock school board did allow football, however, and the Central High Tigers went on to place second in the state championship. Jacoway, *Turn Away Thy Son*, 270.

145. Bates description of activities, to Gloster B. Current, December 31, 1958, Daisy Bates Papers, carton 2, WHS.

146. Jacoway, *Turn Away Thy Son*, 289.

147. Ibid.

148. Stockley, *Daisy Bates*, 190.

149. For a full discussion of this period, see Jacoway, *Turn Away Thy Son*, chs. 14–16.

150. Ibid., 343–45.

151. Kearney, *Daisy*, xxii.

152. Ibid.

153. Kirk, "Daisy Bates"; Stockley, *Daisy Bates*, 181.

154. Stockley, *Daisy Bates*, 204–5.

155. Ibid., 89.

156. In 1961 Bates wrote to a supporter: "I had to give up the presidency of the Arkansas Chapter of the NAACP. Working with the National NAACP, raising funds for the children's education, and contributing what time and money I can for the CORE sit-ins, plus the book is just too much." Daisy Bates to Mrs. Howard Lewis Aller, December 20, 1961, Daisy Bates Papers, carton 2, WHS; Stockley, *Daisy Bates*, 73.

157. Daisy Bates Papers, carton 1, WHS.

158. Kearney, *Daisy*, 79.

159. Ibid., 83. Apparently the rumors were true; see Stockley, *Daisy Bates*, 241.

160. Stockley, *Daisy Bates*, 193; Kearney, *Daisy*, xxiii.

161. A news clipping from a Pine Bluff, Arkansas, newspaper claimed: "As late as June 17, 1962, Mrs. Daisy Bates is still the most hated personality by Arkansas segregationists. Upon completion of her manuscript at New York, she returned to Arkansas where she was greeted by a huge, fiery cross (the KKK's symbol of death)." *Pine Bluff Commercial*, n.d., Daisy Bates Papers, carton 2, SCSW.

162. Stockley, *Daisy Bates*, 242.

163. Ibid., 299; Bates interview with Jacoway, 38–39, SOHP.

164. Bates interview with Jacoway, 32, 41, SOHP.

165. Stockley, *Daisy Bates*, 257–58.

166. Bates interview with Jacoway, 42–44, SOHP; Caillouet, "Daisy Lee Gatson Bates."

167. "Mourners Pay Tribute to Daisy Bates: Funeral Today; 1,000 View Body at State Capitol," *Arkansas Democrat-Gazette*, November 9, 1999.

168. "Daisy Bates Drive Honors [Little Rock] Activist: Signs Label Legacy of Woman of 'Courage,'" *Arkansas Democrat-Gazette*, November 11, 2000; "Senate OKs Bill to Honor Daisy Bates: State Holiday Approved for Civil Rights Leader," *Arkansas Democrat-Gazette*, February 2, 2001; "Clinton to Attend Fund-Raiser to Fix Daisy Bates Home," *Arkansas Democrat-Gazette*, March 26, 2002, 6B.

169. "Daisy Bates: The Triumph of Grace," *Arkansas Democrat-Gazette*, November 5, 1999.

170. Kearney, *Daisy*, 170.

171. Ibid., 153.

Edith Mae Irby Jones
(1927-)

"Brilliant . . . Black Pilgrim, Proud Pioneer" and the Integration of the University of Arkansas School of Medicine

YULONDA EADIE SANO

In 1948, nine years prior to the desegregation of Central High School in Little Rock, Arkansas, by a group of students known as the Little Rock Nine, a more peaceful desegregation took place. On September 6, 1948, Edith Mae Irby became the first African American student to attend the University of Arkansas School of Medicine (now the University of Arkansas for Medical Sciences). A *Life* magazine photographer captured her standing alone in the hallway with book and binder in hand, while white students nearby pretended to socialize but surreptitiously watched her closely. Although Henry Clay Chenault, vice president of the medical school, had proclaimed that Edith would be just like any other medical student in her class, the existence of Jim Crow laws and customs ensured that hers was a unique experience.[1]

Jim Crow limited educational opportunities for African Americans in the South, and secondary schools, public colleges, and universities were all segregated by race. However, in early 1948, the University of Arkansas board of trustees broke with this southern "tradition" and decided to accept black students in its professional and graduate schools. In the spring semester, the School of Law enrolled its first black student, Silas Hunt, and in the fall semester the School of Medicine became the first all-white medical school in the South to admit a black student. Out of the 230 applicants—including 11 African Americans—who had applied for that fall term, the university accepted 90 white students and a lone black student, Edith Mae Irby, a resident of Hot Springs, Arkansas, and a graduate of Knoxville College in Tennessee. Enrolling in medical school was not the last time Edith would be a "first" as she has continued to break racialized and gendered barriers throughout her life.[2]

Edith's story is a compelling narrative of persistence, determination, and faith that belongs in the discourse of the long civil rights movement. She sought to become a physician as a part of the fulfillment of a childhood dream and refused to be deterred from her goal. Without fanfare or legal counsel, she applied to the University of Arkansas School of Medicine. She committed the radical act of asserting her citizenship and her right to equal treatment under the law at a time when African Americans were at best seen as second-class citizens. In addition, she used her fame within the African American community to be a part of the movement that urged black people not to accept the status quo and to demand equal facilities.

Edith Mae Irby was born on December 23, 1927, in Mayflower, Arkansas. She and her siblings, Juanita and Robert Jr., lived with their parents, Robert Sr., a tenant farmer, and Mattie (Buice), a domestic worker. Between 1930 and 1934, the family experienced several tragedies. In 1930, the patriarch of the family died. Edith witnessed the unsuccessful attempts to resuscitate her father, who died from injuries he received while horseback riding. In January 1931, after Robert Sr.'s death, the family was evicted from the farm where they lived and moved in with Mattie's father, who was known as Grandpa Buice, and his wife, whom they called Miss Callie. In 1932, Mattie Irby and her children moved to Conway, Arkansas. While in Conway, Edith was struck with rheumatic fever, which rendered her unable to walk for about eighteen months. Tragedy struck again when Edith's older sister, Juanita, who was then about twelve years old, died from typhoid fever during an outbreak in 1933. A physician had come to treat Juanita once at the Irby home, but due to the family's inability to pay, the doctor did not return for a follow-up visit. Edith maintained that Juanita could have survived if the family had been able to afford a doctor's care. She recalled, "My sister literally bled to death because there was no help, there was no hospital, and there were no doctors to give her any kind of medical attention." Soon after Juanita's death, Grandpa Buice died. These deaths during her childhood, especially her sister's, encouraged Edith to become a physician, "and I was going to see all children" regardless of their family's ability to pay. There was one bright spot during the family's stay in Conway; Mattie Irby gave birth to a baby boy named Louis.[3]

The Irby family left Conway and moved to Hot Springs. There, Edith and her siblings attended segregated schools, and she graduated from Langston High School in 1944. Although she was offered a scholarship to the state-supported college for African Americans, Arkansas Agricultural, Mechanical and Normal College (AM&N), she decided to attend Knoxville College, a small, historically black Presbyterian school in Knoxville, Tennessee. Her favorite high school teacher, whom she consistently referred to as Mrs. Mary Long Martin, taught English and Latin and had attended Knoxville College; Edith was convinced that an education at a private college would be more prestigious.[4]

During the summer before college, Edith worked as a typist at Aldens, a mail-order company in Chicago, Illinois, where she lived with relatives identified only as Aunt Willa B. and Uncle Chester, while saving money for college. By the time she bought new clothes and paid for her ticket to Knoxville from Chicago, however, she only had $60, not enough to cover the tuition of $300. But her confidence in herself and her abilities was unwavering. When she was about ten years old, she babysat for the family of Dr. Ellis, a white physician in Hot Springs whose full name is unknown. Dr. Ellis's mother, who became quite fond of Edith, encouraged her to complete her education and go on to college. Even if she did not have money, the woman stressed, "somebody will give you money." This prediction was fulfilled at Knoxville. After a registrar informed her that no one could make provisions for students without funds except the president of the college, Dr. William Lloyd Imes, Edith went to see him. By the end of their meeting, she had secured a job as an assistant to Imes's secretary in return for her tuition.[5]

Having majored in chemistry, biology, and physics, Edith graduated with honors from Knoxville College in 1948. Before leaving Tennessee, she took the Professional School Aptitude Test (the precursor to the Medical College Admission Test) to qualify for medical school. She returned to Chicago, where she worked at Aldens again. She also enrolled in clinical psychology classes at Northwestern University in Evanston, Illinois. Most African Americans who pursued a medical career in the late 1940s attended one of the two historically black medical colleges, Meharry Medical College in Nashville, Tennessee, or Howard University College of Medicine in Washington, D.C. Edith applied to twelve medical schools, including the University of Chicago, Northwestern, Howard, Meharry, and the University of Arkansas. At the time, she was unaware that Arkansas did not accept black students. In fact, one-third of all the medical schools in the country did not admit African American students.[6]

At the University of Arkansas, located in Fayetteville, racial exclusion was a matter of custom rather than law. It is a land-grant institution that was chartered in 1871 as Arkansas Industrial University, and the board of trustees decided that it would be open to all Arkansans without regard to race. Indeed, records indicate that two African American students enrolled when the university opened in 1872. In 1873, Branch Normal College (which became Arkansas Agricultural, Mechanical and Normal College in 1927 and the University of Arkansas at Pine Bluff in 1972) was chartered to educate black students. Although the University of Arkansas board of trustees did not formally rescind the decision to accept black students, by the end of Reconstruction black students were no longer attending that institution.[7]

Edith credited the vice president of Knoxville College with getting her into the University of Arkansas. He supported her desire to study medicine and provided her with a strong letter of recommendation. She learned about her acceptance into the medical school not by letter but by a phone call from *Time* magazine at her aunt and uncle's home. Based on the medical school's criteria for admission, she was ranked twenty-eighth among the incoming class in 1948. She had also been accepted by the University of Chicago and Northwestern. Many of the medical schools on her preferred list had tuition in excess of $10,000, but the tuition at the University of Arkansas was only $500. "Now, mind you," she emphasized, "I didn't have any money to go to medical school." Nor did her mother have the financial wherewithal to finance her education. Edith had no more money to attend the University of Arkansas than she had when she enrolled in Knoxville College. "In fact," she asserted, "I didn't have as much." Thus, her decision was "the most sensible and economical thing." In addition, the medical school, located in Little Rock, was only fifty miles from her mother's home in Hot Springs.[8]

Prior to the beginning of the academic year, Edith returned to Arkansas where Hot Springs residents—both black and white—contributed money to assist the widow's daughter who had been accepted to medical school. People collected money for the "Fund for Edith Irby" on Central Avenue in Hot Springs. There were church fundraisers for Edith, and some supporters even sent her coins in the mail. One local club owner drove her from Hot Springs to Little Rock for registration in style. She arrived on campus in a "big, long, white Cadillac" with "a bag full of dollar bills, half dollars, quarters, nickels and dimes," the money collected to pay her $500 tuition.[9]

The donations covered her tuition, but Edith was unprepared to pay the laboratory fee, which was an additional fifty dollars. Fortunately, a friend had told her about Daisy Bates, the co-owner of the black weekly newspaper in Little Rock, the *Arkansas State Press*, that was considered "the militant voice of black community protest." Later, Bates became a national figure as the president of the Arkansas State Conference of Branches of the National Association for the Advancement of Colored People and for her support of the Little Rock Nine during the 1957–1958 school year. When Edith went to Bates's office, she introduced herself and explained her financial situation. Bates gave her the money that she needed to complete registration. It was not until years later that Edith found out that the money Bates had given her was Bates's *last* fifty dollars. Thereafter, Bates continued to give her money for books, supplies, and personal items.[10]

Edith could be characterized as a bit naïve when she applied to the University of Arkansas. Having grown up in Arkansas attending segregated schools, she was certainly aware of Jim Crow laws and customs, but she never considered that African American students were not allowed to attend the university. Her goal was neither to desegregate nor to change laws; it was simply to do what was necessary to obtain an education. She explained, "I had spent my whole life getting ready to go to medical school," and she refused to allow segregation, money, or anything else to stop her. Of course, there was some trepidation about being the first black student at the School of Medicine, but Edith was determined. She saw medicine as her best opportunity to help other African Americans.[11]

Edith's enrollment took place in a context of increasing civil rights activity, which had begun in the late 1930s and accelerated in the early 1940s. Black students were asserting their rights to attend state public universities for graduate and professional education, and the NAACP had assisted them through its Legal Defense and Educational Fund, which became a separate entity in 1940. In 1938, the organization had successfully argued on behalf of Lloyd L. Gaines, an African American resident of Missouri who applied to the law school at the University of Missouri, only to be denied admission because the university did not accept black students. The University of Missouri had the only law school in the state. The university offered to pay the tuition for Gaines at an out-of-state institution, but he sought court action to force the university to admit him. Missouri's decision was upheld in the state court but overturned by the U.S. Supreme Court. In *Missouri ex rel. Gaines v. Canada* the Court ruled that Missouri had violated the equal protection clause of the Fourteenth Amendment. In the absence of a state-supported school of law for black people, Missouri was required to admit Gaines. Thus, states had to guarantee equal access to a legal education for both black and white citizens.[12]

Even after the success of the *Gaines* case, southern states continued to circumvent equal access to education for black people. In an effort to maintain segregated institutions, they provided black students with stipends to enroll in out-of-state universities for graduate classes not available at state-supported black colleges. In 1941, Arkansas had no such plan when Scipio A. Jones, an African American lawyer from Little Rock, approached the dean of the law school requesting that the university pay for tuition for his client, Prentice A. Hilburn, a student at Howard University. Nevertheless, the university ultimately provided $134.50 for Hilburn's tuition, thereby postponing a decision on desegregation.

Two years later, the state passed Arkansas Legislative Act 345, providing tuition money for black students who pursued graduate studies unavailable at Arkansas AM&N at out-of-state institutions. Black students were eligible to receive as much as $312 per academic year with a maximum distribution of $5,000, which, ironically, was subtracted from AM&N's funds.[13]

In another victory for desegregation, *Sipuel v. Board of Regents of the University of Oklahoma*—decided in January 1948—the Supreme Court ruled that the university had to admit Ada Lois Sipuel. In 1946, Sipuel, a graduate of Langston University, had applied to the University of Oklahoma College of Law. In an attempt to comply with the ruling in the *Gaines* case, the state hastily set up the Langston University School of Law, and argued that this makeshift professional school qualified as equal access to education. However, the Supreme Court disagreed, siding with Sipuel and the NAACP and requiring the University of Oklahoma to admit her.[14]

The success of the NAACP's court cases may have had an impact on the University of Arkansas's decision to desegregate its professional and graduate schools. When Silas Hunt applied to the University of Arkansas School of Law, Dean Robert Leflar wanted to avoid an equal protection lawsuit. In January 1948, Governor Benjamin Travis Laney proposed creating a regional graduate school for African Americans with help from surrounding states. He urged black leaders to support his plan and a gradual end to segregation. This plan, which would have maintained segregation for the time being, was not well received. Leflar argued that admitting black students but providing separate teaching facilities for them was the better option.[15]

In the spring of 1948, Silas Hunt became the first black student since Reconstruction to attend the University of Arkansas. He had begun his college career at Arkansas AM&N, but his education was interrupted by his military service during World War II. After his tour of duty, he returned to complete his degree and graduated in December 1947.[16] William Harold Flowers, an African American attorney from Pine Bluff who was president of the Arkansas State Conference of NAACP Branches in 1948, advised Hunt on his attempt to enter the University of Arkansas. Although Hunt was admitted to the university, he was not allowed to attend classes with white students. To maintain segregation, professors taught him in a basement classroom alone. Ironically, a number of white students began attending Hunt's separate classes to take advantage of the more favorable student-to-faculty ratio. He was also excluded from the law library and public bathrooms. Hunt obtained his library books through a white intermediary, and the dean permitted Hunt to use his private bathroom. Hunt never completed his law degree. Failing health caused him to withdraw from the university in July 1948, and he never resumed his coursework. Diagnosed with pulmonary tuberculosis, he died in April 1949 at the O'Reilly Veterans Hospital in Springfield, Missouri.[17]

While black students' entry into the law school at the University of Arkansas involved some legal wrangling with the administration, Edith Irby's entry into the medical school took place without any such negotiations. Her admission, she contended, "had nothing to do with civil rights. Absolutely, absolutely none." As civil rights advocates and physicians from around the country reacted to Edith's admission, however, it was clear that many regarded it as a watershed. For example, an August 1948 editorial in the Baltimore *Afro-American* asserted that Edith's admission was "another turning point in the educational history of the South" and declared that "the end of segregation in education, particularly upon the graduate level, is at hand." It may not have been Edith's intent to become a civil rights icon or to break racialized and gendered barriers, but her acceptance and entrance into the University of Arkansas cemented that legacy.[18]

The first black students on all-white campuses often experienced similar challenges: social isolation; exclusion from on-campus housing, libraries, university facilities, and activities; exclusion from or segregation within classrooms and cafeterias; and segregated restrooms. Like Silas Hunt, Jackie Shropshire, who entered law school at the University of Arkansas in the same semester that Edith started medical school, had classes in which he received individual instruction. However, he also shared classes with white students in which his desk was separated by a wooden railing. The railing was eventually removed, but separate areas for studying and dining persisted.[19] For the most part, the black law students described a grudging acceptance of their presence on campus, but George W. B. Haley, who joined Shropshire in law school in the fall of 1949, recalled openly hostile encounters as well. Haley confided to his brother, the writer Alex Haley, that he was told to "go back to Africa," was called racial epithets, and even had urine thrown at him. On one occasion, the law school's black "pioneers" found a hangman's noose in their shared study room.[20]

Most white students at the medical school appeared to be supportive of, or at least indifferent to, Edith's presence. In the late 1940s, many of the university's professional students were veterans of World War II who were eager to complete their educations and begin their careers. In contrast to Fayetteville, with its small black population, Little Rock's black population was much more significant. This may explain why there was more open aggression toward the African American students in Fayetteville. While Edith did not experience much racialized hostility from the students at the university, she noted that some male students resented the women for taking the positions that rightfully "belonged" to deserving male students. Nevertheless, Edith and her white female classmates, Mary E. Arthur and Mary E. Thompson, managed to form close relationships with other students as they studied together and supported one another through medical school.[21]

But Edith's time at the university was not free of Jim Crow restrictions. As with the law school in Fayetteville, bathroom facilities presented a "problem" for the administration. Prior to her enrollment, all of the students and faculty were white; therefore there was no need for separately labeled "white" and "colored" restrooms. Rather than allow her to use the women's restrooms on campus, the university provided a separate facility, with an unmarked door, for Edith's use.[22]

While there were no segregated spaces for Edith in the classroom, she was not permitted to eat in the cafeteria with her fellow students, although she was not required to sit with "the help." Instead, the university set aside a separate study room in the library, where she ate her meals. She remembered that the African American staff made this restriction into a pleasurable experience. They brought in fresh flowers daily and left notes saying "'We love you. We love you.' Well, you know, who couldn't function under that?" Soon, white students began to join Edith in her private room for dining and studying. Although the university prevented Edith from eating in the cafeteria to preserve segregation, white students were allowed to sit in Edith's segregated space. Jim Crow laws and customs generally dictated what blacks could not do, but rarely, if ever, commented on what whites could not do.[23]

By applying to and being accepted by the University of Arkansas School of Medicine, Edith Irby became an icon whose story appeared in *Ebony* and *Life* magazines as well as in newspapers throughout the country. She used her status to encourage others to assert their constitutional rights as citizens. She wanted people to know that "no one should be forced to live deprived of some of the basic needs of life." After studying, she often had speaking engagements at night. She traveled to wherever there was an interested audience—"to the little churches and to the schools for rallies"—and she informed her audiences that they did not have to accept "separate but equal." They should demand better because separate was *never* equal. Community activists feared that if Edith's activities were discovered, she might be expelled from medical school, so they devised an elaborate subterfuge that involved shuttling her to speaking engagements in the back of a hearse from a local black-owned funeral home. A different car was used to drive her to and from the funeral home.[24]

It was during one of Edith's speaking engagements that fellow Arkansas native M. Joycelyn Elders (née Jones), who would become the fifteenth surgeon general of the United States in 1993, saw Edith Irby for the first time. Elders was a student at Philander Smith College, a small, historically black Methodist school in Little Rock, when Edith came to speak on campus. Elders remembered, "Edith Irby cut a high profile" among African Americans in Arkansas. Not only was she "Hot Springs' pride and joy," but the entire black community was proud of her, which was evident from her repeated mentions in black newspapers.[25] Hearing Edith Irby speak influenced Elders's career choice. While in high school, Elders had "hoped" she would be able to get a job at "Mr. Dillard's [department store]." Then, when she began college, she "had the vague idea that it would be nice to work in a lab," but a career in medicine was not something that she envisioned for herself. After all, she had never seen a doctor until she went to college, and "you can't be what you can't see." But after hearing Irby, she "knew with 100 percent certainty that I was going to medical school and become a doctor." After graduating from college and serving in the military, where she was trained as a physical therapist, Elders used her GI Bill funds to enroll in the University of Arkansas medical school in 1956.[26]

Edith read a poem that night at Philander Smith College, "The Ways" by John Oxenham. As Elders recalled it: "Some of us take the high road / Others take the low / And in between on misty paths / The rest walk to and fro." Elders stated, "I was captivated. I thought I had never seen anyone as beautiful or heard anything as moving. I didn't know about anybody else in that hall, but as for me, I knew what I was going to do. I was going to take the high road. All I could think of was that I wanted to be exactly like her and do exactly what she was doing."[27]

After her first year of medical school, Edith earned a scholarship to pay her tuition and expenses. By the time she graduated in June 1952, she had experienced more significant changes in her personal life. Her beloved mother, Mattie Irby, died in March 1950, during Edith's second year of school. A month later Edith married James B. Jones, Ph.D., a professor at Arkansas AM&N. The couple had met during the summer of 1949 when Edith worked on the campus of AM&N. Newspapers from around the country carried the news of her graduation and upcoming internship at the university hospital in Little Rock, another first for an African American. By the time her internship began, some of the prior Jim Crow restrictions were relaxed. She was able to use the dining room along with the white students, professors, and staff. More important, during her clinical training, she treated both black and white patients.[28]

After her internship, Edith Irby Jones remained in Arkansas for six years, working at a "multiple-specialty" clinic in Hot Springs from 1953 to 1959. During this time, she and her husband had two children. James commuted from Hot Springs to Pine Bluff, where he was the director of personnel and guidance at Arkansas AM&N, until he was offered a position as the associate dean of students at Texas Southern University. The family moved to Houston, where Edith did a residency in internal medicine at Baylor College of Medicine from 1959 to 1962. She was Baylor's first African American female resident and only the second African American overall, and there were still Jim Crow barriers to overcome. She completed the last three months of her residency at Freedmen's Hospital in Washington, D.C., because the hospital affiliated with Baylor prevented her from having access to all patients—white and black.[29]

Edith Irby Jones began her private practice in internal medicine in September 1962, opening her office at 2601 Prospect Street in Houston's Third Ward, where she remained until retirement. By 1963, she was chief of cardiology at St. Elizabeth's Hospital and associate chief of medicine at Riverside General Hospital, originally a fifty-bed facility built in 1927 to serve the black population and known then as Houston Negro Hospital. She was also a clinical assistant professor at the Baylor College of Medicine and the University of Texas School of Medicine, all while maintaining a thriving private practice.[30]

Continuing to break barriers, in July 1985 she became the president of the National Medical Association (NMA), the largest professional organization representing African American physicians since 1895. Jones had been a member of the NMA since 1953 and had held high-profile leadership positions in the organization, but she was the first female president in the association's history. During her tenure, she focused on increasing access to health care for African Americans and other minorities, continuing education for health care professionals, and growing the NMA membership.[31] Although President Ronald Reagan's secretary of health and human services, Margaret Heckler, had announced that the nation's health as a whole had improved, and people were living longer, those statistics did not hold true for African Americans or for the poor. Jones introduced an initiative to improve health and racial disparities in morbidity and mortality—focusing on proper nutrition, adequate housing, and curbing detrimental activities like smoking and drug abuse. She argued that many of the diseases that impacted black people's health were exacerbated by poverty, neglect, racism, and stress.[32]

Jones was taking part in a historically (and contemporary) contentious debate by asking: "What is an individual's right in this country to health care?" She asserted that society should "assume responsibility for the health care for the indigent." She was critical of the U.S. health insurance system because the focus was on providing "service at the least cost" and making a profit. She contended that the NMA must be "the conscience for all providers of health care," as well as advocates for African American communities. Jones's NMA presidential farewell address echoed feelings that she had possessed since her sister Juanita died: "All must be free to dream and to have equal opportunities to have the resources of the world shared by all, especially the opportunity to have good health through adequate access to quality health care."[33]

Jones has been honored locally, nationally, and internationally for her work as a pioneer, physician, health care advocate, and philanthropist. The numerous accolades that she has received throughout her career illustrate her importance in the medical community and to both her home state of Arkansas and her adopted home of Texas. The University of Arkansas for Medical Sciences now displays her portrait in the administration building, and the student chapter of the NMA is named for her. She was recognized by President Richard Nixon for her exemplary medical service. She was honored with Edith Irby Jones Day by the state of Arkansas in 1979 and the city of Houston in 1986. She is one of the founders of the Association of Black Cardiologists and was the American Society of Medicine's Internist of the Year in 1988. In 2001, *Black Enterprise* named her as one of the leading black physicians in America. Edith Irby Jones is also respected for her philanthropy. She was a charter member of Physicians for Human Rights. Because she believes that good fortune must be shared, she has funded scholarships for students. In addition to providing free medical services in her community, she has also set up health care clinics in both Haiti and Uganda. Jones was elected to the Arkansas Black Hall of Fame in 1998. More recently, she was inducted into the College of Medicine Hall of Fame in 2004 and the Arkansas Women's Hall of Fame in 2015. Along with nine other medical and health care professionals, she was honored with a marker on the Arkansas Civil Rights Heritage Trail for her efforts to bring about racial equality in Arkansas.[34]

Jones worked well into her eighties, but has now retired. She rarely reveals any negative feelings about her experiences at the University of Arkansas or discusses the impact of racism on her life, but in one of her NMA presidential columns she wrote, "I have observed discrimination in all its forms—blatant and subtle." She handled racial affronts and the pressures of medical school with "quiet dignity." Her way of coping was not to "think about the difficulty." Edith Mae Irby Jones succeeded in spite of the obstacles of racial segregation and exclusion; her strength and persistence are inspirational. As James C. Kilgore, a friend from Hot Springs, wrote in a poem dedicated to her, she proved that no one would "place ceilings on [her] dreams."[35]

NOTES

1. Linda E. Brew, *The Story of Edith Irby Jones, M.D.* (N.p.: NRT Publication Company), 15 (this chapter's subtitle derives from page 49); "Edith Irby Goes to School," *Life*, January 31, 1949, 33;

W. David Baird, *Medical Education in Arkansas, 1879-1978* (Memphis, Tenn.: Memphis State University Press, 1979), 211; Edith Irby Jones, interview by Scott Lunsford, April 3, 2006, transcript, 141, Pryor Center for Arkansas Oral and Visual History, Special Collections, University of Arkansas Libraries, Fayetteville, http://pryorcenter.uark.edu/interview.php?thisProject =Arkansas%20Memories&thisProfileURL=JONES-Edith-Irby&displayName=Edith%20Jones& thisInterviewee=228 (accessed October 25, 2017) (hereafter Jones, Pryor Center interview).

2. Judith Kilpatrick, "Desegregating the University of Arkansas School of Law: L. Clifford Davis and the Six Pioneers," *Arkansas Historical Quarterly* 68 (Summer 2009): 126-27; Baird, *Medical Education in Arkansas*, 211; Harrison Hale, *University of Arkansas, 1871-1948* (Fayetteville: University of Arkansas Alumni Association, 1948), 169.

3. Brew, *Story of Edith Irby Jones*, 1-6; Jones, Pryor Center interview, 6-18; Edith Irby Jones, interview by Kathleen Brosnan and Ramona Hopkins, September 18, 2007, transcript, University of Houston Center for Public History, Houston, Tex., http://classweb.uh.edu/cph/tobearfruit /resources_oraltranscripts_jones_sept07.html (accessed October 25, 2017) (hereafter Jones, interview by Brosnan and Hopkins); Edith Irby Jones, interview by David Goldstein, December 18, 2007, transcript, Houston Public Library Digital Archives, Houston Oral History Project, http://digital .houstonlibrary.org/oral-history/edith-irby-jones.php (accessed May 31, 2012) (hereafter Jones, interview by Goldstein). Edith's younger brother, Louis, was born in 1933.

4. Jones, Pryor Center interview, 29, 70-72, 95. Brew, in her privately published biography of Edith Irby Jones, stated that Mrs. Martin was able to get a scholarship for Edith. However, Edith's interview with the Pryor Center provides the account presented in this chapter. See Brew, *Story of Edith Irby Jones*, 8.

5. Jones, Pryor Center interview, 51-54, 57-58, 72, 78, 94; Brew, *Story of Edith Irby Jones*, 8, 11; P. J. Pierce, *"Let Me Tell You What I've Learned": Texas Wisewomen Speak* (Austin: University of Texas Press, 2002), 140.

6. Jones, Pryor Center interview, 81, 98.

7. Gordon D. Morgan and Izola Preston, *The Edge of Campus: A Journal of the Black Experience at the University of Arkansas* (Fayetteville: University of Arkansas Press, 1990), 3, 9; Robert A. Leflar, *The First 100 Years: Centennial History of the University of Arkansas* (Fayetteville: University of Arkansas Foundation, 1972), 273, 279; Pauli Murray, *States' Laws on Race and Color* (Athens: University of Georgia Press, 1997), 41-42.

8. Jones, Pryor Center interview, 81, 99-100, 104-5; Brew, *Story of Edith Irby Jones*, 11; "Edith Irby Revisited," *Ebony*, July 1963, 58; Jones, interview by Brosnan and Hopkins; Charles Whitaker, "Breakthroughs Are Her Business," *Ebony*, June 1986, 94.

9. Jones, Pryor Center interview, 18, 108-9; Jones, interview by Goldstein; Jones, interview by Brosnan and Hopkins.

10. John A. Kirk, "The Little Rock Crisis and Postwar Black Activism in Arkansas," *Arkansas Historical Quarterly* 54 (Autumn 1997): 282, 285; Daisy Bates, *The Long Shadow of Little Rock: A Memoir* (New York: David McKay, 1962), 3-4, 47; Jones, Pryor Center interview, 109-10; Jones, interview by Goldstein.

11. Whitaker, "Breakthroughs Are Her Business," 94; "First Negro Ready for Graduation," *Spokesman-Review* (Spokane, Wash.), June 15, 1952, 2; "Changing the Face of Medicine: Dr. Edith Irby Jones," National Library of Medicine, http://www.nlm.nih.gov/changingthefaceofmedicine /physicians/biography_175.html (accessed May 9, 2014); Pierce, *Let Me Tell You*, 143; Jones, Pryor Center interview, 106.

12. Missouri ex rel. Gaines v. Canada, 305 U.S. 337 (1938).

13. Guerdon D. Nichols, "Breaking the Color Barrier at the University of Arkansas," *Arkansas Historical Quarterly* 27 (Spring 1968): 5–6; Karen Kruse Thomas, "Dr. Jim Crow: The University of North Carolina, the Regional Medical School for Negroes and the Desegregation of Southern Medical Education, 1945–1960," *Journal of African American History* 88 (Summer 2003): 229; Morgan and Preston, *Edge of Campus*, 11; Leflar, *First 100 Years*, 278.

14. Sipuel v. Board of Regents, 332 U.S. 631 (1948); Robert Bruce Slater, "The First Black Graduates of the Nation's 50 Flagship State Universities," *Journal of Blacks in Higher Education* 13 (Autumn 1996): 83.

15. Kilpatrick, "Desegregating," 127, 129.

16. Nichols, "Breaking the Color Barrier," 16; Kilpatrick, "Desegregating," 132.

17. Kirk, "Little Rock Crisis," 278, 283, 285; Kirk, "'He Founded a Movement': W. H. Flowers, the Committee on Negro Organizations and the Origins of Black Activism in Arkansas, 1940–1957," in *The Making of Martin Luther King and the Civil Rights Movement*, ed. Brian Ward and Tony Badger (New York: New York University Press), 38; John A. Kirk, "They Say . . . New York Is Not Worth a D— to Them: The NAACP in Arkansas, 1918–1971," in *Long Is the Way and Hard: One Hundred Years of the National Association for the Advancement of Colored People*, ed. Kevern Verney, Lee Sartain, and Adam Fairclough (Fayetteville: University of Arkansas Press), 225; Kilpatrick, "Desegregating," 132–34; Nichols, "Breaking the Color Barrier," 17.

18. Editorial, "Arkansas Falls in Line," *Afro-American* (Baltimore, Md.), August 31, 1948, 4; Baird, *Medical Education in Arkansas*, 211.

19. Nichols, "Breaking the Color Barrier," 18, 20; Kilpatrick, "Desegregating," 134–35, 152; Kirk, "Little Rock Crisis," 283; Leflar, *First 100 Years*, 284.

20. Alex Haley, "The Man Who Wouldn't Quit," *Reader's Digest* (March 1963): 54–59, http://www.rd.com/true-stories/inspiring/george-haley-the-man-who-wouldnt-quit; Charles F. Robinson II and Lonnie R. Williams, *Remembrances in Black: Personal Perspectives of the African American Experience at the University of Arkansas, 1940s–2000s* (Fayetteville: University of Arkansas Press), 4; Kilpatrick, "Desegregating," 134, 142.

21. Jones, Pryor Center interview, 139; Jones, interview by Brosnan and Hopkins; Jones, interview by Goldstein; Pierce, *Let Me Tell You*, 142; W. David Baird, *Medical Education in Arkansas, 1879–1978* (Memphis, Tenn.: Memphis State University Press, 1979), 378; Brew, *Story of Edith Irby Jones*, 16.

22. Jones, Pryor Center interview, 116.

23. Ibid., 114–15; Pierce, *Let Me Tell You*, 141.

24. Jones, Pryor Center interview, 127–28, 132; Jones, interview by Goldstein.

25. Joycelyn Elders and David Chanoff, *Joycelyn Elders, M.D.: From Sharecropper's Daughter to the Surgeon General of the United States of America* (New York: William Morrow, 1996), 73; Jones, Pryor Center interview, 35. M. Joycelyn Jones married Oliver Elders during her last semester at the University of Arkansas. Despite having the same last name, she and Edith Irby Jones are not related.

26. Joycelyn Elders, interview by Scott Lunsford, February 14, 2008, transcript, 59, 66–67, 77, Pryor Center for Arkansas Oral and Visual History, Special Collections, University of Arkansas Libraries, Fayetteville, http://pryorcenter.uark.edu/projects/Arkansas%20Memories/ELDERS-Joycelyn/transcripts/TRANS-ELDERS-Joycelyn-Memories-20080214-FINAL.pdf (accessed October 25, 2017); Elders and Chanoff, *Joycelyn Elders, M.D.*, 77; Sara Lomax Reese, "Wisdom of the Elders," *Health Quest* 6 (October 31, 1994): 29; Steve Barnes, "Dr. Elders: Dr. Elders," *New York Times*, October 15, 1989, 75. Elders asserted that the separate dining arrangement for black students still existed when she entered medical school at the University of Arkansas in 1956.

27. Elders and Chanoff, *Joycelyn Elders, M.D.*, 75. These are not the exact words to the poem; it is the way Joycelyn Elders remembered them. Elders graduated from the University of Arkansas School of Medicine in 1960 and became the first black chief resident at the university hospital.

28. Community of Faith, "Dr. Edith Irby Jones," http://www.vimeo.com/39210733 (accessed October 19, 2016); "First Arkansas Medical Graduate to Enter University Hospital," *Journal of the National Medical Association* 44 (July 1952): 316; Jones, Pryor Center interview, 174; "First Negro Ready for Graduation," 2; Brew, *Story of Edith Irby Jones*, 19–20.

29. "First Negro Ready for Graduation," 2; "Edith Irby Revisited," 52; Jones, Pryor Center interview, 154; "Dr. Edith Irby Jones," Arkansas Civil Rights Heritage Trail, http://www.arkansascivilrightsheritage.org/dr-edith-irby-jones (accessed September 14, 2016). The couple had another child after moving to Houston.

30. Jones, interview by Goldstein; Brew, *Story of Edith Irby Jones*, 26, 62; Jones, Pryor Center interview, 157, 180; "Edith Irby Revisited," 52, 54; "Riverside General Hospital History," http://www.riversidegeneralhospital.org/getpage.php?name=houston&sub=About%20Us (accessed July 5, 2014); Eugene B. Perry, "Riverside General Hospital: Formerly, Houston Negro Hospital, Houston, Texas," *Journal of the National Medical Association* (May 1965): 258; "Jones, Edith Irby," in *Marquis Who's Who in the World* (New Providence, N.J.: Marquis Who's Who, 2016).

31. Whitaker, "Breakthroughs Are Her Business," 91, 92; Brew, *Story of Edith Irby Jones*, 41; Edith Irby Jones, "President's Column: Closing the Health Status Gap for Blacks and Other Minorities," *Journal of the National Medical Association* 78 (1986): 485; Jones, interview by Brosnan and Hopkins; Edith Irby Jones, "Farewell Address: Overcoming Challenges to Serve," *Journal of the National Medical Association* 78 (1986): 808.

32. Edith Irby Jones, "President's Column: Preventing Disease and Promoting Health in the Minority Community," *Journal of the National Medical Association* 78 (1986): 19–20; Jones, "Closing the Health Status Gap," 488; Jones, "President's Column: Society's Responsibility for Health Care of the Indigent," *Journal of the National Medical Association* 78 (1986): 95–96.

33. Jones, "Society's Responsibility," 96; Jones, "The Direct Relationship of Health Status to Health Care," *Journal of the National Medical Association* 78 (1986): 271; Jones, "President's Column: Provider/Advocate for the Consumers of Health Care for the Minority Community," *Journal of the National Medical Association* 78 (1986): 175; Jones, "President's Column: Effects of Competition on Access to Care: Will New Trends in Competition Limit Access to Health Care for Blacks," *Journal of the National Medical Association* 77 (1985): 968; Brew, *Story of Edith Irby Jones*, 41; Jones, "Closing the Health Status Gap," 485; Jones, interview by Brosnan and Hopkins; Jones, "Farewell Address," 808.

34. Whitaker, "Breakthroughs Are Her Business," 96; University of Arkansas for Medical Sciences Center for Diversity Affairs, http://cda.uams.edu (accessed October 27, 2017); Mark Richard Mosa, "Doctor Double," *Black Enterprise* 31 (May 2001): 89; "Changing the Face of Medicine: Dr. Edith Irby Jones"; "Jones, Edith Irby," in *Marquis Who's Who in the World*.

35. Jones, "Direct Relationship of Health Status," 271; Whitaker, "Breakthroughs Are Her Business," 94, 96; Brew, *Story of Edith Irby Jones*, 25, 49.

Mary L. Ray
(1880?–1934)

Arkansas's Negro Extension Worker

DEBRA A. REID

Mary L. Ray joined the staff of the Arkansas Agricultural Extension Service on March 16, 1916, as the first Negro home demonstration agent.[1] That position required her to meet with girls and women in rural communities in central and eastern Arkansas. Two years later, on July 1, 1918, she received a promotion to serve as the local district's home demonstration agent for Negro extension work. This position gave her administrative responsibility for a rapidly growing workforce that had been hired with emergency funding to mobilize the homefront during the World War I. Mary Ray covered a lot of territory as one of few female staff members serving black farm families in Arkansas. Her work across the state kept her on the road and aware of the conditions in which rural black families lived. Her job involved personnel management and public relations. She managed as many as twenty-eight women in short-term appointments during 1918. During the 1920s Ray kept busy managing around ten home demonstration agents assigned to work with black farm families. By 1928, Ray had "proved herself very competent" in managing the staff, coordinating state-level training, and negotiating the politics of home demonstration work in the segregated South. Ray worked with the Arkansas extension for eighteen years, with some breaks in her service due to medical leave. In 1934, the Arkansas Agricultural Extension Service reported that she had "retired because of illness and later died [on July 25, 1934] after having served long and capably."[2] She is buried in Oakland-Fraternal Cemetery, a historically African American cemetery in Little Rock. The inscription on her tombstone reads:

RAY
MARY LEE
Died July 25, 1934
A Lovely Home Maker
A 4-H Club Leader
A Friend to Humanity[3]

Women of Ray's professional status often self-consciously documented their lives. Mary L. Ray did not. Her husband, Harvey Cincinnatus Ray, did not mention her in his biographical entry in *Who's Who of the Colored Race*, probably because they married on December 23, 1915, after the editors compiled the listing. Mary's death certificate confirms that even her husband did not know her real age or the identity of her parents.[4] Yet Mary Lee McCrary Ray had a successful career in Arkansas and wielded influence. She functioned in a world that brought rural and urban people together, that emphasized education and self-governance, that furthered local economic development, and that targeted property-owning businesspeople (black farm-owning families). She worked with educated peers, and together they negotiated challenges based in racism, sexism, and anti-intellectualism. Her job was not easy, but her life's work was not unique; her accomplishments are comparable to those of her peers in education and rural reform. The value of Mary Ray's history rests in the ways she, as a professional African American woman in a racist and sexist world, managed to accomplish anything at all.

Ray kept her personal life private, despite her career as a civil servant, but other factors beyond her control further reduced her visibility in the historical record. Ray's ill health sometimes prevented her from participating in extension work at the best of times, but neither could she function fully at the worst of times, for example, during the 1927 Mississippi River flood in Arkansas, when her husband's duties as the district Negro county agent gave him state and national visibility. Her death in July 1934 of course removed her from influence during the rapid expansion of agricultural extension work in southern states prompted by New Deal relief, recovery, and reform policies. The twentieth anniversary of the Federal Extension Service occurred in 1935, and her husband wrote a history of extension work in Arkansas, but Mary had died before then, and H. C. Ray remarried seven months later. Her absence from the anniversary compilations ensured her absence from most studies of extension history in Arkansas. Scholars have explored only selected portions of the history of Negro agricultural extension work in Arkansas in any comprehensive way. Some mention Mary Ray and include excerpts from her annual reports, but they disclose nothing about her involvement in the vibrant middle-class black communities in Little Rock and throughout rural Arkansas. This chapter about Mary Lee McCrary Ray focuses on her influence through her work with Negro home demonstration in Arkansas between 1916 and 1934.[5]

Mary Ray's professional maturation followed paths that other southern rural progressive reformers had trod. From all indications, Mary lived a full life before she met and married Harvey C. Ray and moved to Arkansas. Tuskegee Institute archivists confirmed that she earned certificates in cooking and dressmaking from Tuskegee in 1897 and then taught in private schools until she moved to the frontier to teach at the Colored Agricultural and Normal University in Langston City, Oklahoma.[6] She used her full name, Mary Lee McCrary, while in Oklahoma. She married Harvey C. Ray, a former colleague in Langston City, in late 1915, and they moved from Langston to Little Rock, Arkansas. Her education and previous experience qualified her for the duties she undertook in Arkansas, and she spent the remainder of her life doing Negro extension work for the Arkansas Agricultural Extension Service. This was a federal program implemented in 1914 through a partnership between the U.S. Department of Agriculture's Federal Extension Service and land-grant universities in each state. The programs for women and men had progressive goals aimed at improving agriculture and rural life.

Mary Ray transferred her experiences with formal classroom instruction and community uplift to reach rural children and adults in Arkansas. She emphasized knowledge and skills that progressive reformers believed would make rural families into better farmers. This included financial management and techniques to improve health and nutrition and to stabilize farm economies. She involved women and children in group activities that modeled civic engagement. The club work that resulted required setting agendas, holding regular meetings, and maintaining a visible role in community development. Ultimately, Ray arranged for local support in the form of financial appropriations from county quorum courts. These funds matched state and national moneys that paid extension service employees, including home demonstration agents, and that supported new initiatives, such as movable schools.[7]

Mary Ray undertook these initiatives in Arkansas with confidence attained during her formal training at Tuskegee. Coursework there prepared her to teach in the new common schools and industrial institutes opening across the South. Critics recognized the racist thinking that legitimized this practical education for freed people, and they labeled it "education for a new slavery." Regardless, Ray found that her Tuskegee training could spawn economic development. She took risks as she spent thirty-five years teaching and working with rural families in Alabama, South Carolina, Oklahoma, and Arkansas, furthering that philosophy, and she faced the consequences of legalized segregation despite the relative economic comfort that she enjoyed. She had to travel in segregated conveyances and use "colored only" entrances, water fountains, toilets, and hotels. She worked with young people prohibited from standing on equal ground by white voters. She did not have the right to equal status with her white peers. But she secured positions that put her at the forefront of a growing black professional class dedicated to rural reform during the late nineteenth and early twentieth centuries.[8]

The "separate but equal" world in which Mary L. McCrary Ray lived during her adult life coalesced during her time at Tuskegee when the Supreme Court of the United States issued its decision in the *Plessy v. Ferguson* case in 1896. She entered the workforce with her Tuskegee credentials at the same time that the national government acquiesced to southern states' authority over schools that separated black from white students. She secured her first permanent position in higher education at the new Colored Agricultural and Normal University, the 1890 land-grant institution created to teach black students agricultural and industrial subjects, in the black separatist community of Langston City, Oklahoma Territory. She became "the first instructor of girls in 'domestic economy'" around 1900.[9] The 1902 curriculum focused on practical subjects taught in a sequence aligned with the university's goal of training students to have productive careers. Mary was one of two female faculty members. She established the domestic economy curriculum for girls, including courses in cooking, sewing, and other skills required to "prepare girls to be housewives or to be self-supporting in 'domestic' careers such as dressmaking." The other woman faculty member, Zelia N. Page, the daughter of Inman E. Page, president of the university, and Zelia R. Ball Page, provided instruction in music.[10]

President Page expected the faculty of the Colored Agricultural and Normal University (known as Langston) to be engaged in the community at many levels and not just in intellectual or cultural pursuits. Faculty members helped develop the economic infrastructure in the growing community. They paid rent. Some purchased homes. They bought what they needed at local businesses, and they also opened businesses. By 1906 Mary McCrary operated "a prosperous dressmaking establishment," which likely employed young women who had excelled in her dressmaking courses and who hoped to stay in or near their homes while furthering their careers. A 1912 study of black artisans listed fifty dressmakers and only two milliners in Oklahoma.[11]

Mary McCrary met her future husband, H. C. Ray, when he joined the staff at Langston. He was born on February 2, 1889, in Bunceton, Missouri, and graduated from Lincoln University in Jefferson City, Missouri, in 1911. His alma mater may have caught the attention of Langston's president because Page had served as president of Lincoln for a decade in the late nineteenth century. Whatever brought Ray to Langston, he worked there for two and a half years as farm superintendent and then as an assistant in the Department of Agriculture. During that time Ray studied at Tuskegee Institute, completing academic and industrial arts coursework in 1914. Mary McCrary and H. C. Ray probably interacted during that time since there were few faculty employed at Langston during these formative years.[12]

Farmers' cooperative demonstration work began in Arkansas in 1905, ten years before H. C. Ray gained his appointment. It followed the model established by Dr. Seaman Knapp in Texas in 1903.[13] Knapp, a special agent for the U.S. Department of Agriculture's farmers' cooperative demonstrative work, extended the program to Arkansas with the appointment of J. A. Evans as state agent and A. V. Swatty as district agent. The number of Department of Agriculture employees expanded to four district agents and seven county agents by 1907. In 1909, 4-H Club work began; in 1911, canning clubs began, which expanded into home demonstration work. This growth occurred because of private philanthropy and local appropriations. The process was replicated across the former Confederate states with white administrators and agents working out of 1862 land-grant universities and black administrators and agents working out of 1890 land-grant institutions.[14]

Early cooperative demonstration work focused on the agricultural tasks that men performed, but women sought appropriations as well. Black women educators, including Mary McCrary, watched these developments, perhaps with a sense of anticipation because expansion of the program could mean jobs for women studying domestic science. The General Education Board (GEB), the Slater Fund, and Sears, Roebuck and Company provided millions of dollars to support rural reform across the South. In Arkansas, Sears, Roebuck challenged each county to match a $1,000 donation. If the county raised that amount by private subscription, then Sears, Roebuck would contribute $1,000 for the salary of an agent. White men received appointments as a result, but the influence did not stop there. By 1910, Arkansas legislators had authorized counties to match GEB funds too, thereby encouraging rural reform supported by two private philanthropic organizations without tapping into state operating funds. Regardless of the type of funding, GEB officials believed that "the work [across the South] is far from adequate to the need and the demand. Five hundred Southern counties [out of 1,163 counties] had not been reached at all at the end of 1912; needless to say that perhaps no single county has been exhaustively worked and many have been barely touched."[15]

The GEB funds helped cooperative demonstration work reach fifteen thousand residents in 77 percent of all Arkansas counties during 1912, and the funds did not benefit white Arkansans alone. Agents hired with GEB funds were supposed to include black farmers as demonstrators. Ultimately, black farmers were supposed to be hired to be agents. This occurred in nine southern states, including Arkansas, as of 1912. Individuals who worked with Arkansas's black farmers before the appointments of the Rays have not been documented in any comprehensive way. Yet it appears that at least one black farm agent worked in the state before the Rays arrived. A comparative history of Hot Spring and Lee counties in Arkansas, published in 1937, indicated that officials in Lee County employed a Negro farm agent from 1912 through 1929 with only a one-year gap. The cost for this appointment in 1912 was $75, equivalent to the cost of hiring a white female girls' club demonstrator. This means that three years before H. C. Ray received his appointment as the first Negro farm agent in Pulaski County, with direction to serve African American landowners, Lee County may have met the Sears, Roebuck or GEB funding challenges and hired a black man to do demonstration work with black farmers. Rev. R. E. Bryant filled that position at least from 1917 to 1923.[16]

Mary McCrary would have been familiar with GEB work based on her observations while in Oklahoma. During 1912, the GEB claimed that funds helped cooperative demonstration work reach more than fifteen thousand residents in 55 percent of Oklahoma counties. Annie Peters Hunter became the first black woman appointed to demonstrate canning, starting on January 23, 1912. She did not work in Langston, but in another all-black town, Boley in nearby Okfuskee County, Indian Territory. She worked six weeks during canning season and earned $40 while the white demonstrators earned $75 for equivalent work.[17] Similar appointments occurred in 1912 across the South, including Arkansas. The GEB claimed sole financial responsibility for girls' club work, but implementation depended on a partnership with local funding sources and extension service supervision. Girls' club work focused on canning and poultry. In 1912, the GEB granted $1,500 to the Arkansas Department of Education to start tomato canning clubs.[18] Initially the state hired white women to work with white girls' clubs. An overview of work in Pulaski County indicated the scope: "In Pulaski County four hundred girls aged ten through eighteen living near Little Rock were organized into tomato clubs. Each member grew one-tenth acre of tomatoes and canned them. They also received instructions in making uniform caps, aprons, and tea towels."[19] Black women and their families had to wait two years for these services. In 1914 nine African American women received a total of $2,501, probably for short-term employment doing girls' club work. This was the only time before 1916, when Mary Ray was hired, that black women did demonstration work. One of these women may have been Vivian Young in Lee County, but the women's names and the counties in which they worked await further research.[20]

The Smith-Lever Act of 1914 ended GEB funding for demonstration work. This reduced services to black farm families significantly. Arkansas lost eleven African American workers. But the GEB's support of southern education did not end. Instead, it shifted toward direct support for black students across the South, an agenda already addressed by other funds, including the Jeanes Fund, established by Anna T. Jeanes in 1907 to support "rudimentary education" in "Rural, Community, or Country schools for the Southern Negro."[21] The GEB gained leverage with rural schools starting in 1915 when it dedicated $3,500 to cover the salary of a rural school agent for Negro schools in Arkansas. The rural school agent was supposed to supervise rural homemaker clubs, an opportunity not otherwise available to rural black women. Thus, by the time Mary Ray received her appointment, a network of farm families familiar with extension programs existed. Ray combined lessons learned at Tuskegee Institute with experience gained from her work at the fledgling public 1890 land-grant institution in the territory of Oklahoma to deliver practical instruction to Arkansas farm families. This helped them stabilize their income and make their living conditions more comfortable.[22]

By 1914 the Arkansas Co-operative Agricultural Extension Service's staff included one state agent, one state home demonstration agent, one state 4-H Club agent, three district county agents, several specialists, fifty-two county agents, fifteen home demonstration agents, and the necessary clerical force. Harvey C. Ray joined this workforce before Mary did. As his obituary stated, "Mr. Ray was the first Negro county agent to work under federal appointment" after the U.S. Congress passed the Smith-Lever Act and the state of Arkansas accepted Smith-Lever appropriations. White staff members claimed that "Ray was taken sight unseen on the recommendation of . . . Booker T. Washington." Ray relocated to Arkansas and began work on February 1, 1915. He spent the rest of the year living in Little Rock and working in Pulaski County with black landowners. On December 15, 1915, he became the special agent in charge of work in several more counties (Arkansas, Crittenden, Jefferson, Lee, Monroe, Phillips, and Pulaski).[23]

Mary married H. C. Ray just over one week later, on December 23, 1915. She became the first Negro home demonstration agent under the Smith-Lever protocol in Arkansas on March 16, 1916, teaching domestic science to girls and women in farm homes, gardens, and chicken yards. Job opportunities in Arkansas and

Harvey Ray's employment there apparently motivated Mary to leave her faculty position, marry, and relocate south. Other factors, including dissent among faculty and administrators at Langston over President Page's preference for a humanities curriculum, may have provided added incentive to both Rays to relocate.[24]

Employees in the new Negro divisions of state agricultural extension services came from several 1890 land-grant institutions, including Tuskegee Institute. The appointments of H. C. Ray in early 1915 and Mary just over one year later extended Tuskegee's influence into the Arkansas extension service. Mary had experience working with separatist institutions, where the administrative hierarchy among black staff mirrored that of white staff. But in extension work, the black staff held subordinate positions to all white staff. The administrators at the state level distributed the federal appropriations unequally between the white and black divisions. This resulted in unequal pay despite comparable work and unequal office facilities, transportation allowances, and other financial support. In 1914–1915, the cost for Negro extension work conducted by the two farm agents in Arkansas (Harvey Ray in Pulaski County, February 1, 1915, to December 15, 1915, and the agent in Lee County, October 7, 1914, through December 31, 1915) cost $1,380 total. In 1916, the number of farm agents increased to four and the work cost $2,637; for women, with the appointment of Mary Ray, it cost $341. In 1917, with six male agents, Negro extension work cost $3,017, and with Mary Ray responsible for all the women's work, it cost $1,050. These figures are the complete costs covered by three sources: Federal Extension Service appropriations and state and county funds. The costs indicate the limited remuneration for the work. Mary Ray took a pay cut from the $1,000 that she had earned at Langston in 1912. Her salary when she was appointed to be the local district home demonstration agent for Negro extension work on July 1, 1918, however, came closer to what she had earned at Langston and to the salary of her peer in Texas, Mary Evelyn V. Hunter, who earned $1,020.[25]

Extension services in neighboring states had different strategies to secure funding to keep district agents and farm and home demonstration agents in the field. The Texas Agricultural Extension Service required county commissioner courts to appropriate no less than $300 in matching funds before the service would place an agent in the county. In Tennessee, the opposite situation existed. Counties appropriated zero dollars for Negro extension work, and all funds came from the two state land-grant colleges, the University of Tennessee and the Agricultural and Industrial State Normal School (later Tennessee State University), and from the GEB. Each state set salaries for their agents, and local and philanthropic support affected individual salaries, which reflected power structures based on racist and sexist cultural constructs. By the late 1920s, white male county agents earned more than twice what black male agents earned; white female home demonstration agents earned 75 percent of what white male county agents earned and more than twice what black women earned.[26]

Most of Arkansas's cooperative demonstration staff, including administrators, agents, and specialists (all white), worked out of Little Rock before 1914. The central location in the state's capital seemed logical and helped maintain the visibility of the service in political circles, but it distanced the staff from the land-grant institution in Fayetteville and from farmers throughout the state. The changes that resulted from the Smith-Lever Act included relocation of the business office to Fayetteville and the land-grant college campus, at the behest of the college's president. This did not happen without controversy, and the relocation proved temporary. Most district agents and specialists returned to Little Rock in 1920. By early 1925 the staff worked out of the Donaghey Building at the corner of Seventh and Main in downtown Little Rock even though the building apparently remained under construction.[27] Mary Ray and her husband lived in Little Rock at 2111 Cross Street, and by 1925 they maintained an office at 712½ West Ninth Street. They did not operate out of Pine Bluff, the location of Branch Normal School, an 1890 land-grant institution, or in Fayetteville, where extension service officials worked but where fewer black people lived than in the Mississippi Delta counties. Their home and office in Little Rock gave the Rays ready access to Pulaski County's black population, which they had a duty to serve, but removed them geographically and culturally from the residents of Mississippi Delta counties, which they also were contractually obligated to serve.[28]

Mary Ray traveled from the state capital to the Delta counties during 1916 and 1917 on a regular basis. This allowed her to meet with rural women and their families and to form 4-H and homemaker clubs in communities in Pulaski County and in the two Delta counties that she also served, Phillips and St. Francis. Then in 1918, she had to travel even more given the increased responsibilities associated with the supervision of twenty-eight African American home demonstration agents working on behalf of the war effort. The burden of travel eased slightly in 1919 when the number of home demonstration agents assigned to Mary Ray declined to twenty-one. But the loss of seven agents added different pressures associated with constituents no longer served but still warranting attention.[29]

Mary Ray shared logistical challenges with supervisory staff in Negro extension work across the South, including poor roadways that, at best, resulted in bumpy rides and, at worst, were impassable. Ray and her white peers had to overcome unreliable automobiles, thin tires, and considerable distances between origin and destination. Ray also had to do her job with fewer resources, including a lower salary and no travel allowance, and she had to outmaneuver the obstacles of racial segregation. Black professionals could not stay in segregated hotels, had to use "colored" entrances or walk-up windows at restaurants and lunch counters, and could not use "white-only" facilities in service stations. The segregated nature of travel forced Ray to stay in motels or rooming houses owned and operated by black families or to lodge with friends and colleagues on overnight trips. Ray likely traveled with peers, or with her husband, as often as possible. Staff in other states did this routinely as they delivered programs and attended conferences together. The shared experiences may have lightened the burdens of those in the car, but did not eliminate the logistical, financial, and emotional insults.[30]

Mary Ray and other home demonstration and farm agents depended on black landowning farm families for support during their travels and for engagement to make the Negro extension work programs possible. Ray learned this strategy during her years at Tuskegee Institute and in her work with schools in rural Alabama during the mid- to late 1890s, prior to her relocation to Oklahoma. H. C. Ray had more direct experiences with farm ownership. He grew up on a family-owned farm in Palestine Township, near Bunceton, Missouri, though that farm was mortgaged in 1900. Landowning farmers worked for themselves, often contracted with tenants or sharecroppers to cultivate their properties, and wielded some influence in their communities. Sometimes farm-owning families lived apart from others, but families also clustered near crossroads, railroad depots, businesses such as sawmills, or schools. Black agents targeted these communities because they knew that the landowning families had the potential to help the agents accomplish their goals of rural reform, including improving living conditions and increasing economic independence, and because the agents came from similar cultures, often having been the children of farm owners, educators, or business operators. Families paid taxes on personal and real estate property, and this gave them leverage to lobby at local quorum courts to request appropriations. The goal might be humble, funds for the purchase of a canning retort or pressurized canner, for instance, to help tomato clubs turn their produce into a marketable commodity. The farm-owning families also had homes and yards where they could construct poultry houses to diversify their income or privies to improve sanitation. Thus class consciousness affected programmatic choices.[31]

Harvey Ray engaged with these farm-owning families immediately as a way to establish extension services. Mary Ray built on the groundwork he laid through his work with farm men and children. For instance, Harvey organized the first club for black Arkansas youth, which later became a 4-H Club, in 1915 in Maumelle Township, five miles northwest of Little Rock on the Arkansas River. Two farm-owning couples, James and Virginia Baker and Nathan and Caroline Lee, lived in the community in 1920. The Bakers lived in a section of the township populated by white farm families, but the Lee family lived in a section with a population equally divided between white and black families. Some were educated, some had children, some owned their homes, and some rented. Some were day laborers in the Little Rock Lumber and Manufacturing Company; others were sharecroppers on the farms owned by white and black farm proprietors. Mary cooperated with black farm families in Pulaski, St. Francis, and Phillips Counties to establish homemaker clubs and canning clubs. These served a dual purpose: they diversified the farming economy and also provided evidence of the validity of home demonstration work.[32]

Mary Ray confirmed the value of her work with women and girls through descriptions in the annual reports that she submitted to her supervisors. These emphasized the mutual dependency that existed between the success of Negro extension work and the landowning farm families, small business owners, and community cultural and social centers that featured prominently in her narratives. Her 1916 report, "The Community Fair: A Factor in the Negro Work," indicated that fairs offered a venue to feature these economic success stories and make agricultural extension work visible at the same time. The fairs encouraged friendly rivalry between communities, and their success depended on the involvement of schoolchildren, farm families, technical experts, and agents. In 1918, Ray, with the help of another supervising agent and twenty-four local agents hired with federal funding dedicated to the war effort, worked with schools, churches, lodge halls, and other rural organizations in thirty counties to establish temporary war kitchens and other services. She and her constituents pursued their work "with a view toward helping to care for the nearly two millions of people who are solely dependent upon us and our allied governments for food and clothing."[33]

In reality, most of the "two millions of people" Ray mentioned as needing the services did not get it. The expansion of Negro extension work in Arkansas during World War I helped solidify the program but proved short-lived. The number of agents hired with emergency appropriations returned to the prewar level by 1920, and the agents returned to work with the residents who lived where they worked, who did not have the potential to relocate each January 1 as sharecropper contracts changed. H. C. Ray helped formalize relationships among the male heads of these farm households with the formation of the Arkansas Negro State Farmers' Association in 1920. This still left the majority of agricultural laborers and sharecroppers underserved, however, and gave no credit to farm women and children for the roles they played in sustaining farm ownership. Agents also reached out to tenant farm families and to families that owned more personal property and negotiated better contracts with landowners. Agents refrained from stating their preferences for working with stable farm families and not the uneducated, illiterate, and impoverished workers, but occasionally such sentiments appeared, if only as allusions, in the annual reports. Strikes by agricultural laborers, including sharecroppers and cotton pickers, threatened the security of rural black communities in which Mary and H. C. Ray worked. The agents carefully avoided entanglement in incidents such as the 1919 racial confrontation in Elaine in Phillips County. They stepped lightly because their appointments and the whole of Negro extension work in Arkansas depended on whites' approval. Association with sharecroppers and tenants trying to organize against white planters would have destroyed it. But race and class bias might have also affected the choices of the Rays. In extreme circumstances, H. C. Ray, at least, let his guard down and showed his class bias. He did not specify the race or ethnicity of the working classes, which likely included white, black, and perhaps Mexican laborers, but he conveyed his attitude at the time clearly in his annual narrative report about the 1927 flood: "The bottoms have always been over-run with an abundance of cheap and inefficient labor."[34]

Mary's reports focused more on nutrition and decorum, not activist agendas. This fit the pattern for agent reports across the South. That said, her lessons in community organizing and economic development could be put to use in situations that had the potential to challenge white authority. In 1921 she indicated that lessons in gardening led to successful economic diversification. Girls and women could earn enough money by marketing fresh vegetables, including tomatoes, to attend the annual farmers' conference and short course, a day or two of educational programs designed to meet farm families' needs. One girl in Faulkner County purchased cans and glass jars to preserve the excess produce and still pocketed a profit of $44. Ray did not dwell on tomato production in her "High Points in Home Demonstration Work in Arkansas," appended to her 1922 report. Instead she emphasized the careful planning required to grow the program. She described auto tours of demonstration homes and garden plots that helped county residents see the potential of raising marketable commodities, including sweet corn and tomatoes. Auto tour participants photographed girls harvesting a wagonload of tomatoes at one stop.[35]

Mary Ray dedicated a lot of energy to improving farm families' nutrition. To that end, she described the ways that the "campaign idea" had helped her promote better bread making. She organized a series of meetings that featured a nutrition specialist talking with agents. Then agents met with community organization leaders; those leaders then held demonstrations with their local members. After training, communities held bread-making contests. Winners competed at the county level, and the highest scorers in each county entered the state bread-making contest. Ray indicated that such organizing was not for the faint of heart:

> A very easily discouraged person could not have pushed the work, when we realize the unfavorable conditions under which the initial demonstrations were given.... There are only a few schools equipped for teaching this line of work. But whenever other possibilities failed, the rural schoolhouse was the place chosen.
>
> On bread baking day one would usually see a farm wagon coming to the schoolhouse containing a range and cooking utensils that had been borrowed from some member of the club. Often times a hard fight would have to be made before the stove pipe was subdued and remained intact; suitable wood and water were made plentiful and the many other things so necessary to insure the success of the demonstration. But no one would shrink from their duty when the many anxious, happy, and appealing faces were there, because they wanted to learn.[36]

The programs that Mary Ray described in her annual reports fit the trends evident in black home demonstration reports across the South. Programs such as bread baking reached black constituents with some economic clout, usually farm owners. But these relatively economically viable farm families had limited influence politically. The agents had problems finding suitable locations to deliver their programs and had to create workspaces in locations that served other needs. Ray described a solution in her 1921 report: "The club girls of McGehee [Desha County] raised money and purchased a stove, necessary cooking utensils and placed them on shelves made in a corner of a large classroom. In this kitchenette many demonstrations are conducted before a large class. Perfect cooperation exists here between the agent [Clara Dixon] and the teacher." The demonstrations likely included bread-baking programs and canning demonstrations. Overall, Ray tried to generate visibility for the programs that she, the home demonstration agents, and the clubwomen and girls presented. She did this without threatening the extension service's race-biased hierarchy or jeopardizing white patronage, which was conveyed through quorum court appropriations or permission to conduct demonstrations. The descriptions in her narrative reports emphasized the aesthetic improvements possible through home beautification and blooming gardens or the utility of canning a whole beef, a demonstration often delivered to farm families so they could process an entire beef carcass using appropriate canning methods. These self-help programs depended on individual investment as well as collective and communal action. Any of these could have been perceived as threatening the racial status quo in Arkansas if demonstrators had emphasized the ways the lessons could have empowered poor rural black populations.[37]

Ray used new technology to increase the visibility of self-help programs. She described the ways that county clubs used motion pictures during rallies to increase membership. These likely included the film *Making Negroes Better Farmers*, produced in 1920 by the Federal Extension Service and featuring cooperative demonstration work near Tuskegee Institute in Alabama. Ray also encouraged agents to use photographs to their advantage. The county home demonstration agents included photographs in their monthly and annual reports, as Annie Latimer, the local home demonstration agent in Faulkner County, did in 1923. Latimer's photographs featured displays of canned goods, girls who won bread-baking contests, and members of a community club building a poultry house. One of the photographs of the poultry house under construction appeared in two Arkansas Extension Service publications. Another photograph featured in those publications depicted African American community members canning a whole beef. These illustrations depicted what Mary Ray wanted viewers to see: well-dressed African Americans working on projects to preserve and process foodstuffs, building home, farm, and community. One annual narrative report prepared by white extension administrators conveyed the message: "The negro work is helping to develop thrift and citizenship among members of that race and is making the race more self-supporting and giving them a pride and ambition in improving their homes." This made the extension service, in general, look good. It also did not indicate the inequity in the countryside that kept the majority powerless and impoverished.[38]

Mary Ray's work with women during the 1920s faced numerous challenges. Communities that had prospered during the years when the Rays first established Negro extension work in Arkansas began a steady decline after 1920 as residents aged and the agricultural economy worsened. Owners often remained on their land and involved in their communities longer, but their children and the tenant and sharecropper families left. The combination made it difficult for farm families to maintain and retain their property. This reduced the population density and thus the number of constituents that the agents could serve and increased the challenge to secure the spaces needed for demonstrations. This sequence of events played out across the South. Agents responded in different ways.

The Rays devised a new extension service in 1929, the movable school for Negro farm folk, which allowed the agents to reach residents in counties not served regularly by agents and communities without clubs. Jennie Lou Woodard, formerly the home demonstration agent in Lee County in 1921 and in Miller County by 1924 and the acting local home demonstration agent during Mary Ray's leave due to illness in 1927 and 1928, began as the movable school agent on January 1, 1929. The movable school delivered 1,133 programs and traveled 7,770 miles in a 1928 Ford pickup. Woodard indicated the critical role that support from Mary Ray and her husband played in making the movable school a success. Measurable outcomes included the construction of poultry houses and numerous home improvement initiatives from building sanitary toilets to screening windows and whitewashing structures.[39]

The support Mary Ray provided as an administrator helped make programs in rural communities possible, but her work also employed educated black women and launched their careers. Julia Ada Miller provides an example. Miller was born and raised in Round Lake, Mississippi. She graduated from Tuskegee Institute in May 1924 and apparently worked in Alabama in home demonstration before coming to Arkansas.[40] She then served as the home demonstration agent in Pope County, Arkansas, from 1925 to 1928. A feature called "Negro Work," published in the *Extension Cooperator* (the monthly newspaper published in Fayetteville) mentioned Miller's influence: "The negro girls and women of Pope County who are members of demonstration clubs made an exhibit of their clothing and cooking in Atkins.... The display showed that much good work had been done by the Local Home Demonstration Agent, Julia Miller, who makes her headquarters in Atkins."[41] Miller relocated to Florida to assume a position equivalent to Mary Ray's, the local district home demonstration agent assigned to work with the Negro women of Florida starting in 1928.[42] Miller did not stay there long. In 1931 she accepted the position of home demonstration agent in Kingfisher County, Oklahoma.[43]

The pace of the work exacerbated Mary Ray's ill health. But it took years for her debilitating condition, chronic interstitial nephritis, also known as granular kidney, to kill her. Over seven years, between 1927 and 1934, her condition worsened. She took a ten-month medical leave during 1927–1928, and she wrote about that on the front page of her 1929 report when she announced her return to work. Doctors have observed advanced stages of this disease in middle-aged adults who survived severe childhood illnesses, such as scarlet fever, acute rheumatic fever, or other infections caused by viridans streptococci bacteria.[44]

Mary Lee McCrary Ray died on July 25, 1934. Fannie Mae Boone, the local home demonstration agent in Lee County, dedicated future home demonstration work to Ray's memory: "The home demonstration work and the 4-H club work in the state of Arkansas, among Negroes, are a monument to her untiring efforts. The monument, which local home demonstration agents will set up to honor her, is the building of a program of home demonstration work which will be an everlasting memorial in the hearts of the people who loved her." Boone eulogized her with a stanza that indicated admiration for Ray's work for a noble cause:

> Go to thy grave at noon from all labors cease.
> Rest on thy sheaves, thy harvest work is done.
> Come from the heat of battle and in peace.
> Soldier, go home, with thee the fight is won.[45]

The photograph that Boone used to illustrate her dedication showed Mary Ray and her husband with John B. Pierce, who was the first black agent hired with GEB funds in Virginia in 1906. In 1918 he became one of the U.S. Department of Agriculture's field agents for Negro extension work. During the Depression, Pierce toured the cotton South developing the live-at-home program, and he met regularly with black agents and club members during farmer conferences and short courses. His work included cooperation with female as well as male agents, and Pierce no doubt had enjoyed a long relationship, professional if not personal, with the Rays.

Mary's death certificate has provided few leads to learn more about her early years or to document the context in which she might have developed the chronic condition. The person completing the death certificate wrote "Georgia" as her birthplace and recorded her date of birth as February 21, 1885. At some point thereafter, someone typed over the "5" with a "0," so 1885 became 1880, and this required an adjustment to her age, from forty-nine to fifty-four years. The person completing the form also wrote "Dont Know" [sic] next to the space for the names of her mother and father.[46] Thus, Mary L. Ray's death certificate raised more questions than answers about a woman who spent thirty-five years educating African Americans in several states, eighteen of those in Arkansas, and promoting rural reform.

H. C. Ray provided officials with the information entered on his wife's death certificate. Harvey's lack of knowledge of Mary's parents' identities indicated that he had not met her parents or even talked with her about them. The corrected birth year indicated that Mary had not known her actual birth year or had self-consciously concealed her real age from her younger husband. Either seems plausible.[47]

Succession at work occurred relatively seamlessly because Mary Ray's death did not come as a surprise. Women well informed about Negro extension work and experienced in the programs covered her jobs during her leave of absence and took over when she retired. When Ray died, she left seven home demonstration agents working with African American women and girls in seven counties across Arkansas.

Mary Ray's life and work indicate that relationships transcend geography. Networks of personal and professional relationships helped agents create programs that addressed inequality in the countryside. The farm families with whom Ray interacted invested in their private property and in their community organizations to improve sanitation, nutrition, and economic solvency. The agents invested their energy in these local renewal efforts. The supervisors, including Ray, worked tirelessly to sustain these initiatives. She walked a tightrope between the politics of black communities, where the interests of farm owners did not always reflect the agendas of the majority of landless agricultural laborers, and the politics of white supremacy. She did this through the gender-specific tasks that the extension service expected a home demonstration agent to pursue—making clothing, canning, raising poultry, bread baking, home improvement, and gardening. She also accomplished this work through public engagement outside the parameters of the racialized South. She appeared before local quorum courts to request appropriations. She interacted with her white peers in ways that resulted in visible proof of black home demonstration work. She secured support from cash-strapped locations even when funds became even more limited during economic crises. The moveable school served a purpose during the Great Depression, from 1929 through the early 1930s. But increased appropriations during the New Deal increased agents in the field and made the movable school obsolete.

Mary Ray did not live to see the fruits of those labors. Harvey Ray did not dwell on Mary's accomplishments when he submitted his brief history, "Negro Extension Work in Arkansas," with his 1935 annual narrative and statistical report, in recognition of the twentieth anniversary of Negro extension work in the state. White administrators, however, praised the couple: "Much of the present progress of the Negro extension program in this state can be traced to the work of this pioneering team in establishing a foundation for future accomplishment."[48] Harvey Ray continued with the Negro division of the Arkansas Agricultural Extension Service until he retired around 1953.[49]

NOTES

Generous scholars shared primary sources, including Cherisse Jones-Branch, Arkansas State University; Elizabeth Griffin Hill, author of *A Splendid Piece of Work, 1912–2012: One Hundred Years of Arkansas's Home Demonstration and Extension Homemakers Clubs*; Jeannie Whayne, University of Arkansas; and Gary Zellar, University of Saskatchewan. Cheryl Ferguson, Tuskegee University;

Jameka B. Lewis, Langston University Libraries; and Holly Reed, Still Picture Reference Team, National Archives and Records Administration, responded to research requests. Anita Sego, Eastern Illinois University, affirmed my interpretation of Mary Ray's medical condition. Jana L. Aydt and her interlibrary loan colleagues at Booth Library, Eastern Illinois University, processed numerous interlibrary loan requests.

1. I use the term "Negro" throughout this chapter when it appeared in the official records to designate professional positions.

2. Mena Hogan referenced official Arkansas Extension Service records, including office files, personnel files, and annual narrative and statistical reports as the basis for her "A History of the Agricultural Extension Service in Arkansas," MS thesis, University of Wisconsin, Madison, 1942. Hogan documented Mary McCrary (Ray)'s arrival in Arkansas (139) and included excerpts from her 1918 report (142). For mention of Mary Ray's death, see "Negro Demonstration Work," in *Annual Report: Extension Service, College of Agriculture, University of Arkansas and United States Department of Agriculture Cooperating: Fiscal Year July 1, 1933, to June 30, 1934, with Report of Field Activities December 1, 1933, to November 30, 1934*, Extension Circular 335 (Fayetteville: University of Arkansas, January 1935), 42; Death Certificate, State of Arkansas, Mary L. Ray, July 25, 1934, Little Rock, Pulaski County.

3. J. C. Barnett, "Brief History of Farm and Home Demonstration Work in Arkansas," in *Silver Anniversary: Cooperative Demonstration Work, 1903–1928: Proceedings of the Anniversary Meeting Held at Houston, Texas, February 5th, 6th, and 7th, 1929* (College Station: Extension Service, Agricultural and Mechanical College of Texas, n.d.), 91–96, quote on 94. Hogan, "History," includes one chapter on the Negro division, 136–59, drawing heavily on 1939 material by Harvey Ray, which I have been unable to locate, and on Mary's 1918 report (142) and 1932 report (154–55). Mary Lee Ray, Fraternal (African American) (now Oakland-Fraternal) Cemetery, Pulaski County, Ark., July 25, 1934, gravestone photograph, contributed to Arkansas Gravestones by "excellmoney," August 14, 2008, http://arkansasgravestones.org/view.php?id=43730.

4. "Ray, Harvey Cincinnatus," in *Who's Who of the Colored Race: A General Biographical Dictionary of Men and Women of African Descent*, ed. Frank Lincoln Mather (Chicago: Half-Century Anniversary of Negro Freedom in U.S., 1915), 1:227; Hogan, "History," 139. No marriage license has yet been located to confirm the marriage date or location. See Mary L. Ray Death Certificate.

5. For farm agent or county agent work, see Gary Zellar, "H. C. Ray and Racial Politics in the African American Extension Service Program in Arkansas, 1915–1929," *Agricultural History* 72, no. 2 (Spring 1998): 429–45; Jeannie Whayne, "'I Have Been through Fire': Black Agricultural Extension Agents and the Politics of Negotiation," in *African American Life in the Rural South, 1900–1950*, ed. R. Douglas Hurt (Columbia: University of Missouri Press, 2003), 152–88. "Services for H. C. Ray to Be Today," *Arkansas Gazette*, April 26, 1965, 6B:3, indicated that Ray had been a member of the Bethel African Methodist Episcopal Church in Little Rock for more than forty years and was the superintendent of Sunday school classes and a thirty-third-degree Mason. Mary's involvement in comparable organizations, including women's clubs, remains unknown.

6. Cheryl Ferguson, archival assistant, Tuskegee Library Archives, email to Debra A. Reid, November 6, 2013, confirmed the following: Mary L. McCrary attended Tuskegee from 1893 to 1897; she graduated in 1897 with certificates in cooking and dressmaking; she was a teacher at Mt. Meigs Village School, Mt. Meigs, Alabama, after graduation; she was a teacher in domestic science at Langston University; and she served in extension service housekeeping in Little Rock, Arkansas. For descriptions of McCrary's work in Langston, see Theo Baughman, "Along the Color Line: Mr. Theo. Baughman, the *Plaindealer*'s Globe Trotting Scribe Tells of Negro Advancement in Okla-

homa," *Plaindealer* (Topeka, Kans.), April 16, 1915, 1. I thank Cherisse Jones-Branch for sharing this source. University of Chicago catalogs documented Mary L. McCrary of Langston, Oklahoma, as a student in summer courses, but listed her previous education at Hampton Institute (not Tuskegee).

7. Mary L. Ray submitted annual reports to her supervisors starting in 1916. These describe routines as well as exceptional case studies. The reports of all agents in Arkansas, black and white, female and male, are housed in the Records of the Extension Service, RG 33, National Archives and Records Administration, Southwest Region, Fort Worth, Tex. (hereafter NASW). The National Archives Microfilm Publications issued 106 microfilm rolls of Arkansas reports, arranged chronologically with state administrator reports first, followed by county agent reports. See T848, Extension Service Annual Reports: Arkansas, 1909–1944, available as University of Arkansas Cooperative Extension Service Records, MCL 145, Special Collections, University of Arkansas Libraries, Fayetteville. For an overview of these records, see Joshua Youngblood, "Home Demonstration Records Document Twentieth Century Services to Rural Families," *Arkansian* 6, no. 1 (Spring 2012): 1, 4–5. Some of the annual narrative and statistical reports from state and county agents in Arkansas, 1909–1944, have been digitized, including reports from the Negro agents in Pulaski County, Ray's home county. Hogan, "History," included excerpts of Mary Ray's 1918 report. Elizabeth Griffin Hill included excerpts from Ray's reports from the 1920s in her *A Splendid Piece of Work, 1912–2012: One Hundred Years of Arkansas's Home Demonstration and Extension Homemakers Clubs* (N.p.: [Elizabeth Griffin Hill], 2012), 1920 report, 48, 86; 1921 report, 55; 1922 report, 35–37, 41, 42; 1926 report, 87; 1927 report, 13.

8. Robert E. Butchart, *Schooling the Freed People: Teaching, Learning, and the Struggle of Black Freedom, 1861–1876* (Chapel Hill: University of North Carolina Press, 2010); H. B. Frissell, H. B. Turner, and Alexander Purves, "The Hampton Normal and Agricultural Institute," in their *The Hampton Normal and Agricultural Institute and Its Work for Negro and Indian Youth* (Boston: Geo. H. Ellis, Printer, 1899), 9, 7. This promotional literature for Hampton also conveyed biased opinions: "There is danger that the blacks will lose the trades, which were their best heritage from slavery, unless industrial education is pushed. Young women well trained in domestic science must go out to reconstruct the home" (10). See also Debra A. Reid, "People's Colleges for Other Citizens: Black Land-Grant Institutions and the Politics of Educational Expansion in the Post–Civil War South," in *Science as Service: Establishing and Reformulating American Land-Grant Universities, 1865–1930*, vol. 1, ed. Alan I. Marcus (Tuscaloosa: University of Alabama Press, 2015), 141–71.

9. Zella J. Black Patterson, *Langston University: A History* (Norman: University of Oklahoma, 1979), 226. Mary L. McCrary is listed as an instructor of domestic economy at the Colored Agricultural and Normal University of Oklahoma, known as Langston, in the following publications: *Organization List of the Agricultural Colleges and Experiment Stations in the United States*, Bulletin 111 (Washington, D.C.: U.S. Government Printing Office, 1902), 55; *Organization List of the Agricultural Colleges and Experiment Stations in the United States*, Bulletin 122 (Washington, D.C.: U.S. Government Printing Office, 1903), 61.

10. Patterson, *Langston University*, 154, 226. See Linda Williams Reese, *Women of Oklahoma, 1890–1920* (Norman: University of Oklahoma Press, 1997), for brief biographical information on Zelia N. Page (Breaux), 164–66. Inman E. Page, "1902 Official Report of the President of the Colored Agricultural and Normal University to Governor T. B. Ferguson," transcribed by Tammie Chada, Logan County, Okla., http://www.usgennet.org/usa/ok/county/logan/grads/1902lang.htm (accessed December 31, 2013).

11. Patterson, *Langston University*, 195, 226–27. Richard W. Thompson, "Anniversary Aftermath: Echoes from Tuskegee Institute's Memorable Silver Jubilee: Pertinent Points about People," *The*

Freeman (May 5, 1906), described Mary McCrary as the "proprietor of a prosperous dressmaking establishment at Langston City, Oklahoma." See *The Oklahoma Red Book* (Oklahoma City: Office of the Oklahoma Secretary of State, 1912), 2:201; W. E. B. Du Bois and Augustus Granville Dill, *The Negro American Artisan: A Report of a Social Study Made by Atlanta University under the Patronage of the Trustees of the John F. Slater Fund: With the Proceedings of the 17th Annual Conference for the Study of the Negro Problems, Held at Atlanta University, on Monday, May 27th, 1912* (Atlanta, Ga.: Atlanta University Press, 1912), 73. The study included Indian Territory with Oklahoma.

12. "Ray, Harvey Cincinnatus," 227. Harvey Ray's parents were George and Catherine (Davis) Ray of Bunceton, Missouri. See Harvey Cincinnatus Ray, Graduate Class 1914 Program, Thirty-Third Annual Commencement, Tuskegee Normal and Industrial Institute, Tuskegee, Ala., May 24–28, 1914; *Annual Catalogue of the Colored Agricultural and Normal University Founded 1897, 1911–1912* (Langston, Okla.: N.p., n.d.). Staff lists published by the U.S. Department of Agriculture include Ray as "farm superintendent," *Organization List of the Agricultural Colleges and Experiment Stations in the United States*, Bulletin 253 (Washington, D.C.: U.S. Government Printing Office, 1913), 69; as "agri asst," *List of Workers in Subjects Pertaining to Agriculture and Home Economics in the U.S. Department of Agriculture and in the State Agricultural Colleges and Experiment Stations, Corrected to June 1, 1914* (Washington, D.C.: U.S. Government Printing Office, 1914), 55; as "agri asst," *List of Workers in Subjects Pertaining to Agriculture and Home Economics in the U.S. Department of Agriculture and in the State Agricultural Colleges and Experiment Stations, Corrected to August 1, 1915* (Washington, D.C.: U.S. Government Printing Office, 1915), 78; as "agri asst," *List of Workers in Subjects Pertaining to Agriculture and Home Economics in the U.S. Department of Agriculture and in the State Agricultural Colleges and Experiment Stations, Corrected to December 1, 1915* (Washington, D.C.: U.S. Government Printing Office, 1916), 85; and as "agriculture assistant," *List of Workers in Subjects Pertaining to Agriculture and Home Economics in the U.S. Department of Agriculture and in the State Agricultural Colleges and Experiment Stations, Corrected to January 1917* (Washington, D.C.: U.S. Government Printing Office, 1917), 50.

13. Debra A. Reid, "Racism and Sexism in Rural Texas: The Contested Nature of Progressive Rural Reform, 1870s–1910s," in *Seeking Inalienable Rights: Texans and Their Quests for Justice*, ed. Debra A. Reid (College Station: Texas A&M University Press, 2009), 37–57; and Reid, *Reaping a Greater Harvest: African Americans, the Extension Service, and Rural Reform in Jim Crow Texas* (College Station: Texas A&M University, 2007), esp. 7–113.

14. Barnett, "Brief History," 91–96, said that canning clubs began in 1911, but the General Education Board did not appropriate funding until 1912. Financial backing from Sears, Roebuck may have funded earlier canning demonstrations.

15. Barnett, "Brief History," 91; *The General Education Board: An Account of Its Activities, 1902–1914* (New York: General Education Board, 1915), 37, 49, 56, http://archive.org/stream/generaleducation029311mbp/generaleducation029311mbp_djvu.txt (accessed August 13, 2014).

16. *General Education Board*, 56. See J. V. Highfill and M. C. Wilson, *Progress of Extension Teaching in Lee and Hot Spring Counties, Arkansas*, Extension Circular 397 (Fayetteville: University of Arkansas, June 1937), 7, for the dates of the first three appointments (likely for three different individuals): June 1, 1912–September 30, 1914; October 7, 1914–December 31, 1915; and February 1, 1917–December 31, 1923. See also W. B. Mercier, *Extension Work among Negroes, 1920*, U.S. Department of Agriculture, Circular 190 (Washington, D.C.: U.S. Government Printing Office, 1921), table: "Negro Extension Work—Number of Men and Women Agents and Estimated Cost for Each Fiscal Year from 1908 to 1921, Inclusive," 7. Mildred Grady, "'Famous Firsts' for Blacks in Lee County," in *History of Lee County, Arkansas* (Lee County, Ark.: Lee County Sesquicentennial Committee,

1987), identified Rev. R. E. Bryant and Vivian Young as the county's first farm and home agents, respectively. For a photograph and brief biography of Bryant as a member of the board of trustees of Arkansas Baptist College, see E. C. Morris, *Sermons, Addresses and Reminiscences and Important Correspondence, with a Picture Gallery of Eminent Ministers and Scholars* (Nashville, Tenn.: National Baptist Publishing Board, 1901), 258. The 1920 federal manuscript Census listed Bryant as a farm demonstrator.

17. *General Education Board*; Cecelia Brooks, "'Touch the Bottom and Lift': Black Women Home Extension Agents in Oklahoma, 1912–1935," *Chronicles of Oklahoma* 86, no. 1 (Spring 2008): 88–108; for specifics on Hunter and canning, see 94. See also Ernest E. Scholl, "History of Extension Work in Oklahoma," in *Silver Anniversary*, 84–87, including mention of the appointments sometime between 1910 and 1914 of Russel Council and Anna [sic] Peters, "both colored people of Boley, Oklahoma ... to do work with colored farmers and their families in the vicinity" (86); Jan Scholl and Tanya Finchum, "Annie Peters Hunter: One of the First Extension Home Demonstration Educators," *Forum for Family and Consumer Issues* 17, no. 1 (Spring–Summer 2012), http://ncsu.edu/ffci/publications/2012/v17-n1-2012-spring/scholl-finchum.php.

18. *General Education Board*, 37, 65.

19. Hogan, "History," 46–56. Quote from D. Clayton Brown, "Prosperous Farms and Happier Homes: Arkansas Agricultural Extension Service, 1911–1966," *Prologue* 30, no. 2 (Summer 1996), http://www.archives.gov/publications/prologue/1998/summer/arkansas-extension.html.

20. Mercier, *Extension Work among Negroes*, 7; Hill, *A Splendid Piece of Work*, 10, citing Hogan, "History," 39–49; Grady, "'Famous Firsts' for Blacks," identified Vivian Young as Lee County's first home agent. Canning clubs began as part of cooperative demonstration work in Texas in 1912 when white women were hired for the summer canning season, in cooperation with local chambers of commerce and the Truck Growers Association. See Reid, "Racism and Sexism in Rural Texas," 37–57, esp. 47–52.

21. Alice Brown Smith, *Forgotten Foundations: The Role of Jeanes Teachers in Black Education* (New York: Vantage, 1997); Daniel Kreisman, "The Next Needed Thing: The Impact of the Jeanes Fund on Black Schooling in the South, 1900–1930," *Journal of Human Resources* 52, no. 2 (Spring 2017): 573–620, quote on 577.

22. Earl W. Crosby, "The Struggle for Existence: The Institutionalization of the Black County Agent System," *Agricultural History* 60 (Spring 1986): 131, cited the following on the loss in numbers: letters, Anonymous to Booker T. Washington, August 14, 1914; J. A. Evans to Monroe N. Work, with enclosure "Negro Agents in the United States Farmers' Cooperative Demonstration Work," February 20, 1914, revised to July 9, 1914, typescript, 3, box 988, Booker T. Washington Papers, Library of Congress. Katherine M. Cook, *Supervision of Rural Schools*, Bulletin 10, Bureau of Education (Washington, D.C.: U.S. Government Printing Office, 1922), 23; "A Guide to the Photographs," ser. 1054 "General Education Board, ARK 44—Supervisor of Rural Schools—Negro: Homemaker Clubs," 1915, box 42, folder 412, Rockefeller Archives Center, Sleepy Hollow, N.Y.

23. Barnett, "Brief History," 91–96, quote 94; "Services for H. C. Ray to Be Today"; J. A. Evans, *Recollections of Extension History*, Extension Circular 224 (Raleigh: North Carolina Agricultural Extension Service, 1938), 1–51; Zellar, "H. C. Ray and Racial Politics," 432–33. Polk's Southern Directory Company's 1916 *Little Rock City Directory*, 470, recorded Harvey C. Ray, special agent with the U.S. Department of Agriculture, residing at 2415 Cross Street with George Ray, a black planter, boarding at the same address.

24. For the 1915 turmoil at Langston, see Donald Spivey, "Crisis on a Black Campus: Langston University and Its Struggle for Survival," *Chronicles of Oklahoma* 59, no. 4 (Winter 1981–1982): 430–47.

25. Zellar, "H. C. Ray and Racial Politics," 436, for salaries of black agents averaging 45–50 percent less than those of white agents. For numbers of agents and costs between 1908 and 1921, see Mercier, *Extension Work among Negroes*, 7. For more on the extension milieu in which Harvey and Mary Ray functioned, see, for example, Kathleen C. Hilton, "'Both in the Field, Each with a Plow': Race and Gender in USDA Policy, 1907–1929," in *Hidden Histories of Women in the New South*, ed. Virginia Bernhard et al. (Columbia: University of Missouri Press, 1994), 114–33. More studies exist of the origins and controversies of the southern farm agent system than of home demonstration: Allen W. Jones, "The South's First Black Farm Agents," *Agricultural History* 50 (October 1976): 636–44; Earl W. Crosby, "The Roots of Black Agricultural Extension Work," *Historian* 39, no. 2 (February 1977): 228–47; Earl W. Crosby, "Limited Success against Long Odds: The Black County Agent," *Agricultural History* 57, no. 3 (July 1983): 277–88; Crosby, "Struggle for Existence"; Whayne, "I Have Been through Fire," 152–88. Much has been written about the development of extension programming at Tuskegee Institute, for example, Karen J. Ferguson, "Caught in 'No Man's Land': The Negro Cooperative Demonstration Service and the Ideology of Booker T. Washington, 1900–1916," *Agricultural History* 72, no. 1 (Winter 1998): 33–54, but much less exists on Negro divisions in other states. See Reid, *Reaping a Greater Harvest*; Barbara R. Cotton, *The Lamplighters: Black Farm and Home Demonstration Agents in Florida, 1915–1965* (Tallahassee: Florida A&M University, 1982); and Carmen Harris, "A Ray of Hope for Liberation: Blacks in the South Carolina Extension Service, 1915–1970," Ph.D. diss., Michigan State University, 2002. For McCrary's salary at Langston, see W. B. Richards, comp., *The Oklahoma Red Book* (Oklahoma City: Oklahoma [Territory] Legislative Assembly Council, 1912), 2:201, https://archive.org/stream/oklahomaredbook00okla#page/200/mode/2up/search/langston.

26. The list of costs in each southern state do not convey the complexity of funding: Mercier, *Extension Work among Negroes*, 7–8. For funding strategies and salaries in Texas, see Reid, *Reaping a Greater Harvest*, 45, 89–90. For Tennessee, see Melissa Walker, "Home Extension Work among African American Farm Women in East Tennessee, 1920–1939," *Agricultural History* 70, no. 3 (Summer 1996): 487–502, esp. 489. For salaries at the end of Mary Ray's career, see Gladys Baker, *The County Agent* (Chicago: University of Chicago Press, c. 1939), 201. As of 1935–1936 Negro county agents' salaries averaged $1,500–$1,600, and Negro home demonstration agents' salaries averaged $1,000–$1,100 per year.

27. Hogan, "History," 60; *Annual Report July 1, 1923, to June 30, 1924, with Summary of Field Activities from December 1, 1923, through November 30, 1924*, U.S. Department of Agriculture Cooperating Extension, Circular 193 (Fayetteville: Extension Service, College of Agriculture, University of Arkansas, February 1925), 14.

28. Polk's Southern Directory Company's 1917 *Directory of Little Rock*, 433, recorded Henry Ray, a white clerk, residing at 2111 Cross Street, and Harvey C. Ray residing at 2415 Cross Street with Mary L. Ray, district agent with the U.S. Department of Agriculture, boarding there. Harvey C. Ray's registration card for the draft, dated June 5, 1917, listed his residence at 2111 Cross Street. The 1919 *Little Rock City Directory*, 291, listed H. C. Ray at 2111 Cross Street, but listed Mary L. Ray boarding at 2415 Cross Street (292). For the first time, the 1920 *Little Rock City Directory*, 355, listed Mary L. and Harvey C. Ray residing at 2111 Cross Street. The draft card and all city directories were accessed through www.ancestry.com. Manuscript Census enumerators in 1920 and 1930 recorded Mary and Harvey Ray's address as 2111 Cross Street. Ray maintained an office at 904 Broadway Street, Little Rock, in 1915 ("Ray, Harvey Cincinnatus," 227); an office at 712½ West Ninth Street (*Annual Report July 1, 1923, to June 30, 1924*, 47); and later an office at 610½ West Ninth Street. See "Ray, Harvey Cincinnatus," in *Who's Who in Colored America: An Illustrated Biographical Diction-*

ary of Notable Living Persons of African Descent in the United States, 7th ed. (Yonkers-on-Hudson, N.Y.: Christian E. Buckel, 1950), 430.

29. See Ray, Annual Narrative and Statistical Reports, 1916–1919, RG 33, NASW.

30. I have documented the logistical challenges that black agents faced as they traveled from Texas to Negro extension meetings in other states, which were recorded in the minutes of staff meetings. See Reid, *Reaping a Greater Harvest*, 129, 151. For more on racism and how it affected middle-class travelers, see Susan Sessions Rugh, *Are We There Yet?: The Golden Age of American Family Vacations* (Lawrence: University of Kansas Press, 2008).

31. George Ray, head of household, widowed, with Harvey Ray listed as eleven years old and "at school," Palestine Township, Cooper County, Mo., U.S. Census, 1900, enumeration district 54, 6-B, www.ancestry.com (accessed August 23, 2014). Sources have documented the intention of Arkansas extension administrators to have H. C. Ray work with farm-owning families: Zellar, "H. C. Ray and Racial Politics," 434–35; and Whayne, "I Have Been through Fire," 178–79. For more on black landowning families, see Debra A. Reid and Evan P. Bennett, *Beyond Forty Acres and a Mule* (Gainesville: University Press of Florida, 2014), and for a state-level study that puts extension work into the context of black communities, see Reid, *Reaping a Greater Harvest*. I address specific instances of the success that black women had in commissioners' courts in Texas; Whayne provides an example of Mary J. McCain, the agent in Mississippi County, and the interest the quorum court showed her in 1925 (Whayne, "I Have Been through Fire," 173–74).

32. The residents of Maumelle have made no impression on researchers except for the association with early Negro extension work. More needs to be known about the families in the community in 1915, what if any relationship they had to Harvey or Mary Ray, and what their economic assets really were. U.S. Census, 1920, manuscript returns, Maumelle Township, Pulaski County, Ark.

33. Mary Ray, "The Community Fair: A Factor in the Negro Work," 1916, pt. 4: "The Part Women Are Taking in Community Organization Work in Arkansas," appended to Annual Narrative and Statistical Report, 1916, Arkansas; and Mary Ray, "Report on Home Demonstration Work among the Colored Women and Girls for the Year 1918," appended to Annual Narrative and Statistical Report, 1918, Arkansas, both RG 33, NASW.

34. Zellar, "H. C. Ray and Racial Politics," 433; O. A. Rogers Jr., "The Elaine Race Riots of 1919," *Arkansas Historical Quarterly* 19, no. 2 (Summer 1960): 142–50; Lee E. Williams and Lee E. Williams II, *Anatomy of Four Race Riots: Racial Conflict in Knoxville, Elaine (Arkansas), Tulsa, and Chicago, 1919–1921* (Hattiesburg: Hattiesburg University and College Press of Mississippi, 1972); Whayne, "I Have Been through Fire," 177. Note that Whayne identified the district agent as Hiram C. Ray.

35. For descriptions of the girls picking tomatoes, see Ray, "High Points in Home Demonstration Work in Arkansas," appended to Annual Narrative and Statistical Report, 1922, Arkansas, RG 33, NASW.

36. Mary Ray, Annual Narrative and Statistical Report, 1922, Arkansas, RG 33, NASW.

37. Mary Ray, Annual Narrative and Statistical Reports, 1918–1927, 1928 (prepared by Jennie Lou Woodard), 1929–1934, Arkansas, RG 33, NASW. For brief excerpts from Ray's annual reports, see Hill, *A Splendid Piece of Work*, 1920 report, 48, 86; 1921 report, 55; 1922 report, 35–37, 41, 42; 1926 report, 87; 1927 report, 138. The quote comes from Ray, "Negro Home Demonstration Work," in Annual Narrative and Statistical Report, 1921, section on "work rooms," 2.

38. Photographs of 1923 events appear in Mary L. Ray, Narrative Report of County Extension Workers included in the Annual Report of County Extension Workers, December 1, 1923, to November 30, 1924, Arkansas, RG 33, NASW. Photographs published in *Annual Report July 1, 1923, to June 30, 1924* include livestock judging, 47; and constructing a poultry house and canning beef,

48. See also "Negro Agents Conducting a Community Demonstration in Canning a Whole Beef," *Extension Cooperator* (November–December 1925): 2. The caption in Annie Latimer's narrative report (January 1–November 30, 1923) for Faulkner County read: "Cooperative Work in the Bethel Community. View A: Serving lunch after ½ days [sic] hard work. 25 men, women and girls took part in erecting this poultry house which we completed in one day." The same image was published in *Annual Report July 1, 1923, to June 30, 1924*, 48, with the caption "Negro workers are interested in better poultry. Negro agents helping build a model poultry house along accepted lines" (Records of the Extension Service, RG 33, NASW). Mary Ray's peers in other states described community canning demonstrations in their reports, and they stressed the cooperative nature of the programs, which depended on the collaboration of male and female agents and their club members (Reid, *Reaping a Greater Harvest*, 68–78). For the quotation, see T. Roy Reid's annual narrative report, July 1, 1923, to June 30, 1924, with field observations from December 1, 1923, through November 30, 1924, conclusion to "Negro Home Demonstration Work," in *Annual Report July 1, 1923, to June 30, 1924*, 49.

39. For information on the movable school, with a photograph of home demonstration agent Woodard, agricultural agent C. C. Hardaway, and the truck, see Jennie Lou Woodard, "Annual Report of Moveable School Extension Agent, A: Statistical Section, January 1, 1929, to November 30, 1929"; and Woodard, "Narrative Report of County Extension Workers, Section B: Arkansas, January 8, 1929, to November 30, 1929," both RG 33, NASW, especially "The Effectiveness of the Moveable School in the Future," 21.

40. Forty-Third Anniversary Exercises, Tuskegee Normal and Industrial Institute, Programme, Commencement Day, May 22, 1924; "Florida's Woman Supervisor: Miss Julia A. Miller of Arkansas Gets Appointment," *Modern Farmer* 1, no. 1 (March 1, 1929): 1.

41. "Negro Work," *Extension Cooperator* (July 1926): 4. This coverage warrants attention because it is one of the only mentions, by name, of a black home demonstration agent in the white-centric publication, and it featured Julia Miller, who became H. C. Ray's second wife. While Mary Ray did not share her personal background in public information, Miller appeared in several published sources in several states.

42. "Florida's Woman Supervisor," 1. Miller was headquartered at Florida A&M College, Tallahassee. For more on home demonstration work in Florida, see Cotton, *Lamplighters*; and Kelly A. Minor, "'Justifiable Pride': Negotiation and Collaboration in Florida African American Extension," in Reid and Bennett, *Beyond Forty Acres and a Mule*, 205–28, quotes from Miller's 1931 report, 226n4, 228n22.

43. Brooks, "Touch the Bottom and Lift," 98. Julia Miller remained in Oklahoma even after she married H. C. Ray in 1935 and after they had children. See the entry in the 1940 manuscript Census return for Harvey C. Ray, head of household, with his wife, Julia M. Ray (U.S. Census, 1940, Population Schedule, Langston, Okla.).

44. Mary L. Ray Death Certificate; Oskar Klotz, "Chronic Interstitial Nephritis and Arteriosclerosis," *American Journal of the Medical Sciences* 150, no. 6 (December 1915): 827–34.

45. The words Fannie Mae Boone used to eulogize Mary Ray appear in slightly different form in Rev. Abner C. Kirk, *History of the Churches of the Beaver Baptist Association from 1809–1860* (Pittsburgh, Pa.: W. S. Haven, 1860), 34: "GEORGE I. MILES was a native of Pennsylvania. He was one of four brothers, Baptist ministers. He was at one time agent of the P. B. S. Convention. He removed to the West, where he died. 'Go to the grave, at noon from labor cease, Rest on thy sheaves, thy harvest task is done; Come from the heat of battle, and in peace, Soldier go home, with thee the fight is won.'"

46. Mary L. Ray Death Certificate.

47. Public records identified to date provide four more years for Mary's birth: 1876 per the 1900 manuscript Census return; 1879 per the 1910 manuscript Census return; an implied birth year of 1889 per the 1920 manuscript Census return, given her age of thirty-one years; and, last, an implied birth year of 1898 per the 1930 manuscript Census return, given her age of thirty-two years. Obviously someone other than Mary could have provided her age to Census enumerators, but only a lack of knowledge, poor enumeration, or purposeful obfuscation explains the inconsistency of birth year and age over the years. Her death certificate stated a birth year of 1880 and her age in the mid-fifties, not the mid-thirties. Mary may have adjusted her birth year to be closer in age to the people she most associated with, and this continued as she met and then married a younger man (Harvey Cincinnatus Ray was born on February 2, 1889, and died on April 24, 1965). See "Services for H. C. Ray to Be Today." He is buried in Oakland-Fraternal Cemetery, Little Rock.

48. Hogan, "History," 139–40.

49. "Farm Demonstration Work," part of Ray's 1935 annual narrative report. H. C. Ray was retired by 1957 when his and Julia's third child, Gloria Ray, enrolled in Little Rock Central High School. See "Gloria Cecelia Ray Karlmark," in *Encyclopedia of Arkansas History and Culture*, http://www.encyclopediaofarkansas.net/encyclopedia/entry-detail.aspx?search=1&entryID=726.

Dr. Mamie Katherine Phipps Clark

(1917–1983)

American Psychologist and Arkansas Native

LORETTA N. MCGREGOR

❀ ❀ ❀

Dr. Mamie Phipps Clark was one of the earliest prominent black psychologists in the United States. She was the second black person to graduate with a Ph.D. in psychology from Columbia University; her husband, Kenneth Clark, was the first.[1] Mamie and Kenneth Clark's research contributed to the end of American apartheid when it was used in the historic 1954 *Brown v. Board of Education* Supreme Court decision that ended segregation in public schools.[2] Although Mamie Clark is relatively unknown by many Arkansans, her activism and her training as a psychologist was informed by her experiences in Arkansas and beyond.

Mamie Katherine Phipps was born in Hot Springs, Arkansas, in Garland County on October 18, 1917. Her father, Harold Hilton Phipps, a physician, was born in Saint Kitts, British West Indies, on April 20, 1882.[3] He migrated in 1904 to the United States where he later became corresponding secretary of the Arkansas State National Medical Association and involved in the Arkansas Republican Party.[4] Harold Phipps's medical practice was located at 417 Malvern Avenue in Hot Springs.[5] He was quite likely the only black physician available to African Americans for miles around. In 1920, approximately 1.5 percent of African Americans nationwide held professional positions. The majority of these were educators and clergy members. Black physicians were extremely rare in the early twentieth century.[6] Phipps thus occupied a very important role in Hot Springs's black community. It was not uncommon for black doctors to have an additional source of income, however. They were often underpaid because they served the poorest members of society. Many African American patients simply could not afford to pay for medical care. Thus Phipps operated the Pythian Hotel, the only resort and spa in Hot Springs open to African Americans.[7]

Mamie's mother, Katherine Florence Smith Phipps, a native Arkansan, was born in Hot Springs on April 20, 1892. She and Harold were married on May 4, 1915. Katie Phipps was a housewife and helped her husband manage the Pythian Hotel.[8] She was an active member of the Arkansas Association of Colored Women, founded in 1905, and was the organization's treasurer in the 1930s. Mamie Phipps was also involved in the association and served as president of its junior clubs.[9]

Mamie's older brother, Harold Hilton Phipps II, was born on February 18, 1916.[10] Their childhood was rather atypical for black children in the South during the early twentieth century. She recalled that she had enjoyed growing up in the small town of Hot Springs. The Phippses were very comfortable compared to most people who lived through the difficult years of the Depression. In fact, Mamie believed the Depression had helped strengthen her family ties. She remembered: "How can I tell you I had a happy childhood. I really did. I enjoyed everything. I enjoyed school. I loved school. I enjoyed recreation. I enjoyed the little traveling we did. I was very happy. I can't say it was impoverished; for me it was privileged. . . . it was a very privileged childhood."[11] The Phippses exposed their two children to art and culture. In 1934, for instance, the family traveled to Little Rock to see *The Green Pastures*, a play written in 1930 by Marc Connelly, which portrayed parts of the New Testament through the eyes of a young African American. The play was later adapted into a movie in 1936.[12] They also impressed on their children the benefits of obtaining an education, particularly for African Americans. Mamie attended public school in Hot Springs. She graduated from Langston High School on June 8, 1934, at the age of sixteen and then was strongly encouraged to attend college. Mamie later realized how limited her early education had been because she was legally required to attend segregated schools and its impact on her experiences in college. As she recalled, "I liked everything, and I was very good in math, and I decided to major in math when I went to college. . . . I loved it. The school was poor, and later I realized how much we didn't learn. For example, there was one point when I realized I had learned no English grammar—none. And I had learned no history. But those gaps, you weren't aware of when you were coming through high school. But you could look back and see that the school was very poor. There was hardly anything you really learned."[13]

In the 1930s, African Americans had limited options when it came to higher education. Two of the premier universities for African Americans during that time were Fisk University in Nashville, Tennessee, and Howard University in Washington, D.C. According to Mamie, "Both schools offered [me a] scholarship on merit, but there was more excitement about attending college in the nation's capital and traveling over one thousand miles to study!"[14] In the fall of 1934, Mamie Katherine Phipps left Hot Springs for Washington, D.C. This was not an easy trip for a young black woman at that time. Yet, Mamie was fortunate; her parents could afford to pay the fare for her to take the train to Washington, D.C. However, Dr. Phipps was afraid his young daughter might encounter difficulties traveling alone. He knew the terrors that could befall an unescorted young black woman, especially in the Jim Crow South. Unprotected and unsuspecting women could be abused, raped, exploited, or killed by white men with little or no interference from others.[15] So, he arranged for her to be escorted by a companion, and he purchased a sleeping compartment on the train for them. He instructed Mamie to stay in the room until she arrived at her destination. Mamie and her companion were not even allowed to open the window shades.[16] Phipps arranged for the porters on the train, whom he knew, to protect the pair and to ensure they were fed.[17]

Mamie arrived at Howard University on September 18, 1934.[18] She initially planned to major in mathematics and minor in physics. Her goal was to become a math teacher, but she soon became disenchanted. Clark recalled, "I had made A's in math, but [the head of the mathematics department] consistent[ly] gave me a C, for two semesters, and I just got depressed and discouraged, you know, and so my husband persuaded me, and it didn't take much work, to go into psychology."[19] Women, regardless of their race, were often discouraged from studying mathematics in college. As a result, few female students majored in the subject, and those who did received little or no support from their male peers and professors.

In her junior year, Mamie enrolled in an abnormal psychology course taught by Kenneth Bancroft Clark, an instructor of psychology at Howard. Kenneth had recently received a bachelor of science degree from the institution. He wanted to obtain a Ph.D. in psychology and was currently pursuing a master's degree.[20] Kenneth was a graduate student under the supervision of Dr. Francis Sumner, a Pine Bluff, Arkansas, native and the first African American to receive a Ph.D. in psychology from Clark University in Worcester, Massachusetts (1920).[21]

Kenneth Clark was born in the Panama Canal Zone in 1914 to Arthur and Miriam Hanson Clark. Clark's father had been born in Jamaica and worked as a supervisor for the United Fruit Company. When Kenneth was four, his parents divorced, and he moved with his mother and his two-year-old sister, Beulah, to New York City, where they grew up.[22] Miriam Clark supported Kenneth and his sister by working as a seamstress.

Mamie and Kenneth developed an almost immediate attraction to each other. Mamie also grew fond of the study of psychology. According to her, "my entrance into the professional discipline of psychology came through a close association with my future husband.... I listened when he said one day 'Why don't you take up psychology?'"[23] Kenneth introduced Mamie to Sumner, head of the psychology department, and Dr. Max Meenes, with whom she would later conduct research. Mamie noted, "They were warm, friendly, and eager to have me in their courses.... Kenneth Clark was delighted.... At that time neither one of us realized that in entering the field of psychology we would enjoy a lifetime of close, challenging, and professionally satisfying experiences."[24] Mamie and Kenneth's relationship grew as they exchanged many letters. Finally, on April 14, 1938, during her senior year in college, Mamie and Kenneth married.[25] That same year, Mamie was crowned queen of Howard University's annual May Day festival.[26] She also graduated magna cum laude from the university with a degree in psychology.[27]

Employment opportunities for educated black women were extremely limited in the 1930s and 1940s. Although Mamie Clark lived in the North, there were virtually no jobs in the field of psychology or in academia for black women. Even after completing her Ph.D., she found it difficult to gain adequate employment: "In the security of the almost completely segregated student body at Howard University, it did not occur to me to ask such questions as 'How will a Negro woman fare in the nearly all white male field of psychology?' 'How will a female psychologist manage to satisfy an interest in working with children in a northern society mainly offering services to white children?'"[28]

In the summer of 1938, Clark accepted employment as a secretary in the law office of Charles Hamilton Houston, a prominent D.C. attorney, a placement arranged by Howard University.[29] Houston's law office was frequented by individuals, such as Thurgood Marshall, who were involved in the civil rights movement. Clark described the office as a "hub" for the early planning stages of the civil rights cases that challenged the laws requiring or permitting racial segregation in the United States: "This opportunity to learn, not only about the plans for the eventual repeal of the *Plessy v. Ferguson* case but also to observe firsthand the 'giants' who were preparing these cases, made a deep impression on me."[30] Later, her graduate research would be influenced by the work of these civil rights giants and then used by them to challenge and eventually end legal segregation in the United States.

In the fall of 1938, Mamie Clark enrolled in Howard University's graduate program in psychology.[31] Kenneth had been accepted into Columbia University and was working on his doctorate in psychology and teaching at Queens College in New York.[32] At some point during this time, Kenneth met and befriended Gene and Ruth Hartley. The Hartleys were social psychologists at the City College of New York who conducted research on social issues, such as peace, prejudice, and other minority-related topics. Kenneth suggested to Mamie that she go to New York and talk to the Hartleys about their research because of her interest in child development. The Hartleys conducted developmental research and studied self-identification in nursery school children, using line drawings of black and white children. They were aware that they needed to expand their studies to include more black children in their samples. Therefore, they encouraged Mamie to pursue this line of research because she could help them with access to black nursery school children.

Before meeting the Hartleys, Mamie Clark had visited a predominantly African American nursery school in Washington, D.C., and conducted research with the children. She adapted the Hartleys' approach for her study, which ultimately became her master's thesis, "The Development or Consciousness of Self in Negro Pre-School Children."[33] In 1939, Mamie received her master of arts in psychology from Howard University.[34] Later that year, she and her husband published a revised version of her findings in the *Journal of Social Psychology*.[35]

In 1940, Mamie and Kenneth Clark received a fellowship from the Rosenwald Fund to continue their research.[36] The fund was established in 1917 by Julius Rosenwald, a successful Jewish businessman and a co-owner of Sears, Roebuck and Company. Rosenwald was interested in social issues, particularly those related to the education of African Americans. He created his fund to "advance the lives of Black Americans and to improve race relations."[37] The fund initially focused on building schools in southern black communities. However, in 1928, its focus expanded to granting fellowships to promising black graduate students pursuing professional careers.[38]

Based on her work with the Hartleys, the Clarks' proposal to the Rosenwald Fund outlined a plan to expand her previous research on black school-age children. They developed newer versions of a coloring test and a doll test to use with black children. The Hartleys had originally developed both of these research tools, and the Clarks used the dolls to explore the subject of racial self-consciousness in black children. They were awarded a $1,500 fellowship, which allowed Mamie to enter Columbia University's Ph.D. program in psychology, where her husband was already a student. As Mamie Clark recalled, "My husband, Kenneth Clark, shared my interest and excitement in this research.... While my husband gathered research data in selected northern and southern states, I completed the first year toward the doctoral degree at Columbia University and took care of our first child Katherine Miriam Clark, who was born in 1940."[39] Kenneth completed his studies and graduated with his doctorate in the same year.[40] Their extraordinary, groundbreaking work was supported by the Rosenwald Fund for an additional two years.

Mamie Clark was the only woman of color in her classes at Columbia University. However, the adventurous young woman from Arkansas noted, "This did not pose a problem for me, in retrospect I never anticipated that it would."[41] Yet, she encountered racism and sexism while at the university. Clark's dissertation advisor, Dr. Henry Garrett, supported her research, but he could not imagine a black woman being successful in a white, male-dominated field. In her final year of study, he commented to Clark, "You are, of course, going back home to teach?" This professor had clearly underestimated her drive and determination. As she recalled, "It always amused me that he saw my advanced training in psychology as preparation for a career of teaching black high school students in the south."[42] Clark graduated from Columbia University with a Ph.D. in psychology in 1943, and in that same year gave birth to their second child, Hilton Bancroft Clark.[43]

After completing her doctorate, Mamie Clark sought full-time employment. In 1942, Kenneth had obtained a university appointment at City College in New York. However, employment opportunities were not readily available for educated black women. In light of this, Mamie sought work as a researcher. She was first hired by the American Public Health Association, where she analyzed data gathered on nurses throughout the country. According to Clark, "I was the only black person there. It was a humiliating and distasteful first employment experience, but I stayed for one year to gain the benefit of experience in this type of psychological research."[44] In 1944, she taught psychology and a class called Health for the Citizens at the George Washington Carver School in Harlem.[45] Clark then worked as a research psychologist for the U.S. Armed Forces Institute and the New York Examination Center in the Teachers College at Columbia University. However, in 1946 she secured a position at the Riverdale Home for Children, where she conducted psychological testing on homeless black girls. While working at Riverdale, Clark realized that black children in New York City desperately needed psychological services. The city provided psychological and psychiatric services for white children through a network of "well established sectarian agencies." However, minority children did not have access to such services.[46] After more than a year of lobbying the state of New York for psychological services for children in Harlem, with no success, Mamie and Kenneth decided to establish their own agency. Mamie noted: "The need for such services was so great that my husband and I decided to try to persuade some social service in Harlem to include psychological services for minority children. . . . [The] reaction on the part of the existing agencies [was] so frustrating that my husband and I finally made the decision to establish the services ourselves."[47]

The Clarks were encouraged by friends and family to start their own business but needed financial assistance to make their dream a reality. Mamie's father, Harold Phipps, loaned them $936, which allowed them to rent office space in the basement of the Paul Dunbar apartment complex in the northern section of Harlem in February 1946. They initially named their business the Northside Testing and Consultation Center but in 1947 renamed the facility the Northside Center for Child Development (NCCD).[48] This was the first center to offer full psychiatric, psychological, and casework services to black children and families in Harlem.[49] The NCCD established a board of directors that included public figures in the black community, representatives from the Rosenwald Fund, and philanthropic Jewish leaders.[50]

The NCCD's primary objective was to provide psychological and educational services to minority children and to help their parents cope with the pressures of racism, discrimination, and economic privation. Its goals were informed by the Clarks' research on the negative effects of racial discrimination and social inequities on personality development.[51] Mamie Clark, the NCCD's executive director, envisioned an empowering environment: "Unhappy children and children burdened with emotional problems are deprived of an opportunity to develop their maximum abilities no matter how high their intelligence, and in spite of the good intentions of the parents. Our basic operational principle is that there are no innately bad children: only children who are afraid, or starved for genuine affection and understanding. The center aims to give children in the Harlem area a better than chance opportunity to grow and develop to their fullest capacities for an integrated personality."[52]

Initially, Clark faced resistance from parents who feared that such services would stigmatize their children in the community. However, in time, the parents began to come to the center for services. Many of them were frustrated with the public schools, which often placed minority children in classes for "children of retarded mental development" (CRMD). Black parents argued that their children were often put in these classes without being cognitively assessed, which stigmatized them and eroded their self-esteem.[53]

The Clarks and their staff at the NCCD retested many children and found that the majority of the students had IQs above 70, the cutoff score used for the placement of students into the CRMD classes.[54] After they effectively helped many children and their parents in the New York schools, the NCCD's psychological and psychiatric services became well known and respected. Mamie Clark recalled, "As a result of word-of-mouth promotion and considerable newspaper publicity, a large number of parents brought their children to the Northside Center for psychological testing; and most of these children were subsequently able to return to normal class[es]."⁵⁵ The NCCD also received a $10,000 federal grant under the National Mental Health Act (passed in 1946), which aided their work among Harlem's children.⁵⁶

In the 1950s African Americans intensified their demands for equality throughout the United States.⁵⁷ The Clarks became involved in a lawsuit that would forever change U.S. history. In 1951, the Clarks again encountered Mamie's former advisor, Henry Garrett, this time in a federal courtroom where a Virginia school desegregation case was being tried. The Clarks testified against Garrett in *Davis v. School Board of Prince Edward County* (1952); he opposed school desegregation on the grounds that black children and white children had different talents and abilities and thus needed to be trained in different environments. In other words, Garrett supported "separate but equal" environments for blacks and whites. Mamie Clark battled her former advisor using data she had collected under his supervision. The major findings of her research were that "Negro children became aware of their racial identity about the age of three years; simultaneously, they acquire a negative self-image. Our findings established the fact that self-identification in these children was determined by the larger society's negative and rejecting definition of them."⁵⁸

In September 1952, Kenneth Clark, Isidor Chein, and Stuart Cook wrote "The Effects of Segregation and the Consequences of Desegregation: A Social Science Statement."⁵⁹ The study had been commissioned by the NAACP Legal Defense Fund attorney Robert Carter for use in court to challenge segregation. "The document reviewed the body of social psychological research on the effects of segregation and its role in maintaining prejudice as well as work on the potential effects of desegregation."⁶⁰ The final document, signed by thirty-two prominent social psychologists, including Mamie and Kenneth Clark, highlighted the significance of their research and that of other social psychologists on the self-identification of black children, and was used in desegregation cases in Washington, D.C., Delaware, Kansas, South Carolina, and Virginia. These cases laid the groundwork for the *Brown v. Board of Education of Topeka* Supreme Court case, where Thurgood Marshall successfully used the document in his arguments against segregation in schools, ultimately resulting in the dismantling of legally sanctioned segregation in America on May 17, 1954, when the Court's decision was announced. It was the evolution of the Clarks' early research that led to victory in this case.⁶¹

For many years, Dr. Mamie Phipps Clark was considered Dr. Kenneth Clark's research assistant. In each of their coauthored articles, Kenneth's name appears first. However, this was thought to be necessary given the academic world's view of female researchers. Higher education and science were considered a man's world. Many professional, educated women were marginalized and their accomplishments ignored because of their gender. Kenneth Clark, however, insisted that he always informed people that his wife was the driving force behind their research.⁶²

Mamie and Kenneth Clark built a life for themselves first in Washington, D.C., and then in New York. They lived in Hastings-on-Hudson, a predominantly white community in New York's Westchester County where they were one of two black families. The house was a large fieldstone and wood building with a library and a greenhouse because Mamie loved to garden.⁶³ They maintained strong ties with family and friends in the South, visited Arkansas often, and had a tangential involvement with school desegregation in Little Rock. Although the Clarks helped strike down the concept of "separate but equal" schools for black and white children in 1952, the battle for desegregation continued to rage in the southern states well after the 1954 *Brown* decision declared segregated schools unconstitutional.

Arkansas became a battleground in the fight against segregation, and the Clarks became involved in 1957 when the Little Rock school board decided to implement the Supreme Court's ruling. Nine black students were selected to integrate Central High School, but the Little Rock Nine were harassed daily by white students. Among the nine students was a sixteen-year-old named Minnijean Brown. Minnijean was outgoing, outspoken, lively, and in her own words "didn't fit anybody's stereotype of who a young black woman was supposed to be."⁶⁴ After nearly three months of constant harassment, Minnijean became exasperated. One afternoon, when several white students attempted to block her way in the cafeteria, she "accidentally" dropped her tray, allowing chili to splatter on a white boy standing nearby. She was expelled for the incident. This was the same year that Mamie was chosen Mother of the Year by the Q-Ives, a group of wives of members of Omega Psi Phi fraternity in Brooklyn, New York.⁶⁵ Receiving such an honor was surely prescient.

After Minnijean's expulsion from Central High School, she received death threats and her family feared for her life. Kenneth Clark traveled to Little Rock and spoke with the teenager and her family. As Minnijean recalled, "When I got expelled from Central, Kenneth came to Little Rock and said 'New Lincoln [School] says she can come there.'"⁶⁶ Although the Clarks had two children of their own and a very busy life as community activists and professionals, they took her in. Minnijean Brown moved to New York and became a part of Kenneth and Mamie Clark's family. She graduated from New Lincoln in 1959.⁶⁷

Although Mamie Clark was busy with her family, her work at the Northside Center, and her research, she found time for civic engagement at the national and local levels. In the 1960s, Clark was appointed to serve on the Office of Economic Opportunity's National Headstart Planning Committee and was among those who protested when Mississippi was disproportionately impacted by cuts to its programs.[68] In 1967, she chaired Liaison, a group of black women volunteers in New York who raised money to help African Americans in Sunflower County, Mississippi, in their first campaigns for political office.[69] Clark was a Harlem Youth Opportunities Unlimited board member and also served on the governing boards of the American Broadcasting Company, the Museum of Modern Art, Mount Sinai Medical Center, Columbia University's Teachers College, Haverford College, and the New York Public Library.[70] This was all in addition to heading the NCCD and continuing to speak out about racism's impact on children's development as her own particular form of activism. Indeed, in 1968, she asserted, "The healthier the home, the easier it is to combat race prejudice when it does come up. It's a day to day job. If the parents' attitude is frank and open and without race prejudice, this is what the child is going to learn."[71]

Clark's activism netted her important awards, recognition, and new opportunities. She received the American Association of University Women's achievement award for "her admirable service to the field of mental health" in 1973. News of this honor made its way back home to Arkansas newspapers.[72] In 1974, the NCCD relocated to Schomburg Tower in Harlem. The new multilevel facility provided much-needed additional space and allowed the Clarks to serve even more families and children with psychological needs.[73] Mamie remained its executive director until 1979.[74]

In 1976, Mamie, Kenneth, and their son Hilton established a consulting firm, Clark, Phipps, Clark, and Harris, Incorporated, to assist businesses, government agencies, and educational institutions in need of counseling on human and race relations and on affirmative action programs.[75] And the awards continued to come. In 1981, Mamie Clark and television anchor Mike Wallace received honorary doctorates from Mercy College and Long Island University. Clark's doctor of science degree was for her services to the "mental wellbeing of America."[76]

Dr. Mamie Phipps Clark died of lung cancer in her home in Hastings-on-Hudson, New York, on August 11, 1983.[77] She was sixty-five years old. In October of that year, she was posthumously recognized by the National Coalition of 100 Black Women with the Candace Award for extraordinary achievement.[78] Kenneth died on May 1, 2005, at the age of ninety. The Clarks are both buried in Hastings-on-Hudson.[79]

Although she grew up in Hot Springs, Arkansas, during the height of southern segregation, Mamie Phipps Clark's family's middle-class status insulated her from the worst of the racial indignities many southern black people suffered. Yet, she was keenly aware of the inequalities in black and white lives in the South and in Arkansas in particular. These observations impacted her research and compelled her to document the psychological effects of segregation on African American children. Her contributions ultimately proved critical to challenging legal segregation in American public education and society. A trained psychologist, Clark's research served her well as a community and civil rights activist. This native of Arkansas, who attended segregated schools in her youth, well understood the significance of her work as a means to provide equal and fair services to all children regardless of their location, race, or economic status.

NOTES

1. Alexandra Rutherford, "Mamie Phipps Clark, Developmental Psychologist: Starting from Strengths," in *Portraits of Pioneers in Developmental Psychology*, ed. D. A. Dewsbury, W. E. Pickren, and M. Wertheimer (New York: Psychology Press, 2012), 266.

2. Brown v. Board of Education of Topeka, 347 U.S. 483 (1954).

3. "Negro Physicians Elect," *Daily Arkansas Gazette*, May 31, 1913, 2.

4. U.S. Census, 1920, Population Schedule, Hot Springs Township, Garland County, Ark.; "Negro Physicians Elect," 2.

5. Shirley Abbott, "Mamie Phipps Clark, a Hot Springs Woman who 'Overcame the Odds,'" *Record 2006: Garland County Historical Society* 47 (May 4, 2015): 15.

6. Shafali Lal, "Giving Children Security: Mamie Phipps Clark and the Racialization of Child Psychology," *American Psychologist* 57, no. 1 (January 2002): 20–28.

7. Thomas J. Ward Jr., *Black Physicians in the Jim Crow South* (Fayetteville: University of Arkansas Press. 2003), 136; "Health Your Best Asset," *Pittsburgh Courier*, July 1, 1939, 15.

8. Abbott, "Mamie Phipps Clark," 15; "Health Your Best Asset," 15.

9. "New Negro Federation Organized," *Daily Arkansas Gazette*, December 30, 1905, 7; "Arkansas Clubs Re-Elect Officers at Annual Meeting," *Pittsburgh Courier*, June 30, 1934, 8.

10. Harold Phipps II is listed as Harold Phipps Jr. in Census records. He became a well-known dentist in Pine Bluff, Arkansas.

11. Abbott, "Mamie Phipps Clark," 16.

12. "Hot Springs, Ark.," *Plaindealer* (Kansas City, Kans.), January 19, 1934, 3; "Green Pastures Travels on to New Triumphs," *Courier News* (Blytheville, Ark.), October 6, 1934, 3; "Hollywood," *Hope Star* (Hope, Ark.), March 18, 1936, 3.

13. Abbott, "Mamie Phipps Clark," 18.

14. Mamie Phipps Clark, *Mamie Phipps Clark*, ed. A. N. O'Connell and N. F. Russo (New York: Columbia University Press, 1983), 267.

15. Kim Lacy Rogers, *Life and Death in the Delta: African American Narratives of Violence, Resilience, and Social Change* (Gordonsville, Va.: Palgrave Macmillan, 2006), 41; Danielle McGuire, *At the Dark End of the Street: Black Women, Rape, and Resistance: A New History of the Civil Rights Movement from Rosa Parks to the Rise of Black Power* (New York: Vintage, 2011).

16. Abbott, "Mamie Phipps Clark," 18.

17. It is likely that Phipps hired Pullman porters to watch over Mamie and her companion. Pullman porters were African American men worked who worked as valets for the Pullman Company in sleeping cars on passenger trains all over the country from 1860 to 1969. They attended to the various needs of passengers.

18. Stephen N. Butler, "Mamie Katherine Phipps Clark," in *Encyclopedia of Arkansas History and Culture*, http://www.encyclopediaofarkansas.net/encyclopedia/entry-detail.aspx?search=1&entryID=2938.

19. Ed Edwin, interview of Dr. Mamie Clark, May 25, 1976, Columbia University Libraries Oral History Research Office, http://www.columbia.edu/cu/lweb/digital/collections/nny/clarkm/index.html.

20. Abbott, "Mamie Phipps Clark," 19.

21. Information about Francis Sumner can be found in Robert V. Guthrie, *Even the Rat Was White* (1976; repr., New York: Harper and Row, 2004).

22. "Mamie Katherine Phipps Clark," in *Encyclopedia of Arkansas History and Culture*, www.encyclopediaofarkansas.net /encyclopedia/entry-detail.aspx?search=1&entryID=2938.

23. Clark, *Mamie Phipps Clark*, 268.

24. Ibid.

25. Butler, "Mamie Katherine Phipps Clark," and others have speculated that Mamie and Kenneth actually eloped and were married before April 14, 1938, and that the second wedding occurred on this date.

26. "Howard U Queen Crowned before 500 Admirers," *Washington Tribune*, May 21, 1938, 1.

27. "Socially Speaking," *Pittsburgh Courier*, June 25, 1938, 6.

28. Ibid.

29. Clark, *Mamie Phipps Clark*, 268.

30. Plessy v. Ferguson, 163 U.S. 537 (1896); Clark, *Mamie Phipps Clark*, 268.

31. Guthrie, *Even the Rat*, 205.

32. Ibid., 190.

33. Clark, *Mamie Phipps Clark*, 269.

34. Rutherford, "Mamie Phipps Clark, Developmental Psychologist," 265.

35. Kenneth B. Clark and Mamie P. Clark, "The Development of Consciousness of Self and the Emergence of Racial Identification in Negro Preschool Children," *Journal of Social Psychology* 10 (1939): 591–99.

36. "Survey Shows 24 Have Received Masters in Psychology at H.U.," *New York Age*, March 8, 1941, 2; "68 Given Rosenwald Fund Scholarships," *New York Age*, May 4, 1940, 1.

37. Rutherford, "Mamie Phipps Clark, Developmental Psychologist," 269.

38. Alfred Perkins, "Welcome Consequences and Fulfilled Promise: Julius Rosenwald Fellows and Brown v. Board of Education," *Journal of Negro Education* 72, no. 3 (Summer 2003): 344–56.

39. Clark, *Mamie Phipps Clark*, 269.

40. Ibid., 269.

41. Ibid., 270.

42. Ibid.

43. Ibid.

44. Ibid., 271.

45. "Carver School Offers New, Practical Courses," *People's Voice* (New York), January 29, 1944, 15.

46. Clark, *Mamie Phipps Clark*, 272.

47. Ibid., 272.

48. Rutherford, "Mamie Phipps Clark, Developmental Psychologist," 274.

49. Clark, *Mamie Phipps Clark*, 273.

50. Butler, "Mamie Katherine Phipps Clark."

51. Rutherford, "Mamie Phipps Clark, Developmental Psychologist," 274.

52. "Kids Get a Break at North Side Center," *People's Voice* (New York), February 22, 1947, 14.

53. Clark, *Mamie Phipps Clark*, 273.
54. Kenneth B. Clark and Mamie Phipps Clark, "Report on Scientific Testing of Mentally Slow Children," *People's Voice* (New York), June 29, 1946, 21.
55. Clark, *Mamie Phipps Clark*, 273.
56. "Northside in Opening," *New York Age*, December 14, 1948, 12.
57. Thomas Brooks, *Walls, Come Tumbling Down: A History of the Civil Rights Movement, 1940–1970* (Englewood Cliffs, N.J.: Prentice Hall, 1974), 73.
58. Clark, *Mamie Phipps Clark*, 271.
59. Kenneth Clark, Isidor Chein, and Stuart Cook, "The Effects of Segregation and the Consequences of Desegregation: A Social Science Statement in the Brown v. Board of Education of Topeka Supreme Court Case," *American Psychologist* 59, no. 6 (September 1952): 495–501. This article was the first time that social science research was used in a Supreme Court decision.
60. Rutherford, "Mamie Phipps Clark, Developmental Psychologist," 272.
61. Mamie and Kenneth Clark's groundbreaking research has been cited and replicated in multiple sources.
62. Kenneth B. Clark, telephone communication with author, April 1992.
63. Bryant Rollins, "The Clarks," *Essence*, June 1, 1976, 3.
64. Elizabeth Jacoway, "Not Anger but Sorrow: Minnijean Brown Trickey Remembers the Little Rock Crisis," *Arkansas Historical Quarterly* 64, no. 1 (Spring 2005): 4.
65. "Dr. Mamie Clark to Be Honored by Q-Ives," *New York Age*, May 4, 1957, 18.
66. Jacoway, "Not Anger," 12. The New Lincoln School, founded in 1917 by the Rockefeller Fund, was a private, coeducational school in New York City.
67. "Minnijean Brown Trickey: Civil Rights Activist Who Integrated Central High School in 1957," National Women's History Project, http://www.nwhp.org/whm/trickey_bio.php (accessed August, 8, 2013).
68. "Must Mississippi's Children Abandon Hope?" *Clarion-Ledger* (Jackson, Miss.), March 28, 1968, 15.
69. "Toki Types," *Pittsburgh Courier*, March 4, 1967, 11.
70. "Dr. Mamie Clark Recipient of AAUW Achievement Award," *Fairbanks Daily News-Miner* (Fairbanks, Alaska), September 19, 1973, 7; "First Black Woman Nominated by ABC," *Los Angeles Times*, April 24, 1973, 75.
71. "Race Prejudice Fight Parents' Steady Job," *Troy Record* (Troy, N.Y.), July 26, 1968, 4.
72. "Dr. Mamie Clark Recipient," 7; "Achievement Award Presented by AAUW," *Northwest Arkansas Times*, June 20, 1973, 3.
73. Rutherford, "Mamie Phipps Clark, Developmental Psychologist," 275.
74. Clark, *Mamie Phipps Clark*, 72.
75. "New Consulting Firm Set Up in New York," *Pittsburgh Courier*, March 13, 1976, 2.
76. "Wallace Gives Grads Encouraging Words," *Journal News* (White Plains, N.Y.), May 18, 1981, 10.
77. "Ex-Leader of Children's Center Dr. Mamie P. Clark Dies at 65," *Poughkeepsie Journal*, August 13, 1983, 8.
78. "Awards Honor 11 Black Women," *Town Talk* (Alexandria, La.), October 16, 1983, 65.
79. Abbott, "Mamie Phipps Clark," 20.

Mary Sybil Kidd Maynard Lewis
(1897–1941)

"I'm from the South and I've Got Plenty of Rhythm"

MICHAEL B. DOUGAN

Mary Sybil Kidd Maynard Lewis was an internationally known Broadway star, opera singer, and radio performer. During her short and tragic life during the Jazz Age and the Great Depression, Lewis broke new ground for generations of classical music performers. Her legacy endures due to the extensive recordings she made from 1924 to 1937. Lewis's ties to Arkansas remained strong throughout her career. Sorting out the facts of her very complex life has not been easy, but she was and remains for Arkansans "our Mary."

The woman known to the world as Mary Lewis was certainly not the first celebrity to create an artificial persona, but while she deliberately rewrote significant parts of her life, some elements were unknown even to her. One example is her birthday. Although Mary claimed to have been born in 1900 and later confessed to not knowing the real date of her birth, baptismal records at St. Mary's Catholic Church in Hot Springs, Arkansas, give January 29, 1897, as her birth date and August 29 of the same year for her christening.[1]

Mary's parents were Charles Kidd and Hattie Lewis. Charles reportedly moved to Hot Springs from Chicago. Hattie had possibly been born in Kentucky. Mary's middle name, Sybil, came from her maternal grandmother. Her brother, Joe, was born in 1899. Charles died that same year, and the family fell on hard times. Apparently Mary's mother worked as a domestic, moving her children first to Little Rock and then to Dallas, Texas. Hattie, who was likely unable to care for her children, sent them to an orphanage where Mary's golden curls were cut off and kerosene was rubbed into her head to kill lice. Both children ran away from the orphanage. Joe escaped first and apparently went to live in Chicago with some of his father's kin; Mary was rescued by her mother but then was sent to a family that kept her as a servant and locked her in a rat-infested basement. Mary ran away again one Sunday morning and temporarily reunited with her mother. By age six she was living on the streets of Dallas, where she "danced to hurdy-gurdies" and sang songs. One of her jobs was fetching beer for a grocer's wife who thought that job unsuitable for her own children. Mary's reward for that task was a rotten banana. As a consequence, she developed a lifelong antipathy to bananas. At some point, Mary's mother married Ed Maynard, and Mary took her new stepfather's last name. It seems that Hattie was again unable to care for her daughter, leaving Mary to fend for herself.[2] Destitute, Mary followed a childhood friend to the Settlement Sunday School, which was affiliated with the Hope Methodist Church in Dallas, but she was afraid to attend the service in her poorly dressed and malnourished state. One Sunday evening she fell asleep on the church steps only to be awakened when the preacher's wife, Anna Fitch, stepped on her. After hearing Mary's story, Anna offered her a clean dress in exchange for coming to church. Mary accepted, and that dress, which symbolized her first step out of the slums, became sacred to her. It is still in the Fitch family's possession.[3]

In 1905, Mary was permanently taken in by Anna and her sixty-year-old Methodist pastor husband, the Reverend William S. Fitch. There were no adoption papers or legal agreements. When Mary went to live with the Fitches their first task was to eradicate her head lice. The second was to treat her pernicious anemia. Mary was in such poor physical health that Anna, a former schoolteacher, taught her at home; she began by erasing, as Mary put it, "the patois common to the slums." And she "taught me the wisdom of self-control and of curbing my impulsive temper." Anna was a strict disciplinarian, and Mary was prohibited from dancing and singing the "boisterous songs, heady with the beat of ragtime" that she knew from the streets. Mary recalled that Anna "took me into her household as her own daughter, a child without health, doomed to die before she was ten, without loveliness, without manners or training. In her tight-lipped, relentless way she loved me."[4]

The Fitches also gave Mary, who already had demonstrated musical talent, piano and violin lessons. Soon Mary was given a song, "Jesus Wants Me for a Sunbeam," and was taught to pronounce it syllable by syllable and then word by word even before she could sing it. "I have never ceased to be grateful to her," Mary said later about Anna's rigorous vocal instruction.[5]

Methodist churches were notorious for moving their ministers, and in 1906 Fitch was sent to Eureka Springs, Arkansas, a noted spa town in the Ozarks. There, Mary sang "The Banner and the Beauty of Glory" at a patriotic service and began singing a new song in church each Sunday. Soon Fitch was transferred to Little Rock and then to Judsonia in White County. The town's history book, *That's Judsonia*, described Mary as "the very plain little eight-year-old girl who had sung her solos so frequently in the local Methodist Church." The church sported an orchestra and a much higher quality of music than was common in small towns. Residents later recalled that local audiences "did not receive her efforts with as much appreciation as did those of later years." Fitch, himself a musician and composer, in his "desire for perfection" robbed Mary of musical expressiveness so that her singing "was sometimes almost mechanical." However, a traveling salesman recognized her talent and was heard to remark, "I tell you she's going places."[6]

Around 1908 Mary was invited to sing for pay at a benefit concert in Little Rock. For this occasion Anna taught her "The Holy City," a rather difficult piece for a child her age. This event was a turning point for Mary, who quickly lost her desire to become either a Methodist deaconess or a foreign missionary. This, according to Mary, was her "first touch of being a prima donna."[7]

Meanwhile, age had caught up with William Fitch, and he was moved to Little Rock to serve the mission church. Although the family had only William's small pension and no savings, an inheritance from Anna's father allowed them to build a house in the new Hillcrest addition to Pulaski Heights. The Pulaski Heights development was the work of H. F. (Henry Franklin) Auten, the Methodist, music-loving deacon who earlier had arranged for Mary's Little Rock debut. In addition to being a real estate developer, Auten was also a high-ranking Republican and in 1898 had been the party's unsuccessful candidate for governor.[8]

Built in the Craftsman style common in Hillcrest, the house was Anna's home until her death in 1936. A newspaper account of a "house warming" called it their "first real home." Yet things were not going well. William became increasingly ill, and Mary, exposed again to an urban space, was intrigued by the popular culture that Anna was still determined to root or rather whip out of her. Like many children, she rebelled by running away.[9]

Mary got no farther than the home of H. F. and Carrie Auten, who had two sons near her age as well as an adopted son. For three years, 1912–1915, she lived with the Autens. Mary attended Little Rock High School (renamed Central in 1953), the first time she had ever sat in a classroom, and she took music lessons from Alice Henniger, a well-known figure in Little Rock's cultural life. Mary even started teaching, took lessons on the pipe organ, and became the organist at the Second Baptist Church. "All in all," she recalled, "there is no saying that my musical foundation was not a sound one!" Her public appearances were frequent and included singing for President Theodore Roosevelt when he visited Little Rock in 1905.[10]

In 1915 Mary married her high school sweetheart, J. Keene Lewis, at the Second Baptist Church, and Auten gave the newlyweds a house in Pulaski Heights. Auten died on May 24, 1918, and William Fitch followed on September 28. Perhaps these two losses prompted her to attempt to establish her own identity as an artist. On Armistice Day, November 11, 1918, Mary induced her husband to take her to Chicago where she hoped to find her long-lost brother. Then, just before Christmas, she departed with a traveling troupe. Keene formally divorced Mary in 1920 with her promise to keep his name out of her publicity.[11]

Little evidence exists to confirm Mary Lewis's account of her years on the road. However, she did work at Tait's at the Beach in San Francisco, a famous restaurant at that time. Her big break came when she met Fanchon and Marco Wolff, a nationally known brother and sister show business team. It was Fanchon who solved Lewis's costuming problem; given her impoverished childhood, her growth might have been stunted. However, Lewis was much taller than most of the other girls on stage. "I felt like an elephant among them," she admitted. Instead of the religious and classical material she previously had sung, Mary undertook the popular songs of the Jazz Age, belting them out until she lost her voice and had to "talk" them. "Manny o' Mine" was an audience favorite.[12]

Her next move involved signing with the famed comedy filmmaker Al Christie. Lewis appeared in a number of now presumably lost films, including *The Ugly Duckling*. One film from this period that has been recovered is *A Bashful Bigamist* (1920). Mary saved her money and moved to New York in June 1920. From this point on her scrapbooks and national newspaper coverage provide documentation for her national and international career.[13]

Her first New York job was with the *Greenwich Village Follies* of 1920, which was directed by John Murray Anderson.[14] At first, Mary thought she was being slighted and rounded up another job, which she used as leverage; she soon became the company's prima donna, the star with the leading role and the best songs. Co-star Frank Crumit, who had already launched his recording career, suggested that Mary study with vocal coach William Thorner. She switched from the *Greenwich Village Follies* to the far more prestigious *Follies* produced by Florenz Ziegfeld so that she could spend more time in New York.[15] Ziegfeld reportedly considered her "the most beautiful prima donna he had ever engaged."[16]

The *Follies* of 1921 included stars such as Fanny Brice, W. C. Fields, and comedian Raymond Hitchcock with sets by Joseph Urban, who designed not only all the Ziegfeld shows but fifty-one productions for the Metropolitan Opera. Contributing composers included Jerome Kern, Victor Herbert, and Rudolf Friml. Meanwhile, Mary began lessons with Thorner, working on Puccini's *La Bohème* and studying Italian and French. The *Follies* of 1922 included Will Rogers and featured Mary Lewis in a costume spectacle, "Lace Land," created by Charles LeMaire, who later moved to Hollywood, costumed some three hundred films, and won four Academy Awards. However, his design for Lewis, a lace outfit painted weekly in radium that glowed in the dark when the lights were turned off, most likely cost Lewis her life. What she called "neuritis" and blamed on hard work was most likely the symptoms of radiation poisoning, a disease not formally recognized until 1945.[17]

Following the show's run, Lewis met Otto Hermann Kahn, a financier and a Metropolitan Opera patron, at a party.[18] Kahn convinced her to sing "some snatches" from *La Bohème* and followed that up by attending one of her lessons with Thorner. Then he arranged what turned out to be a nervous audition with the Metropolitan Opera's general manager, Giulio Gatti-Casazza, who decided that she had the voice but needed two years abroad to learn a repertoire and stagecraft. Leaving behind her mother, who had mysteriously reappeared a year earlier, Mary intended to rest on the Riviera and then proceed to Italy. In Paris at a performance of Puccini's *Tosca*, she met Russian soprano Maria Nikolaevna Kuznetsova, who introduced Lewis to her manager, Alexander Kahn—perhaps at that time and certainly in 1930 the European representative of the Wolfson Musical Bureau, one of the largest artist representative groups in the United States. Lewis was given a contract following a successful audition. While studying in Paris, she was told that if she learned the role of Marguerite in Gounod's *Faust* in three weeks, she could make her debut in Vienna. Billed as a star of the Paris Opera, she trod the stage of the Vienna Volksoper for the first time on October 19, 1923, with an all-star cast directed by Felix Weingartner. While Traian Grozavescu, Emmanuel List, and Viorica Ursuleac sang in German, Mary Lewis sang in the original French. Lewis was wise in the ways of publicity, for while this was essentially a routine performance in Vienna, it became a headline story back in America.[19]

Following performances at Bratislava and Monte Carlo, Mary auditioned successfully for the British National Opera Company. Her unannounced debut came in Offenbach's *The Tales of Hoffmann* when the famed English soprano Maggie Teyte became indisposed. Lewis's success in the role led to more performances. Of particular note was the world premiere of Ralph Vaughan Williams's folk opera *Hugh the Drover* on July 14, 1924. The record company His Master's Voice recorded extended excerpts, and Mary Lewis appeared on eight of the ten tracks of "one of the great pioneering records of British music." Lewis later recorded eleven arias for the company, but only four were published. Neither the *Hugh the Drover* recordings nor any from the second session were ever issued in America.[20]

Franz Lehár, the operetta composer, had set his eyes on Mary, and she finally agreed to sing his most famous composition, to be performed in Paris as *La Veuve Joyeuse* (*The Merry Widow*). Following this run, she auditioned for the Chicago Civic Opera Company but also was offered the lead role in Sigmund Romberg's new musical, *Princess Flavia* (1925). Mary was caught up in a maze of conflicting offers and contracts until the Metropolitan Opera signed her on November 5, 1925. Her warm-up consisted of appearing in a variety of venues and on radio. Along the way, she picked up Elmer Zoller as her accompanist; he would remain with her throughout her career.[21]

The Mary Lewis story hit U.S. newspapers even before her Metropolitan Opera debut. Part of the celebration of American exceptionalism was the argument that Americans could learn at home and sing grand opera as well as or better than imported Europeans. In January 1924, the *Atlanta Constitution* under the title "What She Won by Never Having Any Fun" had quoted extensively Mary's coach, William Thorner, who not only offered testimonials on Lewis's successes but also claimed that in America "hundreds of girls are neglecting their voices" who could shine on stage.[22]

Mary Lewis debuted as Mimi in *La Bohème* on January 26, 1926. The audience loved her performance and afterward covered the stage with violets. It was, an unidentified newspaper reported, "the climax of a romantic career seldom paralleled in American musical history." New York at that time boasted a cadre of veteran music critics, and their reviews were mixed, with the great W. J. (William James) Henderson finding her merely "credible." Nevertheless, the Victor Company had had Mary in the studio the month before, and she remained an active recording artist until 1928. Her studio recordings were divided between songs, including a highly regarded version of "Dixie," and arias, of which the "Te souvient-il du lumineux voyage" from Massenet's *Thaïs*, better known as *The Meditation*, became her best seller.[23] Mary Lewis did not become an operatic workhorse, but the prestige associated with the opera house opened concert doors everywhere in the United States.

On March 26, 1926, Mary returned home to Arkansas for a concert; "Mary Lewis Given Greatest Welcome State Ever Knew" was the headline in the *Arkansas Democrat*. She had already performed in Hot Springs, but the Little Rock concert was special. Welcomed by Governor Tom Terral and presented with a golden Key to the City by the mayor, she also visited her eighty-year-old foster mother, Anna Fitch. The concert that evening was as much an emotional event as a musical one. After Lewis departed the next day, Terral sent a letter to banker and opera financier Otto Kahn praising Mary and observing, "God has been good to her in that she has been blessed with a voice that seemed was handed to her by an angel of God." Kahn replied by also praising Mary and expressing his "faith in young American talent" who could then "serve the cause of art in America."[24] Despite these successes, things were about to head downhill.

Vitaphone, which had developed sound for motion pictures, quickly signed Mary Lewis along with Americans John Charles Thomas, Charles Hackett, and Rin Tin Tin, a well-known dog. In 1927, Lewis appeared in *Stars of Vitaphone*, singing a program entitled "Way Down South." The numbers included "Swing Along," "Dixie," and "Carry Me Back to Old Virginny." More ambitious was the filming of *The Tales of Hoffmann* in the old Manhattan Opera House. But according to Vitaphone, Mary got drunk, and her work was unusable. Vitaphone sued Lewis and the music director in a case that garnered national headlines. Henceforth, alcohol began to affect Lewis's work. Still, the company went ahead with a biographical film, *The Story of Mary Lewis*, in 1928.[25]

Meanwhile, Mary had fallen in love. On April 15, 1927, she married German baritone Michael Bohnen in a surprise wedding officiated by New York City mayor Jimmy Walker. Bohnen, who had sung in 21 roles at the Metropolitan Opera and racked up 174 performances, was temperamentally not the ideal husband. But as she walked out on her work engagements and sailed with him to Germany shortly after their marriage, Mary said she was "too much in love to be separated yet." In Berlin, she sang with Bohnen in *Faust* (*Margarethe*), along with Richard Tauber and Heinrich Schlusnus, both noted stars. When Lewis returned to America to make her Chicago debut, Bohnen canceled his engagements and joined her. In October she was again in Little Rock, singing at the new high school. She sang with Bohnen at the Metropolitan Opera in *I Pagliacci* on February 13, 1928. That summer Lewis again canceled her engagements and headed back to Europe. Her managers, threatened with suits for breach of contract, began cutting their ties with the unreliable Mary. Back in the United States at the Metropolitan Opera in 1929 she sang only Marguerite in *Faust*, once with Bohnen and twice with the great Russian bass Feodor Chaliapin. Meanwhile, Bohnen had transferred his attentions to the notorious young dancer La Jana, and Mary filed for a divorce. Both the marriage and the divorce were contentious; after Mary's death, Bohnen told his side of the events to *Stern*, a German tabloid, in 1953–1954. English musicologist James F. E. Dennis opined that Lewis's drinking problems were related to her disastrous marriage to Bohnen.[26]

Free of Bohnen, Mary Lewis recorded on film a verbal contract to make movies in Hollywood with Pathé, a French production company. There were to be two films, one of which would recount her life. As the Depression deepened and audiences thinned, the movie industry was in crisis due to too many musical "talkie" films. Lewis's films were canceled, and Mary sued for breach of contract. Pathé claimed she had violated the "morals clause" and cited some unspecified incident. One known episode was when she collapsed or was hauled off the stage during a Sunday evening national radio show. There was a trip to Hot Springs where she had a tumor the size of a golf ball removed from her uterus. Lewis further suffered from the repercussions of her divorce. She told her mother she had only $180 left, having lost $40,000 when she ran off with Bohnen. Her marriage had been a "bad spell," but "I stick my chin out and say *I will*." Disasters, however, continued. Her last complete role at the Metropolitan Opera was Micaela in Bizet's *Carmen*, and one audience member recalled that she was "drunk as a lord, staggering all over the stage." Her opera career was over.[27]

Having burned her bridges in America, Lewis returned to Europe in hopes of finding work, but, she wrote, "I feel never sure of anything now."[28] Luckily, she landed the soprano lead in a French-language version of Emmerich Kalman's *Gräfin Mariza*. But her European career soon ended, and in September 1931 it was announced that she had married Standard Oil executive Robert L. Hague. The manager of the marine division and a Broadway dandy, Hague had already been married three times.[29]

As the Depression deepened under President Herbert Hoover, Hague and his wife seem to have lived quietly in their penthouse at the Ritz Hotel when not in Europe. Lewis's next public appearance was not until June 7, 1933, on the radio, and at its conclusion she was rushed to the hospital for an emergency appendectomy. In August, when she was asked about her new pink chiffon garden party hat, Mary pointed out that it was designed and made in the United States: "Surely that is good for American business." She was quite likely referring to purchasing American-made products to stimulate the economy during the difficult Depression years.[30]

Although her opera career had ended, Mary was not through singing. In the fall of 1933 she and Irish tenor John McCormack sang at a fundraiser for an African American mission church, St. Benedict the Moor in New York City.[31] On May 18, 1934, she gave a recital at Town Hall that critic F. D. Perkins of the *Herald Tribune* called "a virtual re-debut," for instead of an opera singer's temporary, money-making foray, she "entered auspiciously a new phase which could lead to artistic attainments beyond those of her Metropolitan days." Her recital included German lieder by Brahms, Strauss, Wolf, and Schreker; French chansons by Satie, Duparc, Saint-Saëns, and Debussy; and songs by Chopin and American John Alden Carpenter.[32]

Yet little work followed except a few brief appearances. At one point she was reported to have "a violent dislike to the publicity spotlight," and in 1935 there was a rumor that she had been given "permission" by her husband to resume her work. Instead, more benefit performances followed. On November 17, 1935, for example, she sang "Eili, Eili," the famous Yiddish lament, for the Brooklyn Federation of Jewish Charities. Her subsequent recording, possibly the only one by a non-Jew, is uniquely moving and ranks as one of the outstanding performances of the century. Another piece in her repertoire was "My Man's Gone Now," first sung with *Porgy and Bess* composer George Gershwin at the piano. She and her husband were on the first commercial flight of the German dirigible the *Hindenburg* on its maiden voyage from New York to Germany one year before the blimp burned up at the Lakehurst Air Station.[33]

Apparently, these years also included continued bouts of ill health. Hoping to break this pattern, Lewis returned to Arkansas in 1936 for the state's centennial: "It's after all, home, you know." She stopped in Benton (Saline County), Hot Springs, and Little Rock, where she visited her ailing foster mother.[34]

Her final work consisted of contributing to the National Broadcasting Company's Thesaurus set. These sixteen-inch transcription discs were made for radio station distribution and were not for sale. According to producer Robert B. Stone, Lewis's voice was "badly worn at the top" but still good in the middle register. Three sessions were scheduled, but at the third she arrived intoxicated and walked out of the studio.[35]

Mary's marriage to Hague also collapsed during this time, and she went to Europe to recover. After concerts in Germany and France, she sang in Queen's Hall in London with Gerald Moore, the best-known accompanist of the twentieth century, at the piano. Back in the United States, Robert Hague died from cirrhosis of the liver on March 8, 1939; his affairs were tangled, but he was still legally married to Mary. Unable to collect from the estate, Mary Lewis undertook one last tour to Puerto Rico but was stricken with a throat so swollen that she had to have a silver tube inserted to allow her to breathe. She never recovered. Her mother died on March 11, 1940, and Mary Lewis died on New Year's Day 1941. The press blamed a gallbladder ailment, but a more probable explanation is radiation poisoning. It was typical of the confusion of Mary's worlds that the first funeral service, a public one, was held in New York at St.

Matthew's Catholic Church, while the one at Second Baptist Church in Little Rock was for relatives and close friends. She was interred next to the mother who had so often abandoned her.[36]

Although United Press referred to Mary Lewis as one of the most publicized singers during her lifetime, following her death she was almost forgotten except for a few scholarly articles. Then Alice Fitch Zeman, who found among her great-grandmother's mementos the little dress that had propelled Mary Lewis from the slums to the stage of the Metropolitan Opera House, wrote a biography, *Mary Lewis: The Golden Haired Beauty with the Golden Voice*, which was published in 2001. Zeman had access to the Fitch family's scrapbooks as well as those kept by Lewis herself. In 2005 Marston Records, the premier classical music archival firm, received financial assistance from the Arkansas Arts Council and the National Endowment for the Arts to release a two-compact disc set containing forty-eight of her recordings, thus forever ensuring her place in musical history.

Her contemporary, soprano Jessica Dragonette, called Mary "a touching enigma, evidently bent on destroying herself, in spite of excelling gifts." Such an assessment, valid in its way, fails to take into account her undiagnosed medical condition. The last word came from an unknown Arkansas poet at the time of her interment:

> She has come home like a bird to its nest,
> Home, at last, for a long, long rest.[37]

Born in poverty, Mary Lewis left Arkansas as a young woman and became an international star. Throughout her career, however, Arkansas was never far from her thoughts. She returned to the state on several occasions, but she lived her life on a multinational stage. Lewis's complicated childhood and upbringing informed her experiences as a singer and an actor. She was the essence of a prima donna. Despite her disabilities, Lewis was always a larger-than-life persona. She was the first of her kind from Arkansas.

NOTES

1. The standard biography is Alice Fitch Zeman, *Mary Lewis: The Golden Haired Beauty with the Golden Voice* (Little Rock, Ark.: Rose Publishing, 2001), 1. See also Mary Lewis, "From the Slums, to the Follies, to Grand Opera," *Ladies' Home Journal*, May and July 1927.

2. Zeman, *Mary Lewis*, 4.

3. Ibid., 5. On page 9 there is a picture of a child modeling Mary Lewis's dress, which her foster mother preserved.

4. Ibid., 21–23. Mary loved the woman but hated the restrictive environment. She remained close to her foster mother, but Anna was offended by the newspaper suggestions that she treated Mary cruelly. In the broadest sense, this gap between an elderly Victorian and a young person of the twentieth century was not unique.

5. Ibid., 5–6.

6. Ibid., 24–25; W. E. Orr, *That's Judsonia* (Judsonia, Ark.: White Company Printing, 1957), 290.

7. Zeman, *Mary Lewis*, 26.

8. Tom Dillard, "H. F. Auten: A Man Who Could Not Stand Still," *Pulaski County Historical Review* 60, no. 2 (Fall 2012): 108–15.

9. Zeman, *Mary Lewis*, 28–32.

10. Ibid., 39; "President Guest of Arkansas," *Nashville News* (Nashville, Ark.), October 28, 1905, 1.

11. Zeman, *Mary Lewis*, 40–45. Although she left Little Rock and her husband, she nevertheless kept the surname Lewis, explaining that she had a grandmother with that name. In Michael B. Dougan, "An Arkansas Aria," *Arkansas Times* 21, no. 50 (August 2005): 10–12, I recount how in 1975 just prior to giving a scholarly paper on Mary Lewis I learned about this marriage, which Mary had successfully hid from the public.

12. Zeman, *Mary Lewis*, 47–52. There is an extensive website devoted to Fanchon and Marco: http://www.fanchonandmarco.com (accessed August 23, 2016).

13. Zeman, *Mary Lewis*, 52–54; http://www.filmpreservation.org/preserved-films/screening-room/a-bashful-bigamist-1921 (accessed July 10, 2013).

14. "Mary Lewis in the Greenwich Village Follies, 1920," *New York Times*, September 12, 1920, 76.

15. Zeman, *Mary Lewis*, 55–61.

16. Michael B. Dougan, "'A Touching Enigma': The Opera Career of Mary Lewis," *Arkansas Historical Quarterly* 36, no. 3 (Autumn 1977): 265.

17. Zeman, *Mary Lewis*, 67–76.

18. Ibid., 77–78.

19. Zeman, *Mary Lewis*, 77–81. Technically, in homage to Goethe, the opera was billed as *Margarethe* rather than *Faust*. See also "To Make Herself Mary Garden's Perfect Double," *Courier-Journal* (Louisville, Ky.), October 25, 1925, 89.

20. Zeman, *Mary Lewis*, 82–86. His Master's Voice was the English component of Victor in the United States, Deutsche Grammophon in Germany, Voce del Padrone in Italy, and so on—even extending to Japan Victor.

21. Ibid., 87–93.

22. *Atlanta Constitution*, January 27, 1924, E6, 10. Thorner was quoted as saying he had been backstage at Lewis's Vienna debut, and the audience "nearly took the roof down."

23. Zeman, *Mary Lewis*, 87–104.

24. Ibid., 105–15.

25. Ibid., 112. Apparently none of these works have survived.

26. Ibid., 121–38.

27. Ibid., 139–41.

28. Ibid., 142–45.

29. Ibid.

30. Ibid., 156.

31. Ibid., 149–57.

32. Ibid., 157–58.

33. Ibid., 175–80.

34. Ibid., 209–11. Photographs from the mid-1930s show that Lewis had gained weight.

35. Michael Quinn, "The Radio Transcription Discs of Mary Lewis," *Record Collector* 42 (September 1997): 188–94, reprinted in Zeman, *Mary Lewis*, 212–16. The contents ranged from opera arias to popular songs. Most of the pieces as well as unpublished material from her Victor recordings can be found on *Mary Lewis: The Golden Haired Soprano*, Marston Records, 52047-2 (2005). See also "The Mary Lewis Records: An Appreciation," in Zeman, *Mary Lewis*, 209–11.

36. Zeman, *Mary Lewis*, 194–200.

37. Ibid., 201–3; Jessica Dragonette, *Faith Is a Song: The Odyssey of an American Artist* (New York: David McKay, 1951), 78; *Mary Lewis: The Golden Haired Soprano*.

Mary Celestia Parler

(1904–1981)

Folklorist and Teacher

RACHEL REYNOLDS

Often, those who have made significant contributions receive only posthumous attention. Mary Celestia Parler, a University of Arkansas professor and avid collector and scholar of the oral traditions of the Ozarks, is one such example. While she was not unknown in her lifetime, Parler is someone whose contributions were not fully appreciated until after her death. Indeed, the South Carolina native was a legendary presence on the University of Arkansas campus throughout the 1950s and 1960s, even garnering brief exposure on the nationally televised CBS series *The Search*, but her work as a folklore collector and scholar was often overshadowed by that of her more famous husband, Vance Randolph, and by such nationally renowned collectors as John and Ruby Lomax.[1] Still, during her twenty-seven-year career at the University of Arkansas she and her students assembled the largest cultural collection of sound recordings, texts, photographs, and ephemera from Arkansas and the Ozark Mountains. In addition, she participated actively in the formation of the Arkansas Folklore Society, serving as its secretary-treasurer at the outset and later as archivist.[2] She and Randolph were both mentors to Max Hunter, whose own important collection of Ozark folk songs covered the same region and extended to Missouri and Oklahoma, but Parler's work included more than just songs and is much larger overall.[3] Parler was a lifelong learner and a dedicated teacher to thousands of University of Arkansas students. In the years since her death in 1981, the importance of her work on all these fronts has become increasingly apparent to a great many more people than those who knew her as a scholar, teacher, folklorist, and friend.

Mary Celestia Parler was born on October 6, 1904, in a small village near Sumter, South Carolina, called Wedgefield.[4] She was the daughter of Dr. Marvin

Lamar Parler, a country physician and farmer, and the former Josie Platt, a local historian, writer, and teacher.[5] The family owned three cotton farms but through a series of financial missteps during the Great Depression, Mary's father became distraught and—according to Mary Parler's cousin who lived with the family—it is believed that Marvin Parler committed suicide out of despair over their financial situation. Mary's mother was "forbidden as a child to hum folk songs because they were considered 'worldly.'"[6] Josie Platt Parler's scholarly work, mainly locally published articles and books, centered on the local history of "the High Hills of the Santee," as the area was referred to, and on the lore of its Civil War heroes and the many historic buildings of the region.[7]

Mary grew up surrounded by the stories of rural life and in a place consumed by its identity as a Confederate or southern town. The fact that Parler's mother was a local historian, writer, and collector of stories strengthened Mary's concept of experiencing the culture of her place. Her knowledge of oral tradition was further influenced by Flora Smith, who worked for Mary's mother on the farm and was the young girl's friend and caregiver. Parler said, "Mother never sang the folk songs, but I used to love to listen to Ma'am Flora tell those tales and sing those songs."[8] She learned many anecdotes and songs from Ma'am Flora, and is even recorded in the University of Arkansas Folklore Collection recounting some of them for her students.[9] Her most requested tale was "The Forty-Mile Jumper," which she learned from Smith and first wrote down in 1924 when Ma'am Flora was well into her nineties. The story is the tale of a witch, her two daughters (whom she accidentally beheaded), and two traveling men who get the best of her and discover her hidden stash of treasure.[10] This foundation in collecting stories steeped in local traditional culture undoubtedly supported what became her primary academic pursuit, folklore.

Frances Lott, who was raised as Parler's sister, recalled that Mary was an intensely intelligent child who was always reading: "She was so bright that she was out in the stars."[11] Even in childhood, Mary garnered the reputation of being an interesting character. Robert Mallet of South Carolina, the younger brother of one of Mary's school friends, recalled that she was a trickster with a fiery sense of humor and, in a telling comparison of the day, "a real Tallulah Bankhead."[12] He remembered instances of her, as a young adult, stripping down to take a swim and waving her big sun hat to the onlooking crowd. She gained her primary and secondary education in Wedgefield where, by all accounts, she was an excellent student. When she was in the tenth grade, she decided to take an early placement exam for Winthrop College, a small but well-known women's teaching institution in Rock Hill, South Carolina. She was accepted and entered Winthrop in 1920.[13] Upon the completion of her undergraduate degree in English literature in 1924, she continued her education at the University of Wisconsin, where she began a lifelong study of the works of Geoffrey Chaucer and seemingly lost almost all connection to whatever folkloric roots she had gained through her childhood in South Carolina. In 1925, she completed a master's degree in English literature at the University of Wisconsin.[14] Parler carried her graduate studies further through additional work at the University of South Carolina, University of North Carolina at Chapel Hill, and Brown and Columbia Universities.[15] She began working toward a Ph.D. in English literature, but never finished the dissertation portion. While it is unclear why Parler shifted academic programs so often, one of her dear friends and colleagues at the University of Arkansas stated, "Mary Celestia Parler was eager for life, but she didn't know how to grasp it."[16]

Little is known about Parler's early teaching career. However, the Great Depression and World War II created a fluid environment, and Mary moved around the South. After graduating from the University of Wisconsin and before going to Arkansas, she taught at Bethel College in McKenzie, Tennessee; Andrew College in Cuthbert, Georgia; Florida State College for Women in Tallahassee; and Anderson College, a women's college in South Carolina. At Anderson, she was the faculty instructor for the student newspaper, the *Anderson Independent*.[17] It was while working at Anderson that Parler received and accepted an offer for the position of associate professor of English at the University of Arkansas.[18]

Mary Celestia Parler arrived in Fayetteville, Arkansas, in 1948, starting work at the university while still writing her dissertation on southern dialects based on the works of the antebellum novelist and fellow South Carolinian William Gilmore Simms.[19] At Arkansas, she began teaching classes in folklore and Chaucer in the English department, where she became known to her students as "Miss Chaucer" due to her lively analysis of the material and her love for it, which carried over into her flamboyant teaching style.[20] She was often seen in class or sauntering around campus in a beret with a cigarette firmly perched between her lips.[21] Part of her University of Arkansas distinction would always be that of "campus character."[22]

A colleague in the English department described Mary Parler this way: "She was a special kind of female ... independent, outspoken, able to tell the phony from the real.... She was a product of the old South. In spite of her bluntness, her emotional ups and downs, her almost scandalous behavior at times, she was a lady with a generous heart."[23]

Parler, coming from what was considered a privileged background for a woman of her time, was seen as somewhat of a lovable and admirable oddity by her students and informants. It was a rarity to see a highly educated woman living independently and working in the realm of academia in northwest Arkansas. Her sparkling personality and candor endeared her not only to the subjects of her work at the university but also to her fellow faculty. It is likely, however, that her boldness somewhat inhibited the longevity of her program at the University of Arkansas and the support that it received from the university's administration over time.

During the first year of Mary Celestia Parler's new life in Fayetteville, she was asked to become involved in the formation of the Ozark Folklore Society (later renamed the Arkansas Folklore Society) and to accept the position of secretary-treasurer. Later, she claimed that she had not really been that interested in the folklore society, but found it hard to refuse such nice people.[24] Perhaps her disinterest came from a distaste for formality or because she did not find a folklore society necessary or even found it burdensome at that juncture of her career, but nevertheless, this group of people proved instrumental in encouraging her in her endeavors to collect Arkansiana. According to Parler, when she came to Fayetteville she knew the names of only three Arkansans: the poet John Gould Fletcher, Senator William Fulbright, and folklorist Vance Randolph, who was then living in Eureka Springs and had published several articles on the Ozark dialect.[25] The Arkansas Folklore Society brought her into contact with two of these men and intimately linked her to one of them for the rest of her life.

In the 1930s, there had been a national enthusiasm created for folk culture through a series of regional folk festivals held across the country as qualifying events for the National Folk Festival in St. Louis, Missouri, in 1934. Vance Randolph had worked at organizing one such regional folk festival in Eureka Springs, Arkansas. Randolph found Eureka Springs to be a perfect headquarters for himself as it had become home to a number of writers, artists, and composers who grounded their work in the culture of the place. Randolph's work, including the release of his books *Ozark Mountain Folks* (1932) and *Ozark Folksongs*, volume 1 (1946), had attracted interested luminaries to the area, including the Pulitzer Prize–winning poet John Gould Fletcher.[26] It was in the parlor of Randolph's Eureka Springs apartment that the Arkansas Folklore Society was born.[27]

In 1949, an enthusiastic group of amateurs and scholars formed the society as an opportunity to come together and share information regarding Arkansas's vernacular culture. The prime movers were Vance Randolph, the visiting professor and folklorist Herbert Halpert,[28] Howard Carter (then chair of the English department at the university), professor of English Robert Morris, Mary Celestia Parler, and a few "cotton choppin' hoe hands," including Claude W.

Faulkner and Leighton Rudolph (who is responsible for that description), both also members of the Department of English. John Gould Fletcher was elected the society's first president, mostly out of general admiration and in an attempt to exploit his notoriety in the search for funding for the fledgling society, according to Rudolph.[29] Fletcher was Parler's neighbor in Fayetteville. She visited him and helped with his physical care during his year-long stay there in 1949.[30] She served as the secretary-treasurer of the Arkansas Folklore Society from 1950 to 1960 and in subsequent years was the society's archivist and also served with Rudolph on the Council of Members.[31] A substantial amount of folklore material was collected and reported by the group, and much of what became the University of Arkansas Folklore Collection was included in the folklore society's newsletters, which were created on Parler's recommendation.[32]

Also in 1949, Parler developed the university's first folklore course, became the director of the University of Arkansas Folklore Research Project, and began the compilation of archival materials with the help of her field assistant Merlin Mitchell.[33] The university's folklore holdings amassed by Parler, her field assistants, and her students are an important documentation of the first fifteen years of analog magnetic tape technology, but more important, the collection of 3,640 folk songs (442 reels equaling 137,400 feet of audiotape with transcriptions for them all) is one of the largest collections of its kind. John Gould Fletcher, who had proved so important in launching the folklore society, also promoted the launch of Parler's Arkansas Folklore Archives project. Fletcher joined a group of faculty members, including Robert Morris and George Hastings, in expressing the need to record the rich and varied folk culture of Arkansas to the university, and it agreed to fund a continuing folklore research project.[34]

Parler's recordings in the University of Arkansas Folklore Collection represent a signature contribution to the field. They include several "event" ballads native to Arkansas, a choir of Cherokees singing Baptist hymns, songs collected from immigrants, numerous ballads of the type classified by scholar George Malcolm Laws as "Native American ballads,"[35] fiddle tunes, jokes, and tales. The Ozarkers' versions of the Child ballads, the English and Scottish ballads compiled by Francis James Child, were the focus of Parler's acquisitions.[36] Parler's collection includes a rich tradition of British balladry, the written forms of which can be traced as far back as the thirteenth century. As a folklorist, Parler understood the cyclical nature of folk traditions, that there is a cultural process of waxing and waning, but she also subscribed to the notion that traditional cultures were threatened by the rapid expansion of towns and cities and by the growing technologies of radio and television. This belief fueled her obsession with collecting. Along with other collectors in the early twentieth century,

Parler believed that the United States was on the verge of a cultural apocalypse and that she and her assistants were recording the last days of a disappearing way of life. They worked to document speech patterns, sayings, songs, and tunes that, they believed, would soon vanish from the cultural landscape. Parler was unusual in having the foresight to look beyond the strictly traditional forms and to preserve for posterity original songs written by those she interviewed and recorded, their interpretations of early popular music forms that had been regionalized, and their renditions of folk songs learned from the recordings of performers such as the Carter Family, Jimmie Rodgers, or Woody Guthrie. While she obviously did not hold this material in as high esteem as she did the discovery of a regional version of an ancient ballad, she did keep these recordings in her collection, which was not a widely accepted practice (although, here again, Vance Randolph was her great model). Indeed Max Hunter did not agree with this practice and in fact went to great lengths to keep such material out of his collection.[37]

Parler collected and directed her students to collect widely and thoroughly, including not just the oldest ballads of the British Isles but also songs of more recent vintage and native to North America. While Parler did not create a numbering system for her collection nor cross-reference the recordings and written materials with previous collections, she did use the systems of Francis James Child's *The English and Scottish Popular Ballads*, G. Malcolm Laws's *Native American Balladry*, and Vance Randolph's *Ozark Folksongs* to classify the materials from the University of Arkansas Folklore Collection used in her courses in Arkansas folklore.[38]

By 1949, then, when Parler set out collecting, the changes and additions in the world of folklore scholarship, concerning folk song tradition in particular, had opened the door of inclusion much wider. Not only is the University of Arkansas Folklore Collection, overseen and collected by Parler, one of the largest, but also it is notable for its inclusion of all of the known traditions. It contains songs from English and Scottish balladry, Native American balladry, and African American and European American traditions, including songs from the traditions of Austrian, Italian, and Polish immigrants to Arkansas as well as tales, jokes, and a variety of instrumental music or tunes.

When Parler first started collecting, others said that her task would be arduous. Some even suggested that she would come back empty-handed. Perhaps their doubts were based in the fact that Parler was a woman, and it was not common for women, especially educated women who were not from the Ozarks or from Arkansas, to take to the back roads alone. This was an unexpected sight to most residents of the area. Culturally speaking, it was uncommon for anyone, male or female, to address a stranger with a request for information such as Parler was seeking. It is a testament to Parler's determination and skill that her field recording was so successful. Consistent with her general character, she laughed at the suggestion of failure, and on her first field trip came back with eighteen songs recorded from Virgil Lance of Mountain Home, Arkansas.[39]

One of the distinguishing aspects of the field recordings in the folk song collection is Parler's ability to establish rapport with her informants and consequently obtain large amounts of contextual information, including biographical and other details. Raised in the Deep South as she was, Parler, with her "honey-voiced, bespectacled" nature, vast knowledge, patience, and genuine interest, could draw information from the subjects of her inquiry that initially they might have held guarded.[40] Her interviews remain fascinating. She draws information the way a water girl draws from a well, sometimes accessing the memories of people five generations removed from those who only fifteen minutes before could remember nothing. These skills are most evident in her interviews with people who had experienced oppression. Parler proved able at making people with very different backgrounds from her own comfortable in her presence. For instance, when interviewing Charlotte Stephens, Arkansas's first African American public school teacher, she was able to draw from her songs and stories about her enslaved childhood in Arkansas, a history that was obviously difficult for Stephens to discuss and far removed from the life that she had built for herself and her family over the years. Similarly, there is a great deal of textual information that Parler gathered, dealing with sensitive issues regarding women's bodies, health, and the use of herbal remedies to end pregnancies, cast spells on wanted lovers, and more. The breadth and depth of Parler's collection is greatly strengthened by her ability to build and maintain human relationships and her willingness to listen as much (or more) than she talked. Some of her informants remained friends of hers for years.

Being a professor of folklore at the University of Arkansas gave Parler a unique advantage over many of her collecting colleagues and offered opportunities that substantially enhanced the breadth of her collection. Semester after semester, a parade of eager students filed into her classroom, more often than not with relatives in the area, many of whom sang or played or knew someone who did.[41] She had some of the most popular courses on campus. There was often a waiting list to join. For their term projects, Parler sent her students into the field to record their relatives, friends, and neighbors. They returned with recordings, biographical information, transcriptions, and sometimes photographs of those interviewed. Part of the final grade for the course required that all students, regardless of musical prowess, learn a song from an informant of their choosing and then at the end of the semester perform the song in front of their classmates as she recorded the concert. This served a trifold purpose. The threat of public performance warded off those who might consider her class a "fluff" course,[42] provided Parler with contact information on informants, and significantly diversified the amount of material in the folk song collection. According to friend and colleague Ernie Deane, "Emphasis in each student's collecting effort was on person-to-person interviewing. Necessarily, parents, grandparents, kinfolks, friends, old family servants, elderly neighbors and other individuals became participants in the quest for folklore materials."[43] Students recorded sayings, stories, and songs from their grandparents and the old-timers in town and the surrounding areas. They also left their mark on the folklore collection and in the indexes. Parler cited each student project or report as if it had been collected by a field assistant or other collaborator.[44] Parler's collaborative understanding of field recording, that it was a partnership of information mining, was evident not only in her interview style but also in the egalitarian way in which she represented her students' contributions. She seemingly felt that her role as scholar came in the interpretation and analysis of the material. She spent countless hours compiling permutations of the material generated for the collection, including subcategory lists, and crafting bibliographies to accompany the collection. She nurtured this idea in her students and in the young folk song collectors and performers who crossed her path. Deane continued:

> Mrs. Randolph recalls that virtually the entire village of Bellefonte, near Harrison, became involved in a student's summer project several years ago. People would call in items even after bedtime. In another Ozarks community, 40 elderly women each pieced a simple quilt square for a student whose project was old patchwork designs and their names. Older people when first contacted by students were amazed and then pleased to realize there is a genuine understanding and appreciation of the traditional lore they learned when they were growing up, and that seems to be squelched by the younger generation.[45]

The folk songs were only one part of the University of Arkansas Folklore Collection gathered under Parler's supervision. Stored in Special Collections at the University of Arkansas Mullins Library is a mostly unprocessed collection of some sixty thousand handwritten note cards of "Ozark-isms" that were collected by Parler, her assistants, and her students.[46] They include citations that were organized into eighteen volumes of unpublished typescript: eleven volumes of folk beliefs and superstitions, four volumes of proverbs separated into maxims and adjectival comparisons, two of riddles, and one of ballads and songs in the University of Arkansas Folklore Collection.[47] "Mary Parler did this extensive project herself in addition to all her other duties, including teaching. She contributed this and other materials, to the University without any additional compensation—and, for that matter, with very little resulting recognition."[48]

It is difficult to say why, exactly, Parler never got much recognition. Perhaps the study of common or vernacular culture itself was underappreciated in the university system. Perhaps a change in leadership in the English department in the course of her tenure at the university made support for her work more difficult. A darker hypothesis is that her work has been underappreciated because she was a woman doing what, at the time, was deemed unwomanly work and that she lived in what was considered an unladylike way.[49] Certainly, she was appreciated by her students, and several of them went on to display a folkloric influence in their work or became part of the closely knit realm of Ozark folklore enthusiasts.

While her passion and persistence were largely ignored by the university, others recognized the value of her work. Parler earned recognition for her efforts in 1954 when CBS made her the focus of an episode of the television program *The Search*, a series that highlighted interesting people doing interesting work around the nation. This was the first time that Parler received national attention for collecting Arkansas folklore, and she relished the opportunity to share the work that she and her students had been doing. Parler arranged much of the logistics of the taping and lined up the performers who appeared in the television show, all of whom had been recorded by Parler for the University of Arkansas Folklore Collection. The show offers a glimpse into how charming Mary Parler was both as an individual and as a collector working with hill folks in northwest Arkansas. At the end of the program, Parler is sitting beneath a spinning Alexander Calder mobile at the University of Arkansas Fine Arts Building and offers this argument for the importance of her work:

> At the University of Arkansas we are collecting folklore to preserve some of the elements of a passing culture. It's of value to literary scholars, to social historians, to linguists, to anthropologists, and a source of inspiration to writers, artists, and musicians. But we folklore collectors are impressed by the way these people make their own music. We ask ourselves, "What should music mean to people anyway?" Are we not, as a nation, becoming listeners and watchers of our own culture? Can we learn from these folksingers and folk musicians the *joy* and *vitality* of participating in a *live* kind of music?[50]

The Search had followed Parler as she traipsed through "the wilds" of the Ozarks, heading down dirt and gravel roads in search of "the great-great-great-grandchild" of an Elizabethan ballad, "The Two Sisters." Along with CBS reporter Charles Romine, Parler scoured the hills, going from informant to informant, searching for someone who knew the song. Along the way, she and Romine heard songs, tunes, and tales until, finally, the sought-after song was overheard from a most unlikely source, a young girl named Mary Jo Davis at a play party, which had been staged for the television crew. Mary Jo and her family ended up becoming one of the greatest finds of Parler's collecting career. They recorded 135 songs for Parler, and the family's youngest daughter was perhaps the greatest inspiration to Parler. She saw Mary Jo both as hope for a dying cultural future and an artifact to be presented to the folklore crowd.

Parler eagerly recorded the members of the Davis family and added their extensive store of Ozark balladry to her collection, and she took on Mary Jo as a sort of side project. She recorded several of Mary Jo's songs and began booking singing engagements for her at area folk festivals and college campuses. Parler also brought her along on excursions to folklore society events and introduced her to other local musicians. As Davis recalled, "That was something really very special to me. Mary Parler got acquainted with Mother first. Of course, I was going through my teenage thing that you do, when I first became aware that Mother was singing these songs for Ms. Parler. But one day Ms. Parler and Mrs. Jack Carter . . . came to our house, and I sang a version, or part of a version of 'Barbara Allen.' And I remember them saying 'Oh, we'd like to get Mary Jo to do some singing here or there.'"[51] Parler also took Mary Jo with her on collecting trips:

> I went to Russellville with Ms. Parler. I was making an appearance there at the college and she learned about some old gentleman that lived up in the mountains that knew some old-time fiddle tunes. She would get so excited anytime she heard anything like that. It was on the trail; it was the hunt. I would get caught up because I was with her. So she packed up her gear, and I think we had to rent a car. We took off in the mountains, followed directions, and drove as far as we could until we came to a creek we couldn't drive over. So we walked the rest of the way up the hill, and there was this little house nestled in the woods. They didn't have any electricity. The old man was willing to play; he was willing to accommodate her, but he didn't have any electricity. He said his son had electricity and we'd go down there. . . . We just walked in on these people . . . and they didn't care, so it was fine.[52]

Parler developed ongoing professional relationships with several of the people she recorded over the years, including Doney Hammontree, Booth Campbell, Fred High, and Mary Briscoe, and presented them at festivals and gatherings of folklorists. There are also several nationally notable people recorded in her collection, including Charlotte Stephens, who was enslaved before becoming

Arkansas's first black public school teacher (her life was explored in a brief biography written by the sister of John Gould Fletcher, Adolphine Fletcher Terry). The recordings serve as a wonderful document of Stephens's recollections both as a child and as a young adult.

Two other recordings in the collection highlight people who later became famous for their singing and songwriting. Huntsville native Ronnie Hawkins was a student of Mary Parler at the University of Arkansas and was recorded for the collection shortly before he launched his band, Ronnie Hawkins and the Hawks, which played around Arkansas, Missouri, and Oklahoma. In the late 1950s, the group began touring Canada; eventually, Hawkins's musicians toured and recorded with Bob Dylan and then on their own as the Band. Similarly, Jimmy Morris was recorded by Parler in the 1950s before he made it big in 1959 with the hit record "The Battle of New Orleans" under the performing name of Jimmy Driftwood.[53] Morris was a native of Stone County, Arkansas, a teacher, and an aspiring songwriter when Parler met him. As Jimmy Driftwood, he wrote more than six thousand songs, most of them in a traditional style, and he had a brief but successful recording career with RCA Victor.[54]

Within a few years of their initial meeting, Mary Parler found that Vance Randolph was a kindred spirit, and they naturally complemented each other's professional strengths. The first published collaboration between the two came in 1953 and was called *Down in the Holler: A Gallery of Ozark Folk Speech*, a book about Ozark dialect. In the foreword Vance credited his future wife, Mary, stating that without her help the book would not have been possible.[55] Although she was not credited as an author, she had read the entire manuscript, edited out obscurities, and tidied up the book before publication. This was the beginning of a long collaboration that proved to be mutually beneficial. Randolph saw folklore as a fragile part of culture that he worked feverishly to preserve.[56] He had spent years in the hills of the Ozarks recording the people of the region, driven in large part by his fear that their traditions would all soon be lost. Parler shared Randolph's love for prolific collection, but knew the cyclical nature of folklore and its endurance. The two souls combined a boundless love for and knowledge of Ozarks culture.[57] The working relationship developed further in *The Talking Turtle*, another publication by Randolph, this one a collection of tales.[58] That book is dedicated to Parler, and she is also cited for nine jokes or sayings in his *Hot Springs and Hell*.[59]

At the same time that the professional relationship was being forged, so too was the romantic relationship between Randolph and Parler. Mary acknowledged that after the first or second meeting of the Arkansas Folklore Society, she "took a shine" to Vance.[60] In interviews conducted in 1980, shortly before her death, and included in Robert Cochran's biography of Vance Randolph, she recalled, "Every woman he met fell in love with him. And he was a good-looking old man. I bought a car so I could drive to Eureka Springs [to visit Randolph] when I felt like it—a little second-hand Chevrolet."[61] Randolph appeared taken with Parler as well. The folklorist who was known for his cantankerous behavior found himself flirting with the university's new arrival and being not only cordial but even gallant. He recalled: "She was the best thing that ever happened to me. Here I was, almost sixty years old, walking on the grass holding hands! It took her 'til 1962 to break down and let me marry her, but she did."[62]

The two corresponded through letters frequently during their courtship. While Randolph was still living in Eureka Springs, he wrote an account of a near accident when he was almost struck by a vehicle while attempting to write "Vance + Mary" on the sidewalk.[63] During this same period, Parler remembered getting a note from Vance that read, "Dear Mary Celestia, A woman's place is in the f——ing home. As ever, Vance," and another, a picture postcard, showing Vance in a mule-pulled wagon with the caption "Dear Mary Celestia, that's me on the left."[64] For her part, Parler remembered having "begged" Vance to marry her. Although they disagreed about who was courting whom first, the flirtation that began at the Arkansas Folklore Society meetings in 1950 eventually led to the marriage of Vance Randolph, age seventy, and Mary Celestia Parler, age fifty-seven, in the spring of 1962.[65] Margaret Rule, a colleague of Mary, recalled:

> She used to talk to me about her father, a doctor in one of the Carolinas. She loved him. He was so perfect a man to her that she had never been seriously interested in marrying, though men had been seriously interested in her. Her decision not to marry made her, in my estimation, a person of unusual honesty. Most women eventually will settle for a marriage, whether the man is what they wanted or not. Mary C would have none of that. There was one man she respected, actually was drawn to, but she showed an unaccustomed modesty about it, saying that he was too dignified to be interested in her.... That man was Vance Randolph.[66]

Rule continued, "She was happy to be his handmaiden. She certainly had no interest in being anyone else's, professional or personal; and she could say so clearly. In fact, she was a raspy person much of the time. She had no use for toadying, panting ambition, eager agreeing, or jockeying for place ... all signs of wanting, beyond honor, to rise in the profession."[67]

Randolph had made the move from Eureka Springs to Fayetteville in 1960 during his and Parler's courtship. He had a small house on Leverett Street, and after they married they remained there for several years, moving to a nursing home together in 1975.[68] Mary, who had always suffered from poor eyesight, had grown nearly blind, and the once vibrant Vance was now bedridden. The two passed the time by intellectually sparring and entertaining visitors who came to talk with Vance about his work and their work together.[69]

In 1963, Mary Celestia Parler Randolph published her only book, *An Arkansas Ballet Book*, a compilation of the transcriptions of Ozark ballads that she had collected over the years.[70] The book resembled a large mimeographed poetry chapbook in appearance. There was no contextual information provided for the book's contents. Still, it offers an important point of reference in the folk song collecting of Arkansas and is an interesting artifact of Parler's work with the Arkansas Folklore Archives, a piece of her larger collection of Arkansas folklore materials, which were bound into volumes yet never published.[71]

In 1972, she was granted emeritus status, and she retired from the University of Arkansas in 1975.[72] She and Randolph shared a joyful, though never financially prosperous life in Fayetteville, moving from their quiet life in town into the nursing home together in the year she retired. Randolph died in 1980 and is buried in the national cemetery in Fayetteville thanks to his brief career as a largely bedridden soldier during World War I.[73] Parler returned to South Carolina shortly after his death to live with her sister, Frances Lott, and died less than a year later.[74] She is buried four miles from where she was born, at the Church of the Holy Cross in Stateburg, South Carolina, next to her mother and father. Her gravestone reads, "Gladley Wolde She Lerne and Gladley Teche," an homage to her beloved Chaucer and to a life well lived.[75]

Mary Celestia Parler Randolph's legacy is the collection and archives at the University of Arkansas. Through her tireless work and that of her assistants and students, the lives, memories, songs, stories, and sayings of hundreds of Ozark people were documented. She dedicated her life to recording the lives, music, and culture of the Arkansas people and encouraged a host of musicians, scholars, and students associated with her projects.

As Randolph's biographer and American studies professor Robert Cochran opined, "The only shortcoming [about Randolph and Parler] is that Vance deserved all the attention he got, but he cast a big shadow. Mary never got quite the attention she deserved."[76] In 1983, a fellowship was established in honor of Mary Celestia Parler and her husband in the English department at the University of Arkansas. The fellowship supports graduate students with special interests in the English language, literature, or folklore. According to one of the couple's dear friends, Ernie Deane, who was an Ozarks scholar in his own right and a professor of journalism at the University of Arkansas, the fellowship was established by friends and family in the expectation of "further research and study that can add substantially to public knowledge of regional and national culture."[77] In 2005, the

University of Arkansas Libraries hosted a two-day conference, "A Collector in Her Own Right: Reassessing Mary Celestia Parler's Contribution to Ozark Folklore," which reinforced the importance of Parler's contributions to Arkansas cultural history. Parler's life and work continue to be an inspiration for those who stumble upon her or—like a long-lost ballad—hear about her accomplishments from family, musicians, or scholars. In 2014, the University of Arkansas's Special Collections Department, which has housed Parler's materials for decades, launched an inclusive website offering her collection of Arkansas's cultural treasures to a worldwide audience. That same year, Parler's life and work were the focus of a large multimedia exhibit at the Fayetteville Public Library as part of the Fayetteville Roots Festival in partnership with the Center for Arkansas and Regional Studies and Art of the Rural; there are plans to take the exhibit, in traveling form, on the road and back to the communities where Parler found her inspiration.

NOTES

1. Vance Randolph, *Ozark Folksongs*, 4 vols. (Columbia: State Historical Society of Missouri, 1946–1950). Randolph was an avid collector of Ozark oral traditions. His works on the area are numerous and highly regarded. His field recordings reside at the Library of Congress; see John Lomax and Ruby Lomax, "1939 Southern Recording Trip Field Notes," 1939, Library of Congress. In 1939 John Lomax, honorary consultant and curator of the Archive of American Folk Song (now the Archive of Folk Culture, American Folklife Center, Library of Congress), and Ruby Lomax, his wife, took a three-month, 6,502-mile trip through the southern states collecting songs from the region.

2. Jim Clark, News Service announcement, University of Arkansas, July 25, 1975, Mary Celestia Parler Randolph vertical file, Special Collections, University of Arkansas Libraries, Fayetteville (hereafter Parler Randolph vertical file); Arkansas Folklore Society and University of Arkansas Folklore Research Project, *Ozark Folklore* 1–4 (1950–1958).

3. Max Hunter, *The Max Hunter Collection of Ozark Folk Songs*, 40 vols. (Springfield, Mo.: Springfield-Green County Library District and Missouri State University, 2000). Hunter's audio collection includes many joint ventures between his and Parler's collection. See the special issue dedicated to Vance Randolph: *Missouri Folklore Society Journal* 4 (1982).

4. Frances Lott to Norma Ortiz, July 24, 1986, Parler Randolph vertical file.

5. Yates Snowden, ed., *History of South Carolina* (New York: Lewis, 1920), 5:49–50. There are short biographies of Dr. Marvin Lamar Parler and Josie Platt Parler in this history and reference to Josie Parler's writings. The only mention of Mary Celestia Parler that Snowden included is a poem written by her from the perspective of a child in the Aycock store in Wedgefield, South Carolina, at Christmas time (387–88). See also "Christmas in Aycock's Store," Parler Randolph vertical file.

6. Frances Lott, interview, Folklore Collection, Special Collections, University of Arkansas Libraries, Fayetteville (hereafter Folklore Collection); L. Hardy Wright, draft article written for *Southern Accent*, n.d., Mary Celestia Parler Randolph vertical file, Special Collections, University of Arkansas Libraries, Fayetteville.

7. Josie Platt Parler, "The High Hills of the Santee," *State* (Columbia, S.C.), May 11, 1930, in Parler Randolph vertical file; and Josie Platt Parler, *The Past Blows By* (Sumter, S.C.: Knight Bros., 1939).

8. Wright, draft article.

9. Mary Celestia Parler, "The Forty-Mile Jumper," November 24, 1950, reel 78, Folklore Collection.

10. *Journal of American Folklore Society* 64, no. 254 (October–December 1951): 422–23.

11. Robert Mallet, interview by Rachel Reynolds, August 14, 2002. Frances Lott was a first cousin to Mary Parler on her mother's side of the family. After the death of Lott's mother during her infancy, she was raised by the Parlers. Mary and Frances considered themselves sisters; Lott, interview.

12. Mallet, interview. Tallulah Bankhead was a legendary screen actress in the 1930s and 1940s known more for her temperament and wit than for her performances. This perception of Parler's character followed her throughout her life.

13. Frances Lott to Norma Ortiz, letter.

14. Wright, draft article; Frances Lott to Norma Ortiz, letter.

15. Wright, draft article.

16. This quote comes from handwritten notes made by Margaret Rule, an English professor and friend of Parler. Rule wrote an article called "Mary C" about Parler that was published shortly after her death in the *Grapevine*, a local trade paper (exact date unknown). The notes were provided to me by Rule's granddaughter Sarah K. Moore in Fayetteville, Arkansas.

17. Wright, draft article.

18. Mary Celestia Parler Randolph scrapbook, Special Collections, University of Arkansas Libraries, Fayetteville. The scrapbook contains some articles and announcements by or surrounding Mary Celestia Parler. The majority of the contents are articles or book reviews written by her mother, Josie Platt Parler (signed J. P. or J. P. P.).

19. Leighton Rudolph, interview by Rachel Reynolds, April 26, 2002. Rudolph was a colleague of Parler at the University of Arkansas and one of the founding members, along with Parler, of the Arkansas Folklore Society.

20. Rudolph, interview.

21. Ibid.; Rule, "Mary C."

22. Rudolph, interview.

23. Rule, "Mary C," 1.

24. Wright, draft article.

25. Ibid.

26. Fletcher was married to Charlie May Simon, the daughter of Wayman Hogue. She published a book in 1945 called *Straw in the Sun* about homesteading in the Ozarks in the 1930s. Her father had written *Back Yonder: An Ozark Chronicle* (1932). Randolph said that Fletcher had a long interest in folklore and staged the first folk festival on the University of Arkansas campus in 1949.

27. Robert Morris, "The First Arkansas Folklore Society," *Grapevine* 8, no. 17 (December 9, 1981).

28. Halpert and his family became lifelong friends of and advocates for both Mary Parler and Vance Randolph.

29. Rudolph, interview.

30. Ibid.

31. Vance Randolph, Manuscripts and Correspondence, University Libraries, Special Collections, University of Arkansas, Fayetteville.

32. "Articles from Ozark Folklore," *Mid-America Folklore* 17 (Spring 1989): 26.

33. Mary Celestia Parler Papers, 1950–1980, University of Arkansas Special Collections, finding aid, https://libraries.uark.edu/specialcollections/findingaids/parlerpapers.html.

34. Mary Celestia Parler, "Research in Folklore," *Arkansas Alumnus* (November 1958): 4.

35. George Malcolm Laws, *Native American Balladry: A Descriptive Study and a Bibliographical Syllabus* (Philadelphia: American Folklore Society, 1950).

36. A preference for modern versions of ballads that had been cataloged by Francis James Child was shared by many folk song collectors of the early twentieth century, including Texan Dorothy Scarborough and Parler's protégé, Max Hunter of Springfield, Missouri.

37. Hunter, *Max Hunter Collection*, vol. 1. Hunter's preference, if already becoming out of vogue, was tied to the philosophy of the nation's great pioneering folk song collections, especially that of Francis James Child. Child, a Harvard professor, completed the first modern assemblage of ancient balladry in the final decades of the nineteenth century: *The English and Scottish Popular Ballads* (1882–1898; repr., New York: Dover, 2003).

38. See Child, *English and Scottish Popular Ballads*. Vance Randolph's compendium was published as the four volumes of *Ozark Folksongs*; the material was collected between 1909 and 1946. He offered his own numbering system for the Ozark versions and cross-referenced the ballads found in his collection with Child's numbering system. At the same time that Randolph was collecting, John Avery Lomax was scouring the southern states for folk song materials for the Library of Congress. Lomax published the first collection, *Cowboy Songs and Other Frontier Ballads* (New York: Sturgis and Walton, 1910). Drawing from the western pioneer experience, Lomax attempted to "throw light on the conditions of pioneer life" and capture the information in the songs concerning that "unique and romantic figure in modern civilization, the American cowboy" (xvii). This, along with Randolph's collection of western balladry, offered yet another approach to the study of American balladry and had a direct influence on Parler's methodology. In *Native American Balladry*, Laws did for American song tradition what Child had done for Scottish and English ballads. Pulling materials from the collections of Randolph, Lomax, and other collectors of the 1920s through the late 1940s, Laws presented a collection of 185 songs that fit into all aspects of his definition of ballads native to America and provided a categorical scheme to match Child's, identifying war ballads, ballads of cowboys and pioneers, murder ballads, ballads of tragedies and disasters, among others.

39. Parler Papers, finding aid.

40. Wright, draft article; reels 1–442, Folklore Collection.

41. Lott, interview. There are numerous reels of such material in the collection.

42. Ibid.

43. Ernie Deane, "Ozarks Country," *Springdale News*, April 10, 1984, n.p., in Parler Randolph vertical file.

44. Parler Papers, finding aid.

45. Deane, "Ozarks Country," n.p.

46. Unprocessed material, Folklore Collection.

47. Non-song material, Folklore Collection.

48. Ernie Deane, "The Folklore Collection of 'Mary C.,'" *Ozarks Mountaineer* (May–June 1984): 30–31, in Parler Randolph vertical file.

49. Parler was known for her smoking and drinking, sometimes on campus, sometimes in class. She was often said to have a disheveled appearance.

50. Henwar Rodakiewicz, dir., *The Search*, Information Productions, CBS, November 4, 1954. There is no known online copy of the show, but this link has a snippet: https://vimeo.com/104513648.

51. Alan L. Spurgeon and David Gadberry, "Mary Jo Davis Henderson: Her Life and Contributions to Ozark Regional Folk Music," *Mid-America Folklore* 29, nos. 1–2 (Summer 2002): 9.

52. Ibid.

53. Zac Cothren, "Jimmy Driftwood (1907–1998)," in *Encyclopedia of Arkansas History and Culture*, http://www.encyclopediaofarkansas.net/encyclopedia/entry-detail.aspx?entryID=2187 (accessed September 17, 2013).

54. Ibid.

55. Vance Randolph and George P. Wilson, *Down in the Holler: A Gallery of Ozark Folk Speech* (Norman: University of Oklahoma Press, 1953), vii–viii.

56. Robert Cochran, *Vance Randolph: An Ozark Life* (Urbana-Champaign: University of Illinois Press, 1985), 86–87.

57. Vance Randolph vertical file, Special Collections, University of Arkansas Libraries, Fayetteville.

58. Vance Randolph, *The Talking Turtle and Other Ozark Folk Tales* (New York: Columbia University Press, 1957).

59. Vance Randolph, *Hot Springs and Hell and Other Folk Jests and Anecdotes from the Ozarks* (Hatboro, Pa.: Folklore Associates, 1965), vii.

60. Cochran, *Vance Randolph*, 206.

61. Ibid.

62. Ibid.

63. Ibid.

64. Private collection, Gordon McCann.

65. Randolph, Manuscripts and Correspondence.

66. Rule, "Mary C," 2.

67. Ibid.

68. Cochran, *Vance Randolph*, 218.

69. Ibid.

70. Mary Celestia Parler, *An Arkansas Ballet Book* (Fayetteville: University of Arkansas, 1963).

71. Dr. Leo Van Scyoc, interview by Rachel Reynolds, April 20, 2002.

72. Clark, News Service announcement.

73. Cochran, *Vance Randolph*, 217–25.

74. Lott, interview.

75. The quote comes from "The Clerk of Oxford's Tale" in Chaucer's *Canterbury Tales*.

76. Quoted in Spurgeon and Gadberry, "Mary Jo Davis Henderson," 9.

77. Norma Conner, University of Arkansas News Service article, October 12, 1983, box 3, folder 30, University of Arkansas News Service Materials, 1960s–2000, Special Collections, University of Arkansas Libraries.

Contributors

MICHAEL B. DOUGAN is the Distinguished Professor of History (emeritus) from Arkansas State University, Jonesboro. The author of books and articles mostly on Arkansas history, he has also written biographies and studies in the history of music. His connection with Mary Lewis began when at age sixteen he purchased one of her 78-rpm records. It continued when he arrived at Arkansas State University in 1970 and culminated when he produced a two-CD release from Marston Records in 2005.

GARY T. EDWARDS is an associate professor and the director of graduate history at Arkansas State University, Jonesboro, where he teaches courses on the American South, the early republic, and the Civil War. Edwards was a Fulbright fellow (2009–2010) at the Free University of Berlin and served as a guest professor of history at the Kennedy Institute for North American Studies. He has published journal articles in *Agricultural History*, *Family History*, and *Tennessee Historical Quarterly* and book chapters with various academic presses. Edwards is currently working on a book-length manuscript on the yeoman families of antebellum western Tennessee.

DIANNA OWENS FRALEY received her PhD from the University of Memphis in 2017. Her major field of study is twentieth-century U.S. history, and she is currently an adjunct for both Ozarka College in Arkansas and Drury University in Missouri. She is the author of "Conflicts over the Fugitive Slave Act of 1850," a chapter in *Conflicts in American History: Early National Period and Expansion, 1789–1850s*, and several encyclopedia entries in the *Encyclopedia of Arkansas History and Culture* and *The Early Republic and Antebellum America*.

SARAH WILKERSON FREEMAN, a professor of history at Arkansas State University, has been involved with the University of Georgia Press series on southern women's history since the project began, initially contributing a chapter on the Mississippi educator and feminist Pauline Orr. With coeditor Beverly Bond, she edited two volumes of *Tennessee Women: Their Lives and Times* and contributed chapters to each volume, focusing primarily on women's roles in politics and reform movements. Freeman also wrote a chapter on the public welfare pioneer Daisy Denson for *North Carolina Women: Their Lives and Times*. Her work on Senator Hattie Caraway in this volume on Arkansas women marks the end of her long and productive association with this remarkable series.

REBECCA A. HOWARD is an assistant professor of history at Lone Star College, Houston, Texas. She did her undergraduate work at Texas A&M University and received her doctorate in history from the University of Arkansas. An Arkansas native, she is a scholar of the American South with an emphasis on the Arkansas Ozarks.

ELIZABETH JACOWAY is a native of Little Rock. She earned her PhD in southern history at the University of North Carolina. She has taught at the University of North Carolina, the University of Arkansas (Little Rock), and Lyon College. Jacoway is the author or editor of ten books, including *Turn Away Thy Son: Little Rock, the Crisis That Shocked the Nation*, and a dozen articles.

KELLY HOUSTON JONES is an assistant professor of history at Austin Peay State University. Her interests include American slavery, African American history, the American South, and nineteenth-century rural and agricultural history. She is a member of the executive committee of the Agricultural History Society and a trustee of the Arkansas Historical Association.

CHERISSE JONES-BRANCH is the James and Wanda Lee Vaughn Endowed Professor of History and the director of the ASTATE Digital Press at Arkansas State University, Jonesboro. She is the author of numerous articles on women's civil rights activism. In 2014, she published *Crossing the Line: Women and Interracial Activism in South Carolina during and after World War II* and is the coeditor of *Arkansas Women: Their Lives and Times*. She is working on a second monograph, *Better Living by Their Own Bootstraps: Rural Black Women's Activism in Arkansas, 1914–1965*.

JOHN A. KIRK is the George W. Donaghey Distinguished Professor of History and the director of the Anderson Institute on Race and Ethnicity at the University of Arkansas, Little Rock. His research focuses on the history of the civil rights movement, and he has published numerous prize-winning articles, essays, and books on the subject.

MARIANNE LEUNG teaches high school courses in U.S. history at St. George's Independent School in Collierville, Tennessee. She is passionate about bringing her students into the world of historical research, and they together created a museum exhibit, "A Portrait of Collierville: 1940–1945," which was recognized with the 2017 Award of Excellence by the Tennessee Association of Museums. She received her PhD in American history from the University of Memphis.

LORETTA N. MCGREGOR is a professor of psychology at Arkansas State University, Jonesboro. She served as the department chair for nine years and has taught in higher education for more than twenty-five years. Her professional involvements include membership in the American Psychological Association, where she is on the board of directors for educational affairs. In Division 2: The Society for the Teaching of Psychology, she has served as the associate director of society programming for the American Psychological Association convention and on various committees. McGregor has produced numerous publications and research presentations.

MICHAEL PIERCE, an associate professor of history at the University of Arkansas, Fayetteville, is the author of *Striking with the Ballot: Ohio Labor and the Populist Party*. His essays have appeared in *Labor History*, *Agricultural History*, *Arkansas Historical Quarterly*, and numerous edited volumes. Pierce received his PhD from Ohio State University.

DEBRA A. REID is the curator of agriculture and the environment at the Henry Ford museum (Dearborn, Michigan). Between 1999 and 2016 she taught in the Department of History at Eastern Illinois University. She was inducted as a fellow of the Agricultural History Society in 2015. Her books include *Reaping a Greater Harvest: African Americans, the Extension Service, and Rural Reform in Jim Crow Texas*, *Beyond Forty Acres and a Mule: African American Landowning Families since Reconstruction* (coedited with Evan Bennett), and *Interpreting Agriculture at Museums and Historic Sites*.

RACHEL REYNOLDS is a folklorist, writer, and community organizer living and working in the Ozarks. She is the founder of the Oregon County Food Producers and Artisans Co-op and HomeCorps. She is a frequent speaker across the country on the topic of holistic approaches to community development and sustainability. Her work has been published in the *Journal of Folklore in Education*, *Mother Earth News*, and NPR's *Morning Edition*. Reynolds is a founding member of Art of the Rural and currently serves as the managing director of Artist's Laboratory Theatre in Fayetteville, Arkansas. She is pursuing a PhD in heritage studies from Arkansas State University, Jonesboro.

YULONDA EADIE SANO is an assistant professor of history in the Department of Social Sciences at Alcorn State University (Lorman, Mississippi), where she teaches courses in African American, American, and world history. She received her PhD in history from Ohio State University. Her current research explores the desegregation of secondary schools and medical colleges in the South.

SONIA TOUDJI is an assistant professor of history at the University of Central Arkansas. Her dissertation is "Intimate Frontiers: Indians, French, and Africans in the Mississippi Valley, 1673–1803." She is the author of "Change and Continuity: French and Indian Alliance in the Mississippi Valley after the Treaty of Paris 1763" in *Une Amérique Française, 1760–1860: Dynamiques du Corridor Créole* and "'The Happiest Consequences': Sexual Unions and Frontier Survival of French and Quapaws at the Arkansas Post" in *Arkansas Historical Quarterly*. She is currently working on an annotated edition and translation: *Documenting the Frontier: Jean Bernard Bossu's Nouveau Voyages en Amérique*.

Index

Aaron v. Cooper (1958), 191, 202
Adeline (enslaved girl), 36
Adkins, Homer, 125
Allen, Hannah, 34
Allen, John Mebane, 30–32
Alliance Patriot, 95
Allison, Lucindy, 34
all-white primaries, 125
Alston, Melvin O., 181, 182
Amelia (Parmelia; enslaved woman), 29
America (enslaved woman), 64–65
American Association of University Women, 271
American Birth Control League, 141
American Legion Auxiliary, 167
American Medical Association (AMA), 145, 149–50
Ameringer, Freda Hogan. *See* Hogan, Freda
Ameringer, Oscar, 100, 103–4
Anderson, John Murray, 278
Anthony (enslaved man), 40
Arkansas Agricultural Extension Service: black farmers as agents, 242–43; canning clubs, 242–43; funding for, 241–43, 244–45; girls' club work, 242; landowning farmers and, 246–48; location of staff, 245; New Deal and, 253; origins of, 241; pay discrepancy by race, 242, 244–45; purpose of, 239; staff of, in 1914, 243; white support, reliance on, 248, 249–50; during World War I, 247
Arkansas Association of Colored Women, 263
Arkansas Conference of Social Work, 148
Arkansas Democratic Central Committee, 115, 117
Arkansas Democratic Women's Clubs, 112
Arkansas Education Commission, 161
Arkansas Equal Suffrage Central Committee, 112
Arkansas Eugenics Association (AEA): community support for, 140–41; founding of, 138–39; legislation and, 144–45; Little Rock Birth Control Clinic and, 141–43; name changed to Planned Parenthood Association of Arkansas, 148; respectability and, 139–40, 146. *See also* Cornish, Hilda Kahlert
Arkansas Federation of Women's Clubs, 112, 136, 168
Arkansas Folklore Society, 287, 290–91
Arkansas League of Women Voters, 112
Arkansas Medical Society, 146, 148–50
Arkansas Negro Democratic Association, 125
Arkansas Negro State Farmers' Association, 247
Arkansas Post, 11, 17–19, 20–21
Arkansas State Press, 184, 199–200, 201, 213
Arkansas State Society, 114
Arkansas Teachers Association, 160
Arkansas Women's Democratic Club (AWDC), 117–18
Arnold, Malissa, 41
Arthur, Mary E., 230
Asher, Joseph, 162–63
Ashmore, Harry, 206–7
Aurore, L' (slave ship), 9
Auten, Carrie, 277
Auten, Henry Franklin, 277, 278

Bache, Franklin, 101–2
Bache-Denman Coal Company, 101–2
Baker, James, 247
Baker, Virginia, 247
Ballard, Rice C., 29, 32–33
Ballard plantation, 38–39, 40
Barber, Mollie, 38
Bates, Daisy Lee Gatson: *Arkansas State Press* and, 199, 201; biographers of, 198, 200; black clergy and, 198; on Blossom, 202; book contract and, 213–14; as celebrity, 214; children, lack of, 199; death of, 215; early racialized knowledge, 197–98, 199; edu-

Bates, Daisy Lee Gatson (*cont.*)
    cation of, lack of, 199; family background of, 197–98; health of, declines, 214–15; on her anger, 197–98, 209; insecurity of, 200; Irby and, 226–27; L. C., relationship with, 198–99, 213–14; as leader in Little Rock, 198–99, 202; legacy of, 215; Little Rock Nine, relationship with, 210–11; Little Rock Nine's education and, 206, 212; NAACP, president of state branch and, 169, 191, 198, 201–2; on National Guard, 204–5; outward appearance of, 200–201, 202; perceptions on, 201–2; on school's authorities, 170; on screening process of black students, 203; stress of school desegregation and, 208–10, 213–14; testimony on desegregation of, 197; on Thomas plan, 170; threats against, 203–4, 208–10, 211–12; traditional black leadership and, 200, 201; on WEC, 171
Bates, Lucious Christopher (L. C.), 184, 191, 198–200, 201, 203, 205, 213–14
Battle of Pea Ridge, 73, 74, 80
Battle of Prairie Grove, 73, 80, 84
Baury, Marie Genevieve, 5, 11
Bean, Caesar, 78–79
Bean, Joe, 37
Bean, Mark, 78–79
Bean, Mary, 78–79
Beardsley, Bronson, 47, 48, 53, 54, 57
Beardsley, Marcia, 47, 48, 54, 61, 67
Beardsley, William, 47
Beckman, F. W., 147
Becky (enslaved woman), 34
Benson, Sally Ellis, 133
Benton County, 73, 77, 81, 83, 84
Berger, Victor, 103, 104
Bienville, Jean-Baptiste Le Moyne de, 12, 13
Bill (enslaved man), 33
birth control. *See* Cornish, Hilda Kahlert
Birth Control Clinical Research Bureau, 138, 141
Birth Control Federation of America, 148
Birth of a Nation, The (film), 113
black physicians, 262
Blakely, Adeline, 76–78
Blossom, Virgil T., 169, 202, 203, 204, 206, 207, 210
Bodenhamer, Irene, 122
Bodenhamer, O. L., 119, 122
Bohnen, Michael, 281–82
Bone, Marie Louise, 19

Bone, Michael, 19
Booker, Joseph R., 183, 189, 190
Boone, Fannie Mae, 251–52
Bossu, Jean Bernard, 18
Bourgmont, Etienne de Veniard, sieur de, 15–16
Boys Industrial School, 163
Braly, Amanda, 85–86, 87
Braly, William Carrick, 85–86
Branner, Enid, 145
Branton, Wiley, 203
Brewer, Vivion, 156–57, 171
Brodie, George, 38
Brough, Charles, 112, 162
Brown, Betty, 38
Brown, John, 33, 34
Brown, John W., 38
Brown, Minnijean, 205, 212, 270
Brown v. Board of Education (1954), 169, 201, 262, 269
Brown II (1955), 202
Bryant, R. E., 242
Buford, Mary, 39
Bullock, C. Rice, 34
Burch, Lucy, 110
Burns Detective Agency, 101
Business and Professional Women's Clubs (BPWC), 121, 122
Buttram, Eliza, 81–82
Buttram, William, 82

Cabin and Parlor, The (Randolph), 61–63
Caddo nation, 6, 14
Callery, Ida Hayman, 93, 94, 99–100
Calvert, James, 39
Cantrell, William, 51, 52–53
Caraway, Forrest, 111, 113, 114, 115–16
Caraway, Hattie Wyatt: on African American rights, 121; biographers of, 110; children of, 111, 113, 114; death of, 126; at Dickson Normal School, 110–11; early activism, 111; education of, 110–11; ERA and, 120–21, 122; family background of, 110; as glamorous, 114, 115–16; on Hitler, rise of, 123; on Lend-Lease Bill, 123; on military, 124, 125; New Deal and, 109, 120–21; political career of, 118, 119, 120–26; political interests of, 113, 115, 116; public opinion on, 116, 118, 121, 122; Riversdale mansion and, 115–16, 119; on Roosevelt administration, 109; Senate, elections to, 117, 118–19, 121–22, 125; as "silent,"

118; as teacher, 111; Thaddeus, contrasted to, 129n43; Thaddeus, relationship with, 111; as white supremacist, 121, 124, 126
Caraway, Paul, 111, 113, 114, 115–16
Caraway, Robert Easley, 111, 114, 115, 116, 120
Caraway, Thaddeus, 110–11, 112–13, 114–15, 116–17, 121, 129n43
Carlisle, Nancy, 82, 83–84
Caroline (enslaved woman), 57–58, 70n23
Carroll County, 30, 73, 81
Carter, Howard, 290
Carter, Robert, 269
Casazza, Giulio, 279
Casqui nation, 14
Catlett, Leon, 197, 202
Celia (enslaved woman), 30–32
Central High School, 156–57, 169–73, 191–92, 203, 206–10, 211
Champlin, Margaret, 81
Chatrency, Françoise, 9
Chein, Isidor, 269
Chenault, Henry Clay, 223
Chenier, Catherine Francoeur, 18
Chenier, Jean Baptist, 18
Chickasaws, 5
Chicot County, 29, 32, 33, 38, 39, 40
Child, Francis James, 291, 292
Chouteau, Auguste, 20
Chouteau, Pierre, 20
Christie, Al, 278
Christophe, Leroy M., 192, 220n119
Civil War: in Arkansas, 63, 64; cotton market and, 63; displacement and, 75–84; emancipation and, 79; guerrilla warfare, 72; loyalties, 75; occupation and, 74–75
—women during: autonomy of, 75; enslaved, 76–79; as mothers of soldiers, 84–87; scholarship on, 72; violence and, 81–82; as wives of Union soldiers, 82–84
Clark, Alice, 128n26
Clark, Arthur, 264
Clark, Beulah, 264
Clark, Catherine, 84
Clark, Harold Hilton, 271
Clark, Hilton Bancroft, 267
Clark, Katherine Miriam, 266
Clark, Kenneth Bancroft, 262, 264–66, 267, 269–70, 271
Clark, Mamie Katherine Phipps: on black children's need for psychological services, 267–69; children of, 266, 267; on children's self-identity, 266; civil engagement of, 270–71; at Columbia University, 266–67; death of, 271; education of, 262, 263; employment opportunities, lack of, 265, 267; family background of, 262–63; graduate work of, 265–66; Houston and, 265; at Howard University, 263–66; Kenneth, relationship with, 264–65; as Kenneth's coauthor, 269–70; legacy of, 271–72; Little Rock school desegregation and, 270; as middle class, 262–63, 271; NCCD and, 268–69; Rosenwald Fund and, 266; on school segregation, 269
Clark, Miriam Hanson, 264
Clark, Phipps, Clark, and Harris, Incorporated, 271
Clark, Polly Anne, 82–83, 84
Clark, Reuben, 82–83, 84
coal mining, 93–94
Cockrill plantation, 35, 37
Code Noir, 10
Colbert, James, 22n1
Committee on Public Progress, 146–47
Company of the Indies (Compagnie d'Occident), 9, 11
Conference of Social Work, 143–44
Connelly, Marc, 263
Conway County, 29, 124, 224
Cook, George B., 161
Cook, Stuart, 269
Coolidge, Calvin, 114
Cooper v Aaron (1958), 191–92, 212
Cornish, Edith, 135
Cornish, Edward, 135, 137
Cornish, Edward, Jr., 137
Cornish, Hilda Kahlert: Arkansas Eugenics Association and, 138–41; birth control, interest in, 137–38; children of, 135, 137; Committee on Public Progress and, 146–47; death of, 151; domestic life and, 135–36; Edward, relationship with, 135; family background of, 135; FERA and, 143–44, 147; financial security of, 135–36, 137, 143–44; Little Rock Birth Control Clinic and, 141–43, 144–46; on physicians, 133, 143, 144; public access to birth control and, 134, 148–50; retirement of, 150; Sanger and, 137–39; on segregation, 139–40; as volunteer in social work, 136–37; widowed, 137

Cotnam, Florence, 112, 114, 117, 124
Cotton Convention, 116
Coulange, Marie Françoise, 21
Coulange, Pierre Louis Petit de, 21
Council for Medical Services and Public Relations, 149
Coutume de Paris, 9–10, 16
Cowan, J. Alex, 179
Cowan, Lelia Roberts, 179–80
Cox, James, 30
Crane, Sallie, 32, 39
Cravens, William Ben, 118
Crumit, Frank, 278
Current, Gloster, 203, 207, 209
Curtis, Charles, 118
Cynthia (enslaved woman), 29–30

Dallas County, 36, 37
Daniel, Elizabeth, 41
Daniel, Harriet, 36
Daniel, James, 41–42
Daniel, Mary, 41
Daniel, William, 41–42
Daniel v. Guy, 41–42
Davies, Ronald, 205, 206
Davis, Jeff, 162
Davis, Laurence A., 185
Davis, Mary Jo, 296
Davis v. School Board of Prince Edward County (1952), 269
Deane, Ernie, 294, 299
de Barrios, Jacinto, 14
Debs, Eugene, 96, 103, 104
DeClouet, Alexandre Chevalier, 17, 21
DeClouet, Louise Favrot, 21
Delinó de Chalmette, Jean Ignace, 21
Delinó de Chalmette, Marie Madeleine Broutin, 21
Delinó de Chalmette, Victoire, 21
Delure, Marie, 10
Demazellières, François, 19
Dembitz, Nanette, 190
Democratic National Campaign Committee, 117
Democratic National Convention (1920), 112
Democratic National Convention (1928), 114
Democratic National Convention (1936), 109
Democratic Party's Women's Division, 117–18
Dermott, Lillian Dees, 139

de Soto, Hernando, 14
de Villiers, Balthazar, 17
Dewson, Molly, 117–18
Doak, Julia, 111
Donaghey, George W., 161, 162
Dortch, Charles, 37
Dragonette, Jessica, 284
Driftwood, Jimmy, 297
Dubreuil, Jacob (Jacobo), 18, 22n1
Duc du Maine, Le (slave ship), 9
Dudley, Edward R., 190
Du Lac, Perrin, 21
Du Luxembourg, Raphael, 10
Dunaway, Edwin, 206–7
Dunbar High School, 181–82, 186, 192, 199
Dunn, James H., 41
Du Ru, Paul, 13
Dyer Anti-Lynching Bill, 121

Easely, William B., 28
Eckford, Elizabeth, 204–5
Eckford, Oscar, 208
Eighth Circuit Appeals Court, 189
Eighth Circuit Court of Appeals, 212
Eisenhower, Dwight D., 191, 205, 206, 208, 209
Elders, M. Joycelyn (née Jones), 230–31
elections, presidential, 114–15
Eliza (enslaved girl), 41
emancipation, 63, 65, 76, 77–78, 79
Emily (enslaved girl), 29
enslaved labor: arrival of, 9; Code Noir and, 10; labor of, 10; Native Americans as, 19–20; population of, 16, 18, 30; reproduction of, 10, 19–20; restrictions on, 16–17
enslaved women, 34; children, role of, 36; during Civil War, 76; domestic slave trade and, 28–29; family lives and, 34–35, 37; federal troops, views on, 78; freedom and, 41–42; health of, 38; labor of, 32–38; older women, roles of, 35; population of, 27–28; resistance of, 38–40; scholarship on, 27; sexual exploitation of, 57–58; westward migration and, 29–32; white men's debt and, 28–30
Equal Rights Amendment (ERA), 112, 120–21
Espionage Act (1917), 103, 104
Evans, J. A., 241

Fannie (enslaved woman), 37
Fanny (enslaved woman), 33

Fanny (enslaved woman), 38
Farley family, 77
Faubus, Alta, 170
Faubus, Orval E.: closes high schools, 156, 171–72, 212–13; Eisenhower, meeting with, 206; injunction against, 205; National Guard use and, 169, 191, 204–5
Faulkner, Claude W., 290–91
Faulkner County, 248, 250
Federal Bureau of Investigation (FBI), 205–6
Federal Emergency Relief Administration (FERA), 143–44, 167
Felton, Rebecca Latimer, 127n10
Fergusson, Lou, 32
Finley, Molly, 32, 34, 38
Fitch, Anna, 276–77, 280
Fitch, William S., 276–77, 278
Fitzhugh, Laura Davis, 117
Fletcher, Adolphine Krause, 158, 161
Fletcher, John Gould, 158, 161, 174n8, 290–91
Fletcher, John Gould (son), 161
Fletcher, Mary, 164–65
Flowers, William Harold, 228
Fortuné, Le (slave ship), 9
Fox, Nancy Carlisle, 83
Francoeur, Joseph, 18
Francoeur, Marie Jeanne, 18
free people of color, 17
French and Indian War, 16
frontier, 5–6, 8–14, 51
Fulbright, J. William, 110, 124–25

Gaines, Lloyd L., 227
Garland County, 124, 223–26, 262–64, 271; Irby, Edith, and, 231, 233; Lewis, Mary, and, 275, 280, 282, 283
Garrett, Henry, 267, 269
Garrison, William Lloyd, 48–49
Gates, Frederick T., 181
Gatson, Hezekiah "Babe," 197
Gatti-Casazza, Giulio, 279
General Education Board (GEB), 181, 241–43
Gibbs, William, 180
Giffey, Annie, 187
Gillespie, George, 21
Gilman, Charlotte Perkins, 111
Gipson, John H., 187, 191
Girls Industrial School, 163
Great Depression, 116, 137

Great Flood of 1927, 114, 136–37, 238, 248
Green, Ernest, 192, 205, 206, 212
Green, O. W., 35, 39
Greene County, 38
Green Pastures, The (Connelly), 263
Guy, Abby, 41–42
Guy, John, 41

Hagerty, Thomas, 95
Hague, Robert L., 282
Hale, Brown, 94–95
Haley, George W. B., 229
Hall, Graham Roots, 139
Hall, Jack, 37
Halpert, Herbert, 290
Harding, Warren G., 113
Hardridge, Mary Jane, 37
Harriet (enslaved girl), 29
Harris, Victor B., 190
Harry (enslaved man), 65
Hartley, Gene, 265–66
Hartley, Ruth, 265–66
Hastie, William H., 190
Hastings, George, 291
Hawkins, M. C., 133
Hawkins, Ronnie, 297
Hays, Brooks, 130n61, 206
Hays, Wesley E., 211
Heckler, Margaret, 232
Hempstead County, 30, 31, 37, 40–41
Henderson, William James, 280
Henniger, Alice, 277
Henry, Charles, 148
Henry, Charles R., 145
Hermann, Johann, 80–81, 85
Hermann, Karl, 80–81, 85
Hermann, Lina, 80–81, 85
Hermann, Nani, 80–81, 85
Herron, Francis, 80–81
Hibbler, Frances B., 189
Hibbler, Myles A., 183, 189, 190
High, Elizabeth, 81–82
Hilburn, Prentice A., 227
Hindman, 85
Hitler, Adolf, 123
Hogan, Alice, 95
Hogan, Charlotte Yowell, 95, 96
Hogan, Dan, 94, 95, 96, 98–100, 102–3
Hogan, Daniel, Jr., 95

Hogan, Freda: Callery, relationship with, 99–100; early activism of, 98; on education, 98; family background of, 95; family finances of, 96; father, relationship with, 95, 96; on gender inequalities, 97; *Huntington Herald* and, 98–99; journalism and, 98–99, 102; Oklahoma, move to, 103; *Oklahoma Leader* and, 103–4; UMWA versus Bache-Denman Coal Company and, 101–2; Women's National Committee and, 100–101; women's suffrage and, 100–101; on World War I, 102, 104
—Socialist Party: childhood experiences with, 96–97; leader, 104–5; secretary of state, 100
Hogan, Hazel, 95
Hoover, Hebert, 114–15, 116
Hot Spring County, 29
Hotze, Peter, 174n8
House, Archibald F., 189
Houston, Charles Hamilton, 265
Huckaby, Elizabeth, 201–2
Hudgen, Molly, 36
Hudson, Mabel, 93, 94–95, 105, 107n25
Humphreys, Thomas, 29
Hunt, Silas, 223, 228–29
Hunter, Annie Peters, 242
Hunter, Mary Evelyn V., 244
Hunter, Max, 287, 292

Imes, William Lloyd, 225
infant mortality, 50–51
intermarriage, 18–20
International Planned Parenthood Federation, 150
Irby, Edith Mae (Jones): on access to health care, 232–33; education of, 224–25; family background of, 224; financial situation of, 225, 226, 231; gendered experiences in medical school, 229–30; legacy of, 233; medical school acceptance of, 223–24; motivations for becoming physician, 224; philanthropy of, 233; as president of NMA, 232–33; private practice of, 232; publicity of, 230–31; racialized experiences, 232; racialized experiences at medical school, 230; on School of Medicine, desegregation of, 227; Texas, move to, 232; University of Arkansas, acceptance to, 226; University of Arkansas, acceptance to, public reaction, 229

Irby, Juanita, 224, 232
Irby, Mattie Buice, 224, 231
Irby, Robert, Jr., 224
Irby, Robert, Sr., 224

Jacobson, Laura, 113
Jacoway, H. M., 114
Jameson, Hannah, 37
Jane (enslaved woman), 38
Jeanes Fund, 243
Jefferson, Thomas, 22
Jefferson County, 29, 37, 243. *See also* Trulock, Amanda Beardsley
Jenny (enslaved woman), 30
Jim Crow, 112–13; young black women and, 264
Johnson, Lyndon, 214
Johnson County, 37, 78–79
Joliet, Louis, 8
Jollin, Agnes Francoeur, 18
Jollin, Jean, 18
Jones, James B., 231–32
Jones, Martha, 38–39
Jones, Mary "Mother," 96, 97
Jones, Ralph B., 184
Jones, Scipio A., 183, 190, 227
Joutel, Henri, 13, 15

Kadohadachos, 6
Kahlert, Gertrude, 135
Kahlert, Rudolph, 135
Kahlert, Sophie, 135
Kahn, Otto Hermann, 279, 281
Kennedy, John F., 214
Kerns, Adrianna, 32
Kilgore, James C., 233
Kimball, Nancy Carlisle McGinnis, 83
King, Judson, 93
Kirby, William, 113
Kirkwood, Anne, 51, 58
Kitchen, Wade, 122
Knapp, Seaman, 241
Ku Klux Klan, 211–12; second, 113, 115
Kuznetsova, Maria Nikolaevna, 279

Lamothe Cadillac, Antoine Laumet de, 12
Lance, Virgil, 293
Landrony, Catherine, 18
Landrony, Joseph, 18
Landrony, Marie, 18
Landrony, Marie Antoine, 18

Index

Laney, Benjamin Travis, 228
Langdon, Emma, 97
La Salle, Robert, 8, 15
Latimer, Annie, 250
L'Aurore (slave ship), 9
La Vente, Henri Roulleaux de, 12
Law, G. Malcolm, 292
Law, John, 9, 11
Laws, Clarence, 211
League of Women Voters, 165
Le Duc du Maine (slave ship), 9
Lee, Caroline, 247
Lee, Nathan, 247
LeFevre, Wells, 95, 103
Leflar, Robert, 228
Le Fortuné (slave ship), 9
Legal Defense and Educational Fund, 227
Lehár, Franz, 280
LeMaire, Charles, 279
Lemley, Harry, 212
Lewis, Charles Kidd, 275
Lewis, Hattie, 275–76
Lewis, Jane, 81–82
Lewis, J. Keene, 278
Lewis, Joe, 275
Lewis, John H., 186, 187, 190–91
Lewis, John L., 93, 104
Lewis, Mary Sybil Kidd Maynard: alcoholism and, 281–82, 283; Arkansas concert and, 280–81; Auten family and, 277; biographical information, 275; biography of, 284; Bohnen, relationship with, 281–82; career, decline of, 281–83; death of, 283–84; in Europe, 279–80; family background of, 275–76; Fitch family and, 276–77; *Greenwich Village Follies* and, 278; Hague, relationship with, 282–83; illness of, 282–83; Jazz Age songs and, 278; Keene, relationship with, 278; Metropolitan Opera and, 280, 282; musical training of, 276–77, 278; in New York, 278; orphaned, 275–76; publicity of, 280; recordings of, 279–80, 281, 283, 284; *Ziegfeld Follies* and, 278–79
Liaison, 271
Liggin, Obadiah, 28
Lithia (enslaved woman), 33
Little, Harry, 192
Little Rock Birth Control Clinic: African American women and, 141; closing of, 147–48; as demonstration clinic, 147; middle-class white women and, 142–43; physicians and, 144–46; poor white women and, 141–42; women outside Little Rock and, 142
Little Rock Classroom Teachers Association (CTA), 182–83
Little Rock Housing Association, 167–68
Little Rock Nine, 192, 203–4, 206, 207, 211, 213
Little Rock playground movement, 136
Little Rock school desegregation crisis. *See* Bates, Daisy Lee Gatson; Central High School; Faubus, Orval E.; Little Rock Nine
Lomax, John, 287
Lomax, John Avery, 302n38
Lomax, Ruby, 287
Long, Huey, 116, 119, 120
Long, Rose, 116, 120
Lott, Frances, 288, 299
Loughborough, J. Fairfax, 186, 189
Louisiana Purchase, 21–22
Low, Raymond, 136
Lowe, Caroline, 101
Lucille (enslaved woman), 33
Lucy (enslaved woman), 33

Madison County, 73, 82–83
Magnolia Place plantation, 49
Making Negroes Better Farmers (film), 250
Maley, Anna, 101
Mallet, Robert, 288
Mann, Woodrow, 206–7, 209
manumissions, 40–41
Maria (enslaved woman), 29
Marquette, Jacques, 8
Marshall, Norma Williams, 180
Marshall, Thurgood, 180, 183, 185–86, 204, 269
Martha (enslaved woman), 40
Martha Ann (enslaved woman), 33
Martin, Blanche, 160–61
Martin, Elizabeth, 75, 76, 85
Martin, James, 75
Martin, Mary Jane, 85
Martin, Mary Long, 225
Mary (enslaved woman), 40
massive resistance, 203
Matsner, Eric M., 145
Maxey, Fannie Bean, 78–79
Maxey, Ran, 78
Maynard, Ed, 276
McClellan, John, 122

McClinton, I. S., 211
McCormack, John, 282
McCormack, Margaret, 87–88
McCrary, Mary. *See* Ray, Mary L.
McDermott, Lillian Dees, 148
McGinnis, Elisha, 83–84
McMath, Sid, 206
McRae, Thomas C., 136
Means, Gaston, 113
Mecklin, Louisa, 87–88
Mecklin, Robert W., 87
Meenes, Max, 265
Membre, Zenobe, 15
Metropolitan Opera, 279, 280, 282
Mézières, Athanase de, 8, 19
Miller, John, 122, 205
Miller, Julia Ada, 251
Mills, Ambrose, 30
Mills, Susan, 29–30
Mills, Walter, 180
miscegenation, 41, 57–58
Mississippi County, 111
Missouri ex rel. Gaines v. Canada (1938), 227
Mitchell, Merlin, 291
Monroe County, 36, 98, 243
Montcherveaux, Pierre Julien Chevalier de, 18
Montcherveaux, Susanne Francoeur, 18
Montigny, Dumont de, 13
Moore, Emma, 32, 36
Morris, Jimmy, 297
Morris, Robert, 290, 291
Morris, Sue Cowan (Williams): on civil rights activism, 185; community activities of, 192–93; death of, 193; on decision to file suit, 183; education of, 180; fired from job, 179, 184–85, 190–91; marries Williams, 192; *Morris v. Williams* and, 186–89, 190–92, 193; as named plaintiff, 183; rehired at Dunbar High, 192; teacher salaries equalization case, filing of, 179
Morris v. Williams, 186–89, 190–92, 193
Moss, James, 41
Mothershed, Thelma, 205, 211
Mourning (enslaved woman), 40–41
Murrah, Alfred P., 105
Myhand, Mary, 76–77, 78

Nash, William N., 186
National Association for the Advancement of Colored People (NAACP): in Arkansas, expansion of, 179; Caraway, Thad, on, 113; in Little Rock, 192; Little Rock Nine and, 169, 212–13 (*see also* Little Rock Nine); teacher salaries equalization case and, 179; youth chapter, 202. *See also* Bates, Daisy Lee Gatson
National Committee on Federal Legislation for Birth Control, Inc., 141, 145
National Council of Negro Women's Citizenship Education Committee, 200–201
National Headstart Planning Committee, 270–71
National Medical Association (NMA), 232–33
National Mental Health Act (1946), 269
National Women's Party, 112, 121
National Women's Suffrage Association (NAWSA), 112
Nixon, Richard, 233
northern women, slaveholding and, 46–47, 48–49. *See also* Trulock, Amanda Beardsley
Northside Center for Child Development (NCCD), 268–69, 271
Norton, Mary T., 121

Oakland-Fraternal Cemetery, 237
O'Hare, Kate Richards, 97, 103, 104
Oldfield, Pearl, 115, 119
Oldfield, William, 115
Old Polly (enslaved woman), 39
Olmsted, Fredrick Law, 60
"one-drop rule," 41
O'Reilly, Alejandro, 16
Orren (enslaved man), 53–54
Osage nation, 6–8, 13–14, 20
Overton, Mary, 30
Ozarks: Carroll County, 30, 73, 81; Madison County, 73, 82–83. *See also* Benton County; Parler, Mary Celestia; Washington County

Page, Inman E., 240
Page, Zelia N., 240
Page, Zelia R. Ball, 240
Panic of 1837, 50
Parler, Josie Platt, 288
Parler, Marvin Lamar, 287–88
Parler, Mary Celestia: *An Arkansas Ballet Book*, 299; Davis, Mary Jo, and, 296; death of, 299; education of, 288–89; family background

of, 287–88; interviews with subjects, 293; legacy of, 299–300; Randolph, Vance, relationship with, 297–99; recognition of, 295–96; recognition of, lack of, 287, 295, 299; students of, 293–95; at University of Arkansas, 289–90
—folklore: collecting of, 292–93, 296; disinterest in, 290; early interest in, 288; importance of, 295; at University of Arkansas, 291–92, 293–95
Parnell, Harvey, 117
Pattillo, Melba, 205, 219n91
Pattillo, Solomon, 37
Paulina (enslaved woman), 38
Payne, Harriet McFarlin, 35, 36–37
Peggy (enslaved woman), 28–29
Pelham, John, 34
Perkins, F. D., 282
Perry, Dinah, 35
Peter (enslaved boy), 29
Phillips County, 113, 243, 245, 247, 248
Phipps, Harold Hilton, 262–63, 268
Phipps, Harold Hilton, II, 263
Phipps, Katherine Florence Smith, 263
Pierce, John B., 252
Pike, Albert, 168
Pindall, X. O., 160
Pino, Antonio, 18
Pino, Maria Juana (Marie Jeanne) Francoeur, 18
Planned Parenthood Association of Arkansas, 150
Planned Parenthood Federation of America, 148
Plessy v. Ferguson (1896), 240
Political Equality League of Little Rock, 165
poll tax, 124, 125
poll taxes, 118
Pond, Mary, 29
Pond, William, 29
Powell, Evalyn, 143–44
Powell, Velma, 157, 171
Prairie Place Plantation, 46, 55. See also Trulock, Amanda Beardsley
Price, Myrtle, 117
Progressivism, 162; African American activists and, 165–66
Pulaski County, 39, 112; Cornish, Hilda, and, 136, 139, 149; Ray, Mary, and, 242–43, 244, 245, 247; Terry, Adolphine, and, 165, 167. See also Bates, Daisy Lee Gatson; Central High School; Little Rock Nine
Pullman porters, 272n17

Quapaw nation, 6–9, 11, 13, 15–16

racial etiquette, and titles, 197
Randolph, J. Thornton, *The Cabin and Parlor*, 61–63
Randolph, Vance, 287, 290, 292, 297–99
Rassberry, Senia, 37
Ray, Gloria, 205, 210, 212
Ray, Harvey Cincinnatus (H. C.), 238, 240–41, 243–44, 246–48, 250–51, 252, 253, 260n43
Ray, Mary L.: absence from historical record, 238–39; Arkansas Agricultural Extension Services, hired by, 243; biographical information, 239, 252; black farm owners and, 246; career of, overview, 237; community fairs and, 247; death of, 237–38, 251–52; Delta counties and, 245; educated black women and, 251; 4-H clubs and, 245; H. C., relationship with, 239, 240–41, 243; homemaker clubs and, 245; illness of, 251; at Langston, 240; legacy of, 251–53; movable school and, 250–51; nutrition, focus on, 248–50; Progressivism and, 239; relocates to Arkansas, 243–44; salary of, 244; segregated world of, 239–40, 246; supervisory role of, 245–46; technology, use of, 250; travel of, 245–46; at Tuskegee Institute, 239–40; war effort and, 247
Reagan, Ronald, 232
Reed, Murray O., 189
Reuben (enslaved man), 46, 53–54, 55, 56–57, 59, 60, 65–66
Reynolds, John Hughes, 124–25
Riley, Millie, 197
Riversdale mansion, 115–16
Roberts, Terrence, 205, 206, 212, 221n140
Robinson, Joe, 114–15, 119, 120, 122
Rockefeller, John D., 181
Romine, Charles, 296
Roosevelt, Eleanor, 168
Roosevelt, Franklin Delano, 109, 120, 122, 125
Roosevelt, Theodore, 277
Rose, Nancy, 40
Rose, William, 40
Rosenwald, Julius, 181, 266
Rosenwald Fund, 181, 266

Rudolph, Leighton, 290–91
Rule, Margaret, 298
Ruskin Colony, 111

Salary Adjustment Committee, 182
Sanborn, John Benjamin, 190
Sanders, Ira E., 139–40, 150, 151
Sanger, Margaret, 134, 137–39, 141, 145, 146–47, 150
Sanger, Stuart, 137
Sarah (enslaved woman), 38
Sawyers, Alonzo, 86–87
Sawyers, Henry Addison, 86–87
Sawyers, James, 86
Sawyers, Jeptha Jefferson, 86–87
Sawyers, John, 85
Sawyers, Lucinda, 85, 86–87
Scobee, Russell T., 182, 183, 185, 186
Scott, J. D., 185
Scott County, 95, 161
Sears, Roebuck and Company, 241
Sebastian County, 93, 97, 99, 100, 101, 102
Sedition Act (1918), 103
Seidel, Emil, 98
Settlement Sunday School, 276
Shelton, Laura, 36
Shipp, Agnes Ann Work, 111
Shropshire, Jackie, 229
Shugart, Henry, 39
Shugart plantation, 33
Sigmon, Vivian Lewis, 117–18
Simons, May Wood, 97
Sipuel, Ada Lois, 228
Sipuel v. Board of Regents of the University of Oklahoma (1948), 228
Sitton, Claude, 207
Slater Fund, 241
Smith, Al, 114–15
Smith, Flora, 288
Smith, Gene, 207
Smith, Hay Watson, 140
Smith, Luther Ely, 190
Smith, Mabel, 135–36
Smith, Orlee, 197, 199, 216n6
Smith, Susie, 197
Smith-Lever Act (1914), 243–44, 245
Smith v. Allright (1944), 131n86
Socialist Party of America (SPA): in Arkansas, growth of, 100; Arkansas women and, 93;
Committee on War and Militarism, 102; compared with Democrat and Republican Parties, 94–95; decline of, 105; gender and, 96–97; Huntington headquarters, 94; legacy of, 105; platform of, 95–96; Women's National Committee (WNC) and, 100–101; women's network, 94–95; on World War I, 102–3. *See also* Hogan, Freda
Sophia (enslaved woman), 39
Southern Association for College Women ("College Club"), 160
Southern Claims Commission, 75, 76, 78–79, 81
Southern Tenant Farmers Union (STFU), 120
Spanish settlement, 16–20
Spirit of Cotton tour, 200
State Farm for Women, 136
State Sovereignty Commission, 203
Stephen (enslaved boy), 29
Stephens, Charlotte, 293, 296–97
Stewart, Minnie, 38
St. Francis County, 29, 245, 247
Stone, Robert B., 283
Stop This Outrageous Purge, 173, 213
Stovall, Fanny, 28
Stowe, Harriet Beecher, 61
Strayhorn, Eva, 37
Summer, Francis, 264, 265
Swatty, A. V., 241

teacher salary equalization: early cases, 180; limitations of, 190–91; Little Rock Classroom Teachers Association (CTA) and, 182–83; school boards' reactions to, 180–81, 183, 184–85, 187
Teapot Dome scandal, 113
Technique of Contraception, The (Matsner), 145
Tenns (enslaved woman), 39
Terral, Tom Jefferson, 163, 280–81
Terry, Adolphine Fletcher: activism of, 160–61; on Arkansas schools, consolidation of, 160–61; arts, interest in, 168; biographers of, 157; Central High School desegregation and, 156–57, 169–73; College Club and, 160; death of, 173; as debutante, 159–60; education, 158–59; family background of, 158, 174n8; harassment of, 172; on integration, 172; juvenile justice system reform and, 162–63; legacy of, 173; on lynchings, 159; marriage to David, 161–62; as mother, 162,

163–64, 166; newspapers, use of, 161; other activist endeavors, 167–68; public library system and, 166–67, 168–69; racial awakening, 158, 159, 165; at Vassar College, 158–59; women's clubs and, 160, 166; women's suffrage and, 164–65; YWCA and, 165–66
Terry, David, 166
Terry, David (son), 162
Terry, David Dickson, 159, 161–62
Terry, Mary, 163–64
Terry, Mary Louise, 162
Terry, Sally, 163
Teyte, Maggie, 279
Thomas, Herbert, 170
Thomas, Jefferson, 205, 213
Thomas, Seth, 190
Thompson, Ellen Briggs, 37, 39
Thompson, Mary E., 230
Thorner, William, 278–79, 280
Tom (enslaved boy), 29
Tonti, Henri de, 9
Trimble, Thomas C., 183, 184, 187–89
Trulock, Amanda Beardsley: as apolitical, 61; on Arkansas frontier, 51–52; Beardsley, Bronson, and, 53; Cantrell and, 52–53; children of, 50–51, 52, 53, 63–64, 66–67; children of, education of, 58; during Civil War, 63–65; Connecticut, return to, 66–67; Connecticut, visits to, 58–59; emancipation and, 65; on enslaved labor, 49; family history, 47–48; financial success of, 61; James, marriage to, 48–49; on James's death, 51; Reuben and, 54–57, 62, 65–66; on sectional tensions, 59–60; as slaveholder, 53–54, 56–58; on slavery, 48–50, 61–63, 65; on slaves, purchase of, 56–57; as southerner, 60; as Yankee woman, 46, 47–48, 60
Trulock, Bronson Van Buren Nichols, 50, 63–64
Trulock, Burton, 50, 63–64, 66
Trulock, Elizabeth, 50, 51
Trulock, Eugenia, 50–51
Trulock, Felicia, 50
Trulock, James, 48, 50, 51–52, 53, 61, 69n14
Trulock, James Hines, 29, 52, 59, 66
Trulock, Marshall, 52
Trulock, Nichols, 66
Trulock, Victoria, 50, 66–67
Truman, Harry S., 125, 149

Tucker, Mandy, 35
Turgeon, Angelique Francoeur, 18
Turgeon, Joseph, 18
Turner, George, 33

Ulloa, Antonio de, 16
Uncle Tom's Cabin (Stowe), 61
United Mine Workers of America (UMWA), 93, 96, 98, 101–2, 104
United Nations, 125
United States v. Classic (1941), 131n86
United States v. One Package of Japanese Pessaries (1936), 145
University of Arkansas: "desegregation" of Law School, 228, 229; School of Medicine, 223, 226, 229; segregation of, 225–26
Urban League of Greater Little Rock, 168

Vallière, Don Joseph, 21
Vallière de Vaugine, Marie Félicité, 21
Van Buren County, 79, 86, 95
Vaudreuil, Pierre Rigaud de, 12
Victor Company, 280
Vilemont, Charles Melchoir de, 21
Vitaphone, 281
volunteer work, 136

Wagner-Murray-Dingell Bill, 149–50
Wagner–Van Nuys Anti-Lynching Bill, 121
Walker, Jimmy, 281
Wallace, Mike, 271
Walls, Carlotta (LaNier), 204, 205, 213
War on Poverty, 214
Washington County, 37, 73, 75, 77–80, 81–82, 85–87
Weingartner, Felix, 279
Wesley (enslaved man), 87
westward migration, 29–32, 50–51, 73
White, Bertha Hale Brown, 93, 94–95, 105, 107n25
White, Erline, 121, 122
White, Walter, 182
White County, 277
Whiteside, Garrett, 118, 123
Wilhelmi, Fritz, 80
Wilkins, Roy, 183, 217n45
Williams, Booker T., 192
Williams, Charl Ormond, 121
Williams, Robert M., 183

Wilson, Alex, 208
Wilson, Woodrow, 102, 111, 112
Wingo, Effiegene, 116, 119
Wingo, Otis, 116, 118
Wolff, Fanchon, 278
Wolff, Marco, 278
women politicians, through "widow's succession," 115, 116, 117, 119. *See also* Caraway, Hattie Wyatt
Women's Christian Temperance Union, 115, 162
women's club movement, 136, 160
Women's Emergency Committee to Open Our Schools (WEC), 157, 170–73, 213
women's suffrage, 100–101, 104, 112, 164–65

Woodard, Jennie Lou, 250–51
Woodrough, Joseph William, 190
Working Class Union, 103
Works Progress Administration (WPA), 28, 76
World War I, 102–4, 164
World War II, 168
Wyatt, Mozella, 110
Wyatt, Walter, 118
Wyatt, William C., 110, 111

Young, Vivian, 243

Zeman, Alice Fitch, 284
Ziegfeld, Florenz, 278
Zoller, Elmer, 280

www.ingramcontent.com/pod-product-compliance
Lightning Source LLC
Chambersburg PA
CBHW011721220426
43664CB00020B/2884